The Struggle for the Breeches

The Struggle
for the Breeches

*Gender and the Making
of the British Working Class*

ANNA CLARK

 Rivers Oram Press, London

First published in the United Kingdom in 1995 by Rivers Oram Press,
144 Hemingford Road, London N1 1DE

First published in the USA by the University of California Press,
Berkeley and Los Angeles, California

University of California Press, Ltd.
London, England

A catalogue record for this book is available from the British Library.

Printed in the United States of America
9 8 7 6 5 4 3 2 1

ISBN 1-85489-075-1

The paper used in this publication meets the minimum requirements of
American National Standard for Information Sciences— Permanence of
Paper for Printed Library Materials, ANSI Z39.48-1984.

To my mother,
Sylvia Smith Clark,
for encouraging my writing

and to my father,
David Lang Clark,
for inspiring my love of history

Contents

Illustrations and Tables

Illustrations

Tables

Acknowledgments

In the ten years since I began work on this book, many colleagues and friends have helped with ideas and revisions. First of all, this book owes a great deal to the tradition of the History Workshop movement in Britain, and to the (now sadly defunct) Feminist History group. Both allowed history to flourish outside institutional confines and provided a model for making history accessible, not just academic.

The manuscript began life as a Rutgers Ph.D. dissertation on the London working class. John Gillis and Ellen Ross shared the insights of their own work and read my chapters. Marilyn Morris helped a great deal on the radicalism of the 1790s. Jutta Schwarzkopf shared with me her knowledge of women and Chartism, and Sian Moore provided ideas about a comparison with the north of England. Randolph Trumbach generously pointed me to obscure London legal records. Lyndal Roper and I had interesting conversations about gender theory and history. Rachel Weil and Carol Barash helped to illuminate the mysteries of eighteenth-century sexuality, while conversations with Polly Morris, and her excellent dissertation, illuminated the problem of sexual reputation. Most important, Judith Walkowitz was an excellent adviser, one who could always appreciate my thoughts while pointing out contradictions, inconsistencies, and gaps. She went beyond the call of duty in reading the final manuscript in 1993. Her rigorous critique greatly improved it, although I am sure I did not satisfy all of her concerns.

As this project expanded beyond the scope of a monograph on London to a comparative study of Glasgow, Lancashire, and London, many more people have helped me. My departmental colleagues, especially Julia Blackwelder and William Bowman, critiqued several chapters, improving them with insight from other fields. John Smail, especially, who works on the making of the English middle class in Yorkshire, inspired me with his lucid prose style and theoretical insights and patiently read draft upon draft of my book. Leonore Davidoff, who advised me at the University of Essex, has challenged me for years, listening to each new idea as I emerged from the archives every summer, pointing out the pros and cons, and offering more suggestions for further reading than I have been able to carry out. She carefully read the entire completed manuscript and made suggestions for improvement on every level, from style and structure to substance. In Scotland, Eleanor Gordon allowed me to read the proofs of her book on women and labor in Scotland before publication. James Vernon and Jonathan Fulcher also kindly sent me their informative manuscripts before publication.

At the University of California Press, Erika Büky efficiently shepherded the book through the editorial and production process, and Jane-Ellen Long's meticulous and deeply knowledgeable copy editing greatly improved the final product. Sheila Levine has been an enthusiastic editor, picking excellent readers for the manuscript. James Epstein's work on early nineteenth-century radicalism has always been most helpful to me, and so were his comments on the manuscript. Thomas Laqueur's insights into changes in gender and sexuality have provided me with an important heuristic framework, and his gracious acceptance of my work on Queen Caroline has always been appreciated. His critique forced me to clarify my arguments for the final revision. Theodore Koditschek's own ambitious and innovative study of class formation in Bradford provided me with a model, and his extensive, detailed comments much improved the final version of this book.

Librarians and archivists all over Great Britain have also helped to make this work possible. The British Library's blue dome calmed this researcher as she pored over piles of pamphlets. The staff of the John Johnson Collection of Ephemera in the Bodleian Library, Oxford, and the Goldsmiths Library, University of London, were most helpful. County record office staff, struggling with endless budget cuts, nonetheless patiently exhumed dusty documents. Deserving of special mention are the archivists of the Greater London Record Office, the Guildhall Library, the Lancashire Record Office, and especially the Scottish archives, which are full of neglected riches: the Strathclyde Regional Archives, the Local History Room of the Mitchell Library, Glasgow, and both branches of the Scottish Record Office in Edinburgh.

The years of research for this project were initially funded by a graduate fellowship from Rutgers University and by the Social Science Research Foundation. The University of North Carolina Faculty Development Fund very generously funded five summers of research, which made possible the transformation of a London monograph into a national study. The American Philosophical Society also aided summer research. The first draft of this manuscript was written at the National Humanities Center in Research Triangle Park, North Carolina, funded by the Rockefeller Foundation, which provided a year of uninterrupted thought, writing, and the stimulating company of fellow scholars, especially Steve Goldsmith, Sarah Hanley, Linda Kerber, Mac Rohrbaugh, Shirley Samuels, Mark Seltzer, and Lawrence Stone.

My friends and family have sustained me through the years of research and writing. My graduate student colleagues, Polly Beals, Kimn Carlton-Smith, and Laura Tabili, sustained me throughout those years, and in Charlotte, Lisa Kannenburg and I had useful discussions on labor history. John Smail and Tina Wright continuously provided lovely dinners and the warmth of their friendship. In my home in Durham, North Carolina, Harriet Whitehead and Helen Langa discussed contemporary theory on gender and sexuality with me. Dena Leiter, Bellina Veronesi, and Duffy Baum provided a reality check from outside the academy and forced me to explain some ideas in plain English and two sentences. Cynthia Herrup, Judith Bennett, and Barbara Harris have always been supportive of my academic career. In England, Alison Oram, Julie Wheelwright, Wallie Menteth, Clare Midgeley, Chris Dymkowski, Anna Davin, Meg Arnot, and Henk van Kerkijk provided hospitality and friendship on my summer research trips.

Finally, my mother, father, sisters, and niece have provided me with loving, untraditional family values, close rather than closed-minded.

1   Introduction

Alexander Wilson could be taken as the archetypal artisan of radical working-class history. A poet-weaver who satirized conniving masters, he fled from Scotland to America in 1794, driven by fear of political persecution. Wilson's most successful work, however, was more personal; his "Watty and Meg; Or, The Wife Reformed," sold as many as a hundred thousand copies as a broadsheet. Meg nags her hen-pecked husband, Watty, to stay at home instead of drinking at the alehouse. To silence her scolding, his mates advise him, he should threaten to leave her and go join the army. Terrified of being left alone and unsupported, Meg submits; harmony reigns as they dive under the blankets for another "Hinny-moon."[1]

How could Wilson both advise men to demand submission from their wives and encourage them to defy aristocratic power? This book will attempt to answer such questions by linking the personal with the political in working-class history, depicting the making of the working class as a "struggle for the breeches." The private sphere of marriage was often satirically depicted in popular literature as a bitter contest: the "struggle for the breeches" in which wives tried to rob husbands of their manly control. In politics, too, plebeian men such as Wilson felt they were denied the full manhood of citizenship.

This is, of course, not the first attempt to link the personal with the political in working-class history. In the 1950s, Neil Smelser depicted working-class radicals as irrationally reacting to the loss of their patriarchal authority during the industrial revolution.[2] In response, in his classic *The Making of the English Working Class* E. P. Thompson portrayed working-class activists as rational heroes who forged a working-class consciousness by 1832—but to make his point he neglected the connections between family and political life.[3]

1

As a result, as Joan Scott points out, Thompson marginalized women in his narrative and presented a masculine version of working-class history.[4] Indeed, Thompson explained his project as "a biography of the English working class from its adolescence until its early manhood."[5] By contrast, Barbara Taylor, brilliantly initiating feminist attempts to rewrite the making of the working class, described the innovations of Owenite socialist-feminists from the 1820s to the 1840s.[6] Yet the Owenites were only a small minority of proletarians; the mainstream of the working-class movement adopted quite conservative ideals of masculinity and femininity, eventually excluding women from politics. This book will begin to explain why.

My project will pay homage to the work of E. P. Thompson and Barbara Taylor by re-visioning Thompson's narrative to include gender and by putting Taylor's Owenites in the larger context of plebeian and working-class culture. It will not replace Thompson's history of manhood with a history of working-class women. Instead, inspired by the work of such feminist historians as Leonore Davidoff, Catherine Hall, Joan Scott, and Sally Alexander, it will infuse gender—the social construction of manhood and womanhood—into the analysis of class.[7] The late eighteenth and early nineteenth centuries witnessed significant changes in views of masculinity and femininity, the sexual division of labor, and sexual mores, and these changes were intimately intertwined with the evolution of class politics.

This period saw a shift from a notion of gender as hierarchy to a notion of gender as separate, complementary spheres. Prior to the mid-eighteenth century, men and women were not seen as opposites; rather, people saw gender, like the social structure as a whole, in terms of a hierarchy.[8] For instance, they often envisioned women as flawed versions of men. Men ruled over women, who were seen as men's inferiors, just as gentry ruled over common people, householders over servants, and masters over apprentices and journeymen. The manhood of the master was not the same in degree or kind as the masculinity of his servant. By the early nineteenth century, however, a new ideology of gender as separate spheres had arisen, in which individual men joined together as equals to form the public sphere of politics, while keeping their wives in the private sphere of the home.[9] Putting separate spheres into practice, however, was a class privilege denied to working men and women. Working men were denied political power, and working women could not take shelter in the home, but had to earn wages. This book will demonstrate that the making of the working class was in part a struggle by radicals to universalize this class-bound notion of gender.

To integrate gender into class, it will be necessary to transform the traditional categories of working-class history. I will discuss class formation on four levels: work, community, culture, and class consciousness.[10] For

Thompson and many orthodox Marxists, class first begins with the "common experience" of some men "largely determined by productive relations."[11] In other words, working men gained a sense of their own exploitation at work, feeling robbed of their skill and the profits of their labor. But gender also shaped the division of labor during the industrial revolution, as employers sought to replace skilled men with cheaper female and child labor.[12] In response, working men identified skill with manhood and sought to keep women out of the workplace—at the cost of dividing the labor force. Second, in order to organize to fight against exploitation and injustice, workers had to draw upon the strength of community bonds.[13] But gender shapes the boundaries of communities as well. Did plebeians define their communities according to the male worlds of workshop and pub, or did they include women in the wider circles of neighborhoods and markets?

Third, Thompson's genius lay in exploring working people's "traditions, value-systems, ideas, and institution[s]"—their "plebeian culture."[14] The term *plebeian* is useful for its deliberately vague inclusion of working people in general, defined not by a relation to a mode of production but as the "lower orders," ranging from rough soldiers, laborers, and prostitutes to needlewomen, servants, artisans, and factory workers, and merging into the lower levels of what would become the middle class, that is, small masters, shopkeepers, tradesmen, and publicans. However, as Thompson himself noted, plebeians did not form a *class*, in the sociological sense of a stratum of people who shared a common experience of productive relations and social values.[15] Indeed, gender conflict and clashes over moral values often fissured plebeian culture.[16] The religious respectables scorned the rough libertines; textile workers needed women's help while artisans shunned female labor.[17]

Fourth, it is important to explore how these diverse and divided people attained class consciousness: how, in Thompson's words, did they "feel and articulate the identity of their interests as between themselves, and as against other men whose interests are different from (and usually opposed to) theirs?"[18] For orthodox Marxists, class consciousness simply reflected the structure of economic relations and came into being when workers became aware of the "objective" analysis of their situation.[19] But Gareth Stedman Jones and other historians have correctly noted that the radicalism of working people in the 1830s and 1840s did not simply reflect a socialist analysis of economic exploitation. Instead, Stedman Jones examines the language of working-class radicals—and finds that they borrowed the political language of older republican movements rather than looking forward to socialist economics.[20]

However, while rejecting a rigid notion of class as determined by productive relations, we can still ask how radicals of the 1830s and 1840s attempted to create and define working-class consciousness in their own terms.[21] It is important to consider both the words and the organizational practice of working-class movements. During this period, the nature of working-class consciousness was open-ended—sometimes focusing on the political rights of skilled men, sometimes mobilizing women and the unskilled as part of larger communities. By organizing people in new ways, radicals tried to create a unified class consciousness out of divided communities. And to organize working people, radicals also had to create a rhetoric that resonated with people's diverse experiences and that promised solutions to the traumas of the industrial revolution. Radicals did not foresee socialism but, rather, recast old political solutions to solve contemporary economic ills.

Integrating language and organizational practice is also necessary if we are to understand the role of gender in the working-class movement. Joan Scott argues, for instance, that Stedman Jones ignores the way in which republican citizenship further excluded women from politics by defining them as wives and mothers.[22] Yet it would be a mistake to accept totally Scott's move away from experience to political language.[23] After participating in political movements, some women were able to move temporarily away from domesticity, redefining their political identities and reclaiming rational citizenship for themselves. The tension between women's militant activism and the rhetoric of radical domesticity was an important dynamic of the working-class movement. By combining the study of working people's experience with the analysis of radical rhetoric, this book goes beyond the sterile debate about whether it is economics or language that determines class consciousness.

Infusing gender into class also requires rewriting the traditional narratives of the making of the British working class. Historians often tell the story of the emblematic workers of the industrial revolution, the skilled artisans and the lower-status textile factory workers who replaced them. Marx and Engels depicted textile workers as the classic proletariat, wrenched from their family workshops to the mass experience of the factories, who therefore should have been the vanguard of working-class consciousness. However, Marxist historians have never been able to cope with the fact that many of these proletarians were women and children. In contrast, E. P. Thompson celebrates the artisanal heritage of radicalism, depicting artisans as heroic figures who drew upon a rich cultural tradition to create political and economic resistance. As Craig Calhoun points out, Thompson deliberately neglects textile factory workers, disdainfully portraying their struggles as pale imitations of artisan organizations.[24] Yet the story becomes quite different when examined through the lens of gender: artisans appear less heroic, and textile workers more creative.

Gender shaped the industrial revolution.[25] As Maxine Berg and Pat Hudson point out, "New work disciplines, new forms of subcontracting and putting-out networks, new factory organization, and even new technologies were tried out initially on women and children."[26] Skilled men thus faced competition from these cheaper sources of labor. The most familiar case, of course, is that of the cotton factories, where women and children tended machines whose productivity far outstripped that of a male handloom weaver. But urban employers also sought to undercut the clout of shoemakers and tailors by subdividing the labor process and taking advantage of women skilled at sewing and desperate for work.

This book contrasts the gender relations of artisans and textile workers in the metropolitan areas of London, Lancashire, and Glasgow.[27] I demonstrate that textile workers and artisans found different ways of creating and mobilizing communities, one based on fraternal bonding, the other on cooperative yet still patriarchal relations between men and women.[28] London was a center of artisan culture and radical political activity, facing metropolitan industrialization in the form of sweating rather than mechanization. But artisan culture reached beyond the metropolis to Lancashire and Glasgow as well. Artisans could no longer follow the traditional sequence, from apprentice, to journeyman, and then to the status of master and married man. Unable to afford their own workshops, they focused on creating trade solidarity through a bachelor journeyman culture of drinking rituals and combinations. Unwilling to tolerate lifelong celibacy, an artisan would often marry or cohabit, relying on the woman's earnings to help support the family. However, the artisans' bachelor orientation could easily be warped into misogyny and violence against women, directed both against rival female workers and against wives who complained of time and money spent with workmates in the pub. Artisans followed an exclusivist trade-union strategy directed against not only women but other male workers as well, further contributing to divisions among working people.

Lancashire and Glasgow were both dominated by the cotton textile trade, the vanguard of the industrial revolution. By examining Scottish circumstances in depth as well as those in the more familiar locale of Lancashire, this book extends the story of the making of the working class beyond the English to the British context. Yet textile trade-union struggles failed in Scotland but succeeded in Lancashire, resulting in significantly different gender divisions of labor and politics. Scots workers, however, shared many of the problems and responses of their English counterparts, and they were able to articulate them through a rich yet relatively unstudied popular culture.²⁹ The draconian Scottish legal system fiercely prosecuted Glasgow trade unionists, in the process confiscating their voluminous records and interviewing workers in depth, thereby crippling the labor movement but providing the historian with unusually extensive documentation.

The origins and changes in the gender division of labor in the cotton textile industry constitute one of the key problems in the historiography of the industrial revolution.³⁰ Although historians often consider handloom weavers and other skilled cloth handworkers as artisans, I have found that, in terms of gender relations, they had more in common with textile factory workers than with traditional artisans in apprenticed trades. The textile trades grew so rapidly that employers began to hire weavers without apprenticeship. Unlike apprenticed artisans, handloom weavers and other male textile workers accepted women's work as essential to the proto-industrial family economy; indeed, they were often able to marry early partially because they could count on the woman's earnings. The importance of cooperation between men and women may explain why male textile workers were somewhat less likely than others to commit violence against women. However, as new technology enabled manufacturers to try to replace skilled male factory workers with women and children, the gender division of labor had to be renegotiated constantly. To combat this threat, male workers often tried to emulate traditional artisans by excluding women from their jobs; yet, unlike artisans, they accepted female assistance as auxiliaries. After all, effective strikes required the support of women, through community, workplace, and kinship networks. However, textile communities were still divided among themselves, trying to keep wages up by driving away workers outside their own networks.

While the eighteenth century is often regarded as a golden age of family harmony that was destroyed by industrialization, I demonstrate that, instead, a "sexual crisis" characterized plebeian culture of the time.³¹ Labor mobility and the social changes of industrialization drove up illegitimacy rates between the mid-eighteenth and the mid-nineteenth century, and wife desertion and bigamy seemed all too frequent.³² Some plebeians saw common-law marriage and births out of wedlock as acceptable adjustments to new social realities or, alternatively, part of the enjoyment of a libertine or "rough" lifestyle. A man might be judged as respectable even though he was drank heavily and frequented prostitutes, so long as he was an independent, skilled, and intelligent worker.³³ But this libertine ethos clashed with domestic responsibilities, and wife-beating often resulted. Humiliation and anguish faced young couples when the man was out of work and unable to wed and his pregnant sweetheart was left alone and penniless.

In the rich popular culture of urban areas plebeians found social discourses through which to articulate their dilemmas.[34] *Social discourses* embody often unconscious values but also express a culture's social practices.[35] Artisans and textile workers had different sets of assumptions and ideals concerning work, community, and family. But they shared the popular culture of ballads, caricatures, newspapers, and melodrama. Even if they could not read, they heard snatches of verse bawled on the street, watched plays at street fairs or in penny theaters, ogled the latest caricatures in print-shop windows, and listened to fellow workers read the newspaper aloud.[36] However, the popular literature these people consumed did not derive from an autonomous working-class presence or originate in traditional folk culture; instead, popular commercial publishers plagiarized from both high literature and low, occasionally hiring itinerant ballad singers to write topical songs.[37] They hoped to increase sales by appealing to plebeian experiences of love, marriage, family, and social life, not through realistic depictions but in highly stylized genres of satire, comedy, or melodrama.

Religion, too, provided alternative ways of articulating the traumas of the sexual crisis. My view of religion here will differ from that of Thompson, who depicted Methodism as a masochistic distraction from the real issues of politics; instead, I will argue that sectarian religion spoke to personal dilemmas which early radicalism often ignored.[38]

Until the 1820s, the boundaries between plebeians and the middle class were often quite blurred, for plebeians often shared values and lifestyles with the slightly higher-status middling tradesmen, small shopkeepers, and master artisans. As the nineteenth century progressed, however, successful tradesmen and merchants distanced themselves from their neighbors who were sinking deeper into proletarianization and poverty.

The middle class was the first to develop a coherent class identity. Over the course of the late eighteenth and early nineteenth centuries, separating masculine work from the feminine home became a marker of middle-class status.[39] More than a matter of lifestyle, separate spheres had profound political implications as an ideology. Middle-class reformers defined themselves as more virtuous than either the dissolute aristocracy or the rough plebeians; the private virtue of their wives proved bourgeois men's public probity. Drawing upon the traditions of civic humanism, middle-class reformers defined the citizen as a propertied male householder, thereby excluding most working men, who had no property and often could not afford to maintain a household. This concept of the middle class was decisively enshrined in the 1832 Reform Act, which enfranchised middle-class men and excluded the working class.[40]

As Ernesto Laclau and Chantal Mouffe suggest, political language creates class by drawing hierarchical lines of difference between groups of people.[41] Gendered notions of virtue, expressed in the discourses of civic humanism, separate spheres, Malthusianism, and political economy, justified the exclusion of working people from the privileges of participation in the state. In response, working-class radicals were faced with the problem of creating a positive political class consciousness among demoralized and divided working people. They developed a rhetoric of class consciousness before the working class had been formed in sociological terms, that is, before they had become a cohesive group of people sharing common experiences and values. Radicals had to mobilize fragmented groups of working people into a united "imagined community" of class, creating new forms of political organization as they went along.[42] But which vision of community would shape working-class consciousness? Would radicals mobilize whole communities, including women and children, or would they simply speak to the interests of skilled working men?

In order to unify working people, radicals tried to create a political rhetoric that could convince them they had interests in common and that they could mobilize to defend those interests. I use the term *rhetoric* here because it implies a dialogue, for speakers must persuade their audiences and pressure their opponents.[43] To accomplish the first task, orators had to express the grievances of working people, not by merely describing their hardships or providing a correct analysis of their situation, but by drawing upon metaphors and motifs from popular culture to evoke their audiences' emotion and condense varied experiences into a few potent images, such as that of the aristocratic libertine destroying a happy home.[44] They also had to provide a vision of the future that promised to transcend these hardships and transform plebeian cultures plagued by heavy drinking, sexual antagonisms, and divisions between trades. This vision had to reassure both working men anxious at the loss of patriarchal privileges *and* women weary of hard work and irresponsible husbands.

To wrest concessions from Parliament, radicals had to manipulate the contradictions between political economy and the notion of separate spheres. In shaping these strategies, radicals faced many choices. Would they accept the radical re-visioning of gender in Owenite socialist feminism, or would they reshape the middle-class ideology of separate spheres for their own ends? Would radicals demand the vote on the basis of inherent individual political rights (which could include women), or would they claim manhood suffrage by proving their patriarchal respectability? Some historians and thinkers argue that only the available contemporary discourses can construct consciousness; without them, people have no way of thinking about the world.[45] To be sure, political economy, for instance, shaped the way many people thought in the early nineteenth century. But I am arguing that early nineteenth-century radicals could choose from a variety of ideologies and discourses. Their choices were determined, not by the dominance of discourse, but by the realities of power: their own lack of political clout, and working men's desire to retain control over women at home and at work.[46]

Whereas Thompson tells the story of the formation of working-class consciousness as a heroic, even a melodramatic, tale, my narrative must be more open-ended.[47] By examining diverse plebeian dilemmas and the rhetoric that attempted to address them, we can better understand that the moderation of working-class politics was not inevitable but simply one vision of many "makings" of the working class, one possible result of the "struggle for the breeches."[48]

1

WOMEN AND MEN
IN PLEBEIAN CULTURE

Figure 1.   In Wapping's Distant Realm I Drew My Breath. British Library T.2072 (3). By permission of the British Library.

2 Setting the Stage
Work and Family, 1780-1825

Sitting cross-legged on benches, sewing elaborate topcoats with strong stitches, late eighteenth-century tailors prided themselves not only on their skill but on the fact that they worked in all-male shops away from the home. They needed their wives' earnings—yet they insisted on keeping their workshops sacrosanct (see Figure 1). Even when the press of work forced them to stay up all night finishing a special order, tailors would not allow their wives to assist them. Instead, their spouses kept small millinery shops or, as a last resort, went out to do laundry or char by the day.[1]

In contrast, weavers relied on their wives' and daughters' labor in the task of making cloth. Women had always spun, and they could also wind spindles for their husbands while they rocked the cradle or watched the soup. When spinning moved into the factories, women began to learn to weave, bending over the looms for long hours alongside their husbands and brothers in shops under high, wide windows that were closed tight to keep the yarn soft and clean.

Why did tailors shun family labor when weavers valued it so? After all, artisans and textile workers faced similar problems. Few men earned enough to support a wife and children consistently, for even where wages were high, most trades followed seasonal patterns of frantic labor interspersed with unpaid lulls. As a result, on the one hand the men needed the labor of their wives and children in order for their families to survive. On the other, they faced the threat of having their wages undercut when employers hired cheaper female and child labor in mechanized or sweated processes. But the experiences and responses of artisans and textile workers in combining family and work were very different.[2]

Both patterns were probably rooted in the traditional northern European patriarchal family economy of earlier centuries, where the father functioned as master of a productive unit, whether farm or urban work-shop, and was assisted by his wife and children. Some historians, speculating that women's productive contribution allowed them to enjoy personal power as they melded home and work, have nostalgically imagined the pre-industrial family as egalitarian.[3] However, as Judith Bennett points out, that system always subordinated women, who labored in many urban occupations out of necessity rather than as a means of improving their status.[4]

In any case, by the late eighteenth and early nineteenth centuries the patriarchal family economy had been undermined. Enclosure and the agricultural revolution meant that many families could no longer make a living from the land. They sought instead to earn subsistence in domestic industry, spinning and weaving the raw materials merchants put out to them and receiving cash in return. Families profited as women turned to looms during the brief golden age of the textile industry, the last decades of the eighteenth century. Glasgow and Lancashire textile workers often followed the family labor system, whether outside or inside the home, with the father receiving a wage for the labor of himself, his children, and sometimes his wife.[5] But this system could lead to self-exploitation. As Medick points out, women and children were often paid less than subsistence wages, for it was assumed that they were subsidiary laborers whose chief value lay in providing domestic services.[6] Conversely, single men could not compete with the labor of a whole family.

Urban artisans sought to avoid this problem by keeping their families out of their occupations. As international and national trade grew in scale, the traditional progression from apprentice, to journeyman, to mastership and marriage became impossible, leaving many artisans mired at the journeyman stage. They survived by building on traditional bachelor journeyman culture, with its jovial fraternal bonding, to create fierce, cohesive combinations to keep up skill and status. But this required strict exclusionary policies against cheap, unskilled labor—especially that of women.

This chapter examines these different strategies in the urban areas of London, Lancashire, and Glasgow, analyzing the interaction of work, family, and community. Ultimately, the gender division of labor and workers' responses to it were determined, not by the location of work or the nature of the technology or skills, but by power relations within the family and in the workplace.[7]

London's Family Economies

Artisan culture flourished in the fierce competition and vigorous growth of large cities, and especially London. London's population more than doubled in this period, from approximately 670,000 in the middle of the eighteenth century to 1,379,000 in 1821.[8] In the capital and court center, highly skilled artisans, such as silversmiths, coachmakers and painters, wigmakers, mantuamakers, milliners, clockmakers, carvers and gilders, and cabinetmakers, were known for their expertise in fashioning precision and luxury goods.[9]

Yet the position of an honorable tradesman was never secure. Many London workers may have aspired to be a lower-middle-class master or shopkeeper, but constantly feared the plunge to the miseries of sweated labor in a garret. The opposite trajectory, of course, was also possible. The life of Francis Place provides a perfect example of the vicissitudes of work in the trades. His father was variously a journeyman baker, a master baker, a prison officer, and a publican, ultimately failing in business and dependent on his wife's wages from washing clothes. Place himself was apprenticed as a leather breeches maker, but soon fell into dire poverty as the trade became obsolete. He began again as a tailor and eventually established a successful business.[10]

Pressures on artisans intensified in the nineteenth century, as London's economy was transformed through "metropolitan industrialization."[11] Small workshops continued to dominate London's economy throughout the century, and the exceptional large-scale industries of docking, shipping, and brewing were not significantly mechanized. Men were not replaced by machines in the capital. Instead, many employers turned from luxury goods to the mass consumer market, cutting costs by subdividing tasks so that they could hire cheaper, less skilled labor. Makers of consumer goods provided the bulk of London's work force; shoemakers and tailors were the most numerous male workers.[12] The middling ranks and artisans themselves would buy cheap finery from slop shops, cobbled-together shoes, chapbooks hawked on the streets, or ready-made pies from the corner cookshop, but they could not afford a coat that took a skilled tailor a week to make, or carefully crafted boots of fine leather. As a result, many artisans were forced into the "dishonorable" branches of trades, which meant that they could not enforce apprenticeship and often faced competition from cheaper, female labor. Those who kept themselves in the "honorable," luxury branches of trades such as shoemaking or tailoring combined in fraternal organizations, based on the workshop and pub, to maintain tight control over apprenticeship and to uphold their skill, status, and wages.

Since most journeymen could never become masters, marriage—which had traditionally been postponed until that status was achieved—also became problematic. As one advice book noted, journeymen "must unavoidably struggle under great difficulties by being obliged to support the expenses of a wife and children." The book admonished journeyman not to marry "without he can light upon a woman with a fortune sufficient to raise him above it" by enabling him to become a master.[13] Michael Anderson writes that "towns relying on traditional artisan and trade occupations had more delayed marriage, and higher non-marriage rates."[14] Yet many artisans refused to resign themselves to lifelong celibacy, and delaying marriage made sense only if they believed their condition would improve. Many journeymen, therefore, married or cohabited.[15]

Given journeymen's low wages, women's work was crucial to the artisan family economy. A journeyman's wife wrote to the *Public Advertiser* in 1768 that even though her husband never drank, his wage of nineteen shillings was inadequate to support her and the children; she had to earn enough to pay their rent and buy clothes.[16] In addition, the work of many artisans, such as fashionable tailors, was highly seasonal, periodically requiring a wife's earnings to feed the family. And given the instability of eighteenth-century life—as Peter Earle puts it, the propensity of husbands to turn up in debtors' prison, if not Newgate, to run away and join the army or go to America or take up with another woman, or even to stay at home and fail in business due to bad luck or excessive drinking—wives' earnings often became essential to survival.[17]

Yet, until the end of the eighteenth century, wives rarely assisted their husbands in their trade.[18] "Honorable" trade organizations strictly forbade wives to help their husbands, for they wished to keep up their own skill and status by strictly excluding women from their occupations. Women were allowed only in the "dishonorable" or sweated branches of artisan trades. By the end of the century, however, the pressures of declining piece-rates and intense demand for productivity impelled some "dishonorable" artisans to bring work home to wives and children: a hatter's wife, for instance, could prepare the beaver felt, and a shoemaker's wife could bind shoes. If a man did not have a wife or child who could perform these supplementary tasks, he might have to hire a woman and pay her himself. This fact gave artisans an incentive to keep down the wages of women and children. Furthermore, when a family worked together in one room, the mixture of the shoemaker's leather and last or tailor's thread and cloth with the laundry, pots and pans, and children underfoot could disrupt marital harmony, as Francis Place remembered.[19] And even when women, such as shoebinders, labored in workshops, artisans never incorporated them into the culture of their trade.

Women's participation in the luxury trades declined through the eighteenth century. In the 1760s, Collyer's and Campbell's advice manuals on trades recommended that women learn gold and silver buttonmaking, which required "some fancy and genius" to invent "new fashions"; embroidery, which called for artistic talent; children's coatmaking; and capmaking, quilting, tasselmaking, and gilding. However, as particular luxury items went out of fashion, many of these trades declined. Moreover, by the end of the century men had taken over many of the more lucrative occupations, such as millinery. In those masculine trades where a few women had been able to gain a foothold, girls were increasingly excluded from apprenticeship.[20] Women were so crowded into the remaining trades that no matter how skilled they were their wages were comparatively low.[21]

To supplement their husbands' incomes, some artisans' wives ran a small shop of their own, such as a chandler's or a corner grocery.[22] John Overs described a carpenter's ambition as "soaring no higher than the establishment of his wife in some light business"; for example, the common-law wife of one journeyman carpenter sold coals from a cellar.[23] But business could be difficult to combine with motherhood if a woman had many small children. William Hart, a cooper, remembered that he and his wife took a haberdasher's shop "to sell women's and children's shoes, for my wife to try and get a little to help, but we soon found it impracticable, for my wife had young children to attend to."[24]

Most wives of artisans therefore worked in a narrow range of female-dominated trades, especially needlework, charring and laundry work, nursing and midwifery, and hawking and portage.[25] Since they lacked opportunities for formal apprenticeship, they had to turn to good use the extensive skills they had acquired as girls, and as servants before marriage, in household tasks such as needlework, laundry, and cleaning. A few women found employment as highly skilled laundresses of fine laces and linens, but washing was generally a heavy trade, and certainly not genteel.[26] A song depicted a laundress lamenting,

> To think a poor old soul like me
> Should have to slave like I do,
> I'm fifty turned next lady day,
> Yet in the suds I'm sloshing.
> I strive to earn a crust I say,
> By going out a washing
> Toiling, boiling all the day,
> Rubbing, slushing, sloshing.[27]

Hannah More recounted an affecting tale of an industrious laundress who worked hard to support herself, her children, and a profligate husband, only to have him come home drunk and take her wages, which legally belonged to him.[28]

As L. D. Schwarz observed, artisans' strategy of excluding women from crafts enabled skilled working men to keep up their own standard of living at the expense of their wives and children.[29] The "sexual economy" of London and other metropolitan artisans was thus characterized by complex conflicts of interest between artisans, their families, and single women. A bachelor journeyman culture coexisted dissonantly with the reality that many artisans were married. Excluded from crafts, women remained a pool of low-waged labor available to undercut men, a group skilled in the sewing tasks required for the ostensibly masculine trades of tailoring and shoemaking. Their wages were so low that single women were forced into prostitution or cohabitation to survive, but in turn married women's work undercut that of both single men and single women. Within artisan life these factors produced a slow-burning fuse of gender antagonism at work and within the home. Although these conflicts were particularly marked in London, they also manifested themselves among the artisans of urban Lancashire and Glasgow, who, as will be seen below, shared values and organizational forms with their metropolitan brothers.

The Textile Trades

Spinners, weavers, and other textile workers dominated northern cities. Glasgow, Manchester, and the smaller towns surrounding them had always had a core of artisans and merchants, but the textile industry really fueled town growth in the late eighteenth and early nineteenth century. Population density increased; for instance, "between 1801 and 1851 Manchester more than quadrupled its population to over 300,000."[30] Glasgow's population grew from 77,385 in 1801 to 274,324 in 1841.[31] By 1826 it was the third largest city in the United Kingdom, after London and Manchester.[32]

The cotton textile industry flourished in such areas as Manchester, Stockport, and Glasgow because there an urban core provided a pool of skilled artisanal labor and a rural hinterland provided workers for cottage industries and the first factories. Growth in Lancashire and the Glasgow area followed a pattern quite different from the heterogeneity of London, as homogeneous textile villages merged into urban conglomerations. The small textile villages such as Paisley, Anderston, Calton, Bridgeton, and the Gorbals that later merged into Glasgow still maintained their own distinct identities in the early nineteenth century. In Scotland, cotton employed over 150,000 people in 1814, and most of them were outworkers in spinning and weaving around Glasgow and the southwest.[33]

Changes in textile production spurred population expansion. The Manchester, Oldham, and Bolton areas in Lancashire grew rapidly from the middle of the eighteenth century, and industrial southern Lancashire and eastern Cheshire trebled in population in the first half of the nineteenth. As innovations in spinning machinery increased yarn production, hand-loom weaving spread through the rural areas, especially in northeast Lancashire, where cottagers had often taken in weaving to augment their scanty earnings from the stony ground. By 1811, more than a third of Lancashire's population was involved in the cotton industry, mostly in handloom weaving. Spinning factories, initially established in rural areas to take advantage of water power, further stimulated rural cottage industry. With the invention of the steam-powered mule spinner, factories were established in urban areas such as Manchester as well.[34]

The availability of cheap female and child labor was especially important for the textile industry. Contemporary commentators, who had often lamented that women and children had found few opportunities to help support their families, welcomed the cotton industry for employing those "whose work was formerly unproductive."[35] For instance, several ladies of the gentry set up thread-spinning businesses in towns around Glasgow and the Lowlands to provide suitable female employment.[36]

Soon, the booming cotton trade needed the labor of wives and children as well as men, making the last two decades of the eighteenth century a golden age of domestic industry.[37] Yet the very conditions that fostered textile workers' prosperity ultimately undermined it. Mechanization brought new opportunities for men, such as mule spinning, but employers soon tried to substitute women and children on simpler machines. Families working together could earn a good income, but they also bred more weavers and thus overstocked the trade.

The story of how spinning came to be a man's trade in Lancashire and Glasgow exemplifies the constant shifts in the gender division of labor and in family economies brought about by the cotton industry. The spinning jennies were at first used within the home by women, who could vastly increase their output of yarn and earn more money. In the 1780s, a skilled female jenny-spinner could earn as much as or more than a male weaver.[38] One contemporary writer could not understand why people objected to the machines, for they made a "prodigious difference . . . in the gains of the females in the family." He went on, "If it were true, that the *weaver* gets *less*, yet, as his *wife* gets *more*, his *family* does not suffer."[39] However, male weavers may have felt their traditional marital dominance threatened, while handspinners without access to the jennies found that their already meager earnings had plummeted.

In any case, the jenny-spinners' prosperity did not last long, for the introduction of water-powered mule-spinning machines in the factories undercut their earnings.[40] To be sure, at first country mills employed women and children on light mules, taking advantage of the desperation that forced them to accept low wages. But by the 1790s the advent of steam engines made possible larger spinning mules which required not only skill but strength, so employers began to locate factories in towns with a supply of male artisans. Ralph Mather, a contemporary, alleged that the new machines prevented weavers from using the labor of their wives and children to spin at home and thus made it impossible for their families to survive. As a result, he stated, over 4,000 poor men had to enlist as soldiers or sailors to escape the cries of their starving wives and children.[41] During a labor dispute in 1818, mule spinners protested that before the steam engines were introduced their wives could work at home beating and cleaning bales of cotton for the spinners in the factory, "earning eight, ten, twelve shillings a week, and cook and attend to their families." But now, lamented the spinners, their wives "have no employment, except they go to work in the factory all day at what can be done by children for a few shillings."[42]

At first urban men resisted factory employment, but the lure of a new, highly paid occupation enticed many artisans, such as shoemakers, joiners, and hatmakers, to take up mule spinning.[43] Like other workers, mule spinners initially expected that their wives would help to support the family, either by piecing for their husbands or by engaging in subsidiary cotton-processing tasks. However, mule spinners' high wages seem to have put them in the vanguard of the textile trades: they adopted the breadwinner ideal as early as the 1820s, when high wages enabled them to keep their wives at home instead of sending them to the factories.[44] Their homes, though perhaps only a couple of rooms in a tenement, were tidy and prosperous, often furnished with china, books, clocks, a mahogany bedstead, and kitchen things, and wives could feed their families meat several times a week. They also had large families, for children could earn wages by assisting their fathers or other men.[45]

In the textile industry, unlike the artisanal system, female and child labor was always an indispensable part of the productive unit. The skilled male mule spinners, who ran and adjusted the heavy, complex machines, paid children and young women to assist them as piecers, knotting together broken threads, removing spindles, and cleaning the machinery. Mule spinning was organized around a family labor system, in which adult men supervised and paid female and child labor. When possible, they hired their own relatives.[46] Yet since, more often than not, mule spinners did not have enough children of the right age, they often took on children from other families, as well as women.[47] Even if a mule spinner did not supervise his own children, his power over the process was patriarchal. As we shall see in later chapters, the hold of male mule spinners on their high-paid status was somewhat tenuous. Lancashire and urban Glaswegian spinners resorted to violent union activity to retain their positions against employers' efforts to replace them with female spinners. In Scotland, in particular, country mills economized by hiring cheap female spinners in order to compensate for their lack of technological innovation. Females composed 61.1 percent of the cotton industry work force in Scotland, as compared to 50.5 percent for Lancashire.[48]

Factories employed large numbers of women and children as carders and reelers as well as piecers. For instance, in 1809 forty-one cotton mills in Renfrewshire (near Glasgow, around Paisley) employed a total of 932 men, 2,449 women and 17,792 children.[49] Large pools of single women needed work, especially in Scotland. There, many fewer women married than in England; the proportion of single women averaged around 20 percent of the adult female population, compared to 10 percent in England. Male emigration and the allure of the textile industry, which allowed single women to support themselves, however marginally, may account for the greater proportion of Scottish spinsters.[50] In Lancashire, the textile industry paid women and children higher wages than did other occupations, although their pay still lagged far behind men's.[51]

While male mule spinners created their own prosperity, however tenuous, keeping their wives at home and sending only their children to the factory, handloom weavers initially throve by drawing their wives and daughters into skilled work within the home. They enjoyed the golden age in the late eighteenth century, when weaving was still unmechanized. Weavers held themselves to be superior to cotton mill workers, whom they disdained as degraded, dirty, and unskilled.[52]

Paisley weavers, for instance, attained a good standard of living. Like the mule spinners, weavers could afford to furnish their houses comfortably, and they were renowned for their learning, perhaps because their sedentary work gave them time to think.[53] In 1834 a Glasgow weaver nostalgically remembered that in 1792 "young journeymen weavers occupied the most conspicuous seats in our city churches, dressed in a suit of clothes equal in quality, I believe, to their employers, each had tied and powdered hair, and a pair of boots, and a watch." He was able to set up a respectable household with home and loom shop "in the decentest style of tradesmen."[54]

Weavers prized their independence from supervision and their freedom to pace their work. As John Mackinnon observed from his own experience, during the first decade of the nineteenth century, "Journeymen in many other trades forsook their occupations, and flocked into the weaving districts to learn the trade. . . . One principal cause which induced grown men to learn the trade was the complete freedom from control which a journeyman weaver enjoyed. He was as much his own master as the proprietor of a factory, for the earnings of a weaver could rise to the level of a mason's or a smith's."[55] Weavers viewed themselves as skilled, honorable artisans deserving of respect.

Unlike traditional artisans, however, male weavers owed much of their sense of control and their prosperity to the family-based economy, for they could supervise, and profit from, the labor of their wives and children. Wives helped in the production of cloth most generally by winding "pirns," the Scottish term for bobbins, saving their husbands from having to pay other women to perform this task. Wives also spun, and they helped in the business when their husbands had loom shops. David Gilmour recalls of Paisley that wives would pay their husbands' drawboys (who assisted in weaving) and also fetched yarn from the warehouse and delivered finished cloth.[56]

In the 1790s, when tambouring, a type of embroidery, flourished, weavers' wives and daughters could also earn extra cash at that trade.[57] Merchants gave out the cloth to women who would embroider it in imitation of fashionable Indian cloth. Girls would learn the skill at a warehouse and then work at home, which allowed parents to keep their children there rather than send them out to service. Tambour work also enabled young women to buy furniture and finery. As a clergyman noted disapprovingly, the dress of women was "more showy and expensive than formerly." Young women wore scarlet wool or black silk cloaks and high-crowned hats to church, instead of their old brown shawls.[58] Some Glasgow tambourers even purchased their own seats in church.[59] Tambouring strengthened the family economy by allowing women to work at home.

In both Lancashire and Glasgow, as the factories took away their opportunities for spinning at home, many women also began weaving. Linen and woolen handloom weaving had originally been an artisanal trade with strict apprenticeship regulations, but the great demand for labor, especially after 1790 in the new cotton industry, led employers to hire men and women without indentures.[60] For a few pounds, a skilled weaver would teach other men and women the trade.[61] Since handloom weaving was so easy to learn and, in the early years, so profitable, many Highlanders, Irish, and displaced Lowland agricultural workers took it up, eventually overstocking the trade and reducing wages. By the late 1830s, a fifth to a third of the handlooms in the cotton textile industries of the Glasgow area were operated by women.[62] According to Duncan Bythell, "as early as 1808" half of all weavers in England may have been women and children.[63]

Like tambouring, weaving by wives and daughters in family workshops could strengthen the family economy—but it could also weaken family ties by providing an independent source of income for a single woman. Moreover, since men controlled the wages of their wives, a woman's weaving wage could simply go to support his drinking. In 1799, weavers from Lancashire told Parliament that "if a man enlists, his wife turns weaver (for here the women are weavers as well as the men) and instructs her children in the art of weaving; and I have heard many declare that they lived better since their husband[s] enlisted than before."[64]

But the work of women and children in weaving was associated with the decline of the trade. In times of prosperity, early marriage and the profitability of employing children led to large families, and the constant pregnancy hampered women's wage-earning. Eventually, these children would grow up to be weavers and overstock the trade. Women and children, furthermore, were more likely to work on plain goods, while men worked on the better-paying heavy cloths or fancy work.[65]

The fortunes of handloom weavers oscillated during the Napoleonic wars and plunged precipitously soon afterward. Wages dropped dramatically, and the formerly proud weavers were reduced to a steadily worsening poverty. As a broadside portrayed one weaver's lament,

> When peace kept far off, war and strife
> An' food was cheap, and braw an' rife,
> We made a shift to jog through life
> Wi' moderate toil ay
> An' mony a happy man an' wife
> Liv'd cosh an' gaily.
> An' there when a' is gane [all is gone] thegither
> Wi' scarce ae sark [shirt] to change anither,
> The hungry bairns around them gather,
> O, dool [sorrow] to see them!
> While droopin' dad, and greetin' [weeping] mitherr
> Naught hae to gie [give] them.[66]

The huge supply of very low-paid weavers actually delayed mechanization of the trade. The power loom had been invented by 1793 in Glasgow and was introduced by 1800 to Lancashire, but it was quite primitive until 1813 and not perfected until 1833. In 1813, 2,400 power looms and 240,000 handlooms were in operation; by 1829, there were 55,000 power looms and 225,000 handlooms.[67] To operate the early power looms, mills employed young women almost exclusively, at wages lower than men's, an obvious threat to male handloom weavers. As we shall see, handloom weavers often reacted angrily to this threat to their livelihood, destroying powerloom factories in several localities. However, the fact that many handloom weavers were forced to send their daughters to the factories to supplement the family income muted the direct antagonism between male handloom weavers and female powerloom weavers.[68] In fact, female powerloom weavers mainly competed directly with *female* handloom weavers, for they both produced low-quality muslins while men wove the better cloths.[69]

In general, although the availability of work in spinning and weaving drove up women's wages, they still remained low enough to undercut the position of skilled men. As did artisans, skilled male cotton textile workers fought continual battles against employers' efforts to undercut them by drawing upon this pool of cheap female labor. But for cotton textile workers, unlike artisans, the traditions of the family labor system muted gender antagonism: the subordinate labor of women and children was necessary and accepted, buttressing, rather than undermining, patriarchal authority.

Conclusion

Artisans and textile workers had much in common. Of course, many textile workers were former artisans, and, as we shall see, they initially followed similar cultural strategies in struggling against the threats of deskilling and declining status. However, the sexual division of labor in the textile industry—the essential role played by women's and children's labor—helped to shape different cultural patterns, which, if not exactly egalitarian, potentially allowed more cooperation between the sexes. Yet occupational culture also played a role. When hatters, shoemakers, and other artisans were forced to allow women to work on subsidiary tasks, sexual antagonism, rather than cooperation, seems to have resulted.

The industrial revolution did not represent a simple fall from an idyllic world of the household economy to the degradation of the factory family. Instead, there were continual shifts and negotiations over the gender division of labor. For metropolitan male artisans who had followed an exclusivist strategy of keeping skilled work for themselves and relegating their wives and children to a few low-paid occupations, the introduction of the family labor system meant decline into sweating. For handloom weavers, conversely, the family labor system of cottage industry strengthened patriarchal control and brought prosperity—until their trade declined. Factories allowed mule spinners to employ their own children and allowed their wives to stay at home, but they always faced the threat of undercutting from cheap female labor. In both instances, the potential for tensions existed among the interests of skilled men, their families, and single women.

3 Men and Women Together and Apart

Plebeian Culture and Communities

Historians have often idealized artisan culture as the plebeian prototype of working-class consciousness. They imagine a group of shoemakers or weavers disputing religion and politics over their work, and frequently adjourning to the pub to quaff whisky or ale, sing subversive songs, and debate the existence of God. Their elaborate craft rituals are depicted as the foundation of later working-class solidarity. Their control over skill and workplace organization enabled them to maintain their independence from bosses and priests, and their social bonds created the community cohesion necessary for effective class mobilization.[1]

Yet artisans formed only one strand, and a limited one at that, of plebeian communities. Artisans focused on the workshop and the pub at the expense of the neighborhood and the home, thereby excluding women from their culture. In the nostalgic vision of artisan communities, we are not shown the wives hovering around the door of the pub, trying to coax their husbands home before they spent all their wages. Even when women worked in the same trade as men, artisans refused to admit them into their occupational culture, for they based their honor on masculinity. Not only that, artisans cemented their own solidarity by excluding other, less skilled male workers, as E. P. Thompson admits.[2] Until after the Napoleonic wars, they looked after the interests of their own particular trade, rather than championing all workers' rights. In contrast, although textile workers often emulated and participated in artisan culture, they seem to have valued family, marriage, and neighborhood much more than artisans did, organizing on the basis of kin and community as well as work.[3]

Artisans' focus on the workplace and pub deprived them of other sources of organization within the larger plebeian culture. Whereas the middle class was formed as bourgeois men separated private life from the

25

public sphere, their masculine springboard to political power, plebeians found such a separation between public and private impossible to maintain. Plebeian women labored and socialized among men in workshops, pubs, and streets. In some occupations, men worked at home side by side with their wives and daughters. Thompson himself has stressed how plebeian culture went beyond organization at the workplace, as communities came together to defend their morality through rough music—nocturnal, discordant demonstrations of neighborhood displeasure.[4] As Ruth Smith and Deborah Valenze write, women were particularly active when plebeian communities mobilized around the values of "mutuality," such as food riots.[5] While the predominance of women has sometimes been seen as a hindrance to working-class mobilization,[6] plebeian women were able to create organizational forms that transcended the boundaries between work and home.

This chapter will demonstrate how plebeian culture contained within it both the preconditions for class mobilization and factors which fractured the potential for class solidarity. To be sure, the male bonding of artisans created an intense, powerful cohesion often emulated by other workers. But plebeian men and women also bonded across occupational lines as they socialized in pubs or neighborhood streets, went to market, attended chapel, and organized friendly societies.[7] Furthermore, occupation, ethnicity, and gender—and, as we shall see in later chapters, religious and sexual values—could fissure plebeian communities as well as unite them.[8]

Urban Geography

Community organization first grows out of proximity. Workers could complain to each other as they labored at tailor's benches or bent over their looms and could then plot to strike if masters would not raise wages or shorten hours. They could broaden their concerns and strengthen their organizations if discussions spread beyond the boundaries of small workshops or individual factories. Women could link high food prices with the wage cuts at a particular mill as they bargained over vegetables in the town market. Shoemakers and tailors could compare grievances as they drank ale or whisky together at a pub. Standing at their doorsteps on the street, nursing babies or knitting, mothers could observe not only their children playing but strikebreakers skulking into a mill.

The particular urban geography of a town thus shaped the community organization of its plebeian population. In general, London lacked neighborhood cohesion, as waves of country immigrants seeking work, decayed tradesmen, and ambitious journeymen jostled for scarce housing in old slums and new suburbs. New immigrants accounted for over a third of the

population of London in 1821.[9] To be sure, certain trades clustered in particular neighborhoods: Clerkenwell watchmakers, Spitalfields silk weavers,
the tailors and shoemakers of St. James. Long Acre, conveniently located
near the court, was known for its "coachmakers and subordinate trades of
painters, varnishers, wheelmakers, sadlers and the like."[10] Artisans in these
trades considered themselves "honorable," "organized in their houses of
call, their societies, and their clubs."[11]

As the sweating system and the growing obsolescence of various trades
robbed them of status, many craftsmen had to leave respectable artisan
neighborhoods for less salubrious locations. For instance, honest shoemakers, matmakers, shopkeepers, and lodging house keepers had to seek
shelter in Church Lane, St. Giles, notorious as a refuge for thieves and
receivers.[12] In slightly less seedy Grays Inn Lane, journeymen shoemakers
lived next to a house of ill-fame; which bordered on a lodging house
populated by excessive drinkers, then Roman Catholics, and a few doors
down respectable tradesmen lived next to shopkeepers who received stolen
goods.[13] For working men, then, not the street but the workshop and the
pub defined their community, although their wives could form strong
bonds as they met on lodging house stairways or shopped together in local
markets.

In contrast, both Scottish and Lancashire textile villages were extremely
cohesive, being inhabited largely by men and women all involved in the
same industry. Between 1813 and 1822, in many north, central, and eastern Lancashire villages one-half to one-third of the men listed in the marriage register were handloom weavers. In Stockport during this period,
"approximately 60–70 per cent of the population . . . was supported by
wages earned in [the textile industry,] either as workers or their dependents," and these workers were evenly divided between handloom weavers
and factory spinners.[14] Massive immigration into Stockport and the Lancashire factory towns did not produce anomie and fragmentation as it did
in London.[15] As Michael Anderson has demonstrated, migrants from other
towns and villages in Lancashire tried to settle near their kin in Preston.
Since Preston and other industrial towns such as Stockport were also quite
compact, workers living on the densely populated streets could easily form
communities.[16] The evidence from Oldham also suggests that artisans and
textile workers intermarried, further cementing larger communities.[17]

Men and Women Together in Urban Space

The lives of London's artisans and Lancashire's textile workers differed in
many ways, but they all shared crowded conditions that made any division
between public and private life impossible. Unlike the middle class or even

the late-nineteenth-century working class, where men and women lived in separate spheres, plebeian women and men worked together in crowded tenements, workshops, and factories, socialized and traded on the street, and drank together in pubs. As John Gillis writes, plebeian society was characterized by a wide social network which extended beyond the married couple.[18] Yet it should not be supposed that "rough-and-ready" equality between men and women existed widely. Women participated in market-oriented social life, but they were positioned in it quite differently from men: their incomes were lower, they bore more responsibility for children, and, ultimately, they were caught in an economy in which their sexuality could be marketable.

Unlike the middle class, plebeians could not retreat to a private world of home. In both London and Glasgow, families typically lived in one or two rooms in houses divided up and rented out by enterprising landlords, or, if they were master craftsmen or shopkeepers, they lived above or behind their shops. These rooms could be quite respectable, with a hearth, ma-hogany dresser, prints on the walls, and a few books, or squalid, with only a few rags in the corner, broken-down bits of furniture, and peeling paint. In some occupations, the home also served as the workshop. For traditional artisans, such as tailors, this was a sign of degradation; for handloom weavers, a valued tradition.

Even when the husband worked away from the family dwelling, outside life could still permeate the home. Many women, especially those with small children to look after, took in lodgers as a way to help pay the rent.[19] At least 27 percent of Glasgow households in my 1841 census sample had lodgers. In Preston, 23 percent of all households took in lodgers, and the percentage was higher among textile workers.[20] In London, because children were not allowed in "respectable" lodging houses, even some skilled workers such as carpenters either had to live in "low" neighborhoods or had to pay high rents to become householders and then let out rooms themselves.[21]

Gloomy, stone Scottish tenements could be particularly dismal, for not only a family but also several lodgers, or even two families, typically shared one room.[22] These rooms were not only crowded but often filthy. Many of the inhabitants were recent immigrants from country districts, accustomed to relieving themselves on dung heaps outside doors, a habit they maintained in the closes (courts) of the tenements. Scottish country-women were notorious for their relaxed attitude toward cleanliness, which sprang from the very low standard of living prevailing in rural areas.[23] And the living quarters of Irish immigrants often fell below even the native Scottish standards, as they were crowded into the worst tenements or even into damp cellars.[24]

Until the mid-nineteenth century, both male and female plebeians sought refuge from crowded homes in the pleasures of public life. Through the "social exchange" of public drinking, Hans Medick notes, plebeians "strengthened . . . the bonds of neighborhood, kinship, or friendship."[25] Respectable middle-class families were withdrawing to more private entertainments, but plebeian men and women continued to socialize together in public. In weaving communities, men and women gathered together in neighbors' homes to pass the winter evenings by gossiping, discussing theology, and singing.[26] In Glasgow, the fair was the great occasion for family outings every summer, and wives accompanied their husbands to the market each week to buy provisions. In London, the wives and daughters of respectable shopkeepers and master artisans went to the theater, card parties, and pleasure gardens with their husbands and male friends.[27]

Both men and women frequented pubs and spirit cellars. In 1794 the reforming magistrate Patrick Colquhoun complained that London laboring families—husbands, wives, and children—"have got into the habit of spending their leisure time in pubs, eating and drinking, quarreling and gaming."[28] The parliamentary Select Committee on Drunkenness of 1834 hired investigators to watch the comings and goings of customers in fourteen London pubs for a week. They found that men never made up more than 66 percent of the customers, averaging just over 50 percent.[29] In Glasgow, the police were kept busy every night hauling drunken women, as well as men, off the streets in wheelbarrows.[30] Respectable skilled textile workers took their wives to spirit cellars on holidays. For instance, a Protestant weaver of Bridgeton had accompanied his wife and some friends to take a dram on "St. Monday," when they were attacked by several Irish Catholic weavers continuing a factional dispute.[31] Similarly, cotton spinner John Rowan's alibi when he was accused of attacking a strikebreaker was that he had been spending a sociable evening at a spirit cellar with his wife, his brothers, and his father.[32] According to the old ballad "John Appleby," "John to the alehouse would go, / Joan to the tavern wou'd run, / John wou'd get drunk with the women, / & Joan would get drunk with the men."[33]

Plebeian men seem to have reserved specific times for drinking with their wives and to have kept others sacrosanct to their workmates. For instance, when Thomas Brophy's wife joined him and his fellow Covent Garden porters for a drink, it proved to be their last sociable moment together. She soon left her husband and mates to continue drinking, and when he finally returned home he exploded in a drunken rage and killed her.[34] Bearing the responsibility for feeding and clothing the children, wives usually had a less carefree attitude toward money than their spouses displayed. The wife of a pinmaker complained in 1833 that "her husband wasted a great proportion of his time and money in the society of men composing two clubs called the 'Lumber Troopers,' and the 'Johns,' where he was in the habit of drinking, smoking, and talking, instead of supporting his lawful married wife."[35] In popular literature, wives reviled the sleek, plump publicans' wives who profited from husbands' foolishness. In "A New and Diverting Dialogue Between a Shoemaker and His Wife," an angry woman declared, "[T]he landladies flourish in their rings, gold chains, lockets, and what not, while we and our children have not bread to eat."[36] Medick notes that "the long-term needs of the household had a relatively low priority in the monetary sphere. By contrast, the demand for public consumption in the monetary sphere was extraordinarily high."[37] In simple language, this often meant that husbands squandered their money in the pub while their wives had to scrimp and save at home.

Plebeian Manhood and Artisan Culture

To be sure, plebeian men spent their money on activities which promoted the solidarity of male bonding rather than individual self-advancement.[38] Drinking bound workmen together. Working men spent most of their time when they were not actually laboring waiting for work in a "house of call," where a publican would allocate daily jobs or at least dispense wages on a Saturday night. Men's friendly societies, which often functioned as trade unions, met in pubs. But the pub was not valuable only because it was a place to meet: drink itself lubricated solidarity. Men grew less inhibited and thus became more intimate as a long night of drinking wore on.[39]

However, drinking usually sapped funds needed for family life, and it engendered violence. The shoemaker John O'Neill described his club meetings in rather glowing terms: "Here we sat talking over old philosophy, and new philosophy, law, physic and politics till we could scarcely tell our way home" after numerous hot whisky toddies. But the wives, excluded from these intellectual conversations, only knew that their hung-over husbands were "cross and wranglesome" the morning after. O'Neill himself assented to wives' entreaties to stop the clubs after he woke up from one particularly alcoholic evening to find he had blacked his wife's eye.[40] As Mary Anne Clawson shows, the male bonding of the fraternal club strengthened the patriarchal power of the man in the family.[41]

Yet definitions of masculinity were fraught with tension during this period. Early modern manhood had depended on patriarchal status, whether as the master of a workshop or as a farmer. By the eighteenth century, however, several factors had challenged patriarchal manhood. Separate spheres had modified traditional patriarchy; instead of the husband and father supervising the work of his wife and children in the home, the middle-class man went off to a public workplace, leaving them in the domestic sphere. Respectable, religious bourgeois men prided themselves on keeping their wives and daughters uncontaminated.[42]

In contrast, some men pursued pleasure in a metropolitan libertine culture. Scholars debate the precise meaning of the term *libertine*; it is used here in a loose sense, to describe the search for pleasure as life's primary goal.[43] Libertinism focused on consumption and display, spending rather than saving, excess rather than control. It cut across all classes, especially in London, where debauched aristocrats might carouse with dissolute tradesmen in the cellars of St. Giles.[44] Plebeian masculinity shared many elements with aristocratic manhood, which was "based on sport and codes of honor derived from military prowess, finding expression in hunting, riding, drinking and wenching."[45] Gentlemen duelled to prove their honor; laboring men engaged in formal boxing matches.[46] For instance, when John Humphries Parry insulted a master bricklayer, the bricklayer retorted, "Stand up and fight like a man."[47] Even the *Trades' Newspaper*, which was trying to create a new respectable working-class culture in the 1820s, lauded fighting for honor while condemning commercial boxing, asserting, "An instant use of one's fist, in resentment of an insult or blow, is manly."[48] Nonetheless, to compete with popular apolitical newspapers such as the sporting *Bell's Weekly Dispatch*, the paper featured extensive coverage of prize fights. Personal temperament no doubt turned individual plebeian men either toward libertinism or toward religious respectability. Shopkeepers, shoemakers, porters, and coachmen could all become either Methodists or debauched gamblers. Yet structural factors of artisan life in particular forced many journeymen into the libertine camp. First, artisans' skill and status were constantly being undercut, especially by cheaper female labor. In response, they developed a cult of male solidarity based on the exclusion of women—as well as less "honorable" men—which became their substitute for the prestige of masterhood.[49]

Artisans created a particular type of masculine culture based more on fraternity than patriarchy.[50] The tight brotherly bonds of equals in the workshop or combination acted as a powerful force in unions and created a rich ritualistic culture. Even as their control over work eroded, journeymen's organizations preserved a sense of pride in craft and independence by celebrating their skill with brotherly joviality. As Prothero writes of trades societies, "Men loved the regular lodge meetings, conviviality, rituals, ceremonies, banners . . . and the annual processions and dinner."[51] Craft-based friendly societies formed the basis for combinations and strikes.

Yet artisan solidarity was also quite exclusive. Traditionally, some trades tried to distinguish themselves as higher status than others: butchers above barbers in London, for instance.[52] In Scotland, Alexander Somerville noted that tradesmen and artisans seemed overly conscious of petty crafts distinctions; craftsmen would scorn laborers' sons.[53] In Paisley, handloom weavers on fancy goods such as silk considered themselves superior in culture, craft, and education to the cotton factory workers, although by the late 1820s the latter had become more cultivated.[54]

However, although historians have often stressed artisan attachment to craft, their "property in skill,"[55] Jacques Rancière has recently argued that the most politically active crafts were those with the least skill and, often, the lowest status in the artisan world: tailors, shoemakers, and weavers. They combined to compensate for the lack of interest their craft provided, and they whiled away their time with elaborate social ritual and thought and talk on political subjects.[56] The shoemakers, for instance, had a tradition of tales about the valor of Saint Crispin, their patron saint, which reached back to the sixteenth century. The "Princely History of the Gentle Craft," a chapbook printed around 1750, praised the pleasures of the trade:

> Of all the crafts, the Gentle Craft's the best,
> Their pleasant songs make Labour seem like rest.
> In mirth and comfort all the year they live,
> And unto Strangers oft relief they give.

Male textile workers such as cotton spinners, handloom weavers, and calico printers imitated these traditions in forming their own organizations, complete with membership cards, rituals, and songs.[57] Desperate, like tailors and shoemakers, to keep their status as skilled workers, they knew that they needed a tough, cohesive organization, for women could easily learn their trades.

Weavers and cotton spinners may also have stressed their intellectual aspirations in compensation for their tenuous, if not totally illusive, hold on craft traditions such as apprenticeship. Weavers were especially known for their clubs during the golden age of the late eighteenth century.[58] John McAdam, a shoemaker's apprentice, had a "passion for reading," so he joined a Calton book club composed mainly of weavers and warpers.[59] At age thirteen, James Paterson belonged to "Willie Semple's Club," run by a shoemaker and (exceptionally) his wife for a group of radical weavers who clubbed together to read the newspapers and journals such as the *Black Dwarf*.[60] Charles Campbell, a cotton spinner, joined a club of artisans and mechanics who debated literary subjects and celebrated their patron goddesses "Nature and Art."[61] In London, the Spitalfields weavers had entomological and mathematical societies, and the Cider Cellar in Maiden Lane was "famous for its political debates and arguments."[62]

Not only self-improvement, but a boisterous, rough, even libertine masculinity characterized some elements of artisan culture. David Gilmore recalled that Paisley master weavers were fond of pugilism.[63] Spitalfields weavers amused themselves in the early part of the century by goading bullocks and chasing them through the streets.[64] As Iain McCalman writes, "Within the artisan world distinctions of status had rested more on such factors as position, custom and skill than on the later criterion of respectable behavior." In its furthest extreme, McCalman depicts a "blackguard" culture of disreputable artisans who dabbled in blackmail, brothel-keeping, pornography, and even rape, at the same time as they were developing radical intellectual ideas.[65]

While most artisans did not go that far, libertinism was not a personal aberration but a consequence of the changing realities of journeymen's lives. Traditionally, apprenticeship had been linked to adolescence, whereas journeymen were rowdy young men who settled down only when they became masters and married. When journeymen could no longer hope to run their own workshops, they remained stuck in the bachelor stage of the trade's life cycle.[66] During their single years, journeyman had celebrated their "freedom" with ribald songs and crude rituals.[67] Although many artisans married despite their inability to become masters, they continued to act as if they were still bachelors, retaining their attachment to their mates rather than transferring loyalty to their wives. Although textile workers shared much of this culture, they kept some aspects of patriarchal status which allowed them to modify bachelor belligerence—for instance, cotton spinners worked with young women and children, and handloom weavers typically wove alongside their wives and daughters.

Artisans practiced elaborate rituals of "footings," fining apprentices and journeymen in drink for trivial offenses or as an initiation. Because they all enjoyed the liquid proceeds, footings ensured solidarity, redistributing any surplus income among the group rather than allowing one member to save and advance on his own—or to bring cash home to his family.[68] Most artisan trades kept these drinking sprees inside the bounds of the workshop, among workmates, rather than sharing with wives or other women. Calico printers, however, modified the custom significantly. Like other artisans, they had elaborate drinking rituals, demanding fines from the apprentices which would be contributed to a fund eventually splurged on enormous amounts of whisky. But the women and children of calico-printing villages would join the party.[69] Despite the hangovers that no doubt ensued, this sharing may explain the intense labor solidarity shown in strikes in calico-printing villages.

For artisans, the celebration of bachelorhood cemented their ties to their workmates as the most important in their lives and, even if they were actually married or cohabiting with a woman, evoked a mythical freedom to escape a master's tyranny by simply throwing down tools and tramping to another town—a gesture rarely possible for a man with family obligations.[70] It may also be that their practice of singing misogynistic sexual songs and celebrating mistreatment of women helped them to form male bonds; present only symbolically, women's absence highlighted men's fragile masculinity.[71] At the same time, marriage and fatherhood marked the state of true manhood, and a single man ran the risk of being called a mollycoddle.[72]

Workshop rituals celebrating journeymen's marriages served as rites of passage which expressed this ambivalence. They acknowledged a man's accession to full manhood as a husband, but they also expressed the tension between his obligations to his wife and his commitment to his brother workers.[73] On the day after a workman's wedding in Thomas Wright's engineering plant, all the engineers would hammer on the pieces of metal lying about the shop, creating an awesome cacophony.[74] When C. M. Smith married, his printing office mounted an obscene mock wedding in which the bride was played by a man.[75]

Textile workers, like artisans, celebrated bachelorhood, but they seem to have valued marriage more. Some textile workers' clubs stressed their bachelor nature, functioning as a transitional support system until a man married. Campbell noted that his club was exceptional in that members did not have to be bachelors. In other clubs, only a few men quit or at least moderated their drinking upon marriage, while others persisted in enjoying bachelor indulgences despite their new responsibilities.[76] But the cotton spinners seemed to have encouraged matrimony, perhaps because they could employ their children as piecers and earn enough to support wives at home. The "fine" or footing for marriage was five shillings, but a young man had to pay the society ten shillings for every year he remained unmarried.[77]

Plebeian artisan culture contained many elements in tension. Its chief strength—a masculine solidarity based on skill, physical prowess, and drinking—was also its chief weakness.

Plebeian Women's Networks

Women sometimes resented their exclusion from masculine plebeian culture. According to the ballad "The Ladies Club,"

> The women are all up in arms, for their society and charms
> Are quite neglected now at home, by spouses who abroad will roam,
> Then since in clubs, the men think fit to spend their time, nor wives
>   admit,

The ladies oft' their chains have thrown and have a club formed of
their own.[78]

In fact, women, too, shaped plebeian culture through their own formal institutions and informal networks. However, their mode of organizing differed somewhat from that of plebeian men. While men organized in the
public world to preserve their craft status and improve themselves, as well
as to enjoy the pleasures of libertine culture, women bonded together
simply in order to survive. Like the late-nineteenth-century poor women
described by Ellen Ross, they created "survival networks" in which neighbors offered reciprocal aid.[79] Single women in textiles shared resources in
an attempt to make ends meet on below-subsistence wages. Women's networks also helped wives overcome the dual burdens of wage-earning and
housework, the vicissitudes of childbirth, and even feckless husbands. They
tried to defend each other from the misogyny engendered by libertinism,
sheltering battered wives and deserted pregnant women.

Yet in blurring the boundaries between public and private space, plebeian women's networks differed both from their late-nineteenth-century
counterparts, for whom male and female worlds were strictly divided, and
from men's clubs, which ritualized the separation of work and home.[80] Plebeian women often shocked middle-class observers by their enjoyment
of the pleasures of public life, so different from the increasing seclusion of
ladies in the private world of the home. Still, they could not indulge in
libertinism as easily as artisan men could, for their respectability was much
more fragile, based on sexual reputation rather than skill. Furthermore,
plebeian women's access to female networks varied by occupation and locale, in a range from the intense solidarity of female factory workers to the
isolation of London servants.

When plebeian women organized formally, they established female
friendly societies, whose members usually met monthly at a pub (or sometimes a chapel) to socialize and contribute a small sum, in the expectation
that the club would pay them sickness and/or funeral benefits. The first
female friendly society seems to have been founded in the late seventeenth
century in order to provide annuities for tradesmen's widows, but most
surviving rules date from the 1770s. The rules of female societies were
copied from the standard models published for men's societies, mandating
certain levels of monthly contributions and rules about not working while
receiving sickness benefits.

In 1794, the Friendly Society Act required the registration of these clubs
in England, and more came to be listed publicly, although no doubt many
evaded registration. Most societies were all male, but there were a substan-
tial number of women's clubs. In London, eighty-two female friendly so-

cieties registered, 15 percent of the total of 542 clubs.[81] As women's economic position became more marginal in London, however, the number
of female friendly societies declined, accounting for only 3 percent of the
total of 344 in 1837.[82] They seemed to concentrate in areas where married
women still worked, such as markets, and in neighborhoods where women
labored in tailoring, shoemaking, silk weaving, and watch finishing, such
as Whitechapel, Bethnal Green, and Clerkenwell.[83] In locales where the
textile industry employed many women, the numbers of female friendly
societies continued to be high.[84] In Stockport, 10 percent of the members of friendly societies were female, and women's societies accounted
for one-third of the total number in existence between 1794 and 1823.[85]
The proportions were also high in other industrial areas; the returns of
friendly societies in 1824 indicate that female friendly societies accounted
for 16 percent of the total in Nottinghamshire, 18 percent in Lancashire,
27 percent in Cheshire, and 35 percent in Leicester, all areas with female
employment in textile trades.[86] We do not have consistent information for
Scotland, where at least in the 1790s, an era of political repression, official
permission to form friendly societies was difficult to obtain.[87] Little information survives on female friendly societies in Glasgow, but they flourished in outlying villages such as Kilmarnock (where many women were
employed as embroiderers), Paisley (where women were also employed in
weaving and cotton factories), Irvine, Saltcoats, and Neilston.[88]

Whereas many men's societies were formed on an occupational basis, or
indeed as a cover for trade unions, women only occasionally formed trade-
based clubs. In London, for instance, the United Sisters of Tobacco Pipe
Makers registered in 1805 and the Female Friendly Bookbinders in 1815,
and there were a few societies for female servants and governesses.[89] A
contemporary satirical pamphlet listed a mantuamakers' club and a quilt-
ers' club, suggesting that informal occupational clubs may never have
registered.[90] In Manchester, Birmingham, and the West Country, a small
number of female handloom weavers' societies existed.[91]

Nonetheless, the rules of female friendly societies suggest that women
were conscious that their work was valuable and conferred status. Just as
men's societies did, women's societies required each member to "give an
account of her trade and calling," which implies that these women had
some sort of an occupational identity.[92] A regulation of the Sisterly Society
of Women suggests women's sense of responsibility for wage-earning, for
it gave sickness benefits to "any member afflicted . . . with sickness, lame-
ness or blindnss so as to deprive her of getting a living for herself and her
family."[93] Yet these rules also acknowledged that women were as likely to
assist their husbands or do housework as to follow their own trade. The

Kilmarnock Dutiful Female Friendly Society required its members to be "capable of gaining a livelihood for themselves or managing the affairs of their families." In general societies refused benefit to a supposedly sick member if she were found "working at her trade or calling, or doing any business whatsoever, mending, cleaning, or any housework in her family." Another society adjusted the rules to fit artisans' wives who quilled their husbands' looms, sewed seams for tailors, or bound the shoes their spouses made, by ruling that no woman might receive sickness benefits if she were found "assisting to work . . . whereby she or they whom she assists may receive any benefit for the same."[94] It was sometimes difficult to draw the line between housework and waged work: an Aldgate society excluded women from sickness benefits if they washed or ironed "or anything by which money is earned," but they could sweep the house or cook for their husbands.[95]

Female friendly societies demanded a certain level of prosperity and respectability, making distinctions that suggest nascent class divisions within plebeian society. The level of sickness benefits—seven to eight shillings per week—compares favorably with women's wages in this period, and women had to be able to spare at least one shilling for the monthly subscription. Like male societies, they excluded those who followed dishonorable or unhealthy trades: "no barrow-woman, basket woman, fishwoman, or anyone that gets her living on the streets, shall be admitted to this society."[96]

Friendly society members also tried to uphold moral respectability among their members. A Friendly Society of Women held at the public house of Mrs. Campbell aimed to promote "good Manners and Civil Conversation," perhaps to set themselves off from their rougher neighbors.[97] Societies required that each new member be recommended by another member and "personally examined" not only for physical health but as to moral reputation.[98] In order to uphold good order and respectability, women's clubs fined members who drank too much, quarreled, insulted each other, or swore. Like male societies, they did not give benefits for those injuries caused by fighting (except in self-defense), drunkenness, or venereal disease. Libertine indulgences endangered health as well as respectability.

But these rules also reveal how fragile the line between reputable and disreputable could be. A handwritten note on one set of rules denied funeral benefits to any woman whose husband was hanged for felony, and to any wife who contrived to have her husband impressed into the navy.[99] A Burnley society suspended any member who would "marry or go along with any hired militia," a provision which also suggested possible political resentment.[100] Another excluded women convicted of petty larceny but not those imprisoned for debt, and a similar society excused women from paying membership dues if they were imprisoned.[101] Two societies refused sickness benefits to women whose husbands had inflicted injuries upon them, although it is difficult to know whether it was moral sanction or the frequency of such incidents that motivated this refusal.[102] Another society, meeting in Drury Lane, suggested that members commiserated together about female sorrows. Its rules declared: "That there is many calamities happens to women, that is not proper for the clerk to be present, it is also agreed, that the clerk can be ordered out of the room for half an hour, while she declares the same to the society."

Women shared raucous good times as well as their sorrows at the societies' monthly meetings and annual feasts. A pamphlet entitled "The New Art and Mystery of Gossiping" satirized female friendly society members for meeting only to gossip, drink, and gorge on delicacies, but such indulgences could appeal to vigorous plebeian women. The pamphlet presents a mouthwatering, if comic, picture of the tailors' wives' club annual feast, where they consumed nine geese, six legs of mutton, and french beans, rolling out into Monmouth Street after having smoked "pipes and tobacco" and drunk "royal gin."[103] One can only imagine why the Fore Street Society added the rule that "no member shall commit any indecent act with the victuals" at the annual feast.[104] Moral reformers, of course, disapproved of such independent female pleasure. Sometimes they tried to co-opt female friendly societies in order to inculcate the values of chastity.[105] Yet most independent female friendly societies adopted a definition of respectability which differed greatly from that of middle-class women. By meeting in pubs without their children, who were forbidden to stay in the clubroom, they violated notions of domestic seclusion.

Yet marriage handicapped women's ability to participate in independent organizations. Married women were legally minors who did not control their own wages. A husband could by law forbid his wife to use her earnings to pay for subscriptions, and if she received a benefit payment for sickness or lying-in, he could appropriate it to his own use.[106] Finally, the illiteracy of many women made them dependent on male clerks to keep their records. For instance, only four out of eleven members of the Sisterly Society of Women which met in Shoe Lane could sign their own name.[107]

Despite these difficulties, the fact that many of these societies lasted for some years belies assumptions that women's organizations were fragile and transient. One of the Kilmarnock societies, instituted in 1817, still flourished in 1835. A Thistle and Crown Society registered in 1794 had been alive for twenty years.[108] It is possible that these societies endured because they enabled women to move between work and home. They also provided precedent and experience for later women's radical political organizations.

In addition to the formal organization of friendly societies, plebeian women created an informal and intense social life, based on individual friendships, quasi-kinship networks, female rituals of sociability, and neighborhood bonds. By exchanging information and monitoring local mores, these networks enabled women to survive such hardships of plebeian life as violent husbands and poverty. They also cemented plebeian culture in a solidarity of sharing that reached beyond the workplace.

Women's culture extended beyond the home into the streets. The acceptability of female drinking in plebeian society gave women access to public space and the intimacy intoxication could render. Women drank together as well as in the company of men, and gin seems to have been their favorite drink. As a servant girl to a hatter's wife told Mayhew, "Some women called on mistress . . . , and they had a deal of talkin', and bladherin', and laughin', and I don't know how often I was sent out for quarterns of gin." [109] To the horror of moral reformers, women frequented gin shops, and they even dominated pubs at certain times of the day or week.[110] They drank to get themselves through Saint Monday, the day their husbands took off for drinking—when wives had to do the washing. As a wife in one song complained,

> A friend of mine came in one day,
> 'Twas cold and foggy weather,
> To comfort you says she we'll have
> A drop of max together.
> My husband came in at the time
> I know not what to say,
> But she'll not come again I'm sure
> Upon a fuddling day.[111]

Tea parties provided a more respectable alternative to gin-drinking, but the engineer Thomas Wright complained that lodging houses fostered "joint stock tea partying, gossiping, and other undesirable qualities in women." [112]

A few women were able to live and work together as an alternative to patriarchal marriage. Martha Ridgeway, defending her friend Mrs. Jarman against a defamatory accusation, said they had been "intimately acquainted" for fifty years, as they had come from the same part of the country and had lived together for fifteen years, running a mantua and millinery business and sharing lodgings.[113] But generally only women with independent wages could take advantage of this alternative arrangement. In 1840, there were 50 Spitalfields households where two women worked together at silk looms and 27 where three women worked together, out of 1,936 households where adults worked together.[114] Single Irish female streetsellers also sometimes lived with each other in common lodging houses.[115]

In areas of Lancashire, women migrated to lodge with kin, and Anderson found that same-sex kinship ties such as those of aunt and niece, tended to be the strongest.[116] Female-headed households were common in Glasgow, accounting for 27.5 percent of households in 1821.[117] By 1841, approximately 26 percent of Glasgow households from selected textile districts were all female, and about half of these contained women who worked as powerloom weavers or other cotton workers. Female workers, such as powerloom weavers, seemed to have organized their lodgings on a kinship or fictive kinship basis, living with their aunts or sisters, or several younger women with an older landlady.[118] There was also an unusually high proportion of single women in the Glasgow population, due to a shortage of men and, perhaps, to a plenitude of female employment.[119]

Since the daughters of London working people usually went out to work at a very young age as domestic servants, far from their families, they often sought out aunts, family friends, or sympathetic mistresses to guide them through the world of work and courtship. Foundling Hospital petitioners frequently came from out of town to stay with their aunts and cousins, who would find work for them or shelter them when they were out of place. Anne Riverside came from Exeter to live with her aunt on Carpenter Street, Westminster, where her sister already lived with another aunt.[120] Women in other occupations drew upon the aid of their aunts as well. A poor street seller told Mayhew, "I'm a['']going to leave the streets. I have an aunt [who is] a laundress . . . and I always helped her, and she taught me laundressing."[121] Lacking an aunt, when her parents died Mary Ann Ashford had to seek out "an old friend and countrywoman of my father's" for advice on whether to go into service or to apprentice as a milliner.[122] However, by the late eighteenth and the early nineteenth century, domestic service became more regimented and servants more isolated. Patricia Seleski notes that "maidservants as a group lost easy access to plebeian women's culture."[123]

Late-eighteenth- and early nineteenth-century plebeian women, then, shaped for themselves a culture which defied the increasingly narrow conventions of middle-class life. They stepped out into the public life of streets and pubs and organized themselves to bridge work and home. Yet, as the nineteenth century advanced, they faced increasing controls over their sociability and increasingly rigid definitions of respectability. And even for those women who still enjoyed working together or gossiping in the streets, plebeian women's culture had its limitations. Women did not always help each other; neighbors sometimes ignored battered women's cries for help, and loyalty to male kin or workmates easily overcame the sympathy of sex for women who were used as strikebreakers. Women could also pass judgment on each other on the basis of morality or class status.

Most of all, women's limited monetary resources made it difficult for them to use surplus income to build formal organizations. Northern women, who could get work in nearby textile factories where they would receive their own wages, could sometimes overcome these difficulties. London servants stranded in middle-class neighborhoods and needlewomen slaving in sweatshops faced a forbidding isolation. Nonetheless, female networks set the precedent for a working-class solidarity that could move beyond concerns of the workplace to those of families and the larger community.

Conclusion

The vitality of plebeian communities contributed to the making of the radical working class of the 1830s and 1840s. The practice of sharing, so different from both the condescension of eighteenth-century philanthropy and the harshness of nineteenth-century utilitarianism, became a political principle mandating state responsibility to relieve the poor but also nurtured the working-class organization to demand that relief. And friendly societies provided the precedent for this organization, both among women and among men. The experiences of plebeian women in public life— engaging in heavy or skilled labor, drinking in pubs, participating in riots, and running their own clubs—no doubt helped prepare them for an active political role. This evidence gives the lie to assumptions that later political organizations excluded women simply because they did not go to pubs or were not capable of membership in long-lasting organizations. But it also helps us see how the shape of later radical organizations both derived from divisions within plebeian culture and attempted to transcend them.

Plebeian culture was deeply divided, not only by locale and occupation but by gender cultures. Artisan culture provided the precedents of education and intense solidarity, but it also tended to be both exclusively masculine and exclusive in general. Textile workers, while often imitating the masculine artisan heritage, also created a plebeian culture where the genders could mix at the workplace and in social life, which enabled a sense of solidarity that reached beyond the workplace to draw upon community strength. However, sexual tensions cut across occupational lines. While the blurring of gender roles invigorated popular culture, it also gave rise to acute sexual tension. The strength and independence of plebeian omen threatened their men, who had hoped they would be rulers in their own homes but instead sought solace with their workmates. In turn, women resented the money and time their husbands spent at the pub. Religion and moral values also divided plebeians. As public libertinism faded within the upper and middle classes, it became a stigma discrediting the working class. As morals changed, sexual reputation became a focus for class tensions.

4   Plebeian Sexual Morality, 1780-1820

In the 1780s, Ann Webb lived with a master shoemaker in London and considered herself a respectable woman. Yet their cohabitation scandalized his partner's wife, a deeply religious woman, and she convinced them to marry legally. After they tied the knot, Ann's previous sexual experience seemed to make little difference to her life. The couple continued to prosper; Ann employed a dressmaker and sheltered her young niece, who assisted them by binding shoes. Then tragedy struck: her husband fell in love, bigamously married the niece, and threw Ann out of her home, reducing her to a meager living as a shoebinder.[1] A century earlier or later, Ann Webb and her husband would have been part of a tiny, scorned minority; but during the late eighteenth and early nineteenth centuries, many like them shared such freedoms and troubles.[2] Their story reveals the clash between religious and libertine mores within families and occupational groups, the prevalence of sexual unconventionality among prosperous plebeians on their way to the lower middle class, and the vulnerability of women that accompanied sexual freedom.

Of course, in any era there are people who do not conform to prevailing sexual mores or who cannot live up to their own moral standards. But the period from the late eighteenth through the early nineteenth century witnessed something different—a "sexual crisis."[3] First, rates of premarital sex, illegitimacy, and common-law marriage soared.[4] Clashing moral standards also confused many plebeians.[5] At the further extreme, plebeians could find themselves in a "rough" or libertine metropolitan subculture, among debauched tradesmen's sons, kept mistresses, women who abandoned bad husbands to live bigamously with new loves, belligerent prostitutes, and drunken journeymen.[6]

But for most plebeians, illegitimacy and common-law marriage did not necessary stem from social chaos, but from an alternative plebeian morality. Relatively free from the domination of the church or the upper classes, many plebeians viewed premarital sex after a promise of marriage as completely acceptable.[7] Although we do not have reliable figures for urban areas, P. E. H. Hair suggested from a study of 77 parishes in rural areas that the rate of prebridal pregnancy rose from 16.5 percent in the seventeenth century to 43.4 percent in the period 1750–1836.[8] Plebeians tried to regulate their own mores through gossip and social pressure, ensuring that young men married the women they impregnated.

But this alternative morality had its risks. For instance, marriage did not always follow pregnancy, for economic fluctuations forced many couples to delay or abandon wedding plans. The uncertainties of the market economy, especially for proto-industrial production dependent on world trade, and the inability of journeymen to become masters inhibited marriage and prevented many young men from living up to their responsibilities.[9] English settlement examinations and Scottish kirk sessions records reveal that many women found themselves plunged into destitution and uncertain about the status of their relationships when their men went off to war, especially during the Napoleonic wars, when many joined the militia in order to avoid being impressed. Opportunities elsewhere for soldiering or work aided men to escape a marriage forced upon them by Poor Law authorities reluctant to give parish support to illegitimate children. Many fathers left to seek their fortunes in the West Indies or America, or simply other parts of Britain.

Some plebeians sought refuge from these perils in an alternative subculture of respectable religiosity. In late-eighteenth-century cities, those respectable in the definition of the religious may have been in a minority, adhering to strict standards of behavior and morality to distinguish themselves from the undisciplined multitudes around them. Such respectability was simultaneously an indigenous plebeian response to the difficulties and confusions of rough urban life and a marker of nascent middle-class status.[10] Plebeian respectability and middle-class respectability could be quite different, of course; the shifting definitions of respectability run as a leitmotif in this book. But this was a period of changing status, in which many shopkeepers and tradesmen retained plebeian values, and others were attempting to claim middle-class status by morally elevating themselves from their poorer neighbors—and some could not find a place for themselves.

By the late 1790s, however, the middle class increasingly espoused self-control for men and chastity for women. Attainment of these ideals became a marker of class status as middle-class moralists differentiated themselves from the dissolute aristocracy and the debauched plebeians.[11] They portrayed plebeians as their antithesis, whose faults illuminated bourgeois virtues and who had to be controlled to ensure bourgeois comfort and hegemony. Moral reformers regarded the sexual behavior of the lower classes with horror, even panic. Especially after the French Revolution, they associated sexual freedom with crime, disorder, and even sedition.[12] In 1802, the conservative *Anti-Jacobin Review* fulminated, "Bastardy is now scarcely deemed a disgrace. . . . This species of profligacy, so detestable in itself, and so pernicious in its consequences, both to the individuals, and to the community at large, has increased of late years, especially in the metropolis, to an extent that is almost incredible. Adultery and concubinage in the lower classes of society are unhappily most prevalent."[13]

Regarding plebeian culture from the outside, moral reformers perceived a frightening sexual chaos, with seduction and illegitimacy the first steps on a slippery slope leading to streetwalking.[14] Calling for the establishment of a metropolitan police force, Patrick Colquhoun claimed that 50,000 prostitutes infested London, but he wildly inflated this figure by including 25,000 common-law wives. As was typical of middle-class reformers, Colquhoun defined a prostitute as any woman who had sex outside of legal marriage.[15] Moral reformers attempted to control the familial, sexual, and social lives of plebeians: the pubs, the fairs, and, above all, the women who ranged freely in and out of workplaces, streets, and pubs. They tried to enforce Sabbatarian regulations and close down the lively fairs, which, they believed, lured plebeians from wage labor by enticing them with immoral pleasures.[16] In the eighteenth and early nineteenth centuries, they founded several Magdalen hospitals to shelter weary prostitutes—whom they often equated with seduced women—and subjected them to a severe discipline of penitence and work.[17]

Poor Law reformers regarded bastardy as a key social problem, for who was to support these children? Punishment of unmarried mothers had largely died out. Fathers of illegitimate children could be forced to pay maintenance, but many reformers believed that unmarried mothers should be forced into workhouses to deter them from such behavior.[18] In Scotland, mothers of illegitimate children could receive relief only if they identified the father and expressed repentance in the kirk.[19]

However, middle-class reformers were not the only ones distressed by libertinism; sexual tensions also fissured plebeian culture from within. The insecurity of the market economy often meant that an evening's indulgence could, in the cold light of morning, send a family to ruin when a skill became obsolete or a shop went bankrupt. For women, libertinism could have dire consequences. They had less monetary access to the pleasures of the market culture, more responsibility for their families, and, of course, greater sexual vulnerability, for in a market culture women were not only consumers but commodities, whose sexuality was a measure of their worth.[20]

Weavers and Their Weans: Scottish Illegitimacy

As the Scottish textile industry developed, plebeians were able to gain independence from masters and landlords by working at their own looms or in impersonal factories. In the brief period of prosperity textile workers enjoyed at the end of the eighteenth century, they paraded in city streets after church to eye each other, decked out in finery purchased with their wages as weavers or tambourers. As a moralist complained in 1782,

> It is melancholy to reflect, that, in Glasgow, once distinguished for sobriety of manners, piety and exemplary conversation, where none durst walk the streets, on the Sabbath, unless going to, and returning from *public worship*, well-dressed gentlemen are not afraid to walk through the streets on the Lord's Day, Whistling and Singing, *lascivious women make it their day of holding revels. . . . A Babylon*, a cage of unclean birds.[21]

Glasgow youths rejected the dour strictness of Scottish Calvinism.[22] They chafed at the extreme puritanism of the kirk sessions, which condemned even friendly caresses and public sociability between men and women and sentenced offenders to humiliating public penitence.[23] By the 1830s, the kirk sessions' efforts at discipline had evaporated in Glasgow, although they continued in outlying areas such as Rutherglen.[24]

Rates of prenuptial conception increased steadily from the mid-eighteenth to the mid-nineteenth century. In eighteenth-century southwestern rural Scotland, the prenuptial conception rate was only 11 percent, due to the kirk sessions' vigilance.[25] By the mid-nineteenth century, the premarital conception rate reached 30 percent among urban workers and much higher among agricultural women.[26]

Irregular marriage indicated urban workers' growing independence from the hegemony of the kirk. According to Scottish tradition, couples could live together, acknowledging each other as man and wife, and later ratify their union before the kirk. Parishioners in kirk sessions often declared they had "considered themselves married" for many years before they sought kirk approval.[27] More commonly, a couple avoided the expense and publicity of a regular kirk marriage by appearing before witnesses to be united by a non-ordained celebrant, who could grant them a certificate of their union. Rab Steel, the tollkeeper of Rutherglen, often married

Table 1. Occupations of Men Appearing for Illegitimacy and Irregular
Marriage in Kirk Sessions, 1796–1830

Occupied	Illegitimacy (N = 140)	Irreg. Marriage (N = 125)	Male Population in Parishes (N = 21,282)
Professional/mercan- tile/gentlemen	6.4%	4.0%	6.3%
Weavers/warpers	25.7	23.2	16.5
Other textiles	12.1	12.0	21.5
Skilled trades	26.4	40.8	28.9
Laborers/servants	18.5	10.4	18.9
Miscellaneous (including soldiers and sailors)	10.9%	9.6%	7.9%

Sources: Kirk sessions of St. John's, the Gorbals, and Blackfriars. Population of these parishes from 1831 census, reported in James Cleland, *An Enumeration of the Inhabitants of the City of Glasgow* (Glasgow, 1832), p. 214.

All cases where male occupation given.

couples this way, in a "Scottish marriage of the rough and ready type . . . but as binding and faithfully observed as if it had been performed in a cathedral."[28]

Sexual irregularities were not confined to a distinct "bastard-bearing" subclass, but were spread across all occupational groups, as Table 1 reveals.[29] But weavers and warpers were overrepresented: in Glasgow, although only 16.4 percent of the occupied population, in the three parishes examined they nonetheless accounted for 25.4 percent of the cases of illegitimacy. And in the Gorbals, handloom weavers accounted for 10 percent of the occupied population and 22.1 percent of the illegitimacy cases.

High rates of illegitimacy were also typical of other handloom weaving communities, such as Culcheth, Lancashire.[30] In the early golden age of handloom weaving, the birth of illegitimate children may not have been such a disaster, for some women weavers could support themselves and their children and subsequently go on to marriage. In Culcheth, young women raised their children with the help of their families and supported themselves by weaving. In another instance, Sally Marcroft, from an area near Manchester, could not marry the father of her child because of his parents' objections, but she was able to maintain herself and her son, William, by working as a handloom gingham weaver earning twelve to sixteen shillings a week and living in a cellar. Despite her illegitimate child, her neighbors seemed to have respected her as a "thoughtful and industrious woman." Unfortunately, the depression of 1826 put her out of work and her subsequent marriage to a ne'er-do-well reduced their standard of living.[31]

Handloom weavers may have figured so prominently as unmarried or cohabiting parents because their early independence and, in the early days, their high wages encouraged active socializing between young men and women.[32] In late-eighteenth-century Paisley, where textiles brought a brief flush of prosperity, young men and maidservants met weekly to dance in public houses to the music of fiddlers, a practice that often resulted in early marriages.[33] According to another source, "Dancing parties and rural excursions were common among the young people of both sexes."[34] Margaret Colquehoun, employed as a tambourer in the Gorbals, remembered "what a wonderful merry night she had at the New Year's dancing," even though she became pregnant then.[35]

Many Scottish plebeians accepted premarital sex, irregular marriage, and even births out of wedlock, if men and women lived up to their responsibilities. Among the nineteenth-century Lowlands working class, antenuptial pregnancy was normal and illegitimacy not regarded as a sin. People would note, "At least she didn't steal."[36] A Saltcoats friendly society allowed its members to receive benefits if they had one child out of wedlock—although more would lead to expulsion.[37] Popular literature portrayed premarital or extramarital sex as acceptable as long as men provided appropriate maintenance for mother and child. Robert Burns promised his "Love-Begotten Daughter" his last penny. He scorned the kirk sessions but praised "The Fornicator's Court" of the pub, where neighbors repudiated men who seduced women and then left them pregnant or tried to procure abortions. There was nothing shameful in fornication, he proclaimed; the only shame lay in not accepting the consequences.[38] A later, anonymous radical poem, *The Swinish Multitudes Push for Reform*, celebrated the "soft embrace" of "mutual love" and criticized the kirk sessions for their repressive attitude.[39] Jenny Nettles, the protagonist of a popular song about a poor unmarried mother, admonishes the father, Robin Rattle, to do the right thing:

> Score out the blame,
> And shun the shame,
> And without mair debate o't
> Take home your wain [wee one],
> Make Jenny fain [glad]
> The leel and leesome gate o't [loyal and lovable way of it].[40]

The extremely popular chapbooks by Dougal Graham, such as *The Whole Proceedings of Jockey and Maggy's Courtship with the Great Diversion That Ensued at Their Bedding*, joked about the pleasure women took in sex and the common people's resistance to kirk-session discipline.[41]

It was a matter of honor for men to look after their illegitimate children, even if they did not marry the mother. In Glasgow, compared to rural areas, relatively few men denied paternity: only 11.3 percent in the kirk sessions records, plus another 11.3 percent who never responded to summons.[42] John Holland, a Glasgow laborer, "took his child into his arms and acknowledged it" as his and promised to give Elizabeth Patten, the mother, a little money for maintenance.[43] If a man's sense of honor failed to move him, neighbors tried to enforce paternal responsibilities. When Agnes Wilson became pregnant, a friend of Bryce Jardine, the father, asked him what he intended to do, and Jardine replied that "he had done nothing but what he could rectify and that so long as he had a shilling she and it would get half of it."[44] James Miller, a weaver, also faced pressure from his neighbors when he made Margaret Wilson pregnant. Mrs. Pettigrew told him, "Jamie there may be worse than a wean. If ye have had any concern with her, you should tak wi't." When Margaret fainted in distress, Jamie lifted her up and reassured her, "Ye need not mak such a wark about it, for if the child be mine will [we'll] get it brought up a'tween us."[45] Unfortunately, Jamie, like many other Glaswegian young men, failed to live up to his promise. The alternative sexual morality did not produce a common cultural experience for all plebeians: some young men could evade their responsibilities, but young women were left with the consequences.

London Libertinism and Its Consequences

The experiences of young women in London illustrate more starkly than those of Glasgow the sexual politics of plebeian morality. On the one hand, many Londoners had a flexible view of sexual morality; on the other, sexual reputation produced social tensions in plebeian culture as it became a marker of class difference and a means of controlling women's behavior.

As in Glasgow, illegitimacy and common-law marriage occurred frequently and were accepted in many sectors of plebeian society. London's large middle-class population skewed the statistics to make its illegitimacy rate relatively low. In fact, the metropolitan shortage of work for young women increased their sexual vulnerability. Female servants were particularly likely to be deserted by sweethearts, since they were isolated from families and communities that could enforce paternal responsibilities.[46] The English church courts that had humiliated unmarried or prenuptially pregnant mothers had died out, so this form of discipline no longer deterred young couples. The 1753 Marriage Act made marriage difficult, expensive, and public, requiring either the publication of banns three weeks before the wedding or an even dearer special license.[47] This difficulty encouraged the poor to opt for common-law marriage. According to London Poor Law bastardy examinations from 1780 through 1815, 19 percent of unmarried mothers had cohabited with the father of their child, and a further 13.2 percent had known the father for two or more years.[48] Cohabitation may have increased since earlier in the century, when Nicholas Rogers found that 3.5 percent of the parents of illegitimate children had lived together in relationships lasting two or more years before 1735, rising to 5 percent in 1738–1752. He attributes the growth in the number of these relationships to the inability of journeymen to become masters, combined with their desire for female companionship despite their low wages.[49] And these figures probably underestimate the number of illegitimate children produced by common-law marriages, for such cases appeared only when the relationship broke down or the father went to war or the colonies, died, or sank into destitution.

As we have seen, in the late eighteenth century many London plebeians seemed to have tolerated unmarried mothers and common-law couples as neighbors. Francis Place, a master tailor and influential radical, remembered that in the 1780s, when he was a young man, tradesmen accepted their daughters even if they became kept women or unmarried mothers.[50] In plebeian culture, chastity was not necessarily the most important female virtue: whatever their sexual situation, women could be valued as industrious workers, affectionate mothers, kind friends, and good neighbors. Similarly, according to Francis Place, London tradesmen and their families of the 1780s did not shun sexually experienced young female neighbors if they "were decent in their general conduct."[51] One adultery case deposition noted that although Elizabeth Hicks of Shadwell gave birth to an illegitimate child while her husband was away at sea and was "much given to liquor," she had "no other faults."[52] Mrs. Hannah Vollar trusted Elizabeth Webb enough, even though she knew she was an "unfortunate woman," to make her a partner in her dressmaking business, because she "thought her honest." We know this only because Webb actually turned out to be a thief.[53]

Loss of chastity did not deny women the claims of kinship or compassion. Even if they disapproved of premarital sex, mothers and aunts helped to conceal young girls' shame by sheltering them through pregnancy. One mother's attachment to her daughter's newborn twins far outweighed the stigma of their illegitimate birth. In a touchingly affectionate letter, she offered to set her daughter up in a little shop where she could help look after the "Blessed Babes" herself, offering the consoling advice, "never mind worldly friends whose minds soon change and vary but God's mercies are always lasting if we continue to pray with a fervent desire and endeavour to repair what we do amiss."[54] Even if a respectable woman did not approve of sexual commerce, the ideal of rescuing lost souls might compel her to aid another woman. Unlike upper-class philanthropists, who required the severe discipline of repentance, these women seemed motivated by humanity, by the plebeian principle that they should help others in distress, not only out of compassion but in the recognition that they might one day need help themselves. When Harriet Collins confessed to her fellow lodger, an unemployed servant named Elizabeth Tanner, that she was an "unfortunate girl," Elizabeth merely asked, "cannot you reform and become a servant, it is better than going on the streets." When Harriet tearfully exclaimed, "Thank God, I have found a friend at last," the rather gullible Elizabeth proclaimed, "There is more joy over one sinner that repenteth than over ninety-nine just persons." Elizabeth's joy was short-lived; the next morning Harriet disappeared, along with Elizabeth's bundle.[55] When Mary Ann Sleeford, a Petticoat Lane butcher, discovered that her neighbor Bet Evens picked up men on the streets, she "remonstrated with her on the impropriety of her conduct," but still allowed her children to associate with her and helped Bet to claim maintenance from her estranged husband.[56]

The boundaries between "respectable" women, unmarried mothers, and prostitutes were often blurred. In London, young men and women— children of respectable tradesmen together with prostitutes and thieves— enjoyed themselves at dances and played cards late into the night at coffeehouses and pubs.[57] Impoverished needlewomen sought sexual partners who might help them fend off starvation. Shoemakers often cohabited with the women who did binding for them and could thus exploit them both sexually and economically.[58] Mary Wollstonecraft lamented that the genteel trades of mantuamaker and milliner had been made synonymous with prostitution because wages were so low and the risk of seduction so great from the young rakes who frequented the shops.[59]

Just because a constable or magistrate defined a woman as a prostitute does not mean that she or her friends would have accepted this stigma. Although moral reformers considered unmarried mother Mary Scully a prostitute, she defended herself against this imputation. Trying to swear paternity before a magistrate, she declared, "I am no bad woman. I tried all I could to support his child, and now he wants to make me a common streetwalker."[60] Women whose low wages or unemployment forced them to engage in part-time sexual commerce did not consider themselves to be

Figure 2. City Scavengers Cleansing the London Streets of Impurities!! Copyright British Museum.

prostitutes. Explaining her quarrel with Ann Cottrell, Mary Parker admitted, "I wash and iron, and go to gentlemen's houses sometimes, and she insulted me with that," but she claimed that Cottrell "had no right to charge me with being a common woman of the town." Since she engaged in sexual commerce only occasionally, and then with "gentlemen," she did not consider herself on the same level as a common streetwalker.[61]

Yet London women were often extremely sensitive to the insult "whore," because it reminded them of a perilously possible fate. The drunken streetwalker clothed in rags, grabbing and swearing at male passersby on a freezing winter night, was a familiar and a chilling sight. Furthermore, the insult "whore" inhibited the ability of plebeian women to enjoy a public role.[62] Descriptions of prostitutes as "public women" or "women of the town" brought into question the respectability of other metropolitan women of business: shopkeepers, shoebinders, publicans, porters, and costermongers all engaged in commercial public life.

Even if laboring women did not accept middle-class definitions of sexual morality, they lived in a society where magistrates, charity officials, clerics, and constables could punish them for deviating from bourgeois values. To be identified as a common whore could have serious material consequences for women. Any woman out on the street at night, soliciting men, drinking

in a pub, or merely walking home from work, faced the risk of being arrested by corrupt constables as a common prostitute (as is satirized in Figure 2) and then, unless she was able to bribe them, imprisoned by magistrates.[63] Both women and men often insulted other women as "whores";
this was not a literal description but a symbolic way of regulating female
behavior. The common use of this insult reveals that plebeian culture was
just as implicated in power relations as were middle-class efforts to repress
popular culture. The double standard and sexual commerce still divided
men from women, and women from each other. Prostitutes and married
women competed for men's wages, and men could use sexual insults to
undermine women's public presence.

Anthropologists have long stressed the way insults to female sexual
reputation can be used to control women's freedom in male-dominated
societies.[64] The classic studies focused on Mediterranean societies, where
men's honor depended to such an extent on female relatives' sexual reputation that women were kept secluded, chaperoned, and submissive.[65] The
situation was somewhat different in British society. Although honor was
crucial to patriarchal manliness there as well, women played an important
role in production and were not secluded in private space to protect their
virtue. Instead, gossip served to control women's behavior.[66] By the eighteenth century, argued Polly Morris in her study of Somerset defamation,
gossip about female sexual reputation expressed the contradictions between women's economic and social participation, their low social status in
a patriarchal society, and increasingly restricted notions of respectability.[67]

The power of gossip derived from its ability to erase the boundaries
between public and private life, which made it especially threatening to
shopkeeping, artisan, and laboring women whose sexual reputation could
determine their credit at work. Truly respectable ladies, however, stayed in
the domestic sphere, protected by a man. Female shopkeepers, for instance, lived on the lower fringes of the lower middle class; as business-
women, they worked in the public world to earn the money needed for
respectability. Such women were extremely vulnerable to gossip, both
from neighbors who resented their class pretensions and from men who
were threatened by women in business.

Defamation proceedings gave women legal weapons to defend themselves against the insidious power of gossip,[68] and several hundred women
took advantage of them in the London Consistory Court between 1780 and
1820. Depositions for only 39, or 10 percent, of these cases survive in the
records, but they reveal intimate details of plebeian neighborhood life and
sexual mores. (Ninety percent of defamation cases were dropped, probably
because the complainant could not afford lawyers' fees or because the case

was settled out of court.) Three-quarters of the plaintiffs in the surviving cases were artisans' or tradesmen's wives, or female shopkeepers themselves, and the rest were the wives or widows of attorneys, clerics, or gentlemen. They were particularly concerned to keep up not only their sexual reputations but also their class status, which insult could undermine. But they were also the people most likely to use the church courts to defend their honor; the laboring poor would probably fight it out in the streets, and a genteel lady would never risk the exposure of her private life in depositions.[69] The plaintiffs were also particularly concerned to keep up their credit as public figures: one-quarter of them had their own business or participated extensively in their husband's concerns. Unlike the Somerset women Morris has studied, who were mostly married, half of the women bringing charges in London were single, widowed, or separated.[70] Their recourse to defamation proceedings reflects the vulnerability of women alone in the city.

Tensions over sexual reputation produced shifting and complex relations between women. London women were notorious for their love of gossip and slander. One female friendly society had to modify the rule against "no backbiting or railing against any member in any place" to apply only to the meeting room.[71] Although as we have seen, many women succoured unmarried mothers and neighbors who went on the street, others enforced the code of chastity by shunning "fallen" women. Material concerns often impelled this hostility, for association with a prostitute could damage a woman's reputation. A Mr. Neale reduced his estranged wife's maintenance payments from sixteen to twelve shillings a week because "she was chum to a common streetwalker."[72] Conversely, if a man associated with prostitutes or kept a mistress, he was diverting money from the household exchequer and perhaps exposing his wife to venereal disease. When "respectable" women snubbed their fallen sisters, therefore, they were expressing their solidarity with injured wives rather than with "unfortunate" women. For instance, on reading the divorce case of Dickers v. Dickers, we can feel sympathy for Martha Budgery, the former mistress of Thomas Dickers, who had to go from man to man until one finally married her, but we can also understand why Mrs. Dickers's friends disapproved of Martha, for Thomas's debaucheries had left Ann impoverished and ill with syphilis.[73] Women of the laboring and artisan classes became very angry when prostitutes enticed their husbands or sons to spend household funds. In 1823, a "respectable woman named Roberts" charged two teenage girls with "seducing" her only son "from the paths of virtue and honor" (and employment), depriving her of his wages.[74]

The need to uphold a respectable class status could also impel women to reject "fallen" female neighbors. Most female friendly societies refused to accept common-law wives or prostitutes, and they cut off annuities to widows who were seen as disregarding sexual propriety.[75] When Elizabeth Harrison, the wife of a publican, discovered that her close friend and neighbor in the middle-class enclave of Goodman's Fields was not Mrs. Rea, the wife of a gunmaker, but Mr. Rea's "loose and abandoned" kept mistress, she broke off their formerly warm friendship.[76]

The fluidity of both class definitions and sexual morality during this period increased social insecurity for the ambitious artisans, tradesmen, and middle-class population of London. Keeping the family name unbesmirched seems to have been particularly difficult in the vast crowded parishes of the East End, source of half of the defamation depositions in this study. In these areas prosperous families were few and far between, for most of the middle class and gentry had moved to more salubrious and prestigious neighborhoods.[77] In Spitalfields, for instance, only a few master artisans and silk merchants lived among the thousands of laboring poor families.[78] The riverside districts of Wapping and Shadwell sheltered both the most violent, criminal, and degraded population of thieves and prostitutes, and respectable shipwrights and sea captains who needed to stay near their work.

The women involved in these defamation cases experienced the tensions of these shifting and fluid class definitions.[79] In part, when women gossiped they were succumbing to the importance assigned to sexual reputation in women's lives, drawing upon the moral vocabulary of the dominant class to carry out their own vendettas. But they also defied the linguistic constraints of ladyhood by being loud and aggressive and refusing to respect the boundaries of the newly defined private sphere of domesticity.[80] Lower-class women expressed their resentment at the airs of their ambitious neighbors by insulting them. In turn, in suing for defamation, their victims defied middle-class morality by publicizing shameful insults in order to preserve their private respectability.

Families engaged in bitter disputes over respectability. For instance, one day Lewis Vanderpump and his wife Louisa went to ask his sister, Hannah Book, an East End chandler, why Louisa had been excluded from family gatherings. Much offended, Hannah was recorded as retorting that "if he was so inquisitive to know what his wife has done he should go along with her to the place where she has transgressed." Retaliating, Louisa declared, "You infernal Bawd you have reared all your children to be Whores from their Cradles. . . . If I was to tell all that I know of your daughter Betty she would not wear such a high bonnet as she does." While the neighbors eavesdropped on this loud quarrel, Louisa went on to accuse Betty of sleeping with Louisa's own husband before her marriage to a prosperous merchant.[81] The real problem facing this family was not the rumors of adultery; tension over class status sparked these insults. As a shopkeeper, Hannah Book aspired to middle-class respectability, but she was only a corner shopkeeper on a street inhabited by "inferior" people in the poor parish of St. George's in the East. Although she married off her daughter well, her loud family dispute in the public arena of shop and street endangered her respectability. Conversely, Louisa Vanderpump, resenting the airs her niece adopted upon her advantageous marriage, proclaimed that Betty's respectability veiled loose morals. Similar resentment of class pretensions motivated other women who accused their neighbors of being whores. In this way lodgers, for instance, could express their hostility toward more prosperous landladies. When dressmaker Mrs. Butler quarreled with her landlady, she spitefully declared, "You Ma'am don't put yourself in such a style for you have been a whore to Mr. Horton for these thirteen years."[82]

Several of the women who defamed their upwardly mobile neighbors turned out to be common-law wives themselves. After Ann Morris insinuated that she had rescued her ungrateful niece from a bawdy house, the resulting defamation investigation revealed Ann herself had never been legally married.[83] Similarly, after a butcher named Mrs. Dalby called Mrs. Pritchard a "strumpeting whore," her apprentice let slip that Mrs. Dalby was only a common-law wife.[84]

The fact that women who did not themselves conform to conventional marital morals called other women whores brings into question the connotations of this insult. *Whore* literally means "prostitute," of course, but in the context of neighborhood defamation it may also have meant "unfaithful woman." Common-law wives did not necessarily regard themselves as whores, for they were in stable, monogamous relationships. The word seemed to have a larger meaning as an insult, implying that a woman had no self-respect, that she did not control herself, that she was loud and sexually profligate, that she roamed the streets, that she did not submit to the control of a husband or father. Defending William Swan, who, when she spit in his face, had told Mary Ann Simpson, "Don't you behave like an infamous whore," his friend explained that Swan did not mean to imply that Simpson actually was a whore, only to "convey by these words that her behavior was gross and vulgar like that of a common prostitute."[85]

Although gossiping was a stereotypically female activity, men also gossiped. As they bent over their tools in workshops or downed tankards of ale in public houses, some men spread slander about women. As a song, written in response to "The Gossiping Wife," proclaimed,

All you gossiping husbands don't think your wives to blame
While half the husbands in London are ten times worse than them,
For if the woman gossips surely there's no harm done,
But a gossiping husband neglects his work and will to ruin run.[86]

In the London Consistory Court defamation cases men constituted 53 percent of those who had called a woman a whore. They could use the insult
to restrict the freedom of any woman by undermining her reputation. One
midnight in Mile End Old Town, in the East End of London, John Kendrick
saw his neighbor Elizabeth Greaves step into the street and hissed at her,
"Get in you whore, get in you whore, you have been strolling from home,
who can tell where." As Mary Ashley, who kept a nearby barbershop testified in the resulting defamation case, Elizabeth was not a prostitute but a
respectable married woman on her way to fetch her husband home from
the pub. Greaves was so affronted by this insult—a dangerous accusation
in an area where constables harassed streetwalkers—that she charged Kendrick with defamation in the London Consistory Court.[87] Calling a woman
a whore also allowed individual men to undercut the threat female friendships posed to their power over women. William Taylor, a Blackfriars publican, expressed his jealousy at his wife's friend Mary Sefton, who kept a
nearby coal shed, by shouting at his wife, "You bitch you, you are as bad
as that Gallows Whore over the way Mother Sefton and I'll not stand pimp
for either of you."[88] When William Heberley learned that Mrs. Anna
Spence was sheltering her friend Mrs. Oriel from an abusive husband, he
remarked, "If it were not for that damn'd whore Mrs. Spence Wives would
stay with their Husbands and Husbands with their Wives."[89] As Morris
notes, "Sexual language was used by men to discipline women who challenged their supremacy, and it referred, increasingly, to emerging definitions of femininity that denied the contemporary variety of female material roles."[90]

The double standard meant that a man who boasted of having sex with
a woman damaged only her reputation, not his. Thomas Price, a coach
carver, not only called Amy Price "a common strumpet" as she worked in
her husband's saddlery shop but bragged to all around that "he had picked
her up in the Strand many times for a shilling."[91] A butcher's apprentice
revenged himself on his former sweetheart by circulating doggerel verse in
Whitechapel Market alleging that her mother had locked them in a garret
together.[92] Mathew Moss broke up his friendship with his cousin and her
husband, a collarmaker, by bragging that he had seduced her.[93]

The double standard also meant that men could excuse assaults by
claiming that their victims were streetwalkers, and the police themselves
harassed any woman out late at night, no matter what her occupation.[94]

Although much camaraderie existed between prostitutes and their customers, sexual commerce could quickly ignite the sexual antagonism that
smoldered in plebeian culture. Gossiping men sometimes called their victims "bunters"—beggarly streetwalkers who could be had under a bush
for sixpence.[95] In the song "Smith's Frolic," Smith scorns a prostitute's offer
of sex for five shillings by offering sixpence, an insultingly low price for
anyone but a bunter. When she protests, he retorts,

> You gallows mark'd measly, ill-looking whore!
> Your coffin shall walk before I give you more,
> With that I threw out the strength of my fist,
> And made a blow at her, but chanced to miss,
> . . . I straightaway began for to kick and to cuff[,]
> I lubber'd her head till I thought she'd enough.[96]

Harassing women on the streets at night seems to have been a common
form of amusement for young men in metropolitan areas.[97] In Glasgow,
between 1814 and 1824, an average of 14.8 cases of assault on females appeared before the police courts each month. Most of these attacks took place
in public, chiefly in the streets or the closes (small courts or entrances to
tenements) and in the pubs. Although assaults on women seem to have
become somewhat less frequent by the 1830s, in the 1840s they were still
common enough to excite the ire of magistrates. The fiscal procurator
(public prosecutor) of Paisley said he wanted to make an example of William Miller, who had knocked down a young woman on the street, despite
the fact that "some people would say that the poor girl had no business
being out at night, she was probably drunk, even though they would severely criticize an assault on a lady." Miller was fined over one pound for
this assault. In another case, a weaver was given the uncommonly long
sentence of thirty days for a similar assault.[98]

Interestingly enough, Glasgow artisans in traditional apprenticed trades
were overrepresented as assailants on females, accounting for 36.2 percent
of the assaults, although they made up only 16 percent of the occupied
population in 1820 (see Table 2). Textile workers, especially weavers, were
underrepresented. It is possible that traditional skilled artisans were more
closely tied to an exclusively masculine journeymen's culture of pubs and
workshops, while textile workers often worked alongside women and could
regard them as potential partners, even if only auxiliary ones. In Lancashire, a similar pattern prevailed, although not to such a striking extent
(see Table 3). In the earlier period artisans were somewhat overrepresented
as assailants on women, although this proportion declines after 1821.

Table 2. Assaults on Women in Glasgow, 1813–1824

	Assaults (N = 279)	Occupied Population, 1820 (N = 44,385)
Professional/mercan-tile/gentlemen	6.4%	4.3%
Retail	7.8	12.3
Skilled trades	36.2	16.5
Textiles	24.8	31.1
(weavers/warpers)	(14.4)	(27.3)
Laborers/servants	18.0	31.3
Miscellaneous	6.8%	4.5%

Sources: For occupied population: James Cleland, *An Enumeration of the Population of Glasgow* (Glasgow, 1820), p. 7. For assault cases: Glasgow Police Court books, 1813, 1814, 1815, 1817, 1818, and Anderston Police Court books, 1824, in Glasgow, Mitchell Library, Strathclyde Regional Archives.

No doubt many artisans abhorred sexual violence and yearned for women as practical wives, if not as romantic partners. Yet the structural factors of artisans' lives—delayed and difficult marriage, and the bachelor camaraderie as compensation—may have fostered misogynist, even violent attitudes among some men.[99] Some artisans seemed likely to regard young single women not as fellow workers but as either economic rivals or sexual prey. Young artisans, for instance, socialized in "cock-and-hen" clubs with prostitutes. At first glance, these occasions seemed to provide a space where young men and women could mingle on equal terms:

> This club was held in a large long room, the table being laid nearly the whole length of it. Upon one end of the table was a chair filled by a youth, upon the other end another chair filled by a Girl. The amusements were drinking,—smoking—swearing—and singing flash songs.[100]

But, as Stansell points out, "Sexuality was often the ticket of admission—the key to social pleasure, the coin of heterosexual exchange."[101] Plebeians did not only engage in a market culture by buying victuals and drink; for young women, their most valuable possession was their sexuality. Gillis notes, "Hens were young women who earned their living partly by prostitution [and] the Cocks were young tradesmen," most of

Table 3. Occupations of Men Charged with Assault on Females and to
Keep Peace to Females, County of Lancaster, 1799–1834

	1799–1820 (N = 417)	1821–1834 (N = 446)	Occupied Population, 1831 (N =313,097)
Professional/mercantile/gentlemen	1.7%	1.8%	5.6%
Retail	4.0	2.7	13.2
Skilled trades	19.6	13.9	14.3[a]
Manufactures	35.0	32.0	31.1[b]
weavers	(25.0)	(23.5)	[30–80?][c]
Laborers/servants	27.3	41.0	26.7
Farmers/crofters/husbandmen	5.9	4.2	5.2
Miscellaneous	6.2%	4.2%	3.9%

Sources: For assaults and articles to keep the peace to females: Preston Record Office, Lancashire Quarter Sessions. For occupational tables: 1831 census, PP 1834, vol. 10, pp. 306–9.

[a]This is the percentage of all the artisan trades charged with assault or to keep peace to a female (except wife-beating) and listed in the occupational tables of the census: blacksmith, brass trades, bricklayer, carpenter, carter, chairmaker, clothdresser, dyer, engraver, gunsmith, hatter, ironmoulder, joiner, mason, nailor, painter, pipemaker, plasterer, printer, ropemaker, sadler, sawyer, shoemaker, sizer, slater, stonemason, tailor, tinman, turner, watchmaker, wheelwright, whitesmith.

[b]Of those in manufactures, 96.7 percent were textile weavers, spinners, dyers, and so on. The 1831 census does not break down the category precisely.

[c]At least 30 percent of adult males were weavers. In many areas around Preston and in Oldham, Blackburn, and other large towns in the first two decades of the nineteenth century, 50 percent and in some areas up to 80 percent of males were estimated to be weavers. John K. Walton, *Lancashire: A Social History* (Manchester: Manchester University Press, 1987), p. 110.

whom also had a "sweetheart who was the daughter of some tradesman."[102] Young male artisans thus seem to have differentiated between "good" girls they would marry and other women with whom they would engage in sexual commerce. And sexual commerce often led to conflict; for instance, artisans accounted for 38 percent of those accusing prostitutes of stealing their money as they bargained over the price of sex or recovered from a moment's indulgence (see Table 4).

In contrast, textile workers inhabited a culture based on sexual cooperation. Handloom weavers toiled alongside women weavers or winders in close-knit workshops where romance could easily flower. For instance,

Table 4. Occupations of Men Who Prosecuted
Prostitutes for Theft or Robbery in the Old
Bailey Sessions, 1798–1820 (N = 487; all
whose occupations were listed)

Merchants, clerks, captains, gentlemen	10.9%
Publicans, dealers, shopkeepers	8.0
Artisans and tradesmen	38.4
Laborers, soldiers, sailors, servants	42.7%

Source: London, Guildhall Library, Printed Old Bailey Sessions Papers.

friends saw Catherine Hill and William Taylor "making diversions together" around the looms, with William putting his arms around Catherine's neck as she wove.[103] Similarly, neighbors and workmates observed
John Gray courting Marion Taylor; they watched the pair retreat from the
shop where they wove together to a stable for more privacy.[104] Male and
female textile workers also socialized together. Thomas Whittaker, a Preston cotton-mill worker, accompanied his female fellow workers to dances
in pubs, where they competed for prizes for the best hornpipe.[105] In 1825,
Elizabeth Davidson, a carder in a Glasgow cotton mill, went with a group
of female acquaintances to a pub where one of their number treated them
in celebration of her impending marriage. As the evening wore on, they
joined company with a boisterous group of young men from another mill.[106]
    Of course, even though textile workers seem to have been somewhat
less likely than artisans to assault women, some still committed violence—
one of those boisterous young men tried to rape Elizabeth Davidson. Like
all plebeian men, textile workers faced a choice between a responsible and
a misogynist ethos. Such a choice can be seen in a case from Glasgow in
1828, in which a weaver named Richard Bates was charged with the attempted rape of Mary Martin, a washerwoman and dresser who lived
alone. Bates had been observing Martin for some time, commenting to his
fellow weavers that "she had a fine leg and it was like a beam," and that
"long-legged women" were good in bed. Comparing her leg to a beam, part
of a loom, evokes the song "New Bury Loom," which used weaving as a
metaphor for flirtation and sex ("My shuttle run well in her lathe").[107]
Bates enticed another weaver, William Wood, into visiting Martin with
him, although Wood had protested that "he did not need a sweetheart, he
was already tied." Once Bates had wheedled their way into Martin's room
late at night, Wood went outside to relieve himself, only to hear loud cries
of distress. When he broke down the locked door to find Bates molesting

Martin, Wood burst out, "It was a great shame to abuse a decent woman in her own house." They left, but the next night Bates returned alone and beat Martin badly, while she upbraided him as a "blackguard, brute and libertine." Tragically, although Martin fought him off and escaped rape, the experience shook her so much that she died of a stroke.[108] Men like Bates often bragged of their assaults on women in pubs, while men like Woods may have been more likely to join dissenting congregations where, as we will see in the next chapter, their values of responsibility and sexual conformity could be reinforced and supported in a tight subculture.[109]

Conclusion

Sexual morality provided a dividing line between the classes. Plebeian sexual morality differed from that of the nascent middle class, which regarded as prostitutes all women who had sexual experience outside marriage. Plebeians often valued other moral virtues more highly than chastity, following old customs of premarital sex upon promise of marriage and of common-law marriage if a first marriage had broken down. But the prevalence of illegitimacy and common-law marriage was not due just to an alternative morality. The alternative plebeian morality could not provide an element of a common culture or experience that might have enabled plebeians to form a class. Instead, it was the product of social stresses caused by industrialization, labor mobility, urbanization, and wars. Sexuality became a fault-line for divisions among families and neighborhoods within plebeian culture: between men tied to a bachelor libertine culture and their pregnant sweethearts fearing abandonment, between upwardly mobile shopkeepers and their neighbors, between the religious and the respectable. As the next chapter shows, a minority within plebeian culture sought refuge from this seeming sexual chaos in organized religion, creating their own subculture of respectability.

These changes also constituted a "sexual crisis" because they became a political issue. Trade unionists trying to repel their masters' efforts to employ women insulted their female rivals by calling them prostitutes. Sian Moore has stated that in Bradford, "the existence of a large female factory workforce seems to have coincided with a spate of attacks by men on women operatives."[110] Conversely, in the Queen Caroline affair, the existence of conflicting moral standards serves to explain how plebeians could simultaneously uphold Caroline as an emblem of virtue in contrast to the debauched king, and accept her possible sexual adventures as a matter of course. Later on, sexual issues would put the nascent working class on the defensive, as Malthusians and political economists identified the allegedly unchecked reproduction of the poor as a cause of their own misery and a threat to society at large. The morality of factory girls began to be an issue of intense debate after the 1820s, when they entered mills in large numbers. As the middle class gained moral and political power, the working class as a whole had to choose between libertine and respectable strains of plebeian sexual culture. Ultimately, "respectable" sexual attitudes became hegemonic.

5   The Struggle
for the Breeches

Conflict in Plebeian Marriage

The life of David Love, a peripatetic ballad-writer and former collier, did not follow the pattern of his name, for he found marital happiness difficult to attain. He married his second wife expecting a docile helpmeet, but their relationship soured as the shop they kept together failed and, in his words, she "strove to be master." As he continued in his autobiography, "I would not submit; but asserted my authority, which caused great contention." However, he eventually won her over:

> With her my ground could hardly stand,
> She strove to get the upper hand;
> 'Till eight years join'd in marriage band,
>   Chang'd was her life,
>   She did submit to my command,
>   A loving wife.[1]

In common with many religious and popular authorities, David Love believed marriage should be "patriarchal yet companionate."[2] Contemporary moral authorities made it quite clear that husbands ought to rule—albeit with love. But they feared that submission was "directly contrary to women's inclinations, an order which could be sustained only by vigilant suppression of their unruly drives," as Joy Wiltenburg has observed.[3] The Rev. William Secker both advised husbands to love and respect their wives and stressed, "Our ribs were not ordained to be our rulers. . . . The wife may be a sovereign in her husband's absence, but she must be subject in her husband's presence." Secker warned, "Choose such a one as will be a subject to your dominion. Take heed of yoking yourselves with untamed heifers."[4] John Stephens, a London preacher, declared that woman "is forbidden to aspire to rule, for her Maker designed her for a helper." Women must not brawl, he continued, but must submit themselves to their husbands, while men must not act bitterly or inhumanly toward their wives.[5] The Rev. Mark Wilks, a radical Baptist minister, told men to "rule in love."[6]

Yet as Love found, there was an essential contradiction between the patriarchal and companionate ideals.[7] Plebeian marriage was often a business partnership, for both spouses had to contribute to the family's maintenance.[8] But wives were not supposed to acquire equal authority thereby. The sense of independence wives gained by wage-earning clashed with husbands' desire to dominate, resulting in the "struggle for the breeches" satirized in comic popular literature and more tragically evident in court records of wife-beating.

Happy Families

To be sure, autobiographies reveal that many plebeian partnerships were happy and harmonious, especially when husbands demonstrated respect for their wives' contributions.[9] J. B. Leno praised his wife as "a good mother, an affectionate partner, a wise counsellor, a model of industry."[10] Whatever the faults of his second wife, David Love valued his first wife as "a blooming young woman . . . excellent at working, careful and industrious."[11] Similarly, John O'Neill's wife helped him in his shoemaking business by binding shoes, and he remembered her upon her death during her thirteenth confinement as "a mild, sober, industrious, generous-hearted woman, a good wife, an affectionate mother, a disinterested friend."[12] The cooper William Hart, of London, tried to set up a little shop so that he and his "beloved dear" wife could support their children.[13] Alexander Tannahill, the early nineteenth-century Paisley weaver-poet, enshrined this ideal in his verse "When Johnnie and Me were Married":

> Wi' working late and early,
> We're come to what you see;
> For fortune thrave aneath [thrived beneath] our hand,
> Sae eydent [ardent] aye were we.
> The lowe [flame] o' love made labour light,
> I'm sure ye'll find it sae,
> When kind ye cuddle down at e'en,
> 'Mang clean pease strae [in a clean bed of straw].[14]

In the relative poverty of Scotland, industrious wives were prized even more than in England. As one mother in a popular chapbook advised her son, he shouldn't wed a thin girl who'll "di naething but prick and sew . . . an drink tea, but you maun get ane that can card and spin, and wirk in barn and byre."[15] Indeed, Alexander Somerville, son of farm laborers in the mid

Lowlands, remembered that his mother not only made clothes and engaged in other "domestic toil," but had to "add by outfield labor to the family income," carrying haystacks and performing other heavy farm work.[16]

Weavers and other textile workers were especially likely to seek hard-working wives, for women's work in spinning was essential to the production process, and a weaving wife could contribute even more to the family's earnings. Joseph Gutteridge described his prospective wife as "kind, truthful, and industrious, gaining her living by weaving; in fact, she was just the kind of helpmeet I needed."[17] Joseph Livesey, a Preston weaver, praised a good wife as "sober, affectionate and industrious."[18] In Scotland, the "'slubber spinners' who 'drew long from the Flax on the rock,'" producing uneven yarn, were less likely to find husbands than the fine spinners, who . . . were the object of the pragmatically-tinged affections of males who sought the best spinners as partners, and hence a higher standard of living."[19] A young female weaver in Spitalfields could allure potential husbands by flaunting her "showy ribbons, the ear-drops, the red coral necklaces of four or five strings" she bought with her own wages, for a man would be "disposed to consider the earnings which she can make at her loom as far more advantageous to him than all she could gain or save by the use of a needle, or could benefit him by cooking dinners which his wages do not enable him to buy."[20] Thomas Whittaker, a textile factory worker, remembered that he fell in love with his wife when "we were much together, working next to each other [in the factory]; there were many opportunities of showing kindness and rendering mutual help, and in that way our oneness grew into warm affection."[21] The artisan Gutteridge found his wife "good and kind, true and faithful, and patient under the many difficulties that beset us in after life." He became very angry when her disapproving relatives blocked her employment with him in the factory. Eventually, she supported the family as a weaver when he was unemployed, as well as supplementing his income when he was in work.[22]

Not only wives' industry but their wisdom was valued. "The Weavers' Garland, or a New School for Christian Patience," advises a hard-pressed weaver to abandon his drinking companions and seek solace in his wife's good counsel and industry.[23] James Paterson, a Scottish printer, attended political meetings and holiday rambles with a cobbler and his wife who were "exemplary in conjugal felicity as they were in their habits of industry and sobriety."[24] The Rev. Mark Wilks, a former buttonmaker, remembered of his wife that "never was an attachment founded on a greater equality of esteem, or a stronger reciprocity of friendship. . . . His wife was his companion, and his friend, and he never entered on any step without first availing himself of the benefit of her opinion."[25]

However, wives had to ensure that their husbands did not perceive their advice as undermining patriarchal authority. David Gilmour recalled several types of overt or covert struggles for power within artisan marriages in a Baptist weaving community in Paisley, near Glasgow. Gilmour's neighbor Henry Buchan acknowledged that wives could rule their husbands through manipulation:

> In every case what maistry was contended for, the idea o' marriage in its proper sense is excluded; marriage involving the acknowledgement on the part of each that the ither had the richt to be consulted. . . . A true wife will aye see her highest wisdom in her husband's, an' a true husband will always rejoice in his wife's love o' his wisdom. Mairfortaken that love o' his wisdom gies her a pow'r tae rule owre him an' his household, which a true wife will do, while as the poet says, she 'seems to obey.' [26]

However, this patriarchal partnership was not always so companionate. Gilmour also remembered another neighbor, a radical who "waxed eloquent now and then in defence of liberty and equality, but he was from constitutional tendencies a strong-willed aristocrat, and exercised his family headship, not as a responsibility for which he was accountable, but as an authority that ought and must be obeyed." [27]

Most male autobiographers, unlike David Love, were reluctant to reveal marital misery. As David Vincent notes in his study of working-class autobiographies, such revelations would have been "undignified" for writers trying to depict self-improvement. [28] However, children may have been able to be more critical of their parents' marriages. As John Burnett notes of working-class autobiographies, "The father emerges almost as a stereotype—frequently a drunkard, often thoughtless and uncaring of his wife and children, bad-tempered and selfish, but occasionally over-generous and sentimental." [29]

The very few plebeian women's autobiographies presented a different perspective from that of the men. In the examples I have found, women depict marriage as a pragmatic effort to survive. The Scottish Janet Bathgate described a youthful friendship to another girl in much more intense terms than she used for her later two marriages. [30] Similarly, Mary Ashford remembered a strong attachment to a female fellow servant, but she expressed little emotion when describing her marriages. Ashford accepted her first husband's proposal because she had just lost a place as a servant. They promised to pool their savings and "act fair and candid toward each other." Although he had an irritable temper due to gout, he "exerted himself" on behalf of their family of six children. After her first husband died, she married the widower of a close friend, who said "he knew I should do my duty by him, and he could assist me in rearing his old comrade's children."[31] When Mary Saxby, a peripatetic ballad-singer, left her lover for another man, she lamented, "Here I only exchanged one state of slavery for another."[32] Ann Candler suffered in an unhappy marriage for forty years. Despite her "unbounded" affection for her husband, "he treated me in a very unbecoming manner." When she finally left him, he "wept most bitterly at parting; I was sensibly affected, but had suffered too severely to waver in my resolution." Her resolution may have been strengthened by the fact that her husband was not a good provider and drank away their money when he was not serving in the army.[33] Candler was unusual only in that she wrote an autobiography; her experience of neglect and violence was very common among plebeian women.

The Struggle for the Breeches in Popular Literature

Popular literature often admonished husbands and wives to respect each other and forget their quarrels, upholding the values of companionate, patriarchal marriage. "The Fair Sex Vindicated" asked,

> Who then is your constant affectionate friend?
> 'Tis no sottish companion, I'm sure, whose advice
> Has ruined your children, and cheers you in vice,
> But 'tis your best friend, your affectionate wife,
> Who values your health as she values her life.[34]

William Paul concluded his poem *The Wars of Wedlock* by proclaiming,

> The bliss, you'll find, of wedded life,
> Exceeds its petty jarring strife.
> In brief debate—the jarring theme,
> Is but a stane [stone] in wedlock's stream.[35]

Yet publishers aimed not to inculcate morals but to sell songs. To do so, their productions had to speak to the realities, not just the aspirations, of plebeian life. The ideal marriage was rather difficult to attain, and was in any case not a source of satirical or tragic narrative. Even when songs and tales ended with promises of harmony, they almost always began with assumptions of conflict. Many plebeians felt stuck in unhappy marriages, or at least constantly overheard their neighbors' quarrels. Yet popular songs and chapbooks about marriage did not simply reflect marital misery, either, for dreary reality would not appeal to buyers any more than moralism would.

Instead, popular literature satirized marriage through a variety of rhetorical tropes and ancient images—most notably the image of the "struggle for the breeches," an ancient motif in European popular culture. As Laure Beaumont-Maillet writes, "La culotte, c'est la force, la domination, la liberté,"[36] a crucial yet vulnerable symbol of manhood. A thinly veiled phallic symbol, the breeches symbolized male domination. However, unlike the phallus, they could easily be removed and worn by a woman. Popular culture's representations of wives wearing the breeches evoked male anxieties that women could easily undermine their rightful power, yet also excited laughter by their incongruity. Songs upheld husbandly domination by ridiculing men who were unable to enforce their will on their wives.[37] For example, in a Scottish song, "Will the Weaver," the hero complains,

> Mother dear now I'm married,
> I wish I had longer tarried
> For my wife she does declare
> That the breeches she will wear.

His mother admonishes him, "Loving son give her her due, Let me hear no more from you."[38] Similarly, the wife comes off victorious in a song about marital quarrels over the respective costs of whisky and tea. The husband threatens,

> You impudent jade take care what you say,
> You are bound by the laws of the land to obey,
> And while I am able I vow and declare,
> I will not allow you the breeches to wear.

But the song warns husbands,

> For if you should flail [wives] from head to toe;
> You may depend on it they'll have the last blow.[39]

As Wiltenburg observes, the image of the violent wife could be seen as humorous because it transgressed the passive, subordinate, female role—and rarely occurred in reality.[40]

The motif of the struggle for the breeches could appeal to female readers and purchasers of popular literature as well as to disgruntled husbands. Chapbooks presented men as desiring patriarchal marriage while women dreamed of companionate unions. In the chapbook *The Jealous Man . . .* , the wife declares, "I am your yokefellow, but not your slave; your equal, but not your vassal," and her husband retorts, "I own this all to be true, and yet the breeches belong to me. Is not man lord of the creation? . . . I work for you by day, and drudge for you by night [an allusion to her sexual demands], and yet you are not contented, without superiority over me."[41] In the popular *New and Diverting Dialogue Between a Husband and His Wife*, an impatient woman dragging her husband out of the alehouse threatens to cuckold him when he declares he'll beat her. He accuses her of rebelling against "her lord and Master," but she retorts that he is an "unnatural monster, cruel brute, tyrant," who does not remember "that husbands are to love and cherish their wives."[42]

Many songs, especially those from the eighteenth century, vented female discontent but upheld the overall framework of husbandly dominance.[43] But as female literacy increased in the early nineteenth century, publishers began to circulate songs that provided women with a newly defiant rhetoric against oppressive husbands.[44] Perhaps women sang such tunes over washtubs or at their friendly society meetings, egging each other on against brutal spouses. These rather bitter ballads advised women to fight back in the sex war, to "whack him with a rolling pin," a shovel, a poker, or even a chamberpot.[45]

What was new was that these songs drew upon a language of tyranny and slavery familiar from the political rhetoric of the time. The simple message of one song ran:

> I'll be no submissive wife,
> No, not I—no, not I;
> I'll not be a slave for life,
> No, not I—no, not I.[46]

Publishers tried to increase sales by exposing the sexual antagonism of plebeian life, printing misogynist anti-marriage broadsheets and indignant female responses. "A Woman That Is Plagued with a Man," a retort to "A Man That Is Plagued with a Woman," warned, "A woman had better be laid in her grave / Than suffer herself to be any man's slave."[47] "The Woman That Wished She Never Got Married" seconded this warning, proclaiming, "While you ladies do single remain, /By a tyrant you'll never be hurried."[48]

The counterparts to women's defiance were anti-marriage songs and caricatures that most likely found their audiences in the homosocial worlds of plebeian culture, the pubs and clubs where men drank, sang, and caroused, the arenas where the bachelor culture of journeymen flourished.[49] For example, the *Trades' Newspaper* reported one story about a shoemaker who sang "The Struggle for the Breeches" to a workmate who was so struck by its resemblance to his own marital woes that he dropped dead in a fit.[50]

In song, bachelors vowed to avoid the burdens of matrimony—the expense of childbirth and childrearing, the "self-less" labor for a family, the risk of cuckoldry, and, above all, "those termagant jades who'd still wear the breeches." Men should "kiss and cuddle girls," but when they're pregnant, it's "Time to Say No!"[51] The records of the Foundling Hospital and of the Glasgow kirk sessions bear witness to the reality of the problem of seduction and desertion.[52] In song, however, bachelors adamantly celebrated their state, pointing out that in marriage,

> There's scolding and fighting, while we're delighting
> Our selves with our freedom, while you have this strife.[53]

If men stayed single, resources could be circulated among workmates rather than being saved for the home. "Advice to Sailors" declares,

> For we that are merry and free
> Carouse and merrily sing
> For we have no wives that will scold
> We can both borrow and lend.[54]

Nonetheless, most plebeians eventually married or cohabited, but the loyalty of many husbands to their drinking mates obviously caused tensions between husband and wife. Although these clashes did not necessarily lead to violence, the husbands of popular literature often required that their wives allow them to frequent the alehouse. In radical weaver Alexander Wilson's popular song "Watty and Meg, or the Wife Reformed," Watty complains to his mates in a pub of his unhappy marriage to a scolding wife:

> See you, Mungo, when she'll clash [gossip] on
> Wi' her everlasting clack [scolding],
> Whyles I've had my nieve [fist], in passion,
> Liftet up to break her back!

But his friend Mungo advises, "O, for gudesake, keep from cuffets, [blows]," and advises him that simply threatening to desert her will infallibly keep her in line.[55]

Yet the "humorous" intention of popular literature allowed songs to both mock and condone wife-beating. By its title, the ambiguous "A Fool's Advice to Henpeck'd Husbands," one song ridiculed men who could not control their wives. But it also advised them,

> When your wife for scolding finds pretences, oh
> Take the handle of a broom,
> Not much thicker than your thumb,
> And thwack her till you bring her to her senses, oh.[56]

And a misogynist streak within popular culture meant that some songs and caricatures celebrated the torture of wives as funny and as justified by their shrewishness. The early nineteenth-century Glasgow ballad-singer

Hawkie drew crowds with his "Cure for Ill Wives," which advised the unhappy husband to "nail her tongue to a growing tree."[57] Congregating outside the windows of print shops to see the latest caricatures was a favorite
male recreation. One engraving, "Tameing a Shrew, or Petruchio's Patent
Family Bedstead, Gags and Thumscrews [*sic*]" depicted a man stretching
his recalcitrant wife on a rack. Another viciously portrayed "The Cobbler's
Cure for a Scolding Wife" to be sewing up her mouth (see Figure 3).[58] In
the punchline to a late eighteenth-century "joke," the irate husband declares to his scolding wife, "By Gingo, I will break all the Bones in your
Skin, but I'll have quiet."[59]

The wife-beating cobbler—the protagonist of a whole genre of songs—
may have appealed as an anti-hero, transgressing the patriarchal ideal of
companionate partnership and instead simply celebrating the misogyny of
the degraded artisan who married to obtain domestic services and insisted
on retaining his bachelor freedoms. "The Bold Cobbler" declares,

> I'll let the vixen know,
> That I will be her Master;
> When I to dine set down,
> I'll no more bones picking,
> I will have a bit of brown,
> Or Ma'am she knaps a kicking,
> All skittle grounds I'll see,
> To play a cheerful rubber,
> And if she follows me,
> Dam'me but I'll drab her.[60]

The cobbler's popularity as a wife-beater in popular literature may, to be
sure, be derived from the many puns on his trade; but the puns derived
their humor from an acceptance of violence. For instance,

> And when my wife began to strap
> Why I began to leather
> So where to take her down some pegs
> I drubb'd her neat and clever.
>
> . . .
>
> T'would break my heart to lose my awl,
> To lose my wife's a trifle.[61]

When we look at the incidence of wife-beating, we will see that the violent
cobbler was not only a stereotype but a reality.

Domestic Violence in the Courts

The image of the struggle for the breeches buttressed male dominance by
presenting patriarchal authority as the natural state of things and a wife

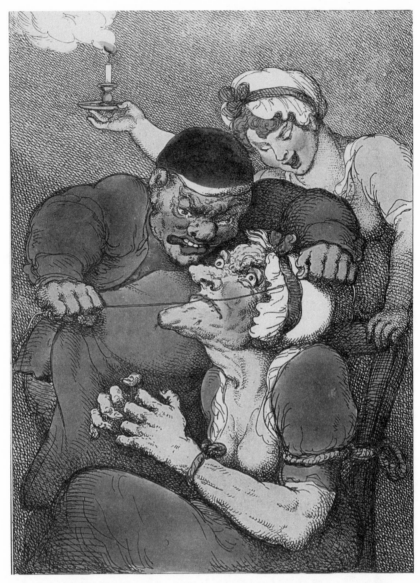

Figure 3. The Coblers Cure for a Scolding Wife. Copyright British Museum.

who refused to submit as aberrant. Even one magistrate described a woman who allegedly beat her husband as wearing the breeches.[62] Police court reporters, who sometimes spiced up their accounts with satire, could use this metaphor to discredit abused wives, ridiculing them as pugnacious termagants.[63] For instance, a *Weekly Dispatch* reporter buttressed George

Parker's claim that his wife Mary beat him by describing her as a "stalwart dame who possessed the power of 'wearing breeches' and refused him his connubial rights." However, in this case, the magistrate found her more convincing and rejected Parker's charge.[64] Similarly, when reporting a marital brawl the *Thistle's* police court reporter observed, "The wife showed marks of no slight description, which showed her husband to be of good pluck."[65]

The image of the struggle for the breeches concealed the reality that men assaulted women in 78 to 95 percent of the domestic violence cases reported in the courts.[66] Many wife-beaters seemed to feel they had a right to abuse their wives, and indeed until 1853 legal authorities equivocated as to whether wife-beating constituted legitimate correction or criminal assault.[67] The alleged ruling of Francis Buller, "Judge Thumb," that a man could beat his wife with a stick no bigger than his thumb was never a legal precedent, but it entered folklore. For instance, the pornographic *Rambler's Magazine* cited it as a charter for wife-beaters.[68] Even in the 1830s, at least one Glasgow magistrate did not take wife-beating very seriously. In a case in which a man had slashed his wife's face, the magistrate told him, "If he had so beaten any other person, than his wife, he would have been punished most severely, but as it was only his wife," he was bound over to keep the peace under a penalty of five pounds if he beat her again. The magistrate next fined a carter, who had whipped his horse till it bled, ten shillings and sixpence.[69]

Scottish men seem to have believed that violence was acceptable as long as it did not involve the use of instruments. For instance, William McFeat, a porter, executed for murdering his wife, denied to the last that "he used any lethal weapon, although he acknowledged that he both struck and kicked her on the night of her death."[70] James Fraser, a shoemaker of Edinburgh, pled guilty to striking his wife on the shoulder with his hand, "but nothing more."[71] George Johnston, a traveling tinsmith, murdered his wife on the road by beating her with a branch, but he pled not guilty, declaring, "I canna deny I struck her, but with no weapon whatever."[72] A "notorious drunkard" accused of striking his "fancy woman" and turning her out claimed, "If I did [strike her], it was only with my fist, for she hid or pawned the poker."[73] Some believed they had a right to beat their wives. An elderly Irish man defended himself before a Glasgow justice against a charge of wife-beating by explaining, "After knowing the law allows a man to beat his wife a little bit, when they're unezy [*sic*], I was just shewing the fists of justice, when she spit clane into my mouth."[74]

Many abused women, however, did not accept their husbands' right to beat them. Sometimes women themselves used the language of popular literature's sex war to express their complaints. Elizabeth Cooney testified that she had been married to John Cooney for only a week "when he began to tyrannise over her."[75] Similarly, the wife of Henry Stracey complained that "her husband was so tyrannical, she lived in constant fear of her life."[76] At least one woman a week appeared before the Middlesex magistrates in the late eighteenth century to complain of her husband's violence. In a three-month period in 1824, fifty-six cases appeared before the Glasgow police court—more than four a week. While it may therefore appear that Glasgow had a higher rate of wife-beating than London, the difference could also be attributed to the fact that the Middlesex court records were recognizances initiated by wives, whereas in Glasgow husbands (and wives) were often charged with "disturbing the neighbors" by fighting, so many cases came to light that wives would not have prosecuted themselves.[77] In any case, we can safely assume that wife-beating was a common occurrence in early nineteenth-century plebeian neighborhoods.

The root cause of domestic violence, then as now, was that abusive men wanted to dominate their wives and used violence to do so.[78] However, to put domestic violence into historical perspective requires an examination of the specific triggers for violence in a particular era. When did husbands believe their authority was being undermined, and what inspired wives to fight back and take violent spouses to court? Nancy Tomes has found that mid-nineteenth-century working-class couples fought over money, drink, and authority.[79] In late eighteenth- and early nineteenth-century Glasgow and London, conflict between plebeian husbands and wives erupted over many of the same issues, but the contradictions between patriarchal ideals, the realities of the family economy, and the pull of plebeian sociability were particular to this earlier plebeian culture.

Wife-beating was not a deviant act caused by unusual pressures of poverty and unemployment, for wife-beaters could be found in all levels of plebeian society.[80] In Old Bailey sessions trials for murders and attempted murders of wives between 1780 and 1845, clerks, tradesmen, and small shopkeepers accounted for 19 percent of the 177 cases in which occupations were known. Laborers accounted for 40 percent of the cases, but their percentage of the London work force is difficult to establish.[81] Skilled working men accounted for 41 percent of these cases in London, and this percentage approximately matches their proportion of the population of London. Only three weavers appeared, although they were the group hardest hit by unemployment. Five carpenters and four tailors were tried, a number roughly proportional to their numbers in the population, but shoemakers were overrepresented at fourteen cases, the largest single occupational group of wife-beaters. In Glasgow, they represented 6.2 percent (16 cases) of the

police court domestic-violence cases, although they made up only 2.9 percent of the occupied population.[82] The discrepancy was less marked in Lancashire, where they composed 3.6 percent (7 cases) of the wife-beaters and
2.7 percent of the occupied population. In both Glasgow and Lancashire,
artisans in traditional apprenticed trades were strikingly overrepresented
as wife-beaters (see Tables 5 and 6).

As in London, textile workers, especially handloom weavers, accounted
for many fewer of these cases than would be expected from their representation in the population. Some textile workers did beat their wives, to be
sure, but it is again possible that the sexually cooperative culture of the
textile industry diminished the incidence of such violence. When husbands
needed their wives' skill at weaving or spinning, domestic violence could
be seen to disrupt a profitable household economy. Conversely, artisans'
domestic violence may have stemmed from tensions between loyalty to the
family and loyalty to the hard-drinking world of journeymen's bachelor
culture.

For families in all trades, the dual responsibilities of husbands and wives
in the family economy could lead to productive partnerships—or to quarrels over the amount of work each performed and the allocation of resources. Proletarianization could increase these tensions, for both partners
often brought in wages, but until later in the nineteenth century, when
husbands often gave their wives a set amount for housekeeping, there was
no clear pattern for which spouse controlled the family budget. Plebeians
knew very well that husbands legally controlled their wives' earnings, but
in practice women did not surrender their wages readily. The social investigator Sir Frederick Eden commented in the 1790s that the legal right of
husbands to claim their wives' wages deterred many industrious women
from earning money, "from a thorough conviction that her mate would,
too probably, strip her of every farthing which she had not the ingenuity
to conceal."[83] Hannah More painted a vivid picture of a woman whose
gambling husband took the pittance she earned: "She bore with patience
her husband's spending all he got upon his own pleasures, and leaving her
to shift for herself; but when he came home, and tore from her what she
had worked so hard for, she could not help weeping and complaining."[84]

Popular literature and witnesses in trials echoed the concerns of social
investigators. From a husband's point of view, a comic broadside mandated
in a mock statute that "every Washerwoman, or any Women going out to
daily work, shall keep one half of her earnings, and the other shall be given
to her Lord and Master, for drinking money."[85] When "Watty" of Alexander Wilson's famous poem finally gains dominance over his wife, he
makes her promise

Table 5. Wife-beating in Glasgow, 1813–1835

	Domestic Violence		Occupied Population	
	1813–1824 (N = 137)	1830–1835 (N = 119)	1820 (N = 44,385)	1831 (N = 94,500)
Professional/mercantile/gentlemen	1.5%	2.5%	4.3%	8.2%
Retail	12.4	5.9	12.3	9.9
Skilled trades	36.5	29.4	16.5	18.9
Textiles	15.3	21.0	31.1	32.4
(weavers/warpers)	(10.2)	(11.8)	(27.3)	(15.2)
Unskilled/laborers	26.3	34.4	31.3	23.7
Miscellaneous	8.0%	6.7%	4.5%	6.8%

Sources: Glasgow Police Court books, 1813, 1814, 1815, 1817, 1818; Anderston Police Court books, 1824, 1831–1832; Gorbals Police Court books, 1835. The figures for 1820 are from James Cleland, *An Enumeration of the Population of Glasgow* (Glasgow, 1820); they are not strictly comparable to the figures for 1831, which are derived from T. C. Smout, *A History of the Scottish People 1560–1830* (London: Fontana, 1972), p. 370.

Table 6. Occupations of Men Charged with Wife-beating,
County of Lancaster, 1799–1834

	1799–1820 (N = 110)	1821–1834 (N = 85)	Occupied Population, 1831 (N = 313,097)
Professional/ gentlemen	2.7%	1.0%	5.6%
Retail	10.6	10.8	12.5
Skilled trades	28.6	22.3	15.0ᵃ
Manufactures	28.8	24.7	31.1ᵇ
weavers	(16.2)	(20.0)	[30–80?]ᶜ
Laborers	15.6	29.4	26.7
Farmers/crofters/ husbandmen	8.3	4.7	5.2
Miscellaneous	5.4%	7.1%	3.9%

Sources: For wife-beating cases: Preston Record Office, Lancashire Quarter Sessions. For occupational tables: 1831 census, PP 1834, vol. 10, pp. 306–9.

ᵃThis is the percentage of the nontextile trades represented as wife-beaters and listed in the occupational tables: blacksmith, brass trades, bricklayer, carpenter, carter, chairmaker, engraver, gunsmith, hatter, ironmoulder, joiner, nailor, painter, pipemaker, plasterer, printer, ropemaker, sadler, sawyer, shoemaker, slater, stonemason, tailor, tinman, turner, watchmaker, wheelwright, whitesmith.

ᵇOf those in manufactures, 96.7 percent were textile weavers, spinners, dyers, and so on. The 1831 census does not break down the category precisely.

ᶜAt least 30 percent of adult males were weavers. In many areas around Preston and in Oldham, Blackburn, and other large towns in the first two decades of the nineteenth century, 50 percent and in some areas up to 80 percent of males were estimated to be weavers. John K. Walton, Lancashire: A Social History (Manchester: Manchester University Press, 1987), p. 110.

That ye'll ne'er, like Bessy Miller,
Kick my shins or rug my hair,
Lastly, I'm to keep the siller [silver];
This upon your soul you swear?

Court records reveal real-life examples. When Daniel Heath set up his wife in a milk walk, he allowed her the silver she earned but kept the gold for himself.[86] Catherine Rolph complained that her husband, a shopkeeper, not only beat her but forced her to give him the money she had earned selling stock neckties.[87]

Women whose small savings or skills gave them independence could be exploited by irresponsible husbands. When Margaret Evans left her husband Daniel Heath on account of his ill treatment, he allowed her only eight shillings a week, although, as we have seen, he had been taking the gold she earned in her milk walk.[88] Similarly, Benjamin Blake had his new wife mind the coal shed he bought with her savings; meanwhile, he told her he worked as a carpenter, but in fact he was spending her earnings on another woman.[89] Although Sarah Purryer and her common-law husband made and sold mats together, he beat her as well as refused to give her money to feed the children. Finally, one night after he had gotten drunk and thrown her down the stairs, she killed him with a mallet-blow to the head. Three years after she had served two months in Newgate for manslaughter, she had established herself in partnership, rather than common-law marriage, with William Umney, a Spitalfields matmaker, and was earning enough to keep a servant.[90]

For women who had their own craft skills, small businesses, or inheritances, marriage could be disadvantageous, but at the same time their experience of public life may have given them the courage to protest against abusive husbands. The wife of John McDonach voiced a common complaint when she told the Glasgow police court in 1829 that she had to support him and the children since he refused to work, and all she had received in return were two black eyes. She assured the justices, "I am willing still to do so," to support the family, but she added, "I think if he does not contribute, he should be bound, at least, to keep the peace." The magistrate sympathized with her but feared that any fine would merely come out of her pocket; all he did, therefore, was to admonish the man, who "went away unconcerned."[91]

Some women went to court because they resented loss of property and independence as well as their husbands' violence.[92] Elizabeth Sims asked a magistrate for a separation because "in the absence of her husband, which frequently happened for some considerable time, she did very well, and got forward, but whenever he returned, he beat her, spent her money, and threatened her life."[93] Similarly, Ann Casson deposed that "prior to her intermarriage . . . she kept a grocer's shop in Edgeware Road and was doing very well when she unfortunately became acquainted with and met her said husband who had little or no property at all."[94] Phoebe Darwell, who kept a tobacconist's shop before she married, lamented, "I had respectability and some money, when I married him; but he has blasted my character, and he has done me every public and private injury."[95] The wife of a dyer from Hume, near Salford, prayed the court to grant her an article of the peace against her husband, who not only led an "idle and dissolute life" but beat her and forced her to spend her small inheritance from an uncle on his support.[96] For such women, husbands represented more of a liability than an asset.

But most plebeian wives, working at charring, washing, or hawking, were paid wages so low that their work could not serve as an avenue to independence. For them, work was only a bitter necessity, especially when a drunken husband contributed little to the family income. "The Drunkard's Wife" complained,

> I am forc'd to get up in the morn,
> And labor and toil the whole day,
> Then at night I have supper to get,
> And the bairns to get out of the way,
> My husband to fetch from the alehouse
> And to put him to bed when I go [*sic*]
> A woman can ne'er be at rest,
> When once she is joined to a man.[97]

In a real-life version of this story, a man named Devon was arrested on suspicion of cutting the throat of his wife, "a sober and industrious woman, [who] dealt in fish, but had the misfortune to live very uncomfortably with her husband."[98] Some wives had to trade support for violence. A laborer defended himself against a charge of wife-beating by claiming that "he was a well-doing man," for in the last week he had earned five shillings and had given four of them to his wife.[99]

Men's drinking eroded the living standards of wives and children. In a poem printed in the *Times* in 1788, a woman bluntly described her husband's cruelty:

> While you drink punch
> And eat your lunch
> And afterwards your dinner
> On tea and bread
> I'm forced to feed
> Spread thin with rancid butter
> My meagre face
> Had you God's grace
> To look at you would shudder.[100]

The wife of the "Drunken Cobbler" of Figure 4 complains that her husband pawned her clogs for money to play at skittles, leaving her for three days "without a bit o' wittles [victuals]."

Alcohol, of course, loosens inhibitions and aggravates any inclination toward violence. Forty percent of the domestic violence cases in the Old Bailey sessions involved drinking by the husband, the wife, or both. The percentage was even higher in Glasgow, where the availability of cheap whisky aggravated the problem. In the Gorbals police courts, 63 percent of the domestic violence cases in 1835–1836 involved a charge of drunk and

11

THE DRUNKEN COBBLER.

A Parody on the "Wife's Dream."

Where is my poor worsted shawl—my bonnet and my chali,
Where is the carpet and the bed, I got upon the tally!
Don't laugh—you pawned my clogs last night, to go and play at skittles,
And you've left me here this three days without a bit o' wittles.

You say I'm walking in my sleep, but don't be foolish Joe,
You'll soon walk to the county-court and promise what you owe.
I wish the skittle ground was burnt—I wish that you were in it,
I'd dance like any dusty Bob, and sing ilke a cock linnet.

... can tell you're drunk again, Tubbs, there'll be the deuce to pay,
Confound the nasty knock'em downs,—you've done no work to day,
'Tis enough to make an angel speak—I never say a word,
You've pawned my only gown and boots, and caged me like a bird.

You have gone on just "any how" since the day that we were wed,
Why don't you join a burial club, that I may wish you dead;
A widow's cap costs but a groat—I'm tired of this strife,
Upon my soul when I get out I'll go and and swear my life!

Last Friday night, as ever was, you went and pawned the bed,
And lost the ticket in your stall—leastways that's what you said,
The things have all gone one by one, there's nothing left behind.
Even my poor bellows is gone that you may mind
the wind.

No, Tubbs, I am not dreaming—I'm too wide awake or you,
I tell you once for all Tubbs, this sort of life wont do;
I am that lawful married wife you swore to love and cherish—
I'll throw myself in the canal, or die upon the parish.

Go to my friends in this state, my friends are not so kind,
You quite forget that five pound loan—and what remains behind;
A good time coming—yes, 'twill be when you are dead,
You nasty, drunken, dirty, snob, sit down and earn your bread.

I'm doomed to starve alive in this tattered petticoat;
All the rags that I stand upright in would not sell for a groat;
I could eat you with a grain of salt—I could upon my life—
I'm known all over London as the Drunken Cobbler's wife.

BIRT, Printer, 39, Great St. Andrew Street, Seven Dials, London.

Figure 4. The Drunken Cobbler. British Library C.116.i.1. By permission of the British Library.

disorderly. Twenty-six percent of the male assailants in the Old Bailey sessions cases were drunk at the time they committed the assault, as were 30 percent of the women. Fifteen percent of the men and 13 percent of the female assailants used their victims' drunkenness as an excuse.[101] Men claimed that their wives were drunkards in order to excuse violence against them, and there were cases of apparently alcoholic women who assaulted their husbands and pawned all their possessions. This problem, too, seems to have been particularly acute in Scotland, where whisky could quickly intoxicate a small woman. If a man drank, his wife might still be able to hold the household together, but if the wife was an alcoholic as well the family was doomed. Working people and social reformers alike tended to see women's drinking as pathological while viewing men's as a normal, if unfortunate, part of plebeian culture.[102] As Stansell points out, "[Female] drunkenness was maddening because it dramatized, however perversely, a woman's determination to serve herself at the expense of others."[103] Yet drinking was not the only cause of violence; the close correlation of drinking with wife-beating in Glasgow may have been due to police primarily arresting men for being drunk and disorderly and only secondarily charging them with assault. Furthermore, as has been observed of the situation today, men may have gotten drunk in order to work themselves up to beating their wives.[104] In her autobiography, Mary Saxby wrote, "I have reason to apprehend, that my husband got drunk on purpose to abuse me."[105]

Drinking crystallized larger issues of competition over access to plebeian sociability and over control of resources. J. P. Malcolm observed of eighteenth-century journeymen and laborers that "their domestic amusements chiefly consist in disputes with a Wife, who finds herself and children sacrificed to the brutal propensities of Drinking and Idleness; and the scene of contention is intolerable, if the lady possesses a high spirit; so entirely so [to] the husband, that he fixes himself for the evening with a party at the public house."[106] Both men and women participated in the free and easy world of libertine plebeian culture, but wives often found their highest priority was to feed the children, while artisan husbands retained their primary allegiance to the homosocial world of workshop and pub. The wife fetching her husband home from the alehouse was the subject of two of the most popular tales about marriage, "Watty and Meg" and "A New and Diverting Dialogue Between a Shoemaker and His Wife." Husbands resented what they perceived to be their wives' "nagging" about their main pleasure in life—drinking with their mates. Archibald M'Lean beat his wife with a poker when she asked him where he had spent the evening.[107]

In turn, women resented the enjoyment their husbands found at pubs and clubs while they starved at home. Another wife defended herself against a charge of stabbing her husband, a butcher, by declaring that he beat her and "kept herself and family without decent clothes, while he went out to the play, dressed like a gentleman, smoking cigars, and stopping out most nights of the week."[108] One printer's wife actually prosecuted a publican for keeping his tavern open too long, because her husband "spent all his earnings at the defendant's house and only brought her three farthings last Sunday."[109] Women resented the freedom and conviviality men found in their pubs and clubs. One woman became so enraged when her husband forbade her to smoke at home although he was enjoying a pint and a pipe at his club, that she disguised herself in his coalheaver's work clothes and went to his pub. There, after imbibing a bit too much porter and tobacco, "with great volubility [she] commenced a discourse on the rights of women." The coalheavers who surrounded her, realizing she was a woman come to spy on them, hauled her to a police court, where her husband declared that "he'd larn her to vear [*sic*] his breeches again."[110]

Wives dreaded the working man's custom of Saint Monday, celebrated by historians as proletarian resistance to capitalist time discipline. In the bitter song "The Fuddling Day, or Saint Monday," a woman laments that on his day off her husband beats her and spends her savings on drink.[111] Conversely, women's social freedom conflicted with the belief of some husbands that their wives should stay at home, under their control and away from temptation. A man whose wife kept two lodging houses defended himself against a charge of wife-beating by claiming that she went out with other men to the Vauxhall Pleasure Gardens.[112] A husband complains in the Manchester song "Gossiping Wife,"

> A gossiping wife I've got for my lot,
> She's such a torment to me,
> She's never at home but to eat and drink,
> At breakfast, dinner and tea,
> But when it's done, and my back is turn'd,
> Away out of the home is she,
> At some neighbour's door with a dozen or more
> With her child upon her knee.
> Then up comes one with a tongue a yard long
> O what do you think I heard,
> Your husband was seen last neight [*sic*], indeed,
> It's true upon my word.[113]

One Glasgow husband defended himself against a charge of disturbing the neighbors by beating his wife by claiming that she was "a bad woman, accustomed to leave his house, and go to the shows." She stated, however, that it was his violence that drove her away from home.[114] Charles Boyle assaulted his wife because she spent too much time at her mother's, but she claimed "she was obliged to do so as he was always murdering her."[115]

The insecurity of marriage may have intensified jealousy, for 20 percent of the protagonists and witnesses in Old Bailey trials cited this emotion as a motive for violence. As the Poor Law records and bigamy trials reveal, men often deserted their wives for other women, and it was by no means uncommon for women to desert their husbands as well. Since common-law marriages were acceptable, at least in the "libertine" sections of plebeian culture, both men and women could readily seek more suitable partners if they were discontented with their first union. For instance, the wife of William King, a working ship's carpenter, left him after his drinking had "reduced his family to indigence," and she went to live with a prosperous hatter at Wapping, who established her in a snug little cottage.[116] Jane Rogers endured the violence of John Dennet, the greengrocer she lived with, for eight years, but finally left him to marry a gardener. Although Dennet drank their health at the wedding, he eventually murdered her.[117]

As Stansell notes, intense romantic love for a spouse could incite jealous rage.[118] When he saw his wife talking with another man on the street, George Edwards knocked her down and kicked her. He justified himself "from the feelings most men possess toward their partners in life."[119] Charles Campbell, a Glasgow cotton spinner, claimed Sarah McVicar as his wife although he had children by a woman who lived in the country. When Sarah repudiated Charles at a dance, he stabbed her to death and then collapsed in remorse, mourning, "I have then murdered her whom I love best in the world."[120] The flexibility of the Scottish marriage law, in which private betrothals could later be recognized as marriages, contributed to this confusion. According to Archibald Alison, cohabitation, private marriages, and bigamy were extremely common among factory workers.[121] For example, during a jealous quarrel Mary Horn, who had been married to a cotton spinner but now cohabited with a butcher, killed the butcher's previous cohabitant, a widow who supported herself and their child by tambouring.[122]

The infidelity of husbands had serious economic consequences for wives, although it was much more difficult for them than for men to draw on the power of the law or popular justice to gain redress. Mary Taylor, for instance, accused her husband of treating her with "inhumanity" by spending all his money on "naughty women" and depriving her of the "necessities of life." The magistrate allowed her a separation and ordered John Taylor to pay her 3 shillings a week, which was certainly not enough for subsistence.[123] Husbands who patronized prostitutes could contract venereal disease and then transmit the disease to their wives. Thomas Dickers, for instance, "a wild debauched profligate," consorted with prostitutes and infected his wife with "the clap." Amelia Brazier fled her husband's syphilitic embraces and charged him before a magistrate with assault, but he told the judge that "he would beat and pox his wife whenever he thought proper."[124]

British society viewed a wife's infidelity much more seriously than it did her husband's adultery. *Conjugal Infidelity*, a popular pamphlet, warned wives with the sad tale of Maria Stent, the unfaithful wife of a butcher who stabbed her in revenge. It painted a pathetic picture of the bleeding wife proclaiming, "You, my dear Henry, were the best of husbands, the most indulgent of men. I was very wicked; O may my fate prove a salutary warning to all bad wives."[125] A husbands who claimed that his wife had been unfaithful could sometimes escape punishment for beating her. In 1804 Francis Morris was found guilty of assaulting his wife, "but it appeared the Lady was not quite so pure as she held herself out to be, he was only sentenced to pay one shilling and be discharged."[126]

A woman making her husband "wear the horns" contended with her "wearing the breeches" as the classic symbol of female dominance in marriage. In a comic dialogue, a drunken shoemaker's wife plots to revenge herself on her feckless spouse by finding some "kind spark" to "graft a pair of horns upon his head." In a similar chapbook, the husband frets, "I dread the horns, I would not be a cuckold for all the world, to be pointed at by everyone, to have a skimmington rode for me."[127]

Domestic Violence and Community Action

Adultery and desertion sometimes incited community action, such as a skimmington or rough music. In these nocturnal rituals, neighbors gathered together to parade the deceived man (or a surrogate) backwards on an ass, to symbolize his reversal of natural male dominance, and they waved a smock on a pole as an emblem of female insubordination. Although a few women took this as a celebration of their defiance, the community generally intended to rebuke the cuckold for his inability to uphold his authority.[128] By the late eighteenth and early nineteenth centuries, however, argues E. P. Thompson, communities practicing rough music had shifted their focus from belligerent wives to abusive husbands.[129] For instance, in the eighteenth and nineteenth centuries in Scotland, the custom of riding the stang was inflicted against violent husbands. Villagers would force men to straddle and ride a "sharpened deal plank or beam" until they promised to reform.[130]

However, this did not necessarily means women's position was better in plebeian society; as Thompson admits, the practice only revealed their defenselessness. And rough music continued to be practiced against violent wives. For instance, a cotton spinner at Hyde complained to the courts that he was beaten up when he tried to stop a crowd riding the stang. They were singing,

> Tink of a kettle, tank of a pan,
> This brassy faced woman has beaten her man.
> Neither with sword, dagger or knife
> But with an old shuttle she'd have taken his life.[131]

Furthermore, rough music was only rarely inflicted on violent husbands, but women needed rescue from domestic violence every day.

Neighbors sometimes assisted abused wives, but only if they screamed particularly loudly or the violence was unusually severe.[132] The neighbors of William Carter, a shopkeeper, insisted that he be tried for murdering his long-suffering wife, whom they had found drowned in a water tub.[133] Men sometimes tried to prevent husbands from assaulting wives, but it was much more likely that female neighbors would interfere. When John Simpson, a Shoreditch hairdresser, was tried for the murder of his wife, Eleanor Evans testified that she had told Mrs. Simpson to leave her husband and come live with her.[134] Elizabeth Ernby warned Abraham Winter to stop abusing his common-law wife, Mary Ann Stone, telling him, "Do not use the woman so ill, for I know to my certain knowledge that she has been a wife to you, and a mother to your children." Unfortunately, he continued beating Mary Ann, and she finally defended herself by stabbing him.[135] When John Ruddle beat his wife for telling him to get his own dinner, a female neighbor heard the commotion and alarmed Ann Baker, whose husband worked with Ruddle. She scolded him, "I am surprized at you, Ruddle, to get ill-using of your wife." Rebecca Bishop, their landlady, also heard the quarrel. She testified, "I asked him, why he made such a noise and such a piece of work in my house for; I asked him whether or no he was not ashamed to use a poor woman so ill?" He retorted that it was none of her business and threatened her.[136] However, neighbors, whether male or female, did not always interfere in domestic matters, and their help could not always prevent domestic homicide. Instead of rescuing Mrs. Riddle, Mrs. Bishop went back to her own room because she feared for the safety of her infant, and Ruddle proceeded to murder his wife. In another trial, Eleanor Burke failed to respond to cries for help from the wife of Edward Welch, a porter who had told Eleanor he would murder his wife, because "there were often such cries; I thought he was beating her, or pulling her hair."[137] Similarly, Sarah Paskin heard Mary Stark cry out, but, as she testified, "it was nothing new to me, as I heard them cry out very often, I continued at my work."[138] In one Scottish case, the plebeian neighbors of Charles Donaldson often heard him beat his wife, but said, "We paid no particular attention to his doing so, as it was his daily practice."[139]

Another form of popular justice romanticized by historians was wife-selling. Wife-selling functioned as a means of popular divorce in an era when legal divorce was available only to the very rich who could afford to obtain a private bill in Parliament. In the typical wife-sale, a husband would put a halter around his estranged wife's neck and take her to Smithfield cattle market or an inn, there auctioning her off for a token amount. The couple often prearranged the auction so that the wife would go to her lover, and many plebeians believed this was an official means of separation. Thereafter, the new union would be recognized as a marriage. Several historians, including E. P. Thompson, have interpreted wife-selling as, albeit a patriarchal practice, at the same time an expression of the independence and creativity of plebeians blocked from legal recourse.[140] So well enshrined in plebeian culture was wife-selling that many people believed it to be legal. In 1797, for instance, when a London flower dealer and a publican's wife wished to marry, they and her husband consulted an attorney to see if a wife sale could make their arrangement legal.[141] As late as 1841, a brushmaker whose wife wished for a separation told her "he knew how to do it legally" and proposed to sell her to her former sweetheart in Smithfield market.[142] In 1784, a Lincolnshire jury refused to allow a man to reclaim his wife from the man to whom he had sold her, thus implicitly accepting the legality of the sale.[143]

Some women initiated a sale or consented to be sold in order to escape a bad marriage and form a new one.[144] For instance, John Lilies, a schoolmaster, defended himself against a charge of bigamy by claiming, "My first wife and I parted by mutual consent; she proposed for me to sell her at Smithfield . . . there were writings drawn up between friends, and we separated."[145] Elizabeth Wood Lloyd told her first husband, a baker, that she wished to go off with a sailor, who sealed the bargain with five shillings and a bottle of wine.[146] A Mrs. Fowle unsuccessfully tried to avoid a charge of bigamy by convincing her first husband to sell her to her second husband at Smithfield market for five shillings and a written transfer agreement.[147] Rebecca Irish told a court that her husband had "no right to claim her," because he had sold her to her lover for a guinea in front of three witnesses.[148]

Nonetheless, the symbolism of women as property is inescapable. It was a plebeian version of civil actions for criminal connection or seduction, which allowed husbands or fathers to claim damages from the seducer of their wife or daughter. Yet wife-selling may have stemmed from a particular misogynist trend rather than representing overall plebeian attitudes toward women. The small amounts for which women were sold could be seen simply as token payments, yet they may have served as a contemptuous expression of how little some husbands valued their wives.[149] Many working people disapproved of wife-selling. For instance, when a "laboring man" exhibited his wife for sale at Smithfield market in 1806, "the public became incensed at the husband, and would have severely punished him for his brutality, but for the interference of some officers of the police."[150] It is significant that London wife-sales took place at Smithfield cattle market, a large male preserve, rather than at Covent Garden or Billingsgate, renowned for their tough, foul-mouthed marketwomen and fishwives who might have hooted down a callous husband. As Menefee notes, by the 1820s and 1830s women increasingly protested against wife-selling, for they saw the practice as "a threat and insult to their sex."[151]

The popular justice of plebeian culture therefore was of very limited assistance to abused wives. Rough music could be used against women as well as for them; wife-sales, however convenient, symbolized women as property; and neighbors could not be counted on to protect battered women.

Conclusion

One of the fault-lines of plebeian culture ran between husbands and wives and fissured the larger community as well. Whether expressed in physical or verbal violence, the contradiction between patriarchal ideals and the reality of the family economy resulted in a struggle for power, resources, and freedom within the family—the struggle for the breeches. Of course, husbands and wives had always struggled over these issues, if the popularity of this theme in songs is any indication, but new sources of tension arose in the late eighteenth and early nineteenth centuries. For all urban plebeians, the libertine pleasures of metropolitan life proved both tempting and perilous. Husbands and wives quarreled over who would spend money at the pub, and the increasing flexibility of plebeian morals could spark flares of jealousy and fears of abandonment. Artisans seemed particularly prone to wife-beating, a phenomenon that may have resulted from the clash between bachelor journeymen's culture and the needs of married life. Textile workers may have worked out more harmonious marriages based on partnership, but neither popular culture nor religion matched practice with an ethic of marital equality.

2

THE SEARCH FOR SOLUTIONS

The confusion felt by plebeian men and women over shifting sexual moralities and marital instability intensified during the era of the French Revolution and continued during the Napoleonic wars fought by the British intermittently from 1795 to 1815. The toppling of the monarchy in France created an apocalyptic atmosphere in which no social or sexual hierarchy seemed safe.[1] While many middle-class reformers initially responded with enthusiasm to the possibility of a new world, the excesses of the Terror quickly drove them to espouse a conservative morality. Rejecting the aristocratic libertinism of foppish gentlemen and flirtatious ladies, they replaced it with the notion of separate spheres, a public sphere controlled by rational, propertied men and a private sphere where pure women were sheltered from the winds of change. However, middle-class reformers did not admit plebeian men into the public sphere or allow plebeian women to remain at home; rather, they expected all plebeians to work at strenuous labor for low wages.

In response, plebeians began to organize to defend themselves against social and economic disruption, but they did not simply attempt to replicate the masculine bourgeois public sphere. Plebeians could not easily separate public from private issues, for their concerns included family disruption, the sexual division of labor, and moral confusion. Although many of the indigenous institutions of plebeian culture, such as artisan combinations, were dominated by men, workers soon found that they needed women's help if they were to mobilize whole communities.

6　Sin and Salvation
Men, Women, and Faith

In September 1797, the elders of the Calton Reformed Presbyterian Church in Glasgow summoned pregnant Janet McEwan before them to confess her "sin" of fornication. She tried to explain to them that a stranger had accosted her on the bridge one evening, "used her rudely," and then "forced" her in a field. It took two months for the dour elders to break down Janet's resolve. In the dark Glasgow November, she finally admitted her "sense of sin" and cowered before the congregation, cloaked in sackcloth, as the elders publicly rebuked her.[1] Men too, faced the discipline of dissenting chapels. A working man stumbling out of the pub after drinking with his mates might be seen by a deacon and summoned before a Methodist chapel meeting to repent or be expelled.

During the eighteenth century, many working people abandoned the established churches in England and Scotland to join such radical sectarian groups as the Methodists or the Scottish Relief Church. The Church of England and the Kirk of Scotland charged pew rents for the few seats available in urban churches, and the sermons seemed bland and complacent to those working people who did attend.[2] In reaction to this spiritual desiccation, John Wesley founded Methodism in the early eighteenth century, evangelizing in streets and fields. He introduced plebeians to a "methodistical" discipline of the soul and a community of the saved. Rejecting Calvinist predestinarianism, Wesley argued that Jesus had sacrificed himself so that all sinners could be redeemed. But this message of hope also infected believers with the gloomy sense of guilt that their heinous sins had required such a sacrifice.[3] Wesley's work inspired all dissenters; Baptist and Congregational dissenting chapels, and in Scotland, Relief and Secession kirks acquired new vigor as the evangelical flame spread.[4]

Why did plebeians accept sectarian religion, which seemed to evade the social and political problems they faced and instead imbued them with an almost masochistic sense of sin? E. P. Thompson interpreted such religious fervor as "sublimation" of the "misery and despair of the eighteenth century poor." Although he admitted that Methodism had positive educational and social results, he claimed that the "social energies denied outlet in public life . . . were released in sanctified emotional onanism."[5] E. J. Hobsbawm commented that "the sect normally dealt with the problems of the proletariat by evading them, or rather by solving them not for the class, but for the individual or chosen group of the elect."[6]

These historians have tended to regard religion as a poor alternative to radical politics; but why not instead ask what sectarian religion provided that politics lacked? Unlike the established churches, radical religion inspired the common people both spiritually and intellectually. Scottish laboring people such as weavers and peasants were intensely interested in theology. The Rev. John Bower of Old Monkland, near Glasgow, reported in the 1790s that "the people are very fond of controversial divinity."[7] Women found in religion an intellectual outlet denied them in politics. David Gilmour, a Paisley weaver, remembered "Motherly women" "deciding to the law and testimony on disputed points of doctrine and religion yet never assuming a position that was not theirs by Nature or Prescription." Religion was much more important to these women than politics, which they refused to discuss.[8]

Radical religion imbued the common people, especially women, with a sense of spiritual equality. Initially, radical religion functioned as a sect: voluntary, dogmatic, and pure, it transcended some of the boundaries of rank and gender.[9] In Scotland, as a result of women's participation in patronage riots, they were allowed to vote in some secession congregations.[10] Some recent writers on early Methodism have stressed its innovative role in allowing women to preach.[11] But did this sexual egalitarianism apply to the earthly as well as the heavenly plane?

Both men and women sought refuge in radical religious sects from the moral confusion and sexual antagonism of plebeian life. The libertine lifestyle could be exciting and enjoyable, but heavy drinking and marital disruption brought emotional and financial woes. As Deborah Valenze observes, many plebeians wandered abroad in search of work, and radical religious sects could provide an alternative home, with discipline and education they could not find elsewhere.[12] However, as the dissenting religious sects became better established, with their adherents marrying and bringing up children in the faith, the early egalitarianism often faded and patriarchalism reasserted itself. Methodists and other dissenting groups formed tight, cohesive communities within the larger plebeian society. They enabled working *men* to find respect and leadership roles denied them in the larger society. Men could become class leaders and preachers, proud of their wider patriarchal role. Moreover, not everyone could live up to the new respectable ideal. Millenarians and antinomians expressed their anguish over the "sexual crisis," seeking an alternative spiritual explanation for the persistence of sin.

Women Preachers in Early Methodism

Methodism served as a barometer or even a catalyst of sexual confusion and its resolution as the movement transformed itself from a sect into an institutionalized church. In its early years, Methodism's focus on spiritual equality provided dramatic opportunities for women. All, regardless of rank, preached Wesley, were sinners, and all could be saved. One of Wesley's hymns declared,

> Outcasts of men, to you I call,
> Harlots, and publicans, and thieves!
> He spreads his arms to embrace you all;
> Sinners alone His grace receives;
> No need for him the righteous have,
> He came the lost to seek and save.[13]

Wesley encouraged believers to abandon their godless families and join each other in "love-feasts" or informal communions. In the earlier years, anyone with a spiritual gift could preach.

Such transgressions of the conventional moral order scandalized adherents of the Church of England. Established churchmen continually reviled Methodism as a disruptive, leveling force, attacking its claim that the individual's religious experience took precedence over religious traditions and family obligations. Opponents spread rumors that Methodist "love feasts" degenerated into orgies—although in fact they were a rather sedate version of communion and prayer—and depicted Methodists' loud preaching, swooning, and visions as unseemly emanations of sexual passion.[14] Just as their spiritual fervor disturbed sedate Anglican practice, critics insinuated, female preaching defied the gender order. Henry Fielding alleged that the famous "Female Husband," who dressed as a man in order to marry several women and swindle them out of their savings, had originally been seduced by a female Methodist. He added that when she disguised herself as a male Methodist preacher, another Methodist man made advances toward her.[15] Similarly, an Anglican cleric capped his lurid anti-Methodist tales with the story of James Stephen, a preacher who traveled with "a young woman in man's clothes" and made a practice of seducing female enthusiasts.[16] In fact,

Methodism was not as transgressive as it appeared but was actually deeply entangled in plebeian culture. Instead of violating conventional morality, it enabled believers to escape the moral confusion of plebeian society. Methodism drew on the vitality and independence of plebeian women, but it never directly challenged patriarchal mores. Rather, unlike the satire of the struggle for the breeches, it provided a respectable place in plebeian culture for women's strength. Female preaching merely extended the continuum from women choosing God over marriage, to female networks, to proclaiming publicly their spiritual fervor.

Methodists organized themselves into small bands and classes that provided believers with an alternative to absent or disrupted families. Often laywomen were married to men hostile to their religious practice or found themselves alienated from unbelieving parents, so Wesley himself sanctioned young women's disobedience of their parents' command that they marry unbelievers.[17] At the same time, Methodism showed the ambivalence toward marriage that was expressed in less spiritual terms in popular literature. Wesley himself wrote that while marriage was a holy state, abstaining from marriage was a gift from God, for the celibate believer could care for God, not the things of this world. Somewhat wistfully, considering his own unhappy marriage, Wesley told the single man, "You enjoy a blessed Liberty from the *troubles in the flesh*, which must more or less attend a married State, and from a thousand nameless domestic Trials, which are found sooner or later in every family."[18] Many Methodist female preachers expressed an unconventional ambivalence about marriage. Elizabeth Evans hesitated a great deal before marriage, for "Christ was all the world to me." When she did marry, she "lost a great glory, but not sanctification; I loved God with all my heart, but had not that clear light, and that burning zeal, and that close union as before."[19] After marriage, however, she and her husband formed a partnership to range far and wide preaching together. Ann Cutler vowed to remain "a chaste virgin to Christ for ever, covenanting with God to live and die in the state."[20]

Methodist women could turn from unbelieving families to the sisterhood of religious women for support, creating their own respectable, educated version of plebeian women's culture. Autobiographies, memoirs, and letters of Methodist women reveal networks of female adherents and intense female friendships. Mary Cooper wrote in much more effusive tones to her friend Mary Anne than to her husband, noting, "My friendship for her glows with undiminished ardor."[21] Jane Cooper, a London needlewoman, wrote to a female friend, "My heart feels pure Union with yours. I love you as disinterestedly as I think I can." Upon her marriage, Mrs. Mary Holder remembered, "I felt much at leaving a large class of young women . . . my band sisters. We were united in the bonds of love, ever glad to meet—but not very willing to part—though sure we still were one in heart."[22] Sarah Crosby, a charismatic female preacher, founded a group of female preachers in Leeds in 1793 called the Female Brethren.[23] Three decades later, in 1821, preacher Ann Carr arrived there with her colleagues Martha Williams and Sarah Healand and founded the Female Revivalists, who, as Deborah Valenze writes, appealed to uprooted and displaced female textile workers.[24] They defined themselves as a "happy, chosen band":

> Still may we to our centre tend
> To spread thy praise our common end
> To help each other on
> Companions through the wilderness,
> To share a moment's pain, and seize
> An ever-lasting crown.[25]

In the early years of Methodism, the fact that the right to preach sprang from a sense of spiritual calling rather than from institutional training gave women the opportunity to claim this spiritual authority for themselves. In many northern areas, women were among the earliest founders of Methodism.[26] Female preachers had access to a power and authority normally available only to men, for the privilege of public speaking was almost unprecedented for women at this time. Only through sectarian religion could a young Nottinghamshire woman of humble origin, Miss Mary Brown, have "preached the gospel in chapels, warehouses, and barns, in squares and the fields, to hundreds, and sometimes thousands of wondering listeners" in London in 1818.[27] Mary Barrit, the sister of a farmer, converted thousands of Lancashire handloom weavers with her fervent preaching.[28] "Praying Nanny" Cutler, a "humble" woman of Preston, traveled in Lancashire and Yorkshire, preaching the new religious fervor and defying the crowds of roughs who harassed local Methodists.[29]

Female preachers' role in public life seems less unusual when seen in the context of plebeian women's economic importance in eighteenth-century cities. Zechariah Taft defended women's preaching by pointing out that "if [women] are allowed to address the other sex in the way of trade and business, and to get money; surely, they may be allowed to address them, upon the subjects which regard the soul, and eternity."[30] Indeed, many prominent Methodist women managed their own business or took an active part in their husband's. While ministers firmly believed that women's place was in the home, they sometimes had to acknowledge the importance of wives' business role in plebeian life.[31] These women had the self-esteem and independence to play an active role in the sect; for instance, Mrs. Lawns, who ran a bakehouse, introduced Methodism into Kilburn, a suburb of London.[32] The first Preston Methodist was Martha Thompson, who was converted when she worked as a servant in London. Her horrified employers reacted to her religious enthusiasm by confining her to a madhouse. Escaping the asylum, she returned to Preston in 1757, married a buttonmaker, and set herself up in business as a milliner to support her religious activities.[33] Elizabeth Evans, a Leicestershire female preacher, worked at lace-mending so that she would not have to live upon the people. She noted, "This I did with great pleasure. I believe I had one of the best places in the town, I had very good wages and could earn fourteen to fifteen shillings per week."[34]

At a time when the middle-class ideology of separate spheres was being developed, with its depiction of women as retiring, quiet, gentle, and submissive, Methodist women preachers drew upon the strength of plebeian womanhood. Mary Barrit was known for preaching "with masculine eloquence and womanly tenderness."[35] When Hester Ann Roe preached, she wrote in her diary, "I was astonished to feel in a few moments every word filled with power."[36] Nanny Cutler prayed loudly, "with great exertion of voice," and confronted local plebeians with their sins, whether they liked it or not.[37] As Deborah Valenze notes, these women gave the traditionally reviled village scold "a legitimate voice."[38] Elizabeth Harper, the wife of a Cornish shopkeeper, continually struggled with her temptation to "too sharply reprove the sins of her neighbors." But she felt "obliged to speak on behalf of the injured. . . . I thought it my duty to speak sharply, though still in love and meekness." These actions could lead to challenging male authority—as Harper found when she "reprov[ed] her husband before Company," for being too "encumbered with the world": she herself was humbled publicly for stepping out of her place.[39] When a magistrate came to the house of Mrs. Richardson, a female preacher in Warrington, and demanded to see the license of the man preaching there, she "raised a storm of prayer about his ears" and drove him out of the house, "beseeching God to turn him into a Methodist preacher.[40] Mary Barrit defied her father and local Methodist preachers in order to preach herself.[41]

Yet Methodism's subversive influence on gender roles was actually very limited, derived from its early emphasis on individual spirituality rather than from any radical notions of female freedom. Seen in the context of plebeian culture rather than middle-class separate spheres, it is clear that eighteenth-century female preachers and their supporters never defied the constraints of gender; they merely stretched and manipulated them. They justified female preaching as necessary to take advantage of a few women's extraordinary spiritual gifts, and they used convoluted arguments to avoid contradicting Saint Paul's admonitions against women speaking in church. Miss Bosanquet wrote that female preaching was consistent "with female modesty and humility" and disingenuously argued that "to entreat sinners to come to Jesus" did not violate the rule that women should be in subjection to their husbands "or usurp masculine religious authority by teaching or meddling in church management." [42] Wesley approved of her preaching only because he believed she had an exceptional call.

As Methodism lost its character as a radical sect and settled down to the work of institutionalizing itself as a church, patriarchal authority reasserted itself in homes and chapels. After 1797, the main body of Methodism grew more conservative. First, the Kilhamites broke off on the issue of power for local preachers, who were often working men. [43] When believers married and had children, membership became hereditary rather than voluntary. [44] In the early days, Wesley encouraged women to defy their parents rather than marry unbelievers, but in 1800 the *Methodist Magazine* told daughters to follow parental choice, stating that daughters were to "transfer obedience from the father to the husband." [45] In 1803 and again in 1810, the Wesleyan Methodist Connection forbade female preaching, which incited the more radical Primitive Methodist Connection to secede in 1812. [46] Women continued to preach in the Primitive Methodist strongholds of Lancashire, Yorkshire, and the southwest. But even within the radical precincts of Primitive Methodism, gender conflict surfaced. Mrs. Dunnel, the first Primitive Methodist traveling preacher, inspired many "pious females" with visions, but she soon got into trouble with male authorities and wreaked "mischief and trouble" on the circuit, according to the historian of Primitive Methodism. [47] And in 1825, the Female Revivalists of Leeds defied the authority of local male leaders and built their own chapel. [48]

But in mainline Methodism, pious Wesleyan women were to abandon preaching and devote themselves to "the retired vale of domestic life," adopting the middle-class ideology of separate spheres. By the early nineteenth century, wives of prosperous artisans and tradesmen were moving out of business activities, and the role of women in Methodism reflected this change. While the late eighteenth-century *Methodist Magazine* had printed many biographies of female preachers, by the early nineteenth century it shunned them, instead preferring to extol the domestic virtues of preachers' wives such as Mrs. Isabella Morrison, "a domestic woman; a lover of home, of neatness, and of regularity in her family," and Mrs. Margaret Worrall, who was too retiring to do public good works but excelled in "domestic life . . . for which her mind was evidently formed." [49] In 1813, the Rev. John Stephens preached in London that a woman's domestic role allowed her to "spend many hours in converse with heaven, and with God, while [her husband] is obliged to attend to all the earthly cares of his farm and merchandise."[50] When the pious Miss Harley gave up her own business to marry, she became "less subject to interruption in the performance of her private and public devotions."[51] London Methodist Mrs. Rich gave up her acting career, and Mrs. Sharland of Marylebone refused to sell fruit on Sunday.[52]

With the disappearance of female preachers, men controlled the positions of power within the chapels, which enabled them to exercise moral discipline over women on the institutional level. Yet the chapels subjected men to moral discipline as well, as Methodists and other dissenters attempted to shape a new vision of respectable manhood.

Moral Discipline Among Dissenting Congregations

As Methodism grew in the late eighteenth and early nineteenth centuries, other dissenting congregations also acquired a new lease on life. They all appealed to a similar stratum of plebeian society, bringing in shopkeepers and tradesmen, but their congregations were usually dominated by artisans. Artisans made up approximately 63 percent of Methodist, Baptist, and Congregationalist church memberships.[53] London Methodist congregations, like those all over England, had always contained a goodly number of tradesmen and artisans, as well as the more plebeian sailors and needlewomen.[54] A Clerkenwell, London, Calvinist Methodist baptism register from the 1830s included one gentleman and one law clerk, along with a machinist and several shoemakers, carpenters, and watchmakers, while a Welsh Methodist chapel in Aldersgate served a more working-class congregation of tailors, shoemakers, hatters, and carpenters.[55] In Lancashire textile districts, Methodism and other dissenting groups burgeoned in the late eighteenth century. Primitive Methodists were particularly strong in smaller industrial towns and villages, and Calvinist Baptists found some followers among weavers and spinners.[56] One Ashton Methodist congregation consisted of 27 percent weavers, 20 percent spinners, and 12 percent followers of other textile trades, as well as other artisans, laborers, and middle-class people.[57] "In [Scottish] small industrial communities—handloom weaving and spinning towns, pit and metallurgical villages," notes Callum Brown, "the Secession and Relief Churches developed as vital focuses of group identity."[58]

Dissenting congregations thus provided an institutional infrastructure for the "respectable" elements of plebeian culture. But they disciplined themselves, rather than accepting the condescendingly moralistic admonitions of middle-class Anglican Evangelicals, who treated plebeians like children in their attempt to reform popular culture.[59] As Theodore Koditschek writes, "The behavior patterns of temperance and frugality that [a Primitive Methodist congregation] instilled in its members represented not so much an imitation of bourgeois values as the working out of a logic of collective self-help."[60]

Yet devout nonconformists also set themselves apart from other working people. For the "moral minority" who felt alienated from their drinking, smoking, swearing neighbors, the chapel provided a self-enclosed subculture that enabled believers to withstand the temptations of the profligate world. For instance, the Bank Top Sunday School in Lancashire faced competition every year from the Whitsun races, and one teacher, Thomas Fildes, noted that "a great majority of the scholars are obliged to work the whole week in Factories with a promiscuous number of hands, many of whom are promiscuous and profligate in the extreme[;] when we recollect the influence of bad company, as well as the effect of ridicule pointed at those who are better inclined, and add on to this the impious lives, and bad examples, exhibited by many of their parents," it is no wonder they found such difficulty in withstanding temptation.[61] When Methodist Barnabas Battersby preached in Poulton, Lancashire, in 1815, "scornful young men pulled faces and laughed" at the congregation.[62] When William Bramwell preached in Preston market place in 1785, "he was mobbed and pelted with mud and filth . . . by a gang of roughs," for most local people were more interested in prize fighting, races, cockfighting, drinking, pigeon racing, and kicking each other with clogs.[63]

Dissenting congregations bound their communities together against the wider plebeian world through moral discipline. The technique of moral discipline originated in the courts of the established church, which had rebuked fornicators and adulterers in the sixteenth and seventeenth centuries, but by the late eighteenth century the English church concerned itself only with private cases of defamation and divorce. The Scottish established kirk continued the tradition in a much more rigid form. By the late eighteenth century, however, established kirk sessions seem to have concentrated on offenses, such as illegitimacy and desertion, that would inflict the expense of child support on the parish. But the kirk sessions' jurisdiction may have also derived from their control over respectability—and salvation.[64] The kirk could refuse to baptize children who were illegitimate or born of an irregular marriage.[65] By rebuking and then absolving people after investigation, performance of acts of repentance, and payment of a fine, the kirk acknowledged that it was powerless to suppress totally an alternative plebeian morality. For instance, the Rev. Thomas Chalmers, an influential reformer in Glasgow, had to give up his efforts to haul couples suspected of premarital sex before his kirk sessions in St. Johns, Glasgow.[66]

But at the same time, the kirk asserted its ultimate moral authority over salvation. Plebeians—especially women—who had inadvertently strayed into libertinism could regain respectable status by undergoing kirk sessions discipline. Whereas in conventional middle-class morality a woman who had once "fallen" was forever degraded, kirk session discipline wiped her slate clean so that she could then marry, confident of salvation.

The moral discipline of dissenting congregations was much stricter. Long before Methodism was founded, dissenting congregations had held monthly or quarterly church meetings in which the moral status of members would be examined. The way chapel members informed meetings about each other's moral peccadillos resembled gossip, but differed from gossip in its legitimacy, its formal punishments, and its clear rules for proper behavior. At chapel meetings members would accuse each other of moral infractions such as drunkenness. If the accusation was upheld, male deacons would visit the offender and give him or her a chance to repent.[67] If the repentance did not seem genuine, the offender would be suspended or expelled as clearly not one of the Elect.[68] Methodists apparently engaged in even more detailed spiritual self-criticism, a sort of religious preventive medicine, at quarterly class meetings where members "had to submit to an examination of every act and feeling."[69] Opponents of Methodism found this practice suspiciously Catholic, describing the Leaders as "Father Confessors."[70] William Benbow voyeuristically described class meetings in his *Crimes of the Clergy*:

> They go around the room, and question thick-headed boobies, silly, old, and enthusiastic young women, as to their feelings: one declares he has been sorely troubled, by the Tempter, with carnal longings after his neighbor's wife, but, praised be to God, he was resolute and made the Tempter flee. Another young and foolish girl, perhaps, says she has been tempted to prostitute her body, but had at last overcome the great Devil through the influence of Jesus Christ.[71]

However ridiculous Benbow made moral discipline sound, it may have functioned much like Alcoholics Anonymous, providing mutual support to help Methodists resist the temptations of plebeian culture.

Either these congregations behaved rather well on the whole, or most moral discipline was informal, for church meeting minute books usually record only one or two cases per year. The possibility of such a confrontation with fellow chapel members must have terrified many into conformity, and probably much informal moral discipline never reached the minute books. For instance, the Old Scots Independent Church of Glasgow complacently reassured itself in 1824 that few members had had to be disciplined in the past year. "When our numbers are considered and the temptations held out in such a large mercantile city where so much allurement and profligacy surrounds the young and inexperienced, the poor and the rich, as individuals, and as a church, we can look only to Him, who has upheld us, and kept us from falling." The church did expel several members on theological grounds, such as upholding the doctrine of universal atonement.[72] But most "sinners" fell from grace for behavioral sins, which could be subtle. The complacency of 1824 masked the fact that between 1812 and 1845, this congregation with a membership averaging one hundred and fifty expelled forty-one persons for behavioral offenses. The most common was drunkenness, accounting for ten cases, but eight were expelled for embezzlement or theft. Covetousness, fornication, falsehood, and "irregular conduct" were the other most common offenses. In 1812, John Barclay was separated from the congregation for "falsehood, covetousness and ignorance." Other expulsions were equally dramatic: Mrs. Adamson, who joined the church in 1798, was pushed out for drunkenness and for "resetting stolen yarn," which suggests that she was a weaver or winder. John Cumming was separated from the church for "want of filial affection," and Adam Fowlds for "gross impurity of mind and manners."[73]

Dissenting churches often found it difficult to insulate their members from the temptations of the surrounding plebeian society. Out of fifty-six cases from the Great Hamilton Street Reformed Presbyterian Church of Calton, a textile district of Glasgow, twenty concerned sexual offenses, such as illegitimacy, fornication, and irregular marriage, fourteen stemmed from drink, fourteen from financial problems ranging from theft to not paying debts, and eight from social infractions. For instance, the elders summoned watchmaker William Logan in 1804 to explain why he engaged in "promiscuous dancing" and belonged to a club that distributed watches by lot. Logan refused to admit that dancing practiced by a few for "amusement" was immoral, but when the congregation rebuked him he apparently agreed to stop. The informal sexual morals of Glasgow plebeian society could also lead to behavior that members later regretted. In 1805 James Bennet was confronted with being a member of several friendly societies and staying out late to drink instead of being "comforted by the practices of family religion." Thomas Forsyth had to apologize for attending a concert and dancing in 1821.[74]

Moral discipline also strengthened men's patriarchal authority within dissenting plebeian society, though not always without a struggle. In late eighteenth-century Paisley, wives superficially accepted their submissive status, but they would take a stand against their husbands on theological questions. In one incident, a dissenting political radical insisted that his wife agree with him on a narrow theological point. Although she could not espouse his views, she avoided discussing the matter until he tried to force her to agree with him publicly. When she refused, he had the congregation expel her—but all the female members left the meeting in protest.[75] Only men could serve as deacons or elders.[76] Women's attempts to rebuke others for misdeeds could therefore be construed as malicious gossip. Only men could have moral authority; the leaders, all men, of the Hinde Street Circuit, West London, seem to have found it necessary to keep a firm rein on the tendency of their women members to "tattle."

Men faced the discipline required to deserve this authority, however, for Methodists, Baptists, and Congregationalists developed a new ideal of manhood as sober, domestic, honest, and successful, quite different from the hard-drinking and pugnacious plebeian masculinity. Religious men cultivated a tender sensitivity that was alien to the aggressive character of conventional eighteenth-century manhood.[77] In the handloom weaving town of Culcheth, Lancashire, Sunday School teacher John Bateman advised young men to adopt "a modest freedom of speech, a soft and elegant manner of address, a graceful and lovely deportment . . . a Sober Masculine piety equally remote from Superstition and enthusiasm."[78] As artisans and tradesmen, dissenting men had to reconcile the conflicting aims of worldly gain and avoidance of Sunday work, for bankruptcy usually meant automatic expulsion from Methodist or Baptist congregations. Given the great instability of trade, this was a difficult standard to meet: the Hinde Street Methodist Circuit censured or expelled eight men for bankruptcy and dishonesty between 1814 and 1830.

Nonconformists also admonished men to avoid the hard-drinking, hard-swearing amusements of their fellow workers. For men who found the workshop culture distasteful, the chapel provided an alternative social life and sense of self-esteem sorely needed by such men as William Hart, a Baptist cooper whose workmates "taunted and jeered him on account of his religion."[79] But many men simply found it too difficult to forswear drinking, which was so inextricably a part of artisan work culture. The Hinde Street Circuit expelled five men for drunkenness. After the New Court Congregational Church expelled a young male member when members reported having seen him intoxicated in the street, he wrote a letter to the Elders in his defense stating that because he worked for a brewer he was "therefore obliged to drink strong ale . . . drinking was allwaise my burden and not my delight."[80]

Dissenters also pressured men to be responsible, sober, protective husbands. Instead of brawling, as couples did in ordinary plebeian marriages, sermons admonished husbands, they should dominate in a mild, loving way and wives should offer affectionate submission.[81] The Manchester Baptist William Gadsby, for instance, advised husbands to "treat [their wives] kindly" while telling wives that "it is the wife's duty to love her husband, and to yield obedience to him in all things." Apparently his female parishioners murmured at this, for he went on to say, "Don't you women start from your pews, recollect it is the word of God. . . . It becomes the wife . . . not to treat the husband as though he ought to have no mind of his own."[82]

Wife-beating was not a major concern of dissenting congregations, however. Although Wesley expelled some members of the Newcastle connection for domestic violence, this offense very rarely occurs in chapel records I have examined.[83] It may be that few dissenters beat their wives, or perhaps husbands stretched the limits of mild correction and did beat them, but their wives felt too much pressure to be dutiful, submissive partners to protest publicly. Scottish kirk sessions also disciplined wife-beaters, but since they were much more likely to believe men than women and they blamed wives for disobedience, such discipline was rarely efficacious.[84] While the Calton Presbyterian Church successfully reconciled separated couples, evidence from other sources suggests that reconciliation came with the cost of wives' submission.[85]

In three cases London chapels censured wives for failing to react with appropriate patience to their husbands' misdeeds. For instance, after her husband was censured for adultery, the New Broad Street Chapel suspended Mrs. Clapp for a year until she revealed "a more humble sense of her own irregularity."[86] The Fetter Lane meeting charged Benjamin Davidge with repeated drunkenness, but also suspended his wife on the grounds that her "temper and conversation with regard to her husband had been very unbecoming. . . . She had frequently indulged herself in such extreme anger, and intemperate language against her husband, and sometimes issued in acts of mutual and personal violence."[87] White's Row Chapel of Spitalfields censured Mrs. Eldridge for some "imprudent behaviour" concerning her husband's "bad moral conduct and unbecoming circumstances," and because she refused to attend the church and had a "very improper" attitude toward it.[88]

Although these examples are few, they fit into a trend in Methodist and Evangelical writings of encouraging abused wives to "endure afflictions with meekness, patience, and humility," to quote an obituary eulogizing one wife.[89] While neither religious tracts nor chapel discipline provided ill-treated women with any means of escaping their husbands, they did give them a sense of self-esteem as martyrs and fed fantasies of divine rescue. For example, a tract contrasted the virtue of the "Good wife," a "bright charmer," with the bad temper of her husband, a "despotic, insolent and rude" butcher. No doubt many wives could identify with the vivid details of his torments, which ranged from beatings to complaints about her cooking to general slovenliness. The only solution the tract offered, however, was for the wife to bear his ill treatment with immovable serenity until her quiet tears had won him over to the cause of religion—and had elicited an apology.[90] Methodist tales encouraged women whose husbands refused to succumb to their saintly patience to believe that "Providence" would save them from violence. Typical is the obituary of Mary Muffin, whose husband "determined to kill her" one night when she was returning from prayer meeting. As he began to swing a cudgel down onto her head, "she cried to God for help," and her husband's arm froze above her, as if it were iron. Humiliated, he begged her to pray to God to restore the motion of his arm.[91]

Adultery, bigamy, and premarital sex worried Methodists and other dissenters much more than wife-beating did. For these issues they were innovative in applying a single standard for men and women. They wished to preserve the family intact as the basis of their chapel organization and to enforce standards of respectability befitting their class aspirations. Yet the rank and file found it very difficult to live up to those standards, given the widespread acceptance of premarital sex and bigamy and the instability of marriage in plebeian culture. For instance, the Bridge Street Wesleyan Chapel in Bolton, Lancashire, expelled nineteen members in 1822 and 1823, mostly for fornication and drunkenness.[92] In Bradford in the 1830s and 1840s, the working-class Prospect Street Baptist Church pushed out 30 percent of its membership for "backsliding, fornication, drunkenness, or other forms of immorality."[93]

Many religious people gave in to the temptations of flirtation, fornication, adultery, or bigamy and suffered agonies of repentance as a result. In the Glasgow Presbyterian church of Calton, a young male member had gotten drunk "in foolish company" and lain down on a bed to rest, awaking to find a young woman beside him. He admitted, with "sorrow," that he had committed fornication with her, but the elders agreed to keep the matter secret if he repented.[94] Samuel Bardsley, a Lancashire man, anxiously explained to his diary that "bundling all night with a young woman" was not a sin.[95] William Swan, a London pastrycook from a devout family, remembered that when he could not afford to marry his pregnant sweetheart, "this brought guilt into my conscience indeed." He was so troubled he felt "there could be no mercy for me" and "continued in much darkness of unbelief," until he finally accepted a less Calvinist doctrine of salvation for all.[96] But others resisted such wallowing in guilt and simply tried to cope with their situation as best they could. In 1825, before the Calton Presbyterian Church, Donald King of Calton was accused of fornication. He "expressed his willingness to submit to the censure of the church," but he also stated that "he was under no promise of marriage to her nor had any intention of doing so, and that he believed her beliefs were the same on the matter."[97] In two cases in the Hinde Street membership, parents connived to marry young couples when the bride was pregnant. In one instance, after Mrs. Nash excused her daughter for living with her fiancé before marriage because they lacked the money for marriage banns, the meeting suspended Mrs. Nash for three months.[98] A couple of years later, a Mr. Cooper told the meeting that the marriage of his son with the pregnant Miss Hornby "was a family concern, he and his wife were satisfied and nobody had any business with it." The Coopers resigned from the chapel under pressure, declaring, "Our consciences acquit us of guilt."[99] Reports of such experiences may have deterred many other prospective members from joining.

Those whose conversion came after they had engaged in a bigamous or common-law marriage had to conceal their past or risk expulsion. In Great Hamilton Street, Glasgow, for instance, three women were reproved for engaging, knowingly or unknowingly, in bigamous marriages.[100] The Fetter Lane Chapel expelled a Mrs. Bough when members discovered that she had cohabited with Mr. Timbrell, passing as his wife for ten years, in the hope that he would marry her.[101] Lodging-house keeper Mary Steens told fellow Methodist Thomas Thompson she would overlook the fact that he already had a wife "as I was steady," or so he alleged at his trial for bigamy.[102] Charles Hill, a member of the Hinde Street Circuit, continued to live with his wife after he found she had been married previously, and after she left him against his will, he declared his wish to marry another Methodist woman. He considered that "God had forgiven him," but the chapel leaders doubted his repentance.[103]

Like Charles Hill, other straying believers sometimes tried to formulate theological solutions to the conflict between unrealizable moral standards and their religious beliefs. Benbow alleged that Methodists just blamed their peccadillos on an external agency: "they covet their neighbours' wives and daughters, then lay the blame on the Devil, which is the effect of their pampered fleshly lust; then they commit the sin, and atone for it in prayers."[104] Other believers dreamed up more iconoclastic justifications. When the New Broad Street Chapel meeting charged Mr. George Davy with adultery, "he confessed the fact but denied the guilt alleging that circumstances relative to his wife's incapacity for the Marriage Duty, made it both lawful and necessary for him to keep another Woman as his concubine." Needless to say, the deacons were unconvinced by his logic and expelled him.[105] Methodist George Heffner drew upon "Scripture authority" to justify his bigamy, quoting the example of Abraham, who had taken two wives.[106] In another bigamy case, a roadside preacher who also worked as a tailor claimed that "he did not have the gift of continence and God told him to marry again."[107] One radical Stockport congregation adopted a flexible version of Christian morality, baptizing several illegitimate children born to women who could not or would not marry the fathers.[108] A Glasgow servant "acknowledged that she had been guilty of taking a ham in a manner that was considered by some, stealing," but she "considered herself injured by her employers."[109]

The tight moral discipline of Methodist communities simply could not respond to the dislocation and despair felt by so many plebeians during the years of the French Revolution and the Napoleonic wars. The promised certainty of heavenly truth could not compensate for the uncertainties of life during times many of all classes perceived as apocalyptic.[110] Methodism gained many adherents during these turbulent years, but it faced competition from the wilder offshoots of revivalism. In London, "mechanick preachers" drew many curious plebeians to Stepney fields, as they held forth on antinomianism, millenarianism, and infidelism, "planted on carts and dunghills, or broken gates, canting, storming and singing."[111] Millenarians such as Joanna Southcott pointed the finger at society's sins, not the individual's, and believed the problem of sin would be resolved by the imminent end of the world rather than by mundane attempts to live a godly life. Antinomian preachers, usually of humble origin themselves, preached to the poor that God would forgive all their sins. Dissenting sects struggled constantly against the tendency of their members to focus on God's forgiveness of their sins rather than on the necessity of avoiding sin altogether. Between 1801 and 1828, the Calvinist New Broad Street Chapel faced a rash of heresy, expelling four men and eight women for antinomian and Southcottian beliefs. For instance, a Mrs. Sorrell and Ann Plows were expunged from the rolls for "embracing sentiments contrary to God's word" which "tend[ed] to licentious practices in themselves."[112] While millenarianism and antinomianism appealed to both men and women, their most prominent adherents found in highly charged spiritual language ways of articulating the sexual antagonism and confusion of everyday life from distinctively gendered viewpoints.

Joanna Southcott and the Prophetesses

A long millenarian tradition justified women's claims to extraordinary spiritual gifts.[113] Luckie Buchan was a Scottish woman who followed Rev.

Whyte out of the Relief Church in 1782, retreating with him from Glasgow to Irvine. She, like other prophetesses, believed herself to be the "woman clothed with the sun" of millenarian prophecy in Revelations.[114] She presented herself as the "spirit of God dwelling in flesh" and, in terms similar to Southcott's, said Mr. Whyte "was the manchild she had brought before." She preached the doctrine of universal atonement and, unlike the Calvinists, proclaimed that "sin does not inhere in the believer." Taking religious authority upon herself, she spent her time "visiting from house to house, in making worship, solving doubts, answering questions, and expounding the scriptures," to the horror of local authorities.[115]

By the 1790s, the time was ripe for more women to claim millenarian spiritual authority. The French Revolution's challenge to conventional political and religious morality convinced many British people that the end of the world was at hand, a feeling intensified during the long, traumatic years of the Napoleonic wars.[116] While many men, such as Richard Brothers, preached this apocalyptic gospel, women were most notable as millenarian leaders, for, like Luckie Buchan, they could take advantage of unusual times to claim the power of prophecy. In the 1790s, three London women—Mrs. Eyre, possibly the wife of a member of Parliament; Sarah Flaxmer, a poor woman living in lodgings; and Dorothy Gott, a Quaker servant—all claimed special spiritual insight into apocalyptic events.[117] Ten years later, Joanna Southcott, a Devon upholstress, had come to London to spread the news of her visions. She founded three London chapels and by her death in 1814 had achieved nationwide fame. She had begun her spiritual career by joining a Wesleyan sect in Devon but the immorality of certain local class leaders soon disillusioned her. As J. F. C. Harrison writes, she and her followers were "sincere, earnest Christians, dependent for guidance on a literal interpretation of the Bible," who longed for something more fulfilling than the respectable round of class meetings and sermons.[118] Unlike Methodists, who wished to encourage self-discipline in their members, Joanna Southcott articulated the grief and confusion her followers felt and offered them a quasi-magical path to salvation, by purchasing a mystical seal which symbolized the grace she claimed God had bestowed upon her. Southcott's urgent, emotional rhetoric drew many believers away from Methodist chapels at a time when the Methodist and Baptist churches were becoming more established and respectable, supporting the government and prohibiting women preachers.[119]

Female prophets justified their authority in the rich metaphorical language of Revelations and Genesis. Like Southcott and Buchan, Sarah Flaxmer proclaimed in 1795 that she was the "woman Clothed in the sun," arrived to herald the Second Coming. Dorothy Gott declared that a divine voice told her to give up housework and concentrate on putting her internal house, her soul, in order.[120] Joanna Southcott announced that God had given her the moral authority as a woman to speak out both on the sexual crisis affecting working people's personal lives and on the crisis afflicting the nation at the time of the Napoleonic wars. The moral authority they claimed was quite different from the sentimental influence advocated by female Evangelicals. Evangelicals wished women would exert their moral influence from within the seclusion of their homes, and they ascribed women's spiritual superiority to the allegedly feminine qualities of tenderness, purity, and nurturance. Southcott, in contrast, rarely concerned herself with the domestic virtues, and Gott explicitly renounced them. Evangelicals also conceived of feminine moral influence in class terms, as exercised through the philanthropy of middle-class women and emphatically not by former domestic servants' visions.

Southcott, like the other prophetesses, spoke publicly about national events and the rise and fall of ministers. Her apocalyptic millenarianism gave her a language in which she could claim national authority, an opportunity available for few other women of her time and class. Southcott told her followers that individual tragedies fit into a larger pattern. In a letter to Jane Townley, her most devoted follower, she wrote of her infant nephew who had died in convulsions that "he was suffering for the nation as she predicted"; in another letter to an afflicted friend, she tried to console her by writing, "Their sufferings are a type to the nation also. But their sufferings will be turned to joy—when the Joys of the Nation shall be turned to sorrow."[121]

Unlike female Methodist preachers, millenarian prophetesses alluded to the sexual antagonism that fissured plebeian culture, often employing scriptural metaphors. All four prophetesses conceived of a great struggle between Satan and "the Woman," citing the verse describing how the Woman would bruise the heel of the serpent in revenge for his betrayal of her in the garden of Eden. Sarah Flaxmer declared that Satan, "knowing that a young woman was to reveal him, has endeavoured to lessen the character of women by his agents . . . but the Lord is not going to call the men into Paradise, and shut the women out."[122]

The prophetesses needed to assert their primacy over male rivals such as Richard Brothers, a prophet who in the 1790s was sympathetic to both the French Revolution and moral reform.[123] Gott attacked Thomas Wright and William Bryan, followers of Brothers, as false prophets. She proclaimed in 1798 that "Our Saviour said there should be wars and rumours of wars, that nation should rise against nation, and kingdom against kingdom, because the dragon in man had fought against the God in the

Woman."[124] Mrs. Eyre, who published her pro-government prophecies in the newspaper the *Oracle* in 1795, declared that Brothers was a false prophet "deluded" by Satan the serpent; she asked him rhetorically, "Why don't thou not come out of thy hole, art thou afraid of a woman? I challenge thee in this public manner—Either thou or myself must be of the devil."[125]

Satan also exemplified masculine ill-treatment of women. Dorothy Gott took the story of Eve and the serpent "as a warning to all females not to put any confidence in the earthly man." After she reluctantly married a non-Quaker footman, she tried to run a millinery and haberdashery shop, but her husband's disapproval and bad debts led to failure, and their next venture, a pub, did no better. She described her husband as "an instrument to strip me of the love of man and this world."[126]

As Barbara Taylor points out, Southcott's prophecies "abounded in images of male villainy and female defiance which aroused women to an anticipation of greater glory." Southcott rewrote the story of the garden of Eden by portraying it as the primal betrayal of women by man.[127] One of her prayers beseeched God to "avenge thy innocent blood on the *serpent's head* which is the devil, that betrayed the innocence of the woman at first."[128] Southcott clearly linked Satan with the many men who betrayed her and other women. She declared, "My heart has been sorely wounded by the malicious lies and inventions of men."[129] She recalled a long series of betrayals by men, beginning with a farmer's son who attempted to seduce her sister and ruined her father to avenge his rejection, and continuing with a sweetheart who later gave a woman an abortifacient that poisoned her, a footman who sexually harassed her and engineered her dismissal, and her employer Wills, who first attempted to seduce her and then sued her for defamation of his adulterous wife.[130]

Southcott's writings thus appealed to women who felt sexually victimized but also pervaded by a sense of sin. More than half of her followers were women, the wives and widows of artisans and small tradesmen, as well as many "nurses, tailoresses, schoolteachers, and servants."[131] Her "strongholds" were in areas where many single and married women worked in the textile industry, including, besides London, Somerset, Devon, Yorkshire, and Lancashire.[132] Hopkins tentatively argues that the majority of Southcott's followers were single women, but he derives this figure from the number of women who signed up for a seal without being accompanied by a husband, father, or other family member. Many of these women may indeed have been unmarried, but some may have been plebeian wives estranged or at least independent from their husbands. While Methodists and Anglican Evangelicals advised women with abusive husbands to submit quietly, Southcott articulated sexual antagonism and advocated marriage to the "divine Husband" who could provide women with the protection they were "disappointed in receiving from their earthly husbands."[133]

As a spiritual leader Joanna Southcott offered redemption and justification to women by transforming Eve from a temptress to a victim, and finally to the savior of man. In a Protestant country, Eve rather than the Virgin Mary was the most potent archetype of woman, a symbol whose roots lay deep in religion and popular culture. As Taylor notes, Southcott stressed that childbearing was woman's "unique mission," one which man could not fulfill:

> Woman brought to Man the GOOD fruit at the first,
> And from the Woman shall the good Fruit burst
>
> . . .
>
> Because no Fruit did ever come from Man,
> Though it is often grafted by his Hand.[134]

She declared that the Second Coming would overthrow the curse of women's subordination inflicted in Genesis.[135]

But when these prophetesses defended the Woman against the Devil, they were asserting their own individual claims to prophetic power rather than any sort of liberation for all women. Ultimately, Southcott failed to resolve the tensions between her prophetic mission, her plebeian female status, and the patriarchy of the biblical tradition. Childbearing was to provide the triumph of her career; a few months before her death, she proclaimed that she was pregnant with Shiloh, the new messiah. Although her followers prepared for a real baby, she was ill, rather than pregnant, and soon died. For decades, however, her followers continued to believe fervently in her message.

Yet if Joanna had married earlier and borne real children, domestic cares would have distracted her from her visions. She wrote, "I looked on matrimony as worse than death."[136] She escaped this fate, unlike so many Methodist female preachers, and preferred to explore femininity on the metaphorical, scriptural level rather than to accept its constraints in daily life.

Antinomianism and Early Nineteenth-Century Manhood

Joanna Southcott solved the dilemmas engendered by living in a world of shifting moral standards by blaming sin on an outside source—masculine villainy—and by asserting that only a woman prophet could combat this

Satan in disguise. Some men, too, had to define the relation of manhood to sin, locating Satan's abode within their own souls to explain their difficulty in meeting domestic responsibilities. William Bryan, a copper-plate printer, experienced his own "battle between God and the Devil in the spirit of man." When he first came to London, he spent his Sundays drinking with friends from home at public gardens and other places of amusement, remembering that "no tongue can describe the distress in mind this brought upon me." Yet after his conversion, he and a friend, carpenter John Wright, repeatedly left their wives without support at the command of the Holy Spirit, including once when Mrs. Bryan was very ill in childbirth.[137] For some men, the antinomian doctrine that humans were powerless to save themselves through good works, since only God could wash away sin through his unconditional grace, spoke to their inability to live up to conventional manhood.

Antinomianism recurrently won popularity in times of social turmoil, for example, among the sixteenth-century German Anabaptists and the English Civil War sects. Seventeenth-century believers could not accept the Puritan assurance that Providence combined with godly living would enable them to better themselves. Providence brought them hardship, not prosperity. While the former optimistic doctrine appealed to the "rising middle classes, antinomianism spoke to the poor and dislocated, stress[ing] the absolute equality of sinner and saved."[138] In the eighteenth century it constantly threatened to subvert Methodism and broke out in such obscure sects as the Muggletonians.[139]

This libertarian doctrine derived, surprisingly, from dour Calvinist theology taken to its logical conclusion. Calvinism declares that in the beginning of time God chose a certain number of people to be the saved, the Elect. This doctrine derived from the Old Testament stress on a "chosen people," but—more significantly for our purposes—also from the notion of God's omnipotence. The reasoning runs as follows: God knows everything and ordains everything that will ever happen; humans are powerless to save themselves, and must rely solely on God's grace. Furthermore, Jesus died on the cross to atone for the sins of the Elect, so they were saved before they were born. The antinomians logically asked, why should members of the Elect bother to avoid sin if they know all their sins have already been forgiven? Furthermore, if God predestined everything that happened, how could anyone expect to resist the temptation to sin, since free will did not exist? In fact, it was presumptuous to suppose feeble human efforts to attain grace could influence God. Wesleyan Methodists often opposed Calvinism on these grounds, for they preferred to hold out a promise of a bargain with God: if believers had faith *and* performed good works, God would save them. Conventional Calvinists simply answered that the virtue of the Elect signified they were the saved. Antinomians rejected both these positions as hypocrisy.

Religious plebeians often focused on God's mercy rather than eternal damnation. For instance, the female revivalists sang,

> Ye scarlet-colour'd sinners, come
> Jesus the Lord invites you home;
> O whither can you go?
> What are your crimes of crimson hue?
> His promise is for ever true,
> He'll wash you white as snow.[140]

Antinomianism was very popular among the Scottish peasants and workers as the furthest extension of Calvinism, and in Manchester, William Gadsby's congregation adopted the doctrine.[141] In Libberton, Lancashire, in the 1790s, the local established kirk minister complained that the "sectarians are preaching antinomian doctrine, sapping virtue and refusing to contribute to the poor rate."[142] Graham notes that the Scottish people "loved men . . . who denounced all teaching of morality as causing men to trust in their 'filthy rags of righteousness.' " While some believed that this view excused a neglect of common moral duties, it was actually founded on a belief that human beings were irredeemably corrupt.[143] There was also a move away from the strict Calvinism of predestination toward a belief in universal atonement.[144] In the 1830s and 1840s the Old Scots Independent Church in Glasgow expelled several members for holding this doctrine.[145]

Although antinomian preachers had many female followers, I believe it is significant that they themselves were mostly men. For them, the doctrine that good tendencies struggled with evil for primacy in the soul of the believer explained their own internal struggle between their desire to live up to responsible manhood and the temptation to drink, commit sexual sins, or abandon work. They claimed that the call of the Holy Spirit took precedence over their domestic responsibilities as respectable husbands.

Most antinomian preachers were male artisans or laborers. James Relly, who was repudiated by Wesley, was a cow farrier; William Huntington (or Huntingdon) held many menial jobs, including that of coal heaver; John Church began as a journeyman ornament-maker; Zion Ward was a shoemaker.[146] Antinomian-tinged Calvinist Methodists were prominent among the "mechanick preachers" who ranted about sin and salvation in Stepney fields around 1800.[147] These preachers attracted those, such as the heretics of the New Broad Street congregation, who could not live up to the strict moral discipline chapel members faced, those who, despite their best spiritual efforts, somehow fell into the sins of adultery, bigamy, Sabbath-breaking, and drunkenness.

Some notorious preachers flaunted their own sinful past in order to illuminate the omnipotence of God, to prove He could wipe away even the foulest of sins. William Huntington, who styled himself "S. S." for "sinner saved," regaled his large congregations with lurid accounts of his own misdeeds, including an incident in which he seduced a young woman and absconded rather than facing the consequences of her pregnancy (see Figure 5). Huntington rose from very humble origins to be wildly successful as a preacher by the 1790s. At first he attracted crowds of poor believers, but then he began to charge for seats in his chapel in order to augment his fortune. His congregation was composed mostly of artisans and tradesmen in the neighborhood of Holborn, who, as an Anglican clergyman complained, flocked to Huntington instead of attending the parish church.[148] Huntington abandoned his first, common-law wife when she proved unable to live up to the respectability demanded by their new prosperity. He took up instead with the widow of the Lord Mayor of London and married her after a long affair. Perhaps his meteoric rise and flexible morals struck a sympathetic chord in ambitious tradesmen who aspired to a higher class but found it difficult to abandon plebeian marital morals.[149]

Robert Flockhart was a Scottish nailmaker, born in 1778, who fell into "uncleanliness in body" serving in the army, until he converted to the Baptists. After leaving the army, he began to roam the streets of Edinburgh, reproving men for going to prostitutes, shouting, "Beware, soldiers, beware! If you go into their house, remember it is the way to hell, going down to the chambers of death." He also visited jails, noting the case of a shoemaker named Gow who had killed his drunken wife in a fit of rage. Gow, deeply repentant, told Flockhart that he had once stolen a bird's nest but replaced it on seeing the distress of the mother bird. "How it was, that a man who had felt such pity for a poor little bird, could experience none for the woman who was his wife, was to [Gow] a mystery he could not understand. To explain it, I unfolded to him the deceitful and desperately wicked character of the heart of man in its natural state." Flockhart believed that men were powerless before sin unless they had God's grace: "I tried to show how totally ignorant we were of the awful crimes we were capable of committing when unrestrained by the preventing grace of God, and exposed to temptation."[150] Flockhart's philosophy may have appealed to men who felt powerless to resist the frustration and temptations of plebeian culture.

John Church became even more notorious than Huntington for the way he used his antinomian doctrine to justify his failure to live up to conven-

Figure 5.   The Relics of a Prophet; or, Huntingdon's Sale. Copyright British Museum.

tional manhood. Church was a foundling who worked for a composition ornament–maker, but, inspired by Huntington, found popular preaching more profitable. Surprisingly, he successfully pursued his career as a preacher despite his notoriety as a homosexual. After being thrown out of Banbury for dallying with several young men, he took a chapel in St. George's Fields, London, and continued to preach even when the *Weekly Dispatch* unveiled his association with the infamous "Vere Street coterie" of homosexual men in 1813, where he allegedly performed mock marriages between two men in a pub.[151] His congregation ignored these accusations and raised enough money to build the Surrey Tabernacle for him, the deeds to which, as he made sure, were in his name. After spending two years in jail for an indecent assault on a boy, he returned in 1819 and preached until at least 1824.

Church's struggles with his desire for men at a time of intense homophobia resembled the inner turmoil of other religious Londoners torn between spirituality and pleasure. Explaining his homosexual tendencies, he wrote, "Even after I had heard, and in a measure, received the truth, still the devil was permitted to deceive me with a sad snare, till the Lord led me to see the difference between the work of the Spirit and the moving of natural passions; the differences between the love of God and those inordinate passions which led me to error."[152] His empathy with the outcasts of society, of which he was one, made him very popular as a preacher despite plebeian homophobia.[153] Indeed, he openly declared that his origins as a foundling enabled him to sympathize with fallen women, whom he saw as more sinned against than sinning.[154] Church's theology was tinged with androgny: explaining the Song of Solomon, he preached that the Holy Ghost and God could appear as "the affectionate Husband, the constant Friend . . . the tender Father, the sympathizing Mother and Nurse . . . the lovely Prince."[155]

Both Huntington and Church avoided the moral scrutiny practiced by Methodist and Baptist congregations. Huntington did not allow his congregation to hold church meetings to examine each other's behavior but himself monopolized the privilege of occasionally expelling "immoral" members.[156] Church explicitly told his followers to "avoid gossiping and tattling about the minister"; he urged them instead to sympathize with each other's troubles and forgive each other's faults.[157]

The scandals over the behavior of Church and Huntington rarely deterred those who were attracted to antinomianism, since such troubles could be taken to prove that God forgave even the most heinous sins. William Benbow, a radical anticlerical campaigner, noted bitterly that prostitutes and other habitués of the St. Giles slum flocked to Church's services, for his doctrine "was very convenient" for those who had "committed sins they were willing to believe it was out of their power to prevent, and glad to have a free latitude to sin in the future."[158] But Benbow, part of a ultra-radical libertine subculture, was exploring the same moral dilemmas that Church, Huntington, and more respectable Methodists all resolved in very different ways: how to escape the turmoil of plebeian culture and develop new standards of manhood, without losing the strength of plebeian autonomy from middle-class moralists.

Conclusion

Sectarian religion did not function in a monolithic way in plebeian culture. On the one hand, sectarian religion's focus on spiritual rather than earthly concerns allowed plebeians such as Joanna Southcott and John Church to transcend, or at least excuse, their failure to live up to conventional ideals. Millenarianism and, at first, Methodism, allowed women to claim a unique moral authority through prophecy. For ordinary dissenting women, religion addressed familial problems that were ignored in radical politics before 1820. At the same time, such women learned organizational skills and acquired a language of protest and a knowledge of the precedent of female heroines which later aided them to join in radical political organizations.[159] This was particularly true in the north, where women took leadership in early Methodism.

On the other hand, radical religion never enabled women to challenge patriarchy directly in ordinary life. Because the role of female prophetesses was anchored in visionary proclamations and in an other-worldly spiritual context, however, their influence was evanescent and could not translate into female authority in the wider society.[160] They found it difficult to transform the metaphorical power of the "woman clothed with the sun" into real political power. Aside from Joanna Southcott, almost no women managed to transcend the masculinity of artisan culture to claim spiritual leadership in London. In the north, radical religion strengthened the tendency within textile communities to combine patriarchal authority and sexual cooperation. For men, dissenting religion provided an alternative role from that of the hard-drinking bachelor or the married misogynist. But it also encouraged men to feel they had a right, even an obligation, to claim protective patriarchal authority over their wives and therefore to demand the privileges of domesticity from the wider society.

Radical religion also had important implications for the eventual formation of the working class. To be sure, the sects, whether millenarian or Methodist, reached only a small number of working people. Church and chapel attendance was particularly low in Lancashire and London, though somewhat higher in Scotland.[161] In the beginning years of the century, the religious formed a subculture within plebeian society. Thomas Laqueur describes the social divisions between "the idle and non-idle classes, between the rough and the respectable, and between the religious and non-religious" as more marked than class divisions.[162] By adopting the values of domesticity, Methodists, as we have seen, allied themselves with the respectable classes and attempted to hasten their own upward mobility. The moral discipline of Methodist and other dissenting congregations bolstered their position as an upwardly mobile minority amid the plebeian masses. By the late nineteenth century, for instance, very few poor laborers attended Methodist chapels; lower-middle-class clerks and skilled workers such as cabinetmakers and printers predominated instead.[163] Methodists and other dissenting congregations thus set the precedent for the fracturing of plebeian society into the lower middle class and the working class.

Sectarian religion, however, also functioned as a vanguard for values and institutional forms later adopted by radical working-class leaders even as they rejected its theology.[164] Radicals could reject Methodist conservatism but retain its self-discipline, moral authority, and the ability to organize new communities of laboring people.[165] Working people founded and controlled Sunday schools in order to educate their children and provide discipline for working-class culture, not to pander to middle-class philanthropists.[166] In Scotland during the 1790s, philanthropists often founded Sunday schools in an attempt to inoculate working people and peasants against seditious doctrines, but to little avail. As Callum Brown notes, the growth of Secession and Relief churches in plebeian communities "alarm[ed] the elites in the wake of the French Revolution."[167] Spirituality could be consonant with politics.[168] For instance, in 1793, the Ashton Methodist Church was divided between the wealthy conservatives and the plebeian Jacobin radicals, and another Wesleyan congregation was later accused of harboring Luddites and trade unionists.[169]

Methodism thus trained working men for positions of moral leadership. Its forms of organization knit together communities and aided in the formation of radical working-class culture—but it also ensured that this culture would be patriarchal.

7 The Struggle over the Gender Division of Labor, 1780-1826

One dark Glasgow evening in December 1809, a few dozen cotton weavers left their wives and children toiling over looms and hurried down dank steps into the back room of a spirit cellar. This was no ordinary evening of drinking and carousing, but a special meeting of the Incorporated Weavers of Glasgow to discuss how to regain the prosperity they had once enjoyed. Following artisan tradition, they resolved to restrict the trade to those who had served an apprenticeship and joined their association. Yet they faced a dilemma. Although the organized weavers ornamented their membership tickets with female figures of Britannia and Justice, they could not decide whether to permit women in their association or to attempt to prohibit them from weaving.[1] Perhaps the married men whose families depended on their wives' and daughters' labor objected to efforts to ban them from the loom, while the bachelors belligerently protested that these females undercut a single man's wage. Unable to agree, the weavers simply postponed the discussion—but in bleak January, and snowy February, and rainy March, they could never resolve the issue and reconcile family needs with trade union strategy.[2]

The weavers were drawing upon a long tradition of artisans combining into a trade union to restrict the unapprenticed—especially women—from working in their craft.[3] They justified their efforts through the notion of "property in skill," clearly assumed to be a masculine quality of honor.[4] However, during the Napoleonic wars, their ability to keep out unskilled workers eroded. Thousands of men were pressed into the navy or joined the militia, then flooded back into the labor market as the fighting waxed and waned.[5] While some trades suffered from the blockade, others boomed with the demand for military materiel such as uniforms.[6] During labor shortages, manufacturers encouraged artisans and textile workers to teach their daughters and wives skills such as shoemaking and weaving, extolling the opportunity to bring more cash into the family. But when unemployment again loomed, employers impatient with their proud mechanics plotted to replace them with docile females on new machines or subdivided labor processes.

In response, workers organized to defend the "moral economy" of their trades against the onslaught of deskilling, mechanization, fluctuating wages, and the decline in apprenticeship.[7] Strikes against women workers, who were often used to introduce machinery and to replace apprenticed workmen, was one of their chief tactics. Between 1806 and 1811, hatters, calico printers, tailors, and framework knitters all struck against women in their occupations, and warpers, weavers, and cotton spinners also expressed concerned over this competition.[8] When these strikes failed to hold back the tide of deskilling, workers petitioned Parliament to improve their lot. In 1813, various trades organized to petition Parliament against the proposed repeal of the Statute of Artificers, which would end the legal requirement of apprenticeship. They defended the honor and pride of their skill and called on the government to regulate the balance of interests between masters and men. When workers argued that employers who hired unapprenticed workers robbed them of what they began to call their "property in skill," they invented a rhetoric to "articulate what they had always assumed."[9] But strikes and parliamentary agitation eventually failed as tactics to keep women and other unskilled workers out of artisan and textile occupations.

That failure had two principal roots. First, artisans' rhetoric could not combat the powerful artillery of political economy. Apprenticeship ran counter to the principle of laissez-faire, which stipulated that employers should hire, at the cheapest possible wages, whomever they wished—including women.[10] Adam Smith, for instance, not only opposed combinations but assumed that even married women must work, stating that "in order to bring up a family the labor of the husband and wife together must . . . be able to earn something more than what is precisely necessary for their own maintenance."[11] Efforts to exclude women from gainful labor offended middle-class moralists who believed poor women's work to be virtuous and necessary. Hannah More, the archetypal Evangelical moralist, on the one hand attacked workers for striking and on the other celebrated poor women's labor, praising the wife who "work[ed] to help the trade," and even the "Affectionate Daughter" who supported her infirm father by working in a coal pit.[12] During the Napoleonic wars, bourgeois opinion often fretted over the specter of men taking over women's jobs, leaving them with no alternative but prostitution.[13] In 1804, the Society for Bettering the Condition of the Poor complained that women's traditional trades had been "grievously and unjustly intruded upon by the other sex" and attributed the misery and immorality of poor women to their exclusion from many trades.[14] Until the 1820s, trade unionists did not counter this view by arguing that they wished to exclude women from work in order to protect them from the contamination of public life. They often relied on their own wives' work themselves; for the poor, women's wages were essential to family survival, and for the more successful artisan, a wife's shopkeeping or needlework contributed to his respectable lifestyle.[15] Instead, artisans wished to keep women out of their skilled, well-paid crafts, not out of waged work altogether; they simply asserted that their own jobs were their property, and women did not deserve the honor of artisan status.

Second, the rhetoric of property of skill condensed into one discourse different divisions of labor within artisan and textile trades.[16] Artisans in traditional trades such as tailoring and shoemaking formally organized their trades through regulated apprenticeships and rituals of craft combinations, all centered on fraternal male bonding that enabled proletarianized journeymen to create intense solidarity with each other and to defend themselves against their masters. When masters hired unapprenticed men and women, they disrupted the traditions of the trade. In contrast, cotton mule spinners and handloom weavers had always needed the subsidiary labor of women and children and had profited from the patriarchal organization of their workshops or factory units. Apprenticeship broke down because learning weaving was easy and lucrative in the late eighteenth century. When the Napoleonic wars disrupted the cotton textile trade, however, artisanal rhetoric seemed useful to weavers and cotton spinners combating employment of women. However, the rhetoric of artisan exclusion contrasted too sharply with the long-established importance of women and children in the textile trade. Even for artisans, the tactic of excluding women from their trades simply created a pool of female, low-waged labor employers were eager to exploit as substitutes for skilled men. The rhetoric of property in skill could not withstand the reality of proletarianization.

Faced with the failure of their rhetorical efforts, workers attempted to develop a variety of strategies to cope with the conflicts between masculine solidarity, family needs, and the reality of women in the work force. As we shall see in this chapter, they could confine women to subsidiary occupations, exploit their low-paid labor, and strike against them—or they could draw upon women's aid in strikes and even demand that women receive equal pay for equal work.

Artisans

Artisans' respectability and independence traditionally derived from skill. As Rule writes, "Skill . . . represented a symbolic capital, an 'honor', the possession of which entitled its holder to dignity and respect as well as imposing the obligation of the proper performance of his craft."[17] But with the increasing subdivision of labor and the production of cheap manufactured goods, much of this skill became illusory, especially in trades involving small consumer products such as hats, shoes, and clothes.[18]

In response, artisans defined "honorable" workers as those who worked in higher levels of the trade and organized themselves into combinations, whereas the "dishonorable" were unorganized and worked for the mass market. By creating a male "moral community," carefully defining who was inside and who was outside, they developed a new definition of honor.[19] British journeymen who labored together in a workshop considered themselves more honorable than those who worked with their families at home, for in the shop they could discuss politics or sing bawdy songs without feminine interference.[20] For instance, brushmaker W. Kiddier reacted with outrage when a rogue journeyman trained several women in the trade. Brushmaking was not difficult to learn, for workers simply dipped bundles of bristles in a pan of pitch. What upset Kiddier was that women invaded the sacred territory of the pan, intruding on male brushmakers' discussions of politics as they carried out their task.[21] Journeymen also had a more pragmatic reason for excluding women and insisting on laboring in the workshop rather than home: there, they could control the labor process and ensure that a married man could not, by obtaining assistance from his wife and children, undercut a single man's wage.[22]

Some trades, such as the bookbinders, solved the problem of maintaining honor in trades threatened by female labor by dividing the trade into different branches, allowing women to work in the less skilled, unapprenticed, low-paid tasks. Men bound the books, but women workers folded and sewed the printed pages. As early as 1779, the journeymen bookbinders formed a union and excluded female sewers and folders from it. Not surprisingly, in 1786 the women workers refused to support the bookbinders' strike. In 1806, however, the women supported the men in a strike over a tea break, but the men still refused to admit the women into the union.[23]

Tailors also followed this tactic fairly successfully until the 1820s. They "channell[ed] female labor into noncompetitive branches," such as army and navy uniform slopwork, which men avoided because of its coarseness and low pay.[24] During the Napoleonic wars the tailors secured considerable wage advances through a male labor shortage and their strong combinations. Their wages increased from twenty-two shillings per week in 1795 to thirty-six shillings in 1813.[25] Not surprisingly, the masters attempted to introduce women in some processes in the skilled branches of the trade, in order to cut wage costs. A few men welcomed the opportunity to augment their wages by taking work home to their wives and children. However, by doing so they endangered the division of tailors into the "Flints" and "Dungs," names evocative of honor or its absence. The former were employed in high-class West End workshops, unionized and apprenticed, while the latter were less skilled and unapprenticed, and sometimes even dishonored themselves by working at home with their families or with women in workshops.[26]

In 1806, the Flints struck when an infirm journeyman took work home to his family, and the same issue inflamed strikes in 1810 and 1811. Yet the masters put the journeymen on the defensive by celebrating the morality of women's waged labor, objecting to the "unnatural system of Husbands and Fathers preventing their Families from earning an honest and comfortable livelihood" by preventing the "Wife and Children from earning one shilling in the way in which the Husband and father can best instruct them!"[27] Newspapers and "canting Methodistical publications," remembered Francis Place, claimed that it was *more* moral to employ women because otherwise they would become prostitutes. Interestingly, the journeymen did not then respond that women's place was in the home; instead, they simply wanted to keep women out of their own trades. Tailoresses, they argued, would deprive the tailor and his wife of subsistence by working in slopshops and therefore undercutting the male wage.[28] The journeymen tailors of London were able to keep women out of the honorable sections of the trade until 1827, when they lost a strike on this issue.

Yet in many trades employers forced men to work alongside women; in others, journeymen could labor only at home, with the assistance of their wives and children. Although journeymen based their culture of honor on a bachelor masculinity, many of them married or cohabited.[29] They faced the problem, then, of how to retain their masculine honor in the face of this female presence. One tactic was to emphasize a belligerent, sometimes even misogynist, masculinity. As we have seen, a man could be a rough, drunken wife-beater and still be respected by his peers for his independence and status at work.[30] As skill and master status became less attainable, fraternal male bonding in defiance of the master became more crucial in developing a sense of honor. Journeymen celebrated their defiance of masters by instructing the young in cheating and stealing and by drinking heavily and fining each other in alcohol for working too fast.[31]

Hatters, for instance, also faced the danger of female encroachment, but their situation was even more difficult than tailors' because women were an essential part of the labor process. Women were employed in the trades to tear or cut the hair off beaver skins; to mix, card, and sort the hairs; and then to form the oval "gores" from which hats were made.[32] However, masters also wanted to employ women to assist in finishing, lining, and binding hats, actions journeymen usually carried out. In 1808 the Stockport hatters struck over this issue. Their general congress declared, "It is unanimously agreed that all women are to be knocked off against [struck against,] to knock one women off at one shop at a time, till it is gone round the trade, and so on until they are all done away with."[33] These efforts failed after the Stockport union was repressed in 1816, and by 1824 London hatters looked with scorn upon the Lancashire hatters who allowed women to "assist" them.[34]

While rejecting women's assistance as finishers, London hatters continued to need women to help them in picking the coarse hairs off the beaver pelts. And here we have a classic example of how journeymen's solidarity took precedence over family needs and led to the exploitation of women by male workers. Hatters relied on the aid of their wives, if not by picking for their husbands, then by earning wages during the off-season when hatters were un- or under-employed.[35] Yet until the 1820s journeymen hatters were notorious for drinking away the family income, and their dissolute workplace culture sometimes undercut their demands for higher wages. It was even alleged that they allowed their apprentices to do their work for them and spent their time gaming and drinking.[36] In 1820, the master hatters scornfully undercut striking journeymen's demands for higher wages by claiming they spent "most of their time in Idleness, Drinking, and Garrett Matches, and Dozenings." Instead of refuting this picture, the journeymen feebly tried to downplay the issue by replying that, like journeymen, some masters drank whereas others were sober.[37] Furthermore, journeymen had an interest in keeping women's wages low. A skilled hatter in regular work could earn two pounds and ten to twelve shillings per week in 1824, but if he did not have a wife to pick the hairs for him he had to pay six shillings to nine shillings and fourpence to another woman.[38] The lower the wages of female assistants (and apprentices), the more the hatter earned. Hatters thus had no interest in defending the rights of women in their trades.

Shoemakers, too, enjoyed a dissolute lifestyle based on male bonding and the exploitation of women's work. Their trade had fallen into patterns of family labor long before others had, and in the eighteenth century their unions were much weaker than those in other trades.[39] As early as the mid-eighteenth century, masters sent out leather to journeymen cordwainers, who would then employ wives and boy apprentices at shoebinding. Un-married women and widows also bound shoes for wages.[40] In good times, some female shoebinders could earn twenty shillings a week, but far more often they earned three to five shillings a week.[41]

A few women even learned the actual trade of making shoes. Many of the wives who assisted journeymen shoemakers were quite skilled, increas-ing the joint income of the family considerably. John O'Neill was able to make three to four pounds per week in the hard winter of 1813–1814 by making snow galoshes with his wife. He remembered that one of his friends was able to earn from "ten to fourteen shillings a day in the brisk season," with the aid of his wife, "an excellent awlswoman." He also re-counted that his half-brother was taught the "art and mystery of the gentle craft" from two former female servants. The wife of one radical journey-man "worked with him on the seat," "a very ready, good craft, and able to make five pairs of women's springs in the day." [42]

Yet women's presence beside men in workshops and their participation in skilled labor did not lead to egalitarian relations in the trade or in the family. Shoemakers fiercely guarded the definition of skill as masculine, refusing to organize women, and their allegiances were to their brother workers rather than to their wives.[43] Historians have depicted shoemakers as archetypal intellectuals and radicals,[44] yet, as we have seen, court records bore out their popular image as wife-beaters. Contemporaries sometimes depicted shoemakers as exploiting their wives' earning power; for instance, the neighbors of the radical journeyman mentioned above reproached him for "indulging in his idle nonsense" while he lived on his skilled wife's labor. When O'Neill, down on his luck, took a cobbler's stall in the street with his wife, passersby mocked, "Oh come and see the woman cobbling, oh crikey can't she pull out! my eye, but that's rare luck for the snob." [45] Shoemakers, like hatters, benefited from the work of a woman in binding shoes for them, and thus they could marry young. The women they lived with were known as "tacks," a word which connotes both the female shoe-binders' function of sewing seams quickly, and a loose, temporary union.[46] To be sure, misogyny was a cultural trend in shoemaking rather than a universal characteristic. In his writings John O'Neill, the shoemaker quoted above, always seems very respectful of women. Unlike women in other trades, shoemakers' wives went on tramp with their husbands, and only married men with families received strike pay, while single men were left to fend for themselves.[47]

Typically, Glasgow shoemakers prized the independence they derived from working at home with the assistance of wives and children, but they relied on journeymen's solidarity—and attempted intimidation of strikebreakers—to keep wages up.[48] For instance, in 1816, striking journeymen visited the home of William Struthers to demand that he join their strike. When he told them he was "obliged to work for the support of his family," they retorted he was "ruining both his own family and others." He had the last word, however: "he again told them he had nothing to do with their family and would look to his own family himself." The strikers' committee gave out a few shillings to several women, perhaps to keep them from working, and they threatened one woman who continued to bind shoes.[49]

This conflict between family needs and union strength was typical of artisans' organizations. Even though shoemakers worked alongside women who were sometimes skilled and often valued their own family commitments, their artisan culture was too powerfully based on fraternal bonding to permit them to overcome the contradiction between masculine honor and women's presence by organizing on a sexually integrated basis.[50]

Weavers

Although historians generally consider weavers to be artisans, the gender culture of their trade differed from that of traditional apprenticed craftsmen. Artisans based their organizations on the assumption that skill was linked to masculinity, an assumption maintained through the regulation of apprenticeship and fraternal bonding in the workshop, but weavers had to recognize that many women could perform the same skilled tasks as men. Therefore they found their chief strength in the autonomy of the family-based workshop and wider community solidarity. John Honeyweaver, a Bolton cotton weaver, testified to a parliamentary committee in 1808 that "women's talent is equal to men's when the work is not too heavy; we have some women whose talent is equal to any man's in the middle kind of work."[51] A silk weaver pointed out in 1818, "My wife is as competent a weaver as I am myself, and as competent to gate, or put in any figure, as I am myself."[52] Since most female weavers worked in their father's or (less often) their husband's workshop, their skill could only benefit the family. But in response to increased competition and overstocking in the trade, organized weavers often had to develop strategies to protect the rewards of skill. They faced a choice between including or excluding women, between sexual cooperation or competition.

Spitalfields silk weavers broke with artisan tradition to incorporate women. Until the 1760s the silk industry in Spitalfields had followed the familiar pattern of men engaging in the skilled work of weaving, as apprentices, journeymen, and masters, and women and children working in the subsidiary processes of dyeing, winding, throwstering, and quilling.[53] Weavers paid "but small wages" to throwsters, who prepared the silk for them, but spinning and winding silk could be more profitable for women, observed Campbell, "if they refrained from the common vice of drinking and sotting away their time and senses." However, winding turned into a sweated occupation when it was done at home, contracted out by poor women who employed others still poorer. Weavers preferred to use their own children at this task. Silk throwsters and winders also used primitive mills that could employ very poor women and children at low wages, which made it "a very profitable business for the master."[54]

Women turned to weaving when the trade of silk throwsters drastically declined in the late part of the century. They worked the ribbon looms rather than the more profitable engine looms, which male journeymen tried to monopolize for their own use. In 1769, male weavers tried to limit women from working in the better-paid branches of the trade, but left a loophole allowing masters to employ anyone in times of war.[55] All attempts to restrict women from working on the looms failed, for weavers profited more from their wives' weaving than from their winding. In 1765 a journeyman testified to the Commons that it was usual for four persons in a family to work on the looms.[56] During times of great demand for British silk, such as the Napoleonic wars, masters encouraged weavers to put their wives and daughters to the trade.[57]

By 1802, Spitalfields journeymen gave up trying to exclude women from weaving and instead tried a strategy of sexual cooperation. For instance, in 1802 Samuel Sholl, a weaver, formed a United Benefit Society for silk workers, incorporating "both men, women, and children" in order to maintain the sick, bury the dead, educate children, and reward merit. A few years later, when masters tried to force women back into silkwinding by paying female workers less and excluding them from regular apprenticeships, the organized weavers successfully lobbied for the Spitalfields Act of 1812, which mandated that women were allowed to complete regular apprenticeships and be paid the same as journeymen.[58] As late as the 1840s, women wove the finest velvets and jacquard brocades and received the same piece rates as men.[59]

But equal piece rates did not put female weavers on a par with men. They were granted a shilling less charitable relief than men, and in bad times there were more women's looms idle than men's.[60] Although wives often hired young maids of all work, their inescapable domestic responsibilities prevented them from producing as much as men or single women, so that although they were paid the same piece rates, they took less money home. Married women's earnings in 1840 averaged four shillings a week, half that of unmarried women.[61] Moreover, silk weaving was not an egalitarian but a patriarchal trade, for husbands controlled their wives' work and wages. Two cases of disputes between journeymen and masters reveal that husbands obtained the silk from the masters for their wives to weave, negotiated over the payment and time of completion, delivered the finished cloth, and received the wages themselves—as was their legal right.[62]

Despite all their efforts to gain organization and protection, the Spitalfields trade went into a prolonged and tragic decline and ultimately disappeared. Francis Place blamed the weavers for their own fate, declaring that if they had kept out female and child labor as had the tailors, they could have retained respectable adult-male wages.[63] But the main problem for Spitalfields weavers was competition from foreign countries and country mills. The Spitalfields weavers had at least tried an innovative and rational solution to the problem of undercutting: that of acknowledging women's skill and incorporating them into the trade.

Although Glasgow women also worked extensively in cotton handloom weaving, weavers there failed to emulate the Spitalfields strategy of sexual cooperation. Instead, they attempted to graft a fraternal, artisan form of organization onto a patriarchal trade, and their unions suffered from the inherent contradictions between the two modes. Whereas male artisans gained autonomy by bonding together against their bosses, weavers gained autonomy by their patriarchal control over their families and employees.[64] Small masters typically employed four to six weavers, including daughters and sometimes wives, along with other, unrelated men and women.[65]

Weavers therefore gained trade union solidarity, not on the basis of male bonding in the workshop against masters, but through community action. Weavers organized themselves into friendly societies, but they also engaged in mass protests that potentially included and supported women. Organized Paisley weavers supported several hundred female clippers when they struck and marched in 1768.[66] In the famous Calton weavers' strike of 1787, the workers marched in organized processions through the streets of Glasgow to protest a 25 percent wage cut and lockout, but they also secretly destroyed looms and forced one strikebreaker to "ride the stang," a form of public humiliation.[67]

By the 1790s and 1800s, however, the influence of artisan culture had become more dominant in weaving. The weaver John Mackinnon remembered that "journeymen in many other trades forsook their occupations, and flocked into the weaving districts to learn the trade."[68] However, the very entry of these former artisans into weaving undermined apprenticeship regulations and led to overstocking and declining wages.[69]

In 1808 the Glasgow weavers fought the deterioration of their trade by organizing into a powerful association with links to Paisley and other areas in Scotland and communications with organized weavers in Lancashire.

Deliberately following the political route instead of rioting and striking, they petitioned Parliament to enforce the old statutory minimum and the apprenticeship system.[70] Drawing upon artisanal rhetoric, they expressed their resentment at their lack of security in their property of skill and asserted their right to the rewards of wages and respect given to other artisans.[71] Now their trade was becoming degraded. They declared:

> Your Petitioners, after serving an apprenticeship, and working several years to acquire a knowledge of their trade, in hopes of afterwards being enabled, by their skill and industry, to earn for themselves and families the means of moderate subsistence, have the mortification to find, after all their pains and attention, that no ingenuity, no exertion or economy on their part, can procure them a competent share of the common necessaries of life, or secure them from the calamities of abject poverty.[72]

This rhetoric claimed that, like traditional artisans, weavers had served an apprenticeship and deserved their just reward. However, apprenticeship rules had never been strict or uniform in cotton weaving, and the skills could obviously be learned in a short period of time.[73] Instead of trying to regain a heritage they had lost, the weavers were trying to reconstruct their trade along the model of traditional artisans. The Weavers' Association tried to insist that only those weavers should work who could prove they had served an apprenticeship and had joined the association.[74] However, the problem remained that many women already wove, and some had even served apprenticeships.

Unlike the Spitalfields weavers, who coped with this problem by insisting that female apprentices serve the same time and journeywomen receive the same wages as men, the Scots tried to ban female apprentices. However, this was not possible: too many families relied on their work. Tensions may have flared between weavers who employed members of their own families and journeymen who regarded women weavers as competition. The Weavers' Association compromised by allowing women who had previously worked in the trade to continue, and allowing weavers to take on women from their own families as apprentices. The association itself did not admit women, however, yet it insisted that only members of the association should work as weavers. Faced with this contradiction, four times the committee of the Weavers' Association postponed discussion on the question of admitting women.

Finally, in 1810, the Calton association of weavers moved that although no new female apprentices could be taken except from the weavers' own families, women whose indentures "bear a date previous to the association

may be received to work journeywork by any of the Members, by producing such indentures or agreements, and becoming regular members."[75] By
1812, when the Strathmig society discussed prosecuting a former member
of their association who had resigned after taking a female apprentice, they
were advised by their lawyer that it was not constitutional to exclude
women, "as they thought it a monopolizing and persecuting spirit to deter
Females from going into the trade."[76] The weavers tried to overcome the
problem of the absolute necessity for weavers to employ their whole families, even at nonunion prices, by providing relief to both men and women,
but even that was not enough for many weavers. One young woman,
whom members of the association attempted to intimidate into working
only at list price, replied, "How will we live if we do not work?"[77] And, in
1812, government persecution crushed the Weavers' Association's efforts
to control their trade by either petitioning Parliament or striking.

Glasgow handloom weavers' attempts to combine artisan organization
with a patriarchal familial trade structure failed. But even as the trade deteriorated over the years, they continued to refuse to adopt the Spitalfields
weavers' solution of incorporating women into trade organizations. Tensions remained between the artisanal male bonding of the Weavers' Association and the family basis of the trade. In 1818 in the political journal of
the Paisley weavers' association, a debate raged over the pros and cons of
female education, perhaps reflecting the misogynist versus the progressive
tendencies in handloom culture.[78] When the Weavers' Association was resurrected in 1824, "an honest Wabster's Rib [weaver's wife] was so alarmed
by the Report of the Association that she conjured her guidman [husband]
not to attend the meeting."[79] The association reiterated their policy about
women weavers, allowing weavers to apprentice only their own daughters.
(They also restricted the number of nonfamilial apprentices to two.)[80] Yet
these efforts failed to halt the entry of women into the trade, already
flooded with male workers.

The new power looms posed the most serious threat to handloom weavers, as they themselves were well aware. Low handloom-weaving wages
delayed the widespread introduction of mechanized weaving until the
1820s and 1830s. Weavers had reacted with anxiety to this threat as early
as 1810, but tension seemed to focus on generational and skill issues rather
than gender. Scottish handloom weavers tended to regard powerloom
weavers as outsiders and refused to organize them.[81] In 1810, the Associated Weavers tried to enforce apprenticeships for powerloom weavers, but
at the same time they voted to expel any handloom weaver who instructed
a powerloom weaver. In the 1810–1811 inquiry in Parliament, Duncan
Lenox complained that boys and girls were employed at power looms

"while men are idle and cannot get a job of work."[82] In 1816 a crowd of two thousand people, probably weavers, tried to destroy powerloom factories in Calton and Dalmarnock and threw stones at the workers. Although women were active in riots against soup kitchens at the same time, the broadsheet reporting the riot made a point of the fact that no women were observed in the anti–power loom riots.[83] Perhaps the masculine, artisanal rhetoric employed by the weavers alienated women who had traditionally participated in community-based actions.

Women were much more involved in weavers' struggles in Lancashire than in Glasgow. They had participated in weavers' riots against cotton machinery in 1779 and had organized their own weavers' friendly societies.[84] Lancashire handloom weavers also mobilized more militantly against power looms. As appeals to Parliament to enforce apprenticeship and minimum wages failed, workers often turned to Luddism, trying to destroy the machinery that undercut their livelihood. Although women were not involved in the secret plans to fire factories at West Houghton, near Manchester, they were very active in the more spontaneous food riots and attacks on powerloom factories that accompanied these activities. A broadsheet alleged that one woman killed in these riots was "extremely violent and insulting to the military."[85] In the arson attack on West Houghton powerloom factory, two teenage girls were spared hanging although they had been seen "with Muck Hooks and Coal Picks in their Hands breaking the Windows of the Building and swearing and cursing the souls of those who worked in the Factory."[86] Since power looms generally wove inferior grades of cloth, the single women who worked them undermined the wages of the less skilled married female weavers, who therefore reacted with hostility to the new factories.[87] Men and women participated together in riots against power looms because they threatened the familial, home-based textile workers' economy.

Factory Workers

Although factory workers have traditionally been seen as the nucleus of the modern working class, E. P. Thompson has argued that their trade unionism was only a pale reflection of the artisan tradition.[88] Craig Calhoun even states that because the factory work force was numerically dominated by young women rather than skilled men, mills were difficult or impossible to organize.[89] To understand the success or failure of factory organization, however, we must investigate trade unionists' ability to create new structures in situations so different from traditional artisan workshops. Skilled men were able to maintain trade union strength only by drawing upon the support of the far more numerous female workers, thus modifying the old artisan heritage to create a new pattern of patriarchal cooperation with women.

For instance, by 1818 Stockport powerloom weavers organized against wage cuts as part of a larger strike wave. As Robert Hall writes, many of them were former handloom weavers, who drew upon their heritage to alternate formal petitions to Parliament with violent strikes and intimidation of strikebreakers.[90] Young women and men as well as children composed the majority of the powerloom work force, and twelve out of the twenty-three sentenced to a month's imprisonment for striking were women.[91] For instance, when factory owner Garsides chose to hire young women from Burton on Trent to replace his striking workers, male and female strikers pelted the women with mud and stones, even holding some under a water pump to dissuade them from working.[92] Clearly, the powerloom weavers were drawing upon the traditions of their own community strength while regarding the young female strikebreakers as outsiders.

But skilled male factory workers such as cotton spinners and tenters (powerloom mechanics) were in the minority within the factories. They needed the support of the far more numerous female mill hands if they were to retain their high wages. Tenters, for instance, were skilled male mechanics who maintained the power looms in Scottish factories. They had often been employed as handloom weavers, but their former workmates tended to regard them with scorn.[93] Nonetheless, the tenters soon set themselves up as an exclusive, skilled trade, complete with artisan rituals and an initiation fee of forty shillings.[94] But to hold on to their status they needed the aid of the female powerloom weavers whose machines they serviced. When Glasgow area manufacturers attempted to employ nonunion tenters and dressers in 1823, the very organized and militant male union of Combined Powerloom Operatives struck their factories. Emulating the cotton spinners who aided them in unionizing, the tenters drank heavily and secretly plotted to shoot "nobs," as they insultingly termed strikebreakers. At one meeting, remembered a weaver's son, they indulged in "a great deal of cursing and swearing and speaking of shooting. . . . They drank half mutchkins of whiskey with sugar and they had five dried speddings and threw the skins and bones at each other."[95] While the male workers secretly and formally organized against "nobs," they could also count on the public belligerence of the female powerloom weavers. For instance, when nonunion tenter Isaac Smith replaced a union man at Mr. Todd's mill in Govan, Glasgow, in 1823, the female powerloom operatives mobbed the mills, behaving, according to horrified observers, in a "particularly outrageous" fashion.[96] After crowds of women outside the factory threw dirt on Smith, Todd sacked several women he identified as ringleaders. In protest, all the women struck for a day. When Todd questioned one of the ringleaders, a sailor's wife, she insolently testified that she had left work because "she was lazy" and declared the women simply could not weave without qualified tenters.

Why were these women so militant in support of the tenters? They seem to have been marginal figures usually considered unorganizable—illiterate, poor women, living in lodgings and not necessarily related to the male workers.[97] Yet somehow tenters were able to create a sense of workplace community across gender and kinship lines, making their own trade union strength possible. As we shall see in chapter 12, they also provided a precedent for independent unions of female powerloom weavers in the 1830s.

In contrast, factory cotton spinners have been notorious both to contemporaries and to present-day historians for their hostility to women, which arose in reaction to employers' attempts to undercut skilled men with cheap female labor.[98] Yet a closer look reveals that the cotton spinners, too, developed a new strategy of patriarchal cooperation with women.

Cotton spinners, like handloom weavers, brought artisan traditions with them from their former trades.[99] Beginning at least in 1792 in Lancashire and around 1800 in Scotland, they formed extremely disciplined, sometimes violent unions that attempted to control access to the trade in order to keep wages up.[100] They were militant, sometimes involved in radicalism, and highly paid. Their status frustrated the employers' reason for mechanization, which was to replace skilled, expensive male workers with cheap female and child labor. As a result, employers often tried to break mule spinners' unions by employing women as spinners.

Yet organized mule spinners in urban areas were able to keep the trade male until the late 1830s in Glasgow and much later in Lancashire. Their success has sparked a debate in labor history over the basis of this gender division of labor. Per Bolin-Hart argues that mule spinning was simply too heavy for women and even for men who were not in the prime of life, for the task involved repeatedly pushing a carriage mechanism back and forth.[101] Employers usually attempted to replace men with women on light machines. They were most successful at this in the country districts, such as Ballingdoch in Stirlingshire, where Archibald Buchanan found that women were "more easily directed than the men, more steady in attendance to their work, and more cleanly and tidy in keeping of their machine, and contented with much smaller wages." A similar strategy was followed at the Catrine works in Ayrshire, nearer to Glasgow. Yet in Glasgow itself, manufacturers preferred to increase productivity by doubling the size of the mule "to the physical limits of the male spinners."[102]

However, women engaged in very heavy labor at this time, shoveling dung on farms and beating cotton in factory cardrooms. Spinner John Jones described their intimidating power:

> . . . the fleecy burdens laid
> On corded frames, where female strength display'd,
> Beats out the refuse—Ah! What dreadful blows!
> Ye Dames, 'twere fatal to become your foes! [103]

Strength, then, was not a male monopoly, but publicly acknowledged skill was. However, females could and did learn the skills of mule spinning, picking them up when they worked as piecers for the adult male mule spinners.[104] Although women were usually employed on the lighter mills, the fact that employers also introduced them on heavier ones to substitute for men indicates that they believed they could profit from the women's skill. As William Lazonick observes, as men's work became heavier women ran a number of spindles only men had been thought capable of a decade earlier.[105] Strength and skill vary a great deal among individuals. Some women are stronger than many men: for instance, a Glasgow female spinner earned thirty shillings a week on a large mule, "more than many of the men."[106]

William Lazonick has argued that men were mule spinners because in supervising women and child piecers they were able to transfer their patriarchal authority from the family to the factory. Employers simply found it easier to allow men to supervise the workers than to employ overseers.[107] James Montgomery advised mill managers that mule spinners should "have the charge of their own work," so that the spinning master would not have to be constantly present.[108] In the end, the mule spinners' union's strength most convincingly explains their ability to monopolize this skilled occupation. As the tenters' union did, the mule spinners' union tightly controlled membership in the trade, violently and secretly intimidating any who defied them. But the power of their union ultimately depended on their ability to gain the support of the majority of cotton mill workers—the women, youths, and children.

In Lancashire, cotton spinners reacted with hostility as early as 1807 when Salford manufacturer George Lee overcame "obdurate" strikes by men by employing women as spinners in his factories.[109] Yet by 1818 the mule spinners managed to gain the support of female and child auxiliary workers in the factories, even though severe unemployment resulted when the men turned out in a massive strike.[110] The men did not object to women's work in principle or claim they ought to earn a family wage; they only reacted with hostility to female competitors for men's jobs.[111] Cotton spinners also expressed their concern over the hardships suffered by children, campaigning in 1818 for the limitation of child labor.[112] In response to this support of women and children as workers, auxiliary factory workers enthusiastically supported the men in their strike. The male spinners put the women "in front of mobs" while the men kept "aloof," for, as the authorities noted, women were far the "worse" in hooting and insulting the strikebreakers.[113] Although the strike forced many women to turn to prostitution for support, upon their return to the factories "surly" women blamed their plight on their employers rather than on the male mule spinners, according to a government observer.[114] Women also incorporated themselves into the larger political culture. For instance, Elizabeth Salt, whose spinner brother was shot by the military in Manchester, published a pamphlet that supported the unionization of cotton workers.[115] Female factory workers also expressed class hostility on the streets of Manchester as they strolled there on Sundays, behaving in such an "insult[ing]" fashion that "their well-behaved superiors" were forced to cross the road to escape.[116]

Glasgow workers took a few more years to overcome simple misogynist techniques of fighting women in favor of patriarchal cooperation with women. According to John Butt, attempts to "terrorize women were fairly commonplace."[117] In 1819 James Dunlop of the Broomward cotton mills near Glasgow employed several women spinners as a means of cutting costs and combating the men's union. In response, several unemployed male spinners planned to "assist in maltreating some of the Broomward Female Spinners" and gathered together pokers and sticks. They set upon a group of women in the street, severely wounding Elizabeth Kelly, although her sisters-in-law escaped. The men also broke into the houses of two other women and their mothers and beat them so severely that one of the older women died.[118] This violence succeeded in forcing Dunlop to dismiss the women. Another mill owner, Mr. Snodgrass, snapped up these by now experienced female spinners, but they could not withstand the unemployed men's attacks and lost their jobs.[119]

The proudly artisanal mule spinners also had to overcome generational conflict with their piecers, whom they paid out of their own wages.[120] For instance, in 1820, just after a failed radical insurrection involving some cotton spinners in Milngarvie, a small town near Loch Lomond, north of Glasgow, the piecers there stopped work until the spinners agreed to pass on more of their wages to them. As the spinning master testified, "The cotton spinners are considered as standing in the same relation to the Piecers as the managers to the spinners." At the same time, the piecers violently intimidated the women and their young children who replaced them in the mills.[121] Two years later, the mule spinners had developed a more cooperative relationship with the piecers and other women workers. When the masters tried to employ strikebreaking spinners from other areas, not only the local spinners but the young female cardroom hands and piecers refused to work, and crowds of men, women, and children threatened the nobs.[122]

Glasgow male mule spinners developed a tradition of patriarchal cooperation with women out of a bifurcated work structure, in which a few male spinners controlled many female piecers. The male spinners fostered a paternalist relationship with their piecers. Witnesses in the prosecutions against strikers often identified themselves as a piecer to a particular spinner, a relationship that would often continue for years.[123] A tray painted with the emblems of the Friendly Association of Cotton Spinners, circa 1820, depicts an adult male spinner holding out his hand to a young girl piecer, with the motto, "United We Stand, Divided We Fall" (see Figure 6). Mule spinners also enlisted the support of workers in other areas of the factory, such as female cardroom hands, who were known for their rough language, irregular hours, and defiance of authority.[124] All the factory workers would join strikes, united in one community against strikebreakers either male or female.

In Glasgow strikes in 1823 against Dunlop's mill and in 1825 against the Broomward mill (owned by Dunlop as well), the mulespinners followed a complex, three-pronged strategy against strikebreakers. First, in a pamphlet war the mulespinners publicly articulated a rhetoric of respectable artisan pride; second, they created a raucous rhetoric of trade solidarity which fueled the riotous support of women and children; third, they anonymously used violent language and actions to threaten their opponents. Their terrorism derived its legitimacy from a shadowy community solidarity which its victims had violated. For instance, in 1823 some cotton spinners "sent two letters to two women employed in the cotton work of Mr. Kerr . . . threatening them . . . and having a cotton and drops of blood drawn at the bottom of the letter [threatening that] these women would be removed or the mill would be destroyed."[125] Despite these threats against female strikebreakers, women and children joined enthusiastically in strikes, congregating boisterously outside mills to hurl taunts and even stones against "nobs." When a crowd of cotton spinners severely beat Alexander Davidson, a strikebreaker, the wife of one of them cried out, "Kill the nob."[126] The spinners encouraged the women and children in their actions. They celebrated Ann McGregor, a young woman jailed for taunting strikebreakers, as a heroine, claiming that she was "a respectable young woman who had joined the crowd, gave a clap with her hands, and burst into a laugh and a cheer"; when she was released, they

Figure 6. Trade Union Emblem of the Glasgow Association of Cotton Spinners. Glasgow Museums: The People's Palace.

presented her with a silver medal and conveyed her home to her parents in a carriage.[127]

As a rhetorical strategy to bind the factory community together, mule spinners created songs in Lowland Scots dialect, thereby enabling women and children factory workers to articulate their pride in the trade. A thirteen-year-old cardroom hand testified that she and her mates sang this dialect song at work:

> We are the braw chick that belongs to the wheel
> That earns their bread by the spinning o't,
> Ne'er let your hearts tumble down to your heels
> But stand on your feet for the Spinning o't.[128]

At the strike against Dunlop's mill, crowds of female piecers and cardroom hands sang threateningly:

> Mr. Dunlop how do ye do
> How many Nobs have ye if your fifth flate were fu [fifth floor were
> torched]

Blin Jocks, blin [blind] and blin may he be
He'll ne'er quit his nobbing till he'll lose his t'other 'ee [eye].[129]

In the official rhetoric of a pamphlet defending their case, however, the spinners took quite a different tone. Instead of using dialect, they wrote mannered, standard English in an attempt to persuade middle-class public opinion of the justice of their case. They paternalistically portrayed the riotous actions of women and children as "shouting and huzzaing . . . harmless exhibitions of feeling, or folly, or weakness." They asked disingenuously, "How are the old Spinners to be answerable for [the] infant conduct [of the piecers], and how could they shut their crying mouths, and hold their playful hands outside the mills." Like the handloom weavers before them, mule spinners adopted artisanal rhetoric, presenting themselves as "tradesmen who are educated to particular modes of skill and labor from their youth, and acquire peculiar habits, which it is impossible for them to change in after life, unless by a violence like the tearing of the flesh from their bones."[130] They contrasted themselves favorably with the masters, who had attained their position only through the "caprices of fortune," when a "more dependent situation" would have better fitted them, "while the operatives in this country possess an informed and genteel behavior, which entitles them to rather more respect and regard than the proud and wealthy are willing to allow them."[131]

However, this was not class consciousness in the sense of working-class solidarity beyond the trade. Cotton spinners wished their craft to be exclusive, even hereditary. Indeed, the spinners later struck against handloom weavers who wished to leave their impoverished trade for a more lucrative one. And when a cowfeeder applied for membership in the union, they rejected him "as the spinners considered he has not got family into the trade" and struck against the mill that employed him.[132] In 1822, cotton spinners wrote to an employer, Mr. Clark, asking why he was taking on "half-learned spinners . . . a parcel of low rascals also bad workmen."[133] And in 1827, William McKay wrote to spinners urging them to support the union "or we will be reduced to one of the lowest class of operatives."[134]

Cotton spinners' actions were predicated on divisions within the working class, for they chiefly mobilized against other workers—single women, and the increasingly marginalized handloom weavers, who sought more lucrative work. Although they successfully developed solidarity among women, men, and children within the factory, that community was limited and local in scope. By the late 1820s, employers became less willing to tolerate male mule spinners' artisanal autonomy and determinedly used female strikebreakers to break down the union, exploiting the contradictions between artisan misogyny, patriarchal cooperation with women, and new notions of masculine respectability.

Conclusion

Artisans and textile workers thus developed divergent strategies to cope with the threat cheaper female labor posed to the skill, status, and wages of male craftsmen. Artisans had long tried to exclude women altogether from their workshops and craft traditions, basing their honor and their defiance of employers on a fraternal male solidarity. As change became inevitable during the Napoleonic wars, artisans attempted to restrict women to subsidiary branches of their trades, or at least to subsidiary processes. Although women labored beside men in tailors' workshops or shoemakers' garrets, sewing seams or binding shoes, the men shut them out of their artisan culture. For many textile workers, by contrast, the labor of women and children had long been an integral part of their trade. This tradition translated into a solidarity of labor which was based in the community, not just the workshop.[135]

However, since the actions of combinations could not always hold back the tide of cheap labor, artisans and textile workers increasingly turned to the public sphere, writing pamphlets and petitions to Parliament demanding a minimum wage and defending apprenticeship. They upheld their tradition of an artisan moral economy, in which a man who had served an apprenticeship was rewarded with wages sufficient to maintain himself and his family respectably, and in which masters could not become rich and overbearing by profiting from the poverty of their workers.[136] However, artisanal rhetoric could be used by trades, such as weavers or tailors, whose experience of apprenticeship and notions of the organization of work differed considerably. Furthermore, the rhetoric had to counter the laissez-faire discourse of middle-class moralists, some newspapers, and many powerful parliamentarians. At this early date, advocates of political economy believed that the work of women and children was not only necessary to support their families but beneficial. For instance, members of Parliament on the Select Committee on Children in Manufacturers persistently asked questions indicating their belief that long hours and low pay for cotton textile workers kept men, women, and children from squandering their earnings on drinking and debauchery.[137] When artisans attempted to exclude women from their occupations, masters accused them of being "selfish" and "monopolizing." When they demanded wages sufficient to support their families, the masters retorted that they would simply spend the money on drink.

Until the 1820s, artisans and textile workers found it difficult to formulate convincing replies to these accusations. References to drinking and debauchery hit close to home, for the carousing that bonded male workmates no doubt deterred many wives from supporting strikes. When masters claimed they should be able to employ poor women to save them from the streets, in response artisans could only bluster about their right to their trade. Organized workers did not yet demand a breadwinner wage in order to protect their wives and daughters from the contamination of wage labor.

To be sure, workers in the first two decades of the eighteenth century laid the groundwork for the later trade union movement. They formed powerful combinations which often defeated employers, and they began to create the infrastructure for the working-class movement as a whole.[138] This period witnessed innovative instances of cross-occupational solidarity, including the campaign for a weavers' minimum wage that was supported by other artisans, the apprenticeship campaign of 1813, and the Lancashire strikes of 1818. But organized workers had not yet gained a sense of class consciousness. A large number of British workers shared the experiences of insecurity if not poverty, deskilling, and unemployment, but many still did not perceive that they had interests in common with other proletarians. While workers often expressed resentment of their profiteering masters, they did not see themselves as locked into two antagonistic classes. Instead, they wished for a return to the days when masters and men shared culture, community, and craft rewards.[139] More important, they were divided among themselves. In many instances, the organized artisans would welcome a man only if he was "not a companion of the low and vulgar part of the community."[140] Traditional artisans in particular limited their organizations to the pub and workshop, determinedly excluding women and therefore limiting their community base. Textile workers were sometimes able to draw men, women, and children together in a kin, neighborhood, and workplace community solidarity, but even then their actions pitted one group of workers against others who were more marginal and vulnerable. Frustrated by increasingly futile actions and weak industrial discourses, working people often concentrated on radical political action, which developed a more inclusive rhetoric and forms of mobilization at an earlier date than trade unions.

8 Manhood and Citizenship
Radical Politics, 1767-1816

In the mid-eighteenth century, reforming gentlemen met in the masculine arena of coffeehouses, banqueting halls, and debating clubs to discuss the issues of the day. With their elegant philosophical rhetoric they formed a rational public sphere that was independent of the corrupt machinations of the state.[1] Excluding women, they defined themselves as manly citizens, whose public participation depended on their private virtue as property-owning, educated heads of households. Theirs was an exclusive club: the cost of society subscriptions, let alone the dinners, also kept out working men.[2] As Lord Cockburn noted, "The *public* was the word for the middle ranks, and all below this was the *populace* or the *mob.*"[3] Plebeian men, unendowed with property, were not thought to have the independence which would give them a political will of their own.[4]

In 1792, a group of journeymen inspired by the French Revolution challenged this exclusion, founding the London Corresponding Society to demand the rights of citizenship for working men.[5] Yet they found it difficult to imagine how they, rough-spoken mechanics without the wherewithal to buy property or even to keep a wife, could place themselves in the tradition of the reforming public sphere. Thomas Paine's notion of inherent human rationality as the basis for citizenship provided an answer. Everyone, regardless of class, was born with the ability to reason and therefore deserved the status of citizenship.

Feminist historians have argued that the focus of the radical movement on rational citizenship excluded women from politics.[6] But Paine's emphasis on reason could be used to argue for female political participation: women intellectuals could assert that women had the power of reasoning too. The exclusion of women from radical politics derived, rather, from the fact that radicals were so caught up in the association of masculinity with political power that they could not carry their philosophical principle to its logical conclusion.

Yet the nature of masculinity remained open to debate. Unable to attain bourgeois manhood, radical men could twist the traditions of civic humanism to assert their own masculinity and ridicule that of their opponents. While some tried to develop a rational, moral manhood, others rooted radical practice in the bachelor masculinity of rough artisan culture, trying to create their own "plebeian public."[7] Like the men of the middle-class public sphere, these radicals tried to separate themselves from the feminine, domestic realms of life, but for both this separation was always illusory. As several historians have noted, public probity increasingly depended on private morality.[8] Working people could not separate the public from the private, for working men were excluded from the public sphere and plebeian women had to work. Family life became a political issue.

Citizenship in the Era of the French Revolution

Eighteenth-century opposition ideology in England had depended on an amalgam of the ancient constitution and civic humanism.[9] In this tradition, only free male householders were citizens—certainly not women, servants, slaves, or mechanics, all regarded as inferior beings.[10] The equality of the male citizen with other men depended on his ability to control and dominate women, children, and servants in his own household.[11] Masculinity therefore defined citizenship. The definition of masculinity, however, was historically mutable. Civic humanists built on the tradition of classical republicanism to argue that the prerequisite for citizenship was independence, which enabled a man to exercise civic virtue, often referred to in the Latin, as *virtus*. *Virtus* connoted masculinity, austerity, force, strength, and autonomy, all qualities which enabled the citizen to put public concerns above private interests.[12] Eighteenth-century thinkers who opposed the ruling party denounced the aristocratic oligarchy as the antithesis of *virtus*, as being instead effeminate, degenerate, and corrupted by luxury.[13] The ideal citizen was the benevolent country gentleman, who looked after society's interests rather than being bought off by the government. By the mid-eighteenth century, however, the middle class became increasingly self-confident and desirous of political rights. The middle class thus began to portray themselves as "citizens": both in common usage, as citizens of a city (as in *burghers*), but also as those whose status as property-owning, tax-paying heads of households made them most deserving of political participation.[14] In their efforts to dominate local government, they began to claim the public sphere for themselves.[15]

By the 1760s, the Wilkes affair began to expand the notion of the public, as plebeian urban citizens joined the opposition. Wilkes published attacks on the king and his favorites, which led to his prosecution by the Crown. Despite his conviction—or because of it—he was elected a member of Parliament for Middlesex in 1768. Unlike most of Great Britain, London came close to the civic ideal of widespread citizenship for all propertied men, for in Westminster and Middlesex forty-shilling freeholders were enfranchised. Crowds of tradesmen, shopkeepers, weavers, and coalheavers enthusiastically took up the cry of "Wilkes and Liberty!" For Wilkes and his supporters, liberty included religious and sexual license as well as political rights. A man could be respected for his contribution to the public interest, while indulging in debauchery in private. Wilkes's publication of the pornographic *Essay on Women*, his gambling, and his abuse of his wealthy wife did not trouble many of his supporters. In fact, in recognition of his struggles for constitutional rights they joined together to pay off the debts he had incurred as an "extravagant libertine."[16]

However, these ideas of masculine virtue were coming to be contested.[17] The virtue of the citizen had always been tied to military prowess, but by the mid-eighteenth century it also became linked to exclusive heterosexuality. Wilkes himself accused two political enemies, George Stone, Archbishop of Armagh, and Lord George Sackville, of mutual sodomy, and the latter of military cowardice as well.[18] And some radicals disapproved of Wilkes's excesses. Those interested in morality advocated a turn away from libertinism toward the domesticity of middle-class patriarchy. They criticized bachelors as selfish and praised "domestic life and friendship as a source of virtue." Middle-class domesticity thus buttressed public probity as classical republican notions of the citizen as head of household were combined with the new Evangelical morality: this definition of masculinity included not just the public qualities of autonomy and strength but the private values of paternal responsibility, sobriety, and piety.[19]

Yet the Wilkesite agitation posed the question of whether plebeians had a place in politics. Although Wilkes eventually supported extension of representation to "the meanest mechanic, the poorest peasant, and day laborer," most of his colleagues in the movement simply wanted a more rational franchise covering all property-owning men.[20] In 1776 Major John Cartwright created a constitutionalist justification of universal manhood suffrage by claiming that the ancient constitution of medieval times had given all men the vote; yet he assumed the lower classes would continue to be deferential.[21] Even by the time of the French Revolution, many middle-class reformers, such as those of the Society for Constitutional Information, believed the vote should be given only to men whose property gave them independence from bribery and influence.[22] Its chairman, Henry

Flood, sponsored a bill in 1790 which would extend the suffrage, but only to resident tax-paying (male) householders, therefore "exclud[ing] great numbers of the lower orders."[23] In London, the high dues of the established middle-class radical groups, the Society for Constitutional Information and the Friends of the People, excluded plebeians.[24]

However, some more radical middle-class reformers promised to speak for and cooperate with laboring men. Provincial reform societies in Manchester and Glasgow were open to both middle-class and plebeian men. Middle-class reformers such as the lawyer Thomas Muir, frustrated at the failure of a ten-year campaign for burgh reform, reached out to laboring people, distributing Paine's works to weavers and other workers in and around Glasgow.[25] The Friends of the People affiliated with the more elitist groups in London but set subscription prices low to encourage laboring men to join.[26] In 1792, a soldier reported to the Home Office that "all the lower ranks, particularly the operative manufacturers, with a considerable number of their employers, are poisoned with a rage for ideal liberty that will not readily be extinguished."[27] Norman MacLeod, a member of Parliament who attended the 1793 Convention of Scottish radicals, protested that although Scottish farmers, manufacturers, and artisans were better educated than their English equivalents, they had *no* representation in Parliament.[28] Similarly, in Lancashire, Yorkshire, and the Midlands, radical reformers began with an alliance between more prosperous and plebeian men. But soon plebeian Jacobins, perhaps inspired by strikes and food riots, began to form their own radical societies. Especially outside Manchester, these informal groupings of weavers, artisans, and factory workers became independent, self-educated, and increasingly radical.[29]

They then had decide how to define themselves as political subjects. At one point a member of the London Corresponding Society proposed to form a section composed solely of "housekeepers" (those who leased a house), adopting the tradition of the male householder citizen to a more plebeian level, but the others indignantly turned him down, arguing that property "may be evidence of industry and economy, but it is not a general test of moral rectitude."[30] The dissidents seem to have formed a separate General Association of Householders, a group of shoemakers, tailors, pastrycooks, and cheesemongers who could afford only two- to four-shilling subscriptions but regarded men who did not pay taxes as having "no will of their own in the political sense."[31]

But many members of the London Corresponding Society were not householders but bachelor lodgers "whose practice [it was] to go to a public house from their workshops after the labor of the day, to have their supper, and then regale themselves with a pint or pot of Beer, and smoak their pipes, and convers about the news of the day."[32] They did not fit into the middle-class notion of the public sphere, whose members' independence was guaranteed by their ownership of property and dominance of dependents. Instead, their political strength derived from fraternal and community bonds; the individual was powerless. None of the traditions of civic humanism, the Glorious Revolution, or classical republicanism could provide adequate precedents for such men's claims to citizenship.[33]

The answer, as we have seen, appeared in 1791 with the publication of Thomas Paine's *Rights of Man*. Paine provided a radically new rationale for citizenship which derived from pure egalitarianism and had wide appeal. Paine cut across the old assumptions of civic humanism by arguing that all men deserved political representation because as humans they had access to reason. All men were born equal, declared Paine, created equal by God. Paine's work had enormous influence, selling hundreds of thousands of copies, in large part because his simple, straightforward, and vivid language was much more accessible to common people than civic humanism was.[34] Previous middle-class radicals had claimed to speak *for* working people, but Paine allowed them to speak for themselves: men had political rights simply because they were men. Did this mean men in the generic sense of humans, however, or did it mean men as masculine beings, that is, not women?

While thinkers such as John Cartwright argued that women could not defend their country in the military and therefore had no right to representation,[35] Paine's ideas were potentially gender-neutral. Although Paine acknowledged gender differences, he did not, unlike Locke, stress gender subordination as natural. For Locke, the individual male was considered to be equal to other men in the public sphere, but his status as citizen derived from his status as head of household in the private realm, where nature mandated female subordination.[36] In the abstract, Paine's notion of citizenship could apply to women because it was not essentially dependent on the association of masculinity with the power of the head of household. He rejected organic models that depicted society as a gendered body, complete with the natural subordination of plebeian hands and female heart to masculine head; instead, he proclaimed, a Nation "is like a body contained within a circle, having a common centre in which every radius meets; and that centre is formed by representation."[37]

The notion of citizenship could open up the possibility for women's political participation. In France, women such as Olympe de Gouges argued that if the suffrage was an inherent human birthright, then women should enjoy it too.[38] And in Britain, a few male radicals considered the possibility of female citizenship, although it was never a central preoccupation for

them. Thomas Cooper, in his reply to Edmund Burke, supported the political rights of women.[39] William Hodgson noted that he intended to write
a treatise on female citizenship, but he never published one.[40] A writer
in the radical Norwich periodical *The Cabinet* "argued unequivocally for
adult female suffrage . . . yet even he recognized that most men would
laugh his arguments out of court."[41] The ultra-radical and land reformer
Thomas Spence said that "Female Citizens have the same right of suffrage
in their respective parishes as the men; because they have equal property
in the country, and are equally subject to the laws." However, Spence went
on to say that "in consideration of the delicacy of their sex [females] are
exempted from, and are ineligible, to all public employments" (presumably
meaning public offices).[42]

Some British women intellectuals tried to develop notions of women's
citizenship. Most notably, Mary Wollstonecraft argued that women should
be industrious so that they could be independent citizens, rather than
dependent parasites like the aristocracy. Women deserved citizenship, she
pointed out, for as rational mothers they contributed to civic virtue.[43] Mary
Hays echoed her friend, writing that girls should be educated in "some
ingenious art or useful trade by which a young woman could hope to gain
an honest and honorable independence."[44] This was quite an original interpretation of the tradition of civic humanism, detaching the notion of independence from masculine power over a household and replacing it with an
independence derived from industry—but not from masculine property in
skill. Wollstonecraft did not see women as utterly different from men, nor
did she see them as the same as men.[45] "Humanity" meant, rather, breaking down rigid gender differentiations: women should acquire "manly virtues," while men should become "chaste and modest."[46] This strategy allowed Wollstonecraft to claim citizenship for women as reasonable human
beings, without denying women's experiences.

Despite Wollstonecraft's publications, few women participated in Jacobin activity.[47] Generally, radical women advocated a concern for the larger
issues of oppression and poverty rather than for the specifics of women's
rights. For instance, the pseudonymous "Tabitha Bramble" wrote a letter
to the hated Henry Dundas, Lord Advocate for Scotland, denouncing "the
wanton cruelty, the perversion of justice" of his government. She hoped
that some brave person would rid the country of such a "pest" as Dundas:
"Some Male, or rather more likely some Female hand, will direct the Dag-
ger that will do such an important Service and Britain shall not want a
Female Patriot emulous of the fame of Mlle. Cordet [*sic*]."[48]

Female friendly societies might have provided a means for women to be
mobilized into radical activity. A spy noted that "A Society of Women"

met at the same pub as a division of the London Corresponding Society (LCS) in Bermondsey. At one point the LCS moved to establish a society of female patriots, although it is not known if this ever occurred.[49] In Scotland, the wife of a radical reformer was denied permission to form a female friendly society because, it was alleged, she had practiced using the guillotine on hens in her back yard.[50] Spitalfields silk weaver Andrew Larcher wished to put together the resources of friendly societies for radical purposes and advocated admitting "Women of every occupation, country, and persuasion" as "Sister Members." To be sure, "Brother Members' Wives" were apparently considered as covered by their husbands.[51] However, there is little evidence that female friendly societies were mobilized in the 1790s for radical purposes.

Why did Jacobins fail to organize women in the 1790s, and why did so few women take up what openings there were for female participation in the radical movement? Part of the explanation lies in the fact that most radicals devoted little thought to recruiting women, and associated reason with masculinity so stringently that there seemed no point in doing so.[52] But we must also ask why radical politics would interest women. The prevalent masculine definition of citizenship, despite Mary Wollstonecraft's efforts to reshape it, left little space for any but the most intellectual woman to imagine herself as a political actor.

Furthermore, despite the blunt eloquence of Paine and Wollstonecraft, their abstract reasoning lacked the narrative drive that could connect politics to popular culture for ordinary working men or women and could provide them with new political identities rooted in old traditions.[53] And when forced onto the defensive, radicals often abandoned even their abstract, gender-neutral logic to seize ammunition from the masculine traditions of British political discourse. When conservatives attacked the very humanity of laboring people, most notably Burke in his description of them as the "swinish multitude," radicals gendered their language once again. Burke and his compatriots seemed to view the common people as animalistic, degraded, irrational.[54] In response, Paine asserted, "It is time that Nations should be rational, and not be governed like animals, for the pleasure of their riders."[55] Another radical work asked people to consider that if they had no representation, "Are you not thus degraded to a level with the very cattle in the field, and the sheep in the field, which are a property to those who rule over them, and have no power to say, why are we bought and sold?"[56]

But to demand the rights of "men," reformers had to assert not only that they were humans, not animals, but that they were men and women, rather than an undifferentiated mass. Burke denounced the French Revolution for destroying social rank and therefore reducing people to the level of animals. He lamented, "On this scheme of things, a king is but a man; a queen is but a woman; a woman is but an animal; and an animal not of the highest order." For Burke, a binary understanding of gender was horrifyingly crude. Instead, there were proper gradations of rank, gentlemanliness, and ladyhood, to be differentiated from mere masculinity and femininity by the practice of chivalry, "that nurse of manly sentiment."[57]

Radicals criticized Burke for his assumption that gentlemen and ladies were innately different from and superior to ordinary men and women. In her *Vindication of the Rights of Man* (which preceded her more famous work) Wollstonecraft upheld the innate dignity of poor men and women against Burke's view of humanity as a feeling to be ascribed only to the nobility. Wollstonecraft attacked Burke's hypocrisy in lamenting the pain inflicted on royalty but ignoring the injustices endured by poor English men and women: "a *gentleman* of lively imagination must borrow some drapery from fancy before he can love or pity a *man*." She went on to extend this argument to women: "Your tears are reserved . . . for the downfall of queens, whose rank . . . throws a graceful veil over vices that degrade humanity; whilst the distress of many industrious mothers, . . . were vulgar sorrows that could not move your commiseration."[58] The "vices that degrade humanity" probably referred to rumors of Marie Antoinette's heterosexual and lesbian affairs, circulated by ultra-radicals at the beginning of the French Revolution.[59] The deist William Hodgson claimed that the rich "pillage and ravage their fellow-citizens to support themselves in the most shameful debauchery . . . [indulging] inordinate and desolating passions, that reduce them in the eyes of the honest and virtuous man, far below the level of the beasts of the field."[60]

Male radicals counterposed their own virility with the femininity of aristocratic corruption and decadence. Even Paine pointed out that a title "reduces man into the diminutive of man in things which are great, and the counterfeit of woman in things which are little. It talks about its fine *blue ribbon* like a girl, and shows its new *garter* like a child."[61] William Godwin complained, "The dissipation and luxury that reign uncontrolled have spread effeminacy and irresolution everywhere."[62] While this trope stemmed, of course, from a long tradition of civic humanism, radicals used it in a new way, to assert their own manliness at the expense of the upper class. Radicals even argued that noble Whiggish reformers had abandoned the masculine virtues of their revolutionary seventeenth-century ancestors. *Pigott's Political Dictionary*, for instance, declared that "Effeminacy is now perfectly well described in Fop's Alley, at our Opera House, . . . by the descendents of Hampden, Sidney, Russell," and other seventeenth-century radicals.[63]

However, radicals could not simply adopt the masculine traditions of civic humanism, for that philosophy presumed a separation between public, political, and private, domestic concerns. Such a separation was simply not possible for working people, who were more concerned with issues of food and work than with the intricacies of political thought. In order to appeal to them, some radicals articulated a wider version of politics based on "humanity," in the sense of an empathy—derived from the experience of hardships—for the sufferings of others, rather than the condescending pity of bourgeois humanitarian philanthropists.[64] Whereas the concept of liberal citizenship in civic humanism ignored the needs of families and assumed that only the concerns of individual males were relevant to politics, Painite politics, with its concern for the welfare of families, potentially appealed to women. For instance, in part 2 of the *Rights of Man,* Paine proposed government payments upon marriage and childbirth among other social benefits.[65] Thomas Spence, a utopian radical who believed land should be common property, expanded the notion of natural rights by saying that even animal mothers had the right to provide food for their children out of the bounty of nature, a right the aristocracy was trying to deny to human mothers. However, Spence identified women only as mothers, as embedded in the natural world, and his appeal to women could be read as an effort to goad apathetic men into activism by portraying them as so unmanly that their wives have to demand their rights themselves. By 1795, the LCS was responding to repression by holding mass meetings that addressed "a range of more urgent popular grievances" such as food shortages and high taxes, appealing to the family concerns of many working people who had been apathetic about constitutional issues.[66]

For radicals, claiming the rights of fatherhood and motherhood was a way of asserting their humanity. They complained that government corruption and oppression prevented them from marrying and raising children. These complaints reflected both the personal concerns of bachelor journeymen, who were not paid enough to support a family, and the political problem that as lodgers rather than householders they were not considered to be independent citizens. Thomas Bentley, a linendraper, was prosecuted for printing a pamphlet that declared, among other grievances, that "thousands of men and women are kept from marrying and drawn into whoredom by the certainty of not being able to support a family."[67] *Pigott's Political Dictionary* defined "wedlock . . . as that happy and enviable state, which but few can enjoy in wicked and unprincipled governments."[68] A Nottingham broadsheet of 1793 claimed that under a "Free Parliament," the poor would be relieved of "the enormous load of Taxes," and "Parents will no longer consider the encrease of a family as a burden but as a blessing."[69] In a reference to Burke's infamous phrase, Thomas

Spence complained that "Swine are excluded the conjugal life."[70] While at least two male radicals advocated divorce, most Jacobins ignored this topic, for admitting family breakdown among the poor made it difficult to defend them as paragons of family virtue—or to counter anti-Jacobin propaganda that radicals would destroy marriage.[71]

The London Corresponding Society tried to appeal to working men as husbands and fathers. In 1797, trying to rouse delinquent members, the LCS asked if they had stopped attending meetings because "the pittance of the Labourer well provides him with Food, comfortable clothes, and fills his little Cot with cir'cling pleasure?"[72] They must respond, it claimed, to "the voice of reason, and the tears of suffering humanity . . . in the name of . . . your famished wives and weeping children, to rally around the standard of liberty," and prove, "by your virtuous, peaceable and manly conduct, that you are worthy of being free."[73] Similarly, the militant pamphlet *The Happy Reign of George the Last* told men, "If you love your wives and children, or yourselves, you will not always consent to have needless and enormous contributions raised upon you."[74] *A Warning to Tyrants* said that by declaring war, "Ambitious tyrants . . . trample on the dearest ties of social affection, and burst the closest connections of life; the affectionate husband, the industrious father, is torn by their venal ruffians from the sharer of his comforts and cares; for ever separated from the engaging dependents on the daily product of his labor!" Even in the best of circumstances, "The occupation of a Swinish Multitude . . . can hardly procure subsistence for a wife and family, as considering the present enormous taxes, seven or eight shillings a week is scarce sufficient to provide bread for one."[75]

However, while such claims may be taken as the germ of the idea of the breadwinner wage, the notion that a man should earn enough so that his wife and children would not have to labor was not widely circulated at this time.[76] The Jacobin Mary Hays obliquely pointed out the absurdity of the assumption that wives were dependent by pointing out "the number of poor hard-labouring women, with large families (the support of which is thrown by a profligate husband wholly upon them)."[77] But such criticisms could not be aired when plebeian men were trying to define themselves as husbands and citizens by depicting women as passive and helpless.[78] An LCS pamphlet reporting on the crowd attack on the houses of Mrs. Hardy and Mrs. Thelwall, whose husbands had been dragged from their homes and imprisoned for sedition, lamented, "The delicate sensibility of the female character was wantonly sported with. The wound recently inflicted by the ruthless hand of power, was again torn open by the mournful recollection, that their husbands were not present to defend them against premeditated assault."[79]

Yet when radicals spoke of food, war, and employment, women, far from playing the role of passive, helpless victims, responded with energy. In 1793, when rumors circulated at a large open-air London Corresponding Society meeting that the members were plotting to "lower the price of provisions," women in the large curious crowd cried, "God bless them."[80] Food riots, in which women had always participated vigorously, sometimes acquired a radical context. Women dominated food riots in Manchester, for instance, and "bitterly" defied troops.[81] In 1793 in Inverness, citizens prevented a boat loaded with grain from sailing away from the dearth-stricken town. Upon a signal, "almost every man from the Lamp manufactory and many women, a number from the Thread Manufactory and a Crowd of Journeymen from the different incorporated trades particularly weavers came to their assistance" and stoned constables. The magistrates noted disapprovingly, "Of liberty and equality they are constantly talking, and of making Laws and fixing prices on every necessity of life."[82] In 1797, Scottish women were active in riots against recruitment into the militia, which spread into stone-throwing at the houses of the schoolmaster, the minister, and the magistrates.[83] By 1800, authorities feared that another wave of food riots had been begun by "active and ill-disposed persons, who instigate the boys and women to be riotous, in hopes of promoting general confusion."[84] Indeed, radicals in Lancashire and elsewhere began to make the connections between politics and economics more explicit by distributing handbills calling working people to demonstrate for lower prices and higher wages.[85]

Yet it would take more than another decade for a broad-based movement to emerge that included women and was organized around issues of survival. Male reformers usually wished to disassociate themselves from women, whom they associated with riots rather than with rational organization.[86] The delegates of the Convention in Scotland in 1793 denounced riots and made clear that they did not want to attack property.[87] The London Corresponding Society published a pamphlet entitled *Reformers No Rioters*.[88] In his *Spirit of Despotism*, written in 1795, Vicesimus Knox refuted the notion that the Gordon Riots proved the "People" incapable of enlightenment—"for I cannot call a fortuitous assemblage of boys, beggars, women and drunkards the People." Instead it is clear that for the Whiggish radical Knox the "People" were male citizens, who could be educated into a "manly" rationality.[89] In Manchester in 1800, according to John Bohstedt, "a committee of organized craftsmen warned their brother workmen against the folly of food riots." As men's organizations grew more formal, women were relegated to the discredited sphere of crowd violence.[90]

Furthermore, any attempt to draw women into politics ran up against anti-Jacobin propaganda that used conservative sexual ideology to tar radicals.[91] They distributed pamphlets claiming that Thomas Paine was a debauched wife-beater who failed to support his own mother.[92] In a simple counterpropaganda dialogue, William Jones claimed that radical attacks on aristocratic authority would unnaturally undermine familial hierarchy. He declared that in reality, "the children are not equal to the Mother, nor the Mother to the Father; unless where there is Petticoat Government, and such Families never go on well; the Children are often spoiled, and the Husband brought to a gaol."[93] Hannah More circulated "Cheap Repository Tracts" warning plebeians, both men and women, to work quietly and spend their evenings tending to their families instead of discussing radical politics in the pub.[94] Once Godwin revealed Mary Wollstonecraft's premarital affairs, all female radicals were stigmatized as sexually immoral by association; indeed, sexual morality became a touchstone of political probity under an Evangelical regime.

As Jacobins widened their vision to demand relief for the poor, middle-class reformers often abandoned the cause, fearful on the one hand of losing their property to revolution, and pressured by government repression on the other. In Scotland by 1793, the government had effectively squelched middle-class support for radicalism by transporting some middle-class reformers to Australia and stripping Jacobin schoolteachers, attorneys, and clerks of their jobs.[95] In 1794, the mechanics of Paisley signed a petition for peace, but William Carlile assured the Lord Advocate for Scotland that "there is no place in Great Britain where the Middling and higher class of Citizens are more loyal and attached to the Constitution than Paisley."[96]

After the excesses of the Paris Terror repelled many English middle-class reformers, they tried to stress civic humanism's exclusion of working men.[97] An anti-Jacobin propagandist, Edward Hamilton, compared mechanics to slaves in their incapacity to exercise political rights.[98] Middle-class men explicitly justified as the price of civilization's progress the inequality that made possible their own cultivated lifestyles.[99] The "progressive and improving" middle class distanced itself even more from both the "effete aristocracy and the licentious rabble," using Evangelicalism to justify obedience to the established order as well as to serve as a means of moral reform.[100]

As revolution and government repression led many working people to retreat from activism, plebeian society was divided between the radicals and the loyalists. Fights erupted in Glasgow and Manchester between the short-haired Jacobins, known as "Croppies," and the repentant former radicals in their blue Volunteer uniforms, who wore oak sprigs in their hats to denote loyalty to king and country.[101] Some of those who retained their radical convictions modified their private morality. Some men, such as

Charles Pigott, who had written and published libertine, obscene satires against the government (inspired by the French) in the early 1790s
emerged sober and sedate from several years of imprisonment for sedition.[102] In the late 1790s many members of the London Corresponding Society retreated into self-improvement and private upward mobility.[103] Yet
radicals such as Francis Place and William Godwin sought to improve
themselves through education, aspiring to a rational radical ethics. They
rejected the middle-class, Evangelical version of morality as hypocritical
and elitist. Place, for instance, advocated birth control; Godwin, free love.

Nonetheless, the move toward self-improvement further closed off possibilities for women's political participation, for it was linked with respectability and domesticity, characteristics thought antithetical to female radicalism. As a result of the broader franchise of city districts and the physical
location of Parliament there, London radicalism continued to focus on constitutional and electoral issues defined in terms of masculine citizenship.

Libertinism, Ultra-Radicalism, and Masculinity

While many Jacobins retreated into respectability and constitutional politics, such a refuge was not possible or desirable for many plebeian men.
Instead, they simply went underground into ultra-radicalism, shaping
their own version of radical manhood out of their heritage of libertinism
and the bachelor journeymen ethos. This libertine subculture provided a
safe haven for many radicals when the Prime Minister Pitt persecuted
them during the 1790s, the long, dark years of the Napoleonic wars against
France. They met in pubs, under cover of the free-and-easy drinking clubs,
and concealed their subversive messages in the verses of bawdy songs. Lord
Conclurry complained, "If the business conducted was treason, it was carefully wrapped up in the jokes, and the ribaldry commonly said or sung in
such places."[104] However, this retreat into libertinism further closed off
possibilities for women's involvement in politics, for it could easily descend
into misogyny. As we have seen, journeymen organized into trade unions
often evinced, at best, indifference and, at worst, misogynist hostility toward women workers. Rather than celebrating family values, they continued the bachelor lifestyle of journeyman culture. Indeed, some of the ultra-
radicals, as MacCalman notes, found "maintenance of children a terrible
'clog' and burden and farmed them out." Libertine ultra-radicalism flourished most luxuriantly in London, where several ultra-radical leaders were
indicted for rape or brothel-keeping, but their cultural style also took root
in the artisan culture of other metropolitan areas, such as Glasgow.[105]

These radicals stressed their virile heterosexuality, for bachelors' sexuality was politically suspect at this time. The government and its advocates
tried to play on the image of British virtue as opposed to French vice to

whip up support for the war effort, accusing the French of effeminacy, decadence, sexual anarchy, and sodomy. An 1803 broadsheet depicted French soldiers declaring, "They have called us Sodomites, and they shall not call us so for nothing; as their handsome Footmen, and Farmers, and their lusty young labourers will find. . . . And we will ravish their wives, and their daughters, in the bargain!"[106]

The government thus tried to exploit homophobia, which was then at its height, fomented by an increasing number of executions for sodomy. This increase was no accident: the public hanging of sodomites could serve to distract the people from radical unrest.[107] Popular anxiety was also excited when a sodomitical subculture was discovered in London in 1810. A coal merchant, a Bow Street Runner, a butcher, a blacksmith, a bargeman, and a coalheaver were found to be homosexuals associating together at the Swan Pub in Vere Street, where antinomian preacher John Church would conduct humorous marriage ceremonies between men.[108] Confounding conventional masculinity, the pub customers took female names, so that "Fanny Murray and Lucy Cooper [were] now personified by an athletic Bargeman [and] an Herculean Coalheaver."[109]

The underground subculture of Church and his Vere Street friends thus appealed to the same plebeian stratum as the radical libertines: people unable or unwilling to subscribe to conventional morality. It was perhaps in part this uncomfortable resemblance between the two subcultures that led radicals to exhibit a virulent homophobia. They turned the conservative propaganda images of French sodomites against the government by exploiting homophobia for their own ends. Some of these radicals preyed on the homosexual subculture through blackmail.[110] More publicly, others delighted in unveiling clerical and aristocratic sodomites to expose the hypocrisy of the government's role in regulating morality.[111] The radical printer William Benbow devoted an entire volume to the sexual peccadillos of all types of clergymen, with a concentration on sodomy.[112] After being blackmailed, Lord Castlereagh, a British foreign minister, committed suicide to conceal his putative homosexuality.[113]

But radical homophobia also stemmed from the fact that many plebeians and their leaders did not fit conventional models of masculinity and morality. To compensate, they employed their heterosexual virility as a marker of power and put down their opponents as sodomitical. To counter the Reverend Thomas Fysshe Palmer's accusation that Maurice Margarot had started an abortive mutiny as they were transported to Australia, Scottish radical Margarot in turn accused him of making homosexual advances.[114] The upper-class radical leader Henry Hunt responded to hecklers who criticized him for leaving his wife for another woman by accusing them of belonging to the Vere Street gang and even insinuating that another radical leader, William Cobbett, engaged in "unnatural practices."[115] Hunt's homophobia was part of his persona of virile heterosexual radical manhood.[116]

Radicals shaped the old attack on aristocratic corruption and effeminacy into a new anti-government attack on dandies, asserting their own heterosexual manhood in the process. Dandies excited disapproval for their attention to their appearance, which made them seem like sexual objects rather than subjects, and therefore feminine.[117] Their extravagant and parasitical lifestyle (they refused to wear watches, which would imply an attention to business) was linked to the excesses of the court.[118] George, Prince of Wales, squandered immense sums on mistresses, gambling, and drink, and some aristocrats were thought to have more unconventional tastes. For instance, the radical periodical the *Black Dwarf* insulted a "new race of men" who "wear stays, and drink God to save the King, in dandy punch. Their gender is not yet ascertained, but as their principal ambition seems to be to look as pretty as women, it would be most uncharitable to call them men."[119] This motif spread from London to Scotland. A Glasgow broadsheet claimed that radicals had invented the name "dandy" to insult well-dressed men, and satirized dandies as so tightly encased in their elegant cravats they were unable to fight.[120] And the *Spirit of the Union* warned radicals against the "Dandy Corseteers," in a thinly veiled insult against the middle-class men who joined the Volunteers to put down discontent:

> How exquisitely pretty,
> In whalebone armor cas'd
> Each dandy walks the city
> Exhibiting its waist;
> While at its side, a porter blade,
> Its heavy musket bears
> As on it hies, to join its squad,
> Of dandy corseteers.[121]

By undermining military masculinity radicals attempted to undercut the war-hero masculine image that had done so much to buttress popular patriotism.[122]

Attacks on dandies were also clearly linked with a belligerently misogynist manhood. The Paisley *Weavers Magazine* published a satirical "Matrimonial Creed," proclaiming, "The man is superior to the woman, and the woman is the inferior of the man, yet both are equal and the woman shall govern the man." It also reprinted a verse, "The Hen-Pecked Dandy," about

> The Demon of Fashion Sir Fopling bewitches—
> The reason his lady betrays—

> For as she is resolved upon wearing the breeches,
> In revenge he has taken the stays.[123]

These quotes alluded both to Wollstonecraftian ideas of female equality and to the "struggle for the breeches," depicting strong women as unfairly trying to dominate their husbands.

Radicals, then, attempted to buttress their demands for parliamentary reform and universal manhood suffrage by attacking the masculinity of their aristocratic opponents, thus undermining their claims to rule. However, radicals faced the problem that their opponents attacked the idea of universal suffrage as absurd by pointing out that if people were naturally equal, women should vote as well as men.[124] The *Gorgon* feebly argued in response that "females are too much occupied by domestic affairs" to take part in politics.[125] However, Mary Ann Tocker, who braved a libel trial to expose political corruption, inspired many other women with her forthright public radicalism and even led Thomas Hardy to write anonymous letters to the *Black Dwarf* calling for women's rights.[126] Many radicals responded with surprise, ridicule, or sentimental condescension to the idea of women participating in politics. One anti-feminist, writing under the nom de plume of Roderick Random in the *Black Dwarf*, advised "sweet revolutionary termagants" to expose dandies as unmanly instead of making ridiculous demands for political rights.[127] In 1818, the *Black Dwarf* reacted to "female politicians" with an elaborate fantasy about women lawyers and clergymen, archly insinuating, "Gladly we would embrace such legislative bodies." The editor speculated that if women were given political rights, men would be allowed only to be nurses and milkmaids.[128] Clearly, they could conceive of women in politics only as an unwelcome reversal of gender hierarchy, a loss of male potency. The Paisley *Weavers Magazine and Literary Companion* was somewhat more open-minded, publishing a lively debate about the potential of women for education. Some argued that women were capable of profiting from a liberal education, which would fit them to be companions for "men of sense." But behind this apparent feminism lay a willingness to attribute the ills of the poor to women. "It is solely on account of the uninformed state of the female mind that the greater part of ill-breeding, ignorance, and immorality exists."[129] Frustrated by this hostility and ambivalence, a militant radical woman proclaimed,

> Though the rule of the sex you amply portray
> O'er the milder dominions of life:
> We had rather, believe me, our characters play
> In the national drama of life.

No more shall our masculine tyrants prevail
Or laugh at the slaves which they made us.
. . .
Torn and mangled your rights, you have ours betrayed.[130]

Conclusion

Since its inception, plebeian radicalism had encompassed two divergent traditions, Painite egalitarianism and civic humanism, which had very different implications for gender politics. Paine's notion of inherent human rights broke free from the conventions of political thought and, as the militant women discussed above realized, opened up the possibility of female citizenship. Instead of following this path, plebeian radicals combined the fraternal solidarity of their old artisan culture with the masculine rhetoric of civic humanism to demand radical male citizenship. By 1819, however, the limitations of libertine ultra-radicalism were becoming apparent. It appealed only to a specific segment of plebeian culture, metropolitan artisans, and failed to mobilize the vast majority of British working people. Some radical men began to listen to women's complaints and to reconceive their politics to include sexual cooperation. Even the *Black Dwarf*, impressed by the eloquence of anonymous female correspondents, became more hospitable to women's political activity. Finally, the tension between Painite egalitarianism and masculine ultra-radicalism began to be resolved in a way more favorable to women. Radicals began to turn away from the extremes of the old blackguard radical culture and to stress a new respectability. The Spenceans, for instance, abolished smoking, drinking, and vulgar toasts and songs. However, male radicals attacked Janet Evans, who instigated this change, as a "Dulcinea" who "wore the breeches," dominating her husband.[131]

Misogyny could not prevail against political necessity, however. Only when radicals would speak to the issues of family and work would they appeal to whole plebeian communities, women as well as men. And only then could they combat the middle-class moral offensive: when commentators attacked the poor as degraded, radicals once again celebrated domestic virtues:

> For strange to say
> These immoral brutes
> Vie even with princes in parental love
> And conjugal affection.[132]

By linking the personal to the political, radicals began to redeem—and expand—Paine's promise of egalitarianism.

9 A Wider Vision of Community, 1815–1820

The end of the war and the passage of the Corn Laws in 1815, which sent food prices and unemployment soaring, brought family issues to the forefront of radical politics. In response, radicals began to augment the notion of plebeian citizenship based on fraternal bonding around constitutional concerns to a wider conception of citizenship based on the needs of families. Lacking the clout of property ownership, radicals needed to tap the power of numbers—to replace the "public" with the "People."[1]

To create the "People" required two tasks: finding forms of organization that could mobilize plebeian communities, and inventing a political rhetoric that would speak to working people.[2] Feminist historians have suggested that women were much more likely to participate in informal, community-based actions such as food riots, defending cooperative values rather than individualist political rights. As popular movements organized formally, they argue, women faded from their ranks.[3] Yet this intriguing insight must be modified in order to understand radicalism between 1815 and 1820. While radicals, especially in the north, imbued their movement with greater discipline, they combined with that formality the old spontaneity of food riots and spectacle. As a result, not only did more women participate in the movement, but plebeian men who had been alienated by abstract constitutional arguments joined in agitation as well. Increasing formality did not necessarily exclude women; rather, in the north women's experience in organized religion, strikes, and friendly societies helped them to participate in radical activism. As radicals learned to link politics with the personal suffering that war, dearth, and famine brought to plebeian families, women as well as men, whole communities as well as individual committed activists, began to join the movement for change. In the process, radical men and women transformed their notions of masculinity and femininity.

Women and Northern Radicalism

Although economic hardship hit London too, the wider vision of radical community was particularly widespread in northern textile districts such as Manchester, Stockport, and Glasgow. Northern activists combined a concern for the issues of labor, family survival, and war with the traditional radical focus on the Constitution and the liberties of the people.[4] Clearly, this was a movement dominated by the laboring classes; although they often asked the middle and upper classes for their support they rarely received it, except from men like Cobbett and Hunt.[5] One radical journal declared, "The People are the labouring people, who produce most of the wealth, and who are facing starvation."[6]

And for the first time, radicals began to define the People as including women. For example, the weaver Samuel Bamford welcomed women's political participation and initiated a motion to allow them to vote at meetings.[7] By 1819, women had established female reform societies in Stockport, Manchester, and Blackburn.[8] In the textile villages around Glasgow, women organized to write addresses for meetings, engaging, if only as auxiliaries, in the political dialogue.[9]

The northern movement also drew sustenance from the rich infrastructure of both male and female friendly societies.[10] For instance, according to Robert Glen, in Stockport "there were thirty-seven female societies in existence at some point between 1794 and 1823, or about one-third of the total." While Glen points out that "the female groups were not noted for their extreme views on either political subjects or industrial relations," the very experience of organizing meetings themselves no doubt helped northern women set up their own radical female reform societies.[11] As early as 1813, a time when magistrates were closely scrutinizing friendly societies for radical and industrial activity, the Manchester Friendly Sisters found it necessary to fine "any member who speaks against the king or his government or against the constitution of this realm or uses any seditious language." In fact, no discussion of religion or politics was allowed, which suggests that some women members were radicals and others were not.[12] Of course, many female friendly societies existed in London as well, but male radicals were relatively uninterested in mobilizing women's support there until 1820.

Why were northern radicals able to organize women on a much more extensive basis than Londoners were? First, whereas London artisans primarily drew on the fraternal solidarity of workshop and pub or even descended into misogynist ultra-radicalism, northern textile workers knew that they depended on women's auxiliary labor in cottages and factories. As we have seen in the previous chapter, hostility toward women workers was certainly present among northern workers in the Luddism of 1811–1814 and other waves of strikes against women workers. But especially toward the end of the decade, trade unionists were learning to be more cooperative. By organizing around networks of kin, neighborhood, and community, male radicals drew women into strikes and political unions, where they could begin to integrate consciousness of economic and political concerns. For instance, Elizabeth Salt, whose spinner brother was shot by the military in Manchester in 1818, not only supported the unionization of cotton workers but inveighed against the rich, the Corn Laws, the Combination Laws, and Malthusianism.[13]

Radical religion provided another precedent for women's political activities in Lancashire and Scotland. In Scotland, women who were uninterested or uncomfortable with politics would be willing to speak on religion, thereby acquiring a voice and organizational experience which served them well when radicals finally appealed to them.[14] The tradition of female preaching was much stronger in Lancashire and Yorkshire than in London, allowing women in the north to learn to articulate their beliefs by combining political with religious rhetoric. For instance, the Manchester Female Reformers' Address of 1819 told upper-class women that "all the Prophets were Reformers, and also the Apostles; so was the great Founder of Christianity . . . and if Jesus Christ himself were to come upon the earth again, and to preach against the Church and the state, . . . his life would assuredly be sacrificed by the relentless hand of the Borough-Judases; for corruption, tyranny, and injustice, have reached their summit; and the bitter cup of oppression is now full to the brim."[15]

Another way women's participation was encouraged was in the call for abstinence from taxed "luxury" articles, which was spearheaded by Cobbett, Carlile, and Hunt.[16] In 1819, many Glasgow reformers resolved to abstain from tea, whisky, ale, and tobacco, so that they could not be insulted from the pulpit as drunken fools and would no longer have to pay taxes to their rulers. At one meeting of the local radical association, a "sinecure teapot" was produced "with the gudewife's compliments to be smashed by the leader." Women carried inverted gill stoups (whisky glasses) and teapots at demonstrations along with placards proclaiming, "No luxuries."[17]

Radicals were able to draw women into the political dialogue of radicalism through a new style of politics which combined plebeian mass action and love of theater with disciplined analysis and organization. In the process they mobilized whole communities. At a great meeting for reform in Glasgow in 1819, an observer described thousands of "men and women four and four arm and arm . . . with silken banners waving over their heads, and bundles of rods in the ends of poles emblematic of unanimity, and large brooms to sweep away corruption, and caps of liberty of all colors."[18] John Urie described a Kilmarnock meeting where "bands of men, and women, too, might be seen approaching from all directions" with banners and bagpipes, and a "cap of liberty" carried on a pole by "a masculine, good-looking amazon."[19] The weaver John Mackinnon remembered that young women marched from the weaving village of Anderston toward Glasgow with their cap of liberty, forming two of the ranks of a procession.[20] In Middleton, Lancashire, young wives and girls led the column to Peterloo, dancing and singing to the music of the accompanying bands, and "comely and decent-looking youths" parading with laurel branches were followed by men with banners and caps of liberty.[21]

When radical women presented beautifully embroidered caps of liberty to male leaders, they were clearly being used as symbols of purity and virtue, as opposed to aristocratic corruption. As James Epstein notes, radical women also depicted themselves as modest mothers reluctant to engage in politics. While it might seem that these women thus accepted a passive, ornamental political role, their actions contradicted their words.[22] Women had to use modest language because they faced vitriolic attacks for their activities. In Stockport, conservatives described female radicals as "the most degraded of the sex," engaged in "disgusting and abominable" efforts to "ruin society."[23] The anti-radical press viciously attacked the many women who had appeared at a radical meeting in Galston near Glasgow. The deceptively named *Reformer* declared, "I mourn the degradation of my country. . . . The heart sickens at the tale; women, Scottish Women! introduced on a stage to mimic the most degrading fooleries of the Poissards of Paris, during the maddest moments of revolutionary frenzy."[24] A anti-radical caricature entitled "The Belle Alliance" tried to arouse plebeian men's anxieties by grotesquely depicting female reformers donning breeches on a radical platform while, below, an emaciated man wears a shirt (see Figure 7). In a Cheap Repository Tract, an abashed radical admits, "Why I must own that since our Debby has turned speechmaker, the children are all in rags, and I can't get a clean shirt."[25]

Because male radicals had to abandon their former ambivalence about women as politicians in order to defend female reformers, their notion of women's role expanded. Even Cobbett countered the anti-radical *Courier's* misogynist invective by declaring, "Just as if women were made for nothing but to cook oatmeal and to sweep a room! Just as if women had no minds!"[26] Women's participation in politics enabled them to begin to weaken the old association of femaleness with effeminacy and weakness by creating a new notion of radical virtue. For instance, a print celebrating the

Figure 7. The Belle-Alliance, or the Female Reformers of Blackburn!!! Copyright British Museum.

Female Reformers of Manchester portrayed a heroic female figure trampling corruption.[27]

While the stress laid on virtue gave the notion of radical womanhood a vague resemblance to the middle-class concept of separate spheres, the two differed in important ways. Whereas the purity of the middle-class woman depended on her seclusion from the public sphere, radical women asserted that domestic concerns must become political issues. Echoing Spence, they declared they were forced to enter politics since their "oppressors and tyrannical rulers" had refused women their natural right to feed their children.[28] They saw themselves as responsible for their families: the Manchester Female Reformers said, "We can no longer bear to see . . . our husbands and little ones clothed in rags. . . . Dear Sisters, how could you bear to see the infant at the breast, drawing from you the remnant of your last blood, instead of the nourishment which nature requires?" The Blackburn Female Reformers combined the standard critique of the "borough-mongering system" with specific images of domestic misery: "Our houses which once bore ample testimony of our industry and cleanliness . . . are now alas! robbed of all their ornaments. . . . We cannot describe our wretchedness, for language cannot paint the feelings of a mother, when she beholds her naked children, and hears their inoffensive cries of hunger and approaching death."[29]

In some ways these women were indicating the inadequacies of the tradition of republican language to comprehend the realities of domestic life. Despite these new, more positive connotations of womanhood, female radicals still had to contend with the strong association of armed masculine might with citizenship. They sometimes apologized for their own feminine weakness, but they also sought precedents for women's military activity to fit themselves into this tradition. For instance, women aggressively demanding food for their children admitted, "We cannot boast much of female courage," but then reminded themselves, "We are not without proof in the history of women who have led armies to the field."[30] And it must be remembered that during the Napoleonic wars the exploits of female soldiers and sailors were often celebrated, providing a female fantasy of adventure and escape.[31]

Women earned their place in radical politics in 1819, when one hundred women and girls were wounded in the Peterloo massacre, a cavalry attack on a Manchester working-class meeting.[32] Mrs. Wilson, a leader of the Manchester female radical union, visited London after Peterloo to raise money for arms, where she attended "meetings at the White Horse tavern with a loaded pistol tied up in her handkerchief and threatened to use it on several occasions."[33] Yet most women were not eager to engage in armed struggle. And in late 1819 and early 1820, a turn toward insurrectionary strategies shut women out of radical activity. The Cato Street conspiracy and Glasgow uprising both failed, however, and national events soon brought women back into politics.[34]

The Queen Caroline Affair

In 1820, George III finally died and his son became George IV. Almost immediately an enormous scandal erupted when Caroline of Brunswick, the new king's long-estranged wife, returned from exile to claim her own crown. George IV started divorce proceedings against her in the House of Lords, but the bill was dropped by Parliament in November, and Caroline died of a bowel obstruction the next March.[35] The agitation around Caroline's cause is important in the history of radical politics because it provided a catalyst for three tendencies: first, it enabled radicals to develop a populist political language that could mobilize a mass movement; second, it decisively transformed radical notions of manhood; and third, it established a place in politics for women's issues as well as for women activists.

George had imported his bride from Brunswick, Germany, to entice Parliament, by the promise of an heir, to pay off his enormous gambling debts. As soon as Caroline gave birth to Princess Charlotte a year later, the couple separated. Even as George busied himself with his mistresses, he encouraged rumors that Caroline had an illegitimate child, despite the Delicate Investigation of 1806, which refuted this notion. In despair, Caroline finally went into voluntary exile in 1814. Because the prince was so unpopular and so profligate himself, Caroline became the darling of the opposition and of the populace.[36]

When Caroline returned to England in 1820, large processions, meetings, and delegations met all over Great Britain to support the Queen, and both the conventional and radical press covered the affair obsessively. The government was extremely anxious about the agitation, for, at worst, it would ignite the Jacobin republicanism that had been smoldering since the 1790s; at best, it discredited the king among those who desired a respectable monarch. Government anxiety was particularly acute in Lancashire and the Glasgow area, for plebeian anger over the Peterloo massacre and the abortive Scottish insurrection of 1820 was still high. Radicals in Lancashire both agitated for the queen and secretly made pikes for drilling at mass meetings.[37] In Lanarkshire, near Glasgow, a Mr. Grant reported that the disaffected in Lanarkshire and elsewhere were hoping that London would see an uprising on 19 July by supporters of the queen.[38] However, the government was even more worried about the broad-based, albeit uneasy, Carolinite alliances. Caroline accepted supporters ranging from Whigs interested in promoting parliamentary reform and embarrassing the government; to shopkeeper radicals such as Alderman Wood, who defended England's "traditional liberties" and Manchester dissenters; to influential populist writer William Cobbett; and to more plebeian ultra-radicals such as the shoemaker William Benbow.[39] Although the insurrectionary potential of the Caroline agitation was highest in the north, it also transformed London radical politics by finally pushing them out into the community and forcing a responsiveness to women's concerns.

The Caroline affair enabled the movement to reach beyond the thin level of committed radicals and trade unionists to mobilize huge numbers of working people.[40] The issues of the affair grew out of the long tradition of radical republicanism discussed above: the role of the king, the problems of personalized politics and corruption, and the use of Parliament in the form of the House of Lords to infringe upon subjects' liberties were all central constitutional issues.[41] However, constitutional politics had previously been somewhat too arcane and abstract for a not very well educated populace. Radicals had since the 1790s attempted to develop a more concrete, popular language to bring these issues home to the people, and the Caroline affair at last enabled them to do so successfully.[42]

In the Caroline affair, radicals learned to draw upon the vitality of plebeian popular literature to create a new political language that could speak both of high royal politics and of family crises in the same breath. Instead of trivializing radical politics, the transformation of popular literature into overt political language made mass mobilization possible. In popular forms such as nursery rhymes, melodrama, and satire, radical writers such as Cobbett and William Hone could convey their messages to a huge audience of the illiterate and the barely literate.[43] No longer were small groups of committed male radicals confined to debating republicanism in the upstairs room of a pub. Instead, mass marches of men and women together could be planned and carried out. Even the apolitical and illiterate could not avoid hearing Carolinite ballads sung on the street and seeing caricatures in printshop windows, and almost anyone could puzzle out the words of Carolinite broadsheets pasted on kitchen walls in villages all over England.[44]

The Caroline affair thus enabled radicals to create a true dialogue between leaders and the people in political rhetoric: she addressed mass meetings in speeches written by Place and Cobbett, and her supporters would respond, identifying her as a mirror of both their woes and their virtues.[45] The "Artisans, Mechanics, and Labouring Classes" of Manchester, alluding to Peterloo and economic distress, told the queen, "The same power which scourged us, is now oppressing you."[46] Caroline became an embodiment of abstract constitutional issues, somewhat like Justice or Britannia but much more vivid and concrete: the Caroline affair forced issues of gender and sexuality to the forefront. Caroline's function as a multivalent symbol allowed her radical supporters to project onto her a variety of moral interpretations in disparate genres of popular literature, from libertine satire to moralistic melodrama.[47]

Radical propaganda combined republican invective with traditional popular forms of caricature, rough music, and song. Caricatures of the king as a dandy or crowned with the cuckold's horns undermined perceptions of his manliness. Many songs and caricatures referred to the "horns" that traditionally bedecked the deceived husband and to the marrow bones and cleavers that produced the rough music to ridicule him.[48] These satires did not just point out George's failures as a husband; rather, they undermined the legitimacy of his rule, for, as we have seen, "manly virtue" was often cited in political debate.[49]

Satire and farce celebrating Caroline as a lusty, defiant wife also spoke to plebeians on both a political and a personal level.[50] While some plebeians, like the middle class, saw Caroline as a symbol of endangered purity, to others the question of her chastity was irrelevant, either because they believed philosophically in sexual freedom or because they accepted bigamy, cohabitation, and premarital pregnancy as ordinary facts of neighborhood life.[51] Some of the very radicals who joined forces with Alderman Wood had savagely criticized him the year before for repressing prostitution, which they defended as a social necessity.[52] Even many of the more respectable male radicals, from the free-thinking Richard Carlile to Cobbett, not only criticized the double standard that allowed a profligate king to put his wife on trial, but they justified Caroline's action in taking a lover. Place, who firmly believed that marital sexual intercourse was necessary to every woman's health, wrote in his unpublished memoirs, "I cared nothing for the queen as the queen, she had been ill-used by her husband . . . and all that could be said against her was that she kept a man, a fine handsome fellow, that was no concern of anybody's and if she liked to do so, it was a matter in which she ought to have been indulged in without scandal."[53] The *Examiner* defended Caroline's behavior as merely following the freer customs of the Continent and declared that the king, by his abandonment of Caroline and his flagrant adultery, had positively incited her to take a lover.[54] In his *Republican*, Carlile advanced a more Godwinian morality by writing, "If it were true she had an affair, it would be justified in the eyes of every reasonable being."[55]

These attitudes were shared on a less theoretical basis by many plebeians. One supporter of Caroline, reported an observer, "thought the Queen a whore—but he would be damned if any woman should be ill-used, whore or no whore."[56] The spy "J.N." took the liberty to warn the government that the loyalty of the soldiers was being undermined by the prostitutes of Westminster, citing as typical the woman he overheard declaring to a soldier, "Dam your Eyes if you present arms [against pro-Caroline demonstrators] you shall not come to bed to me I am for Caroline I am a whore and if she has had a chance stroke is that any reason she is not to be Queen."[57]

The Caroline affair led to a decisive change in radical manhood. While the ultra-radical libertine tradition was known for its misogyny, to take Caroline's side implied a respect for women. Unlike traditional rough music, which disciplined unruly wives, the broadsheets about Caroline defended women's rights, turning the sexual politics of popular literature upside down. In contrast to popular songs and radical satires that jokingly justified beating insubordinate wives, broadsheets supporting the queen often disapprovingly portrayed the king as a wife-beater (see Figure 8). For instance, William Benbow caricatured him as "an infirm elderly gentleman . . . lately left his home, just after dreadfully Ill-using his Wife about *half* a crown."[58] By depicting the king as a wife-beater who should submit to the magistrates himself, caricaturists reversed the usual relation of women to the law. Indeed, Benbow's caricature "The Blanket Hornpipe" shows a circle of lower-middle-class London women tossing George in a blanket—a traditional female revenge on wife-beaters.[59]

T. Wooler of the *Black Dwarf* drew upon this satirical popular tradition to celebrate belligerent wives, although with an ambivalence unsurprising considering that only a few years before he had printed satires *against* women's political participation.[60] In one issue, he noted, "There are wives who will not be frightened at their husbands—the song says, 'Women, like a thundercloud, always run against the wind.' " A few months later, he wondered

> how any of the cabinet ministers dare go home to their wives. Does not their treason to the sex, their gross insults to the claims and rights of women procure for them some troublesome curtain lectures? . . . The bad temper of the wife of a great law lord would merit praise on such occasion, if . . . she would break his head with a fish ladle.[61]

On a less overtly political level, James Catnach published a humorous sheet called "Petticoats Is Master" that, while clearly about George and Caroline, echoed women's defiantly anti-marriage songs:

> Now wives when e'er your husbands try,
> To keep you from your rights-O,

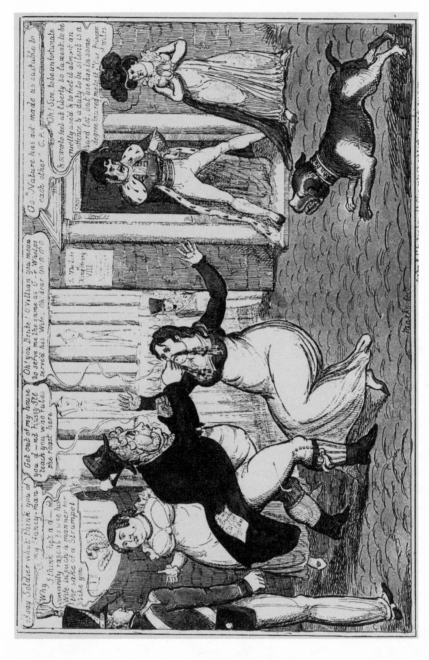

Figure 8. A R——L Example! or a Westminster Blackguard Illusing His Wife.
Treasury Solicitors 115/326, Public Record Office, Chancery Lane.

> Take my advice . . . don't sigh nor cry,
> But face him hard and tight-O,
> Then bang him in, and bang him out,
> And wap him round and round about,
> Nor flinch an inch, but make him shout,
> Oh! Petticoats is Master![62]

The dominant mood of the Caroline affair, however, was a more moralistic one, combining radical religion, melodrama, and the republican critique of aristocratic decadence. Even before Caroline's return, radical preachers had used biblical language to attack the corruption and luxury of George IV's tenure as Regent.[63] A playbill for a performance entitled *The Voice of Nature* explained that "the Moral is a Lesson to Kings, shewing them, the true road to honor is the path of virtue, and by having laws with an even balance, distributed alike to the Rich and the Poor."[64] Given the antics of the Regent at the time, asking that the monarch be virtuous could be seen as rather subversive. In fact, Scottish authorities prosecuted preacher Neil Douglas for comparing the Regent to Belshazzar, the decadent king of Babylon in the Bible. However, the aptness of the comparison made the prosecution untenable, and he was acquitted.[65] At a Middleton meeting in 1816, a mechanic declared that "it was impossible for a Reform to take place whilst the Leaders of the Constitution were going on in wantonness and lust."[66]

Melodrama also conveyed a moralism that reached beyond the religious minority to a wider public. Melodrama was already highly politicized in its portrayal of poor maidens as the embodiment of virtue and aristocratic libertines as the epitome of vice, class-laden metaphors of economic and sexual exploitation that in turn imbued political rhetoric with a deep emotional power. The image of the aristocratic libertine and the virtuous heroine who defied him was first exploited for its political connotations by late-eighteenth-century radical novelists such as Henry MacKenzie, Robert Bage, Thomas Holcroft, and Mary Wollstonecraft. By the beginning of the nineteenth century, these plots had been taken over by newly popular theatrical melodramas, which heightened their contrast between virtue and vice, purveying a deep emotionalism far removed from the Godwinian rationalism of the earlier versions.[67]

During his Regency George IV had long been described in the terms used for fictional aristocratic libertines.[68] And, as MacCalman has pointed out, "In the eyes of many ultra-radicals, Caroline was already the heroine of gothic-romantic fantasy."[69] However, some radicals, such as Francis Place, resisted this personalization of political analysis, arguing that "it is not so much a *personal* oppression under which we suffer; there is no fell monster among us, who with his satellites is deflowering our daughters, and insulting our wives; but it is a *political* oppression, a tyranny exercised over our property" through unfair taxes.[70] But such radicals abandoned these reservations in 1820 when they realized that political invective could generate mass agitation only if it used the language of popular culture.

Radical use of the popular imagery of melodrama solidified an ideal of chivalrous masculinity and began to dissolve the old misogynist libertinism. Melodrama enabled working men to imagine themselves as chivalrous heroes saving innocent maidens from aristocratic libertines, rather than as the irresponsible ruffians usually portrayed in the middle-class press. Chivalry appealed to religious and nonreligious men, to those from poor laboring backgrounds and to those with aspirations toward middle-class status. It gave the radicals needed respectability in their campaign for Caroline.

The concept of chivalrous manhood also promised to smooth over some of the gender antagonism within the culture of working people. Whereas journeyman culture had often celebrated a bachelor libertinism, scorning marriage and portraying wives as unwanted nags, chivalry promised a respectable, responsible masculine ideal. On the level of rhetoric, the Caroline affair encouraged working men to portray themselves as defenders of women against sexual exploitation and enabled radicals to appeal to both men and women. The *Black Dwarf* declared, "No man would basely forfeit the love and esteem of his wife, his daughters, his sisters, or his mistress, by calmly suffering the violation of every female right in the person of his Queen."[71] Hone wrote that the king's treatment of the queen "is a very novel case to see a woman publicly insulted by a man. . . . The ruffians who attack them, meet with no quarter; they are object of general odium and contempt; they are hunted from society; they are known only amongst us, by the designation of MONSTERS."[72]

Chivalry, however, entailed a portrayal of women as weak and in need of protection, a picture incongruous with other images of Caroline as plucky and adventurous. Hone's call for a manly defense of the queen came straight out of the rhetoric of separate spheres: "The beauty—the goodness—the very helplessness of the sex are so many . . . sacred calls on the assistance of every manly and courageous arm."[73]

The many plebeian women who ardently supported Caroline tried to create for themselves a more dignified political role than that of glorified termagant or of passive victim of melodrama.[74] Cobbett noted that when Caroline made her way to the House of Lords to stand trial, "Hundreds of women were seen crying in the streets; and . . . these tears came from those who have been despitefully and insolently termed the 'lower orders.' "[75] The Caroline affair not only provided an arena for criticism of the double

standard, but it expanded the possibilities for women's political participation. Radical women organized ceremonial deputations to the queen,
garnering, for a laudatory address, as many as 17,642 signatures from
the "married ladies of London."[76] In the north, female friendly societies
named themselves after her.[77] A Liverpool newspaper disapprovingly reported on a procession of over five thousand men and women celebrating
Caroline's victory, "for we have our clubs of women as well as men."[78]

The Caroline affair justified women's entry into the political dialogue
and enabled them to speak on the problems of war and depression. The
married female inhabitants of Halifax, for instance, celebrated Caroline's
innocence and mourned the loss of their husbands and sons "in the wars
of ambition, and the battles of false glory."[79] A few women began to write
popular ballads and pamphlets. For instance, Eliza Treager declared in a
song printed by the commercial publisher John Pitts,

> Now's the time and now's the hour
> When England's Queen with legal power,
> Shall crush her foes and on them shower,
> Revenge from Caroline.[80]

In turn, male radicals tried to appeal to women, as in the pamphlet *The
Queen and the Magna Charta* (1820), which bears a frontispiece dedicated
"to the ladies of Great Britain" and depicts Britannia with a banner inscribed, "To assert the Rights of Man / To avenge the Wrongs of Woman."

The Caroline affair brought not only women but women's concerns into
the center of the dialogue of radical rhetoric. During the Peterloo era they
supported their husbands' grievances and expressed concern for their children, but the Caroline affair enabled them to speak to their own rights in
marriage. Caroline herself declared to the female inhabitants of Beverley,
"My own sex are more particularly interested in my triumph over my
enemies. If my matrimonial rights are illegally annulled, theirs eventually
may be rendered less secure."[81] The "Ladies of Edinburgh" responded,

> The principles and doctrines now advanced by your accusers, do not
> apply to your case alone, but if made part of the law of the land may
> hereafter be applied as a precedent from every careless and dissi-
> pated husband to rid himself of his wife, however good and innocent
> she may be; and to render his family, however amiable, illegitimate,
> thereby destroying the sacred bond of matrimony, and rendering
> all domestic felicity very uncertain.[82]

Catnach published a song asking British women to support the queen:

> Attend ye virtuous British wives,
> Support your injur'd Queen,

> Assert her rights; they are your own,
> As plainly could be seen.
> Could you sustain the injuries,
> Your Queen has undergone?
> You answer no, her cause is yours,
> Then make her cares your own.[83]

The popularity of defenses of Caroline's purity inhibited a more open emergence of a radical critique of chastity, but this female activism should not therefore be seen as conservative. The ideology of separate spheres upheld the double standard and counseled women to accept their woes in submissive silence. Caroline's supporters instead took to the political sphere and to the streets.

Plebeian women defended their own dignity in defending Caroline against opponents who portrayed them and her as unwomanly amazons, viragos, illiterates, and prostitutes. The *Morning Post* described the women who presented addresses to her as "shameless females, who tearing off the veil of modesty with unprecedented audacity, insulted the King." An indignant "Englishwoman" wrote to the same journal that Caroline's supporters were the sort of women who declare, "Our sex have as much right to yours to liberty and I am for the rights of Women forever."[84]

In contrast, Caroline's plebeian supporters drew upon their own culture's definitions of female character. While defending Caroline's chastity, they refused to accept sexual purity as the sole definition of female virtue. Like those London female shopkeepers and servants who sheltered prostitutes and unmarried women, they felt compassion for Caroline's fate. In fact, they reversed the former negative connotations of *effeminacy* (as in "the effeminate aristocracy") by celebrating a womanhood that encompassed the virtues of courage as well as purity.

Popular literature about Caroline drew not only upon the stereotype of the passive victim of the aristocratic libertine but upon a tradition of female heroism exemplified by ballads with titles like "The Undaunted Female" and "Female Intrepidity."[85] *The Magic Lantern*, a pamphlet by "A Wild Irish Woman," evokes the female sailor ballads of the time in describing the queen's return to England:

> So great was the hurry of England's sad Queen
> That she ran up the ropes as a sailor she'd been;
> And took instant possession of a vessel to carry
> Her and her friends, not one moment to tarry.[86]

In a broadsheet entitled "Character of the Queen," Benbow portrayed Caroline's travels to the Middle East as a bold adventure in search of knowledge during which "she encountered difficulties, toils and dangers, such as no human being ever before voluntarily encountered; and in cases of the greatest peril, when even sailors were alarmed, she was never known to discover fear."[87] Another caricature portrayed her as the Celtic warrior queen "Boadicia, overthrowing her enemies."[88]

Radicals held up Caroline's courage and supposed education as models for other women to emulate. Benbow, for example, published another broadsheet entitled "Glorious Deeds of Women" that cited Joan of Arc, Charlotte Corday, and biblical heroines as precedents for Caroline and as examples for women to follow.[89] In response, Caroline lauded the "superior degree of intellectual cultivation" recently acquired by English females, and she stressed women's rationality.[90] The descriptions of Caroline as a rational, educated, adventurous, and courageous woman went far beyond the limitations of the femininity prescribed by the doctrine of separate spheres. Anne Cobbett, William's daughter, described Caroline as " a real *good woman*, kind, charitable, feeling and condescending toward every creature, she possesses wonderful courage, presence of mind, fortitude, promptness in action. . . . She is very industrious."[91] As a crossing sweeper told Mayhew in 1850, "She was a woman, she was."[92]

Yet the iconography of the Caroline affair never challenged the fundamental principles of sexual difference, but only expanded the limits of womanhood. Above all, Caroline was regarded as a mother, and women identified with her forcible separation from her daughter and her bereavement at her daughter's death in 1817. But she was a heroic mother; a caricature entitled "Oh My Mother!" portrays her standing between Britannia and the British lion defending her daughter as Charlotte ascends to heaven pursued by politicians flinging arrows of lust, greed, and corruption.[93]

On one level, this celebration of motherhood was rather conventional, enabling women to organize politically without emulating Mary Wollstonecraft's radical sexual stance. But on another level the agitation over Caroline expanded and politicized notions of motherhood just as the actions of radical female reformers at Peterloo had.[94] "Females of Newcastle on Tyne," writing to the *Black Dwarf*, lauded the queen's rationality and courage while defining their own roles as "wives, mothers, and daughters . . . cherishing those sentiments of respect for the sacred principles of religion, justice, and humanity."[95]

Conclusion

Radical politics did begin by excluding women, but it eventually broadened its scope to include them. First, Painite notions of citizenship could allow for female participation based on reason, a precedent which allowed female intellectuals to join in the movement. Second, the radical conception of politics was widened. Working men simply could not restrict themselves to abstract constitutional issues; hunger and poverty were important issues for them as well as for women and children. Third, excluded from the middle-class masculine public sphere, radicals were forced to draw upon the power of numbers, mobilizing male and female members in neighborhoods and workplaces. The masculine "public" was transformed into a "People" composed of both women and men. Radicalism flourished by creating a political dialogue between activists and people, by speaking in a popular voice and also responding to people's concerns.

To be sure, after Caroline's death women's political participation once again diminished. But their activity in 1820 and 1821 set an important precedent for women's participation in later political dialogues. Radicals could not marginalize women in the Caroline affair, for their own issues had mobilized the populace. Yet women were not *just* defending "traditional communal morality"; rather, they were, in an inchoate way, hoping for a revision of traditional values. In defending Queen Caroline's rights as an abused wife, radicals were admitting that the rights of women were a political issue. In speaking to women's sense of victimization and holding up a manly ideal of chivalry rather than libertinism, the propaganda for Caroline promised a new harmony between working men and women, a resolution of the sexual antagonism that plagued them. But it also *displaced* this sexual antagonism onto the royal marital woes instead of directly addressing the problems of marital misery in plebeian culture.

However, the agitation decisively shifted radical men away from a misogynist libertinism toward the chivalrous ideal. Even in London, radical activists and trade unionists found that the ideal of chivalry and the cult of domesticity were potent tools for propaganda. In the north, although misogyny and sexual competition continued occasionally to rear their ugly heads, radicals and trade unionists stressed cooperation between the sexes, casting women in the role of valued auxiliaries. Most important, the Caroline affair brought into full flower the trend toward augmenting the abstract political discourse of citizenship with an inclusive political rhetoric of community, drawing upon people's experiences of family breakdown, unemployment, and hunger and transforming them through popular metaphors into a message of mingled hope and anger.

3

DOMESTICITY AND THE MAKING OF THE WORKING CLASS, 1820 -1850

By the 1820s and 1830s, contemporaries began to refer to "the working class" or "the working classes," and this section will follow that usage. However, this is not to imply that working people had begun to share common experiences or that they lived in an autonomous class culture. Rather, the working class was first defined in negative terms when Parliament passed the Reform Act of 1832, which enfranchised the middle class while deliberately excluding working men. E. P. Thompson ends his *Making of the English Working Class* at this point, arguing that the trade union and political strands of the radical movement had finally come together, enabling working men to react by creating their own class consciousness.[1] But he had been criticized for concentrating on artisanal leadership.[2] In contrast, the Marxist-Leninist John Foster celebrates northern industrial workers as the fierce proto-socialist vanguard bent on seizing state power, but he seems confused by the fact that so many of his ideal proletariat were female textile workers.[3]

By incorporating gender and extending our examination of the making of the working class from the 1820s forward into the 1840s, a more open-ended view of class formation can be obtained. The "working class" should not be seen as an ideal theoretical construct, but as an ever-changing creation of radicals choosing from different strategies in their attempts to unite working people. Owenite socialists had begun to advocate an egalitarian vision of society, challenging conventional sexual morality, denouncing tyranny in marriage, organizing women along with men, and demanding truly universal suffrage.[4] Yet Owenites remained a tiny minority among working people. Trade unionists, factory activists, and radical republicans tried instead to unite the working class, by adopting a notion of domesticity, demanding access to the public sphere for working men and protection in the private realm for their women.

Why did domesticity prove so much more persuasive than Owenite egalitarianism? After all, textile communities and northern activists had already begun to pioneer the incorporation of women into radical movements, and many plebeians could not or would not conform to conventional morality. And the idea of domesticity—that men should go out into the public world while sheltering their wives in the home—was not indigenous to plebeian culture, in which both husbands and wives had been expected to contribute to the family economy. Nor did middle-class moralists impose it from above as part of an effort to co-opt radical movements, for the middle class believed poor women's work to be both virtuous and desirable—and they refused to admit working men to the privileges of the public sphere.

By stopping in 1832, E. P. Thompson omits the ways in which gendered notions of political and economic virtue contributed to the negative definition of the working class. Malthusians depicted unchecked working-class procreation as the cause of overpopulation and unemployment. This philosophy informed the New Poor Law of 1834, which separated husbands from wives and parents from children in grim workhouses. Political economy justified Parliament's failure in 1833 to pass effective legislation to protect poor women and children from the abuses of the factory system.

The struggles against the New Poor Law and the factory system mobilized many working people beyond the narrow band of urban artisan radicals, incorporating women, textile workers, and the unskilled into the working-class movement. Yet the egalitarian potential of this broad-based coalition faded when radicals adopted the rhetoric of domesticity to defend working-class families. To be sure, the libertine satires inherited from the Queen Caroline affairs and the sexual radicalism of the Owenites lost their persuasive power when the New Poor Law and the reformed Parliament seemed to undermine the right of the poor to family life. Therefore radicals stole the notion of domesticity from middle-class moralists and manipulated it to demand the privileges of separate spheres for working-class, as well as middle- and upper-class, men and women. Domesticity proved to be a potent rhetorical weapon—but also a double-edged sword.

10   Sexual Radicalism and the Pressure of Politics

In the 1820s, radicals began to pay serious attention to the sexual crisis which had plagued working people for decades. To resolve the conflict between sexual pleasure and the difficulty of supporting children in hard economic times, some radicals promulgated birth control information. Owenite socialists addressed endemic marital conflict by attacking the inequality and exploitation of women in patriarchal marriage. Yet working people—and the working-class movement as a whole—soon rejected these ideas. Why? These were not wild-eyed schemes dreamed up by intellectuals distant from the realities of working-class life. In both instances, radicals drew upon the experiences of working people in love, sex, and marriage to propose solutions not far removed from the existing popular culture. After all, large sectors of plebeian society frankly accepted sexual pleasure, and the common motif of the "struggle for the breeches" presented marital conflict as a tussle for power. Yet issues of morality had always divided plebeian society, with some rejecting libertinism in favor of religion. True, some plebeians had enjoyed sexual freedom, but many others, especially women, experienced cohabitation, bigamy, and unmarried parenthood as traumatic tragedies. As Barbara Taylor eloquently points out, the increasingly hard economic times left women simply too vulnerable to challenge the security of conventional morals and marriage.[1] This chapter does not explore changes in sexual attitudes on the personal level, but it is clear that these experiences of uncertainty influenced working people's willingness to accept radical ideas about sexuality.

This chapter concentrates on the political reasons why sexual radicalism could not succeed in the 1820s or 1830s, although sexuality and marriage became important political issues at that time. Radicals' critique of conventional morality stemmed from their analysis of society as a whole. Yet

179

middle-class moralists identified plebeian promiscuity as symptomatic of working people's general indiscipline. James Kay Shuttleworth, for instance, linked the "source of social discontent and political disorder" in congested large towns with "the moral leprosy of vice."[2] Political economists defined the middle class as self-controlled and virtuous and the working class as animalistic and depraved.[3] And dominating the debate was the increasingly influential doctrine of Malthus. As Thomas Laqueur writes, "Thomas Malthus made the seemingly irrepressible power of sexual desire the central axiom of his work on population."[4]

Malthus pessimistically argued that the population would inexorably outstrip the means of subsistence.[5] Influenced by Malthus, David Ricardo and others promulgated the "iron law of wages," which held that there was a limited fund available for wages in a capitalist economy. If wages were too high, workers would marry early and produce many children, whom they would train in their trade, thus overstocking the labor supply, and inevitably driving wages down. At first Malthus pessimistically believed that vice and misery were inevitable consequences of an uncontrollable drive to procreate, for working people could do nothing to avoid their fate. Eventually, Malthus and his followers grudgingly admitted that by employing "moral restraint"—delaying marriage or forgoing it—working people could improve their lives, although only by sacrificing family love.[6] To enforce this program, many Malthusians, following their master, believed the Poor Law should be abolished altogether, for relief artificially fed those for whom there was, in Malthus's words, "no room at nature's table," depriving the rest of their due and encouraging the poor to reproduce.[7] A program of that severity was politically impossible, but even before the New Poor Law was passed in 1834, several proposals in Parliament attempted to introduce Malthusian principles by sharply restricting relief. In 1817, the Committee on the Poor Law assumed that a subsistence wage should allow a man to feed only himself and two children. Any additional children should be sent to the workhouse and fed on bread and water, thereby freeing their mother to work for wages.[8]

A harsh religious morality infused these economic prescriptions. Evangelicals such as Glasgow minister Thomas Chalmers intertwined political economy with the doctrine of atonement, proclaiming that only suffering would ensure moral salvation. It was the sin of sexual self-indulgence that caused working-class poverty, they believed, rather than low wages or unemployment.[9] To oppose Malthusianism and the social policies it inspired, radicals had to develop a rhetoric about the family, sex, and marriage that could repudiate these insulting images as well as unite working-class men and women with disparate moral views. The importance of sexual symbolism in the struggle against Malthusianism eventually overshadowed the radical desire to challenge conventional morality.

Radicalism, Sexuality, and Birth Control

The Malthusian prescription that working people must forego or delay sex and matrimony offended many radicals, who had long complained that hard times prevented poor people from marrying. Many working people believed that having children was a human right and that sexual activity was necessary for health. Yet radicals often recognized as well that sexuality was problematic for working people: too many children caused hardship, and bitterly disintegrating marriages brought heartache. They disagreed, however, on the solution. For some, the answer was to transgress the boundaries of conventional morality; rooted in the libertine subculture, ultra-radicals advocated prostitution as a palliative for delayed marriage, and a few even kept brothels and published pornography to raise cash.[10] However, after radicals succeeded in capitalizing on Queen Caroline's image of sexual purity, libertinism became an underground, marginal current within the movement. The more respectable, self-improving strain of radicalism began to dominate the alternative politics of sex. For instance, radicals Francis Place and Richard Carlile supported birth control, not out of libertinism, but because they believed in "liberal enlightenment ideas of individual freedom and social utility," as Iain McCalman notes.[11]

Francis Place, a prosperous tailor whose radical roots reached back to the London Corresponding Society, tried to apply political economy to benefit working people. He believed firmly that the only way laborers could improve themselves was by restricting the labor supply. But he rejected Malthus's claim that "a man has no right to exist, if another man cannot or will not employ him."[12] The poor, he claimed, were neither more nor less dissolute than the upper class. In an age when journeymen could no longer hope to become masters and artisans often found their skills obsolete, no matter how long they waited they would never attain the economic security desirable for marriage, since wages would not increase with age and savings were impossible on subsistence earnings. If working men could use contraception to control their fertility, they could marry early, which would in turn improve morality by preventing fornication.[13] Place circulated handbills and published articles in the *Black Dwarf* and the *Trades' Newspaper* claiming, in addition, that if the poor could use birth control they could control the labor supply and have more time to press for political reform.[14]

On the surface, it would not seem that Place's proposal would have been foreign to plebeian moralities. The Malthusian and Evangelical advocacy of celibacy certainly did not appeal to many working people, who were accustomed to common-law marriage and premarital sex.[15] Despite Place's ascent into respectability, he retained some elements of plebeian culture, believing, for instance, that sexual intercourse was necessary for health—perhaps especially so for women.[16] His birth control handbill declared that among "healthy married people sexual intercourse is unavoidable, as it is wholesome and virtuous."[17] He believed that virginity was harmful to women and led to "disorders of the uterus" and that women who married late produced weak children.[18]

Control of fertility had always been an issue for working people, for many unmarried couples separated when the woman became pregnant, and in times of unemployment an addition to the family could be a burden rather than a joy even for the married. Plebeians tried a variety of contraceptive methods to control fertility. Condoms were too expensive, but working people often practiced withdrawal.[19] Place claimed that working people, especially the journeymen tailors whom he knew very well, often resorted to abortion, although only crude poisons and instruments were available.[20]

To give the working class a somewhat more effective and certainly a safer means of birth control than abortion, Place distributed handbills that provided information on how to use a vaginal sponge soaked with vinegar or lemon. After he started circulating these tracts, Place received letters from working men around the country who were sympathetic to birth control. For instance, William Longson, a Manchester weaver, wrote to agree with Place that mentioning the parts of generation in discussing birth control was not immoral, for the information would permit early marriages.[21] A journeyman shoemaker from Norwich asked Carlile for birth control information because he could not support even the four children he already had. An anonymous old man remembered that in his village women had for forty years taken something to "have as many or as few children as they liked," but unfortunately he did not know what the substance was.[22]

Place's moral values derived not only from plebeian experience but from the principles of the Philosophic Radicals. He was a disciple of the utilitarian philosopher Jeremy Bentham, who believed in political economy but, unlike so many of his contemporaries, rejected Evangelicalism in favor of total rationalism. Unlike most radicals, Bentham also repudiated the notion of "nature"—there was for him no such thing as natural rights or natural morality, only the principle of utility, the determination of what would bring the greatest happiness to the greatest number. This logic led Bentham to conclude that sodomy should be decriminalized: he could find no rationale for its prohibition, since same-sex love did not increase the population.[23] Many plebeian radicals, however, were strongly attached to the romantic notion of "nature," from which followed natural rights and natural needs. For instance, Place had to overcome Carlile's objection that birth control was "unnatural." Place responded, echoing Bentham, that "it is prejudice and not reason to talk of Natural and Unnatural as you have done. . . . Nature is a blind dirty old toad, and must be met with reason when she is likely to do harm to mankind."[24]

Carlile, eventually convinced by these utilitarian arguments, wrote and published *Every Woman's Book, or What Is Love*, which gave working people information about birth control. However, unlike Place, who wholeheartedly believed in separate spheres and militantly advocated the exclusion of women from waged labor, Carlile espoused a relatively feminist philosophy of birth control, especially as the 1820s ended. Birth control, he argued, would improve women's position because it would encourage early marriage, allowing women to indulge their sexual appetites without fear of dangerous abortions or unwanted pregnancies, and providing men with an alternative to frequenting prostitutes. Carlile valued women as colleagues in his struggle for the freedom of the press, asking them to assist in his shop and to sell unstamped, therefore illegal, periodicals in the streets. Susanna Wright, for instance, a Nottingham lace-seller, eloquently defended Carlile's publications in court and unflinchingly advocated birth control and women's rights.[25] While Carlile was imprisoned, his wife ran the business. Their marriage, however, was very unhappy, and he eventually left to form a free union with feminist Eliza Sharples.[26]

Carlile's philosophy on gender combined the ultra-radical with the traditional. On the one hand, he denied the importance of sexual difference: to the philosopher, men and women "vary . . . but little as to external form or internal character. He finds they possess the same passions, have the same desires, live by the same means with the difference of the female body being the body qualified to breed." According to Angus McLaren, Carlile's advocacy of birth control derived from his anticlericalism; Carlile believed that women should control their own destinies rather than submit to "God's plan."[27] But on the other hand, he retained a belief in "nature," arguing that birth control would prevent "unnatural gratifications" such as onanism and pederasty.[28]

Place and Carlile, however, could never free birth control from its association with Malthusianism, which most working people found insulting. Children were an economic asset, especially in textile districts, and, more important, they provided meaning in working people's lives. The assumption of Malthusian political economy that laboring people should breed or not breed according to economic circumstances reduced them to the level of animals, a metaphor that had been politically charged ever since Burke had denigrated them as the "swinish multitude."[29] To discourage working people from procreating was to deny them their humanity, to imply that they were not worth reproducing. Even though Place and Carlile denounced Malthus's and Bentham's more cold-blooded theories, birth control still went against the centrality of fatherhood and motherhood to working-class identity. Unlike Carlile, working people associated birth control with prostitution and "unnatural acts" such as sodomy. When Place had some young men distribute his birth control handbills at a market to the wives and daughters of mechanics and tradesmen, alleged the *Trades' Newspaper*, "an indignant crowd" dragged the men to a magistrate.[30] Characteristically, William Cobbett violently denounced Carlile's and Place's birth control tracts as "diabolical" and "monstrous" for "teaching young women to be prostitutes before they are married."[31] Instead, Cobbett celebrated the "natural" morality of early marriage among rosy-cheeked village lads and lasses obeying the Bible's admonition to be "fruitful and multiply."[32] Carlile's defense of pornographic publishers' freedom of speech (despite his austere disapproval of their works) and his inclusion of a naked Adam and Eve on the cover of *Every Woman's Book* must have offended the many deeply religious members of the radical culture.[33]

For many radical women who defined their political role as that of militant mothers defending their families, birth control violated their raison d'être and threatened their reputation. When Place sent his handbills to Mary Fildes, a Stockport radical leader, hoping that as a community leader she would spread his doctrines, she responded by sending the tracts to the attorney general and wrote that "as a woman, a *Wife*, and a *Mother*, . . . I feel indignant at the insult that has been offered to me."[34] Birth control also insulted the vigorously heterosexual manhood of ultra-radicalism, which had turned away from bachelor misogyny to a celebration of marriage and fatherhood. In 1821, the *Black Dwarf* satirized Malthus, declaring that his policies would lead to a "board of emasculation in every parish . . . to take care that Nature did not break through the provision of an act of Parliament."[35]

Anti-Malthusian radicals denounced birth control as just another upper-class vice, "unnatural" and akin to sodomy. The *Black Dwarf* alleged that birth control advocates "are preparing the way for further experiments which may end in the grossest abominations; and extend the infamous practices which have so shamefully disgraced so many *ornaments* of the *church*, and pillars of the *state*."[36] Here the *Black Dwarf* was referring to the recent scandal in which the bishop of Clogher, a prominent member of the Society for the Suppression of Vice, had been caught having sex with a guardsman.[37] Reporting on the exposure of a homosexual pub, the Barley Mow, in 1825, the *Trades' Newspaper* editorialized that the "indignation" at sodomy exhibits a "manliness of feeling" which should extend to repudiating "the advocates and eulogists of certain practices for regulating the population of the country."[38] Carlile's former shopman, William Haley, who turned conservative, accused Place of turning male youths into "catamites" and females into prostitutes, of employing "emasculated wretches" and associating with someone notorious for "unnatural practices."[39]

Radicals also opposed birth control on more philosophical and political grounds. The *Black Dwarf* argued, "It is not by diminishing their numbers, but by sharpening their intellects, that the condition of the human race is to be bettered."[40] A correspondent in the *Trades' Newspaper* tried to make a distinction between private and public issues. Place and Malthus, he claimed, "would reduce the whole matter to a question between Mechanics and their sweethearts and their wives; but . . . the whole matter rather resolves itself into a question between the employed and their employers . . . between the taxpayers and the tax inflictors." Another correspondent wrote that Place "diverts [Labour's] thoughts from the inhuman use of machinery, monopoly and paper money, to which ALONE they owe their sufferings."[41] The effort to restrict sexual and marital issues to an apolitical private sphere was doomed to failure, however, among working people. The hegemony of Malthusianism, with its attack on the reproductive lives of laboring people, meant that working-class activists had to confront the politics of private life.

Owenism and the Radical Attack on Patriarchal Marriage

The most radical challenge to conventional ideas about the class system and relationships between men and women came from the Owenites. Owenism was at once a visionary, "scientific" scheme and an articulation of the experiences of sexual freedom and sexual antagonism within plebeian culture. Owenites attacked inequality in every sphere, blaming it all on the selfish spirit of capitalism, private property, and patriarchal marriage. They wished to replace that spirit with a more communal, loving ethos. To transform society, they founded utopian communes, and they also spread their doctrines more widely through trade union organization and publications such as the *Pioneer*. The founder of Owenism, factory owner Robert Owen, and his son, Robert Dale Owen, advocated birth control. They believed that sexuality was natural and healthy, in women as well as in men. Carlile and the Owenites also advocated free unions instead of conventional ties, as a way to avoid the unhappiness of failed yet inescapable marriages.[42]

By the early 1830s these ideas had spread beyond the rather advanced circles of déclassé intellectuals to proletarian radicals, as cooperative socialism became a working-class endeavor independent of Owen. In 1830, Owenite marriage ideas reached Glasgow when William Cameron, a working-class radical, preached there on the "Evils and Remedies of Domestic Life."[43] Owen's 1835 tract, *Lectures on the Marriages of the Priesthood in the Old Immoral World*, spread these doctrines widely across Britain. Benjamin Gray lectured in Glasgow in 1836 that men and women should be "drawn by the silken cords of affection, and bound only by the strong feeling of moral duty."[44]

Owenite sexual radicalism was not a foreign importation but a political articulation of existing practice in working-class culture. Cohabitation and marital separation were widely practiced and accepted among many sectors of plebeian society.[45] In recognition of this situation, Benjamin Gray, for instance, wanted to modify the existing Scottish practice of irregular marriages by allowing registration of both marriages and divorces with legal officers.[46] However, Owen's ideas could also appeal to the libertine strain within plebeian culture, with their focus on the harmful effects of suppressing sexuality, especially male sexuality, since, as Barbara Taylor insightfully points out, Owen described sexuality as a "natural force . . . beyond the control of human will," and attacked "compulsory monogamy" for thwarting the natural affections.[47]

The Owenite critique of marriage took on a feminist tone. Although Owen himself was not particularly feminist, his followers Anna Wheeler and Richard Thompson had begun to publish devastating attacks on marital unhappiness in the 1820s, comparing women to West Indian slaves, denouncing masculine tyranny, and presenting the gain of women's political rights as the solution to sexual woes.[48] As working people began to debate marriage in Owenite periodicals, complaints that had been articulated only in the popular language of the "struggle for the breeches" now acquired a political voice. Eliza Sharples, for instance, declared that women deserved the suffrage because they were "subject to more abuses than the men."[49] In contrast to the defensive attitude of the *Trades' Newspaper*, which urged wives to be submissive, domestic, apolitical creatures,[50] Owenite periodicals repudiated violent husbands and gave women a forum. Whereas the struggle for the breeches validated male dominance and ridiculed women's resistance, Owenites took gender inequality in marriage seriously. James Morrison linked violence with the unequal living standards of plebeian husbands and wives, writing that a working man could "go to a coffee house every night, and read the papers," keeping half his wages for himself, while his wife "is working from morning till night at housekeeping. . . . Her wages come from her husband, and they are optional. . . . If she complain, he can damn and swear."[51] He repudiated working men's "tyrannical power" over their wives and pointed out that "an operative may thrash his wife with impunity."[52] "Zero" in the *Crisis* compared women to black slaves, because both groups could legally be beaten.[53] Women themselves also wrote to the *Pioneer* revealing their marital unhappiness; as one complained, not only must she slave for subsistence, but "if she offers the least resistance [to her husband], it is thrust down her throat with his fist."[54] "Gertrude," another correspondent, believed marriages would be happier if "man [would] try and remain satisfied with a more domestic life" instead of neglecting his wife by frequenting endless meetings.[55]

Yet Owenite periodicals set out assertions of women's woes alongside misogynist attacks on women as vain, ignorant creatures who held back the working-class movement.[56] And the Owenite critique of marriage and conventional sexual morality itself failed to appeal to large numbers of women. Many working-class women reacted angrily to Owenites who criticized conventional marriage; a group of Paisley women, for example, insulted and stoned a female Owenite lecturer.[57] In a time of economic depression, they were simply too vulnerable to desertion by lovers and husbands to afford to embrace such a doctrine. Owenite free love could be seen as a political excuse for plebeian libertines to carry on as they had always done—seducing and abandoning poor women.[58] The Owenites could not heal the wounds of unhappy marriages and the confusion caused by clashing moralities and hard times.

The New Poor Law

Whatever position individual working people might have taken on the marriage question, the brutal imposition of the 1834 New Poor Law forced them on the defensive, cutting off any possibility that the Owenite critique on marriage could gain a wider radical resonance, for opposing the New Poor Law required radicals to defend working-class morality rather than undermine its shaky foundations.

Influenced by Malthusianism, the New Poor Law represented a dramatic change from the previous system. Under the old Poor Law, the poor could receive "outdoor relief" of a loaf of bread or a few shillings, enabling them to remain in their homes and keep their families together. Although the old Poor Law was admittedly an imperfect, ramshackle, expensive system, it embodied the principle that the poor had at least a minimal right to relief. Its irrationality and cost, however, appalled many Malthusians. Utilitarians such as Edwin Chadwick knew that political reality prevented them from doing away with poor relief altogether, but they hoped a severe reform would rationalize the system. The New Poor Law enshrined the Benthamite notion of "less eligibility," which meant that the living standard of a pauper receiving state relief should be less than that of the poorest independent laborer. By mandating that the poor could receive relief only in austere workhouses, where they would be fed a diet carefully calibrated barely to keep them alive, the promulgators of the reform intended to deter the poor from asking for assistance.[59] The basic premise of the New Poor Law seemed to be that paupers had only the most tenuous right to subsistence, and no right at all to a family life. This represented a dramatic and, to working people, a shocking change from the old Poor Law.

The problem of overpopulation, which was blamed on "improvident marriages," motivated the creators of the New Poor Law. Both Evangelicals, who denounced sexual indulgence as a sin, and Utilitarians, who feared that reproduction would overstock the labor supply, believed that the workhouse system should deter the poor from marrying and reproducing.[60] Poor Law officials could no longer give family allowances or admit some children into a workhouse while the rest of the family stayed at home. Relief could be granted only if the entire family sold all its possessions and entered the workhouse. The regulations separating wives from husbands and children from parents ostensibly saved expense but really followed Malthus by attempting to prevent couples from producing infant paupers.[61] Pat Thane argues that the New Poor Law embodied the concept of the "stable two-parent family, primarily dependent upon the father's wage," and the notion that the "poverty of women and children was thought to be remediable by the increased earnings of husbands and fathers."[62] While Thane is certainly correct to argue that the New Poor Law slighted the problems of deserted, widowed, and single mothers by assuming they would be dependent on a man, the New Poor Law cannot be said to support the breadwinner wage. Granting working men higher wages, even to support a family, would have violated the principle of the iron law of wages and encouraged marriage. The Poor Law reformers wanted to deter the poor from marrying and having children in the first place. Only those men who could somehow earn enough to support a family should take a wife; otherwise they should be content to remain low-paid bachelors.

For Benthamite Nassau Senior, preventing births in general was more important than preventing bastardy, so he opposed the old system of encouraging unmarried fathers to marry the mother of their children. Previously, any pregnant woman whose child was likely to become chargeable to the parish could appear before a magistrate and swear its paternity. Parish officials would compel the father of the illegitimate child to contribute to its support, usually levying two shillings a week. If he refused to pay, they could jail him or (although illegally) force him to marry her. Senior believed that such marriages would produce large numbers of legitimate pauper children. He therefore wrote a clause freeing unmarried fathers from any obligation to support their children and instead requiring the mothers to go into prison-like workhouses to receive relief.[63] Senior's bastardy clause, primarily motived by Bentham, gained support from Evangelicals, who believed women should pay for their sins.[64] Defending the bastardy clause in Parliament, Bishop Blomfield claimed that it was the "law of God" that an unmarried mother should bear a heavier burden than the father.[65]

The Poor Law commissioners believed it was futile to attempt to restrain male licentiousness through legislation, yet they depicted unmarried mothers as "shameless and unprincipled" harlots who blackmailed rich men and oppressed poor men, completely disregarding the function of the old Poor Law in enforcing the plebeian custom that marriage followed betrothal and sexual activity.[66] While they regarded unmarried fathers as victims in this context, in general they depicted the poor as animalistic and irrational: "Can we wonder if the uneducated are seduced into approving a system which aims its allurements at all to the weaker parts of our nature—which offers marriage to the young, security to the anxious, ease to the lazy, and impunity to the profligate?"[67]

Working people protested violently against the New Poor Law, especially its bastardy clauses.[68] Only Francis Place's and William Lovett's London Working Men's Association, impelled by their alliance with the utilitarian Philosophic Radicals, even tepidly and temporarily supported the acts. The ultra-radical *London Democrat* warned that metropolitan men were ignoring the dangers of the New Poor Law, the unstamped radical press fiercely denounced the act, the various London Chartist organizations included opposition in their manifestos, and parish officials and radicals united to mount many protest meetings.[69]

Northerners opposed the introduction of the New Poor Law in 1837 in a much more violent, yet organized, fashion. Following on the heels of the agitation for factory acts, paternalist gentlemen such as Richard Oastler and John Fielden initially formed the anti–Poor Law movement. But skilled workers, and even female operatives such as Eliza Dixon, joined in as well.[70] As Cecil Driver writes, "Chapels and public houses in remote villages rang to the denunciation of itinerant speakers while Oastler and Bull . . . led demonstrations in the larger towns," with rhetoric such as Oastler's "Damnation, Damnation, to the fiend-begotten, coarser-food New Poor Law."[71]

Working-class radical men feared the New Poor Law would emasculate them and reduce them to the level of animals. As the London Democratic Association declared in its manifesto of 1838, the "accursed New Poor Law" sprung from a "pretended philosophy that crushes, through the bitter privations inflicted upon us, the energies of our manhood, making our hearts desolate, our homes wretched . . . thus does this hypocritical, Malthusian philosophy . . . trample on the best feelings of humanity."[72] The *Spitalfields Weavers' Journal* denounced the New Poor Law and philanthropists' efforts to dissuade men from marrying until the age of twenty-five as an insult to women. Ostensibly quoting a working-class wife, a verse pronounced,

> Lord help us! This is a plan:
> Can a thing wearing breeches believe he is still a man?
> I hate all these brawlers of natural sedition,
> If children are curses, why don't they petition
> The God of all Nature to alter his creatures
> That man might till twenty-five shun women's features,
> If heard not, and prone to continue such courses,
> Better do by the men as they do by the horses.[73]

To refute the New Poor Law's promulgators' attacks on working-class morality, activists linked them to birth control and infanticide. They were infuriated by the publication of a pamphlet by "Marcus" which literally advocated gassing infant paupers. Although a satirist or agent provocateur may have written the pamphlet, its matter-of-fact discussion of infanticide merely took Bentham's private musings on the subject to their extreme and thus undercut utilitarian credibility.[74] The *Northern Liberator* addressed its venom "to you who have tacitly countenanced schemes for prevailing upon the people to outrage nature by preventing the fruitfulness of their wives, and by the actual murder of their infant children; to you who accused these peaceable, excellent and industrious people of vice, guilt, and idleness." It published a melodramatic tale about a virtuous but starving family forced into a workhouse, where a husband is prevented from seeing his dying wife and a male keeper attempts to violate their son.[75]

Working people objected to the separation of husbands and wives and parents and children in the workhouses as Malthusian, "inhumane," "unchristian," and "at variance with the laws of God and man."[76] The *Weekly Dispatch* editorialized, "Perhaps the worst and most decidedly un-English part of the new system is, the separation of mothers from their children, husbands from their wives, in the New Bastiles, and the driving *men* from the marriage bed to sleep with *boys*."[77] The Reverend John Hart of Middleton, near Manchester, implored working people to resist with violence; he portrayed "widows calling upon husbands and children upon fathers, who are husbands and fathers no more; God has determined to give them vengeance if they continue to rob, murder, and oppress the poor."[78] Bronterre O'Brien fulminated that the policy severed "the deepest ties of human nature, without regard to habits, feelings, sympathies, constitutional ailment, or human passions."[79]

Women demonstrated with vehemence against the New Poor Law, for they were deeply concerned about the bastardy clauses and the separation of mothers from their children.[80] John Watkins pointed out that under the system, "Nor wife, nor mother, she is not deemed a woman; she is called a PAUPER; a being degraded far below humanity."[81] Opponents encouraged women to demonstrate against the New Poor Law. Richard Oastler fulminated against the Poor Law report, telling "English Mothers" that "the same Parliament, which secured the Pensions of the King to the Prostitutes and Bastards in High Life, has branded you with the epithet of W——e! Now, Women of England, Women of the Working Classes—will you bear it? will you submit?"[82] Peter Bussey, a Bradford radical, declared to women, "I know you can fight the battle better than your husbands; I want you to come forward, I was going to say like men (loud laughter) but like women."[83] "Fight the battle" was not just a figure of speech. In Mansfield, Nottinghamshire, an angry crowd surrounded an assistant commissioner and vowed, "especially the infuriated females, to tear him to pieces."[84] During Oastler's parliamentary campaign in Huddersfield, working-class women went in gangs "from shop to shop threatening to withdraw their patronage if the proprietors would not vote for Oastler."[85] At Elland, Yorkshire, determined women ambushed some assistant Poor Law commissioners as they came out of a meeting, knocking them down and rolling them in the snow.[86]

But the anti–Poor Law movement did not just allow women to vent their feelings in traditional crowd action; it also gave them a voice and a place in politics. Elland women, like thousands of others in Middleton, Barnsley, Staleybridge, Northampton, and other towns, sent petitions to Queen Victoria and Parliament denouncing the New Poor Law. Mrs. Susan Fierly opened the meeting which passed the petition by "exhorting the females present to take the question of the repeal of the bill in their own hands, and not to rely on the exertions of others . . . but at once to assert the dignity and equality of the sex." The Elland women objected to the separation of families in the workhouse and particularly opposed the bastardy clause for driving their daughters to "child murder and suicide."[87] The London Female Chartist Association denounced the New Poor Law as "cruel, unjust and atrocious," citing the plight of women forced to give up their children to the workhouse because they could not support them.[88] Mary Ann Walker presented the hardships experienced by women under the New Poor Law as a central argument for the Charter.[89] "Sophia" asked, rhetorically, why, if poor husbands and wives were to be separated to prevent the birth of paupers, aristocratic "State pensioners" should not also be subject to this "Malthusian Law."[90]

Like the Queen Caroline affair, the bastardy clause agitation gave women a political context in which to express their sexual vulnerabilities. But it also limited the way they could explore this issue. The Owenite critique of marital tyranny and advocacy of free unions and divorce as a solution were not politically expedient in the anti–Poor Law campaign. For instance, when Elizabeth Hanson, a Yorkshire agitator, denounced the New Poor Law for separating husbands and wives in the workhouse, the *Globe* newspaper attacked her credibility on the grounds that she herself was separated from her husband. She could only reply defensively that there was a difference between forced and voluntary separation.[91] The anti–Poor Law battle thus undercut the credibility of Place's birth control movement and Owenite free love, especially in northern campaigns dominated by fiery radical Methodists such as the Rev. J. R. Stephens. He pronounced that the poor must trust God rather than those "who philosophise love into wayward lust, make a mockery of marriage, call the purest and profoundest of our affections the prejudices of education. . . . They know nothing of the application of 'steam' to factory machinery, or of 'gas' to the humane project of 'painless extinction' for every child born above two in a family." For Stephens, Benthamite or Owenite social "science" paralleled the technological juggernaut that ruined the livelihoods of the poor handloom weavers and alienated factory workers who made up his following (see Figure 9).[92]

The critique of the bastardy clause also forced a shift in radicals' accounts of female sexuality. Plebeian ballads depicting women as actively desiring were highly problematic, but at least women were seen as clever agents rather than passive victims. At first, the Owenite *Pioneer* denounced the bastardy clause as punishing a natural act: "While nature woos her, as it were, to love and joy, harsh custom, with a sterile frown, forbids."[93] But in order to argue against misogynist Evangelicals and utilitarians who portrayed unmarried mothers as scheming seductresses, the *Poor Man's Guardian* declared that women consent to sex only under promise of marriage: "It is their softness and affection alone which cause them to yield to their husbands," for they have little sexual drive. Women were seen not only as asexual but as passive, weak victims. Although this

Figure 9.   Heaven and Earth. Copyright British Museum.

line effectively defended working-class women against Evangelical smears, it also undermined women's agency. The *Poor Man's Guardian* went on to say that women were "the weaker vessels," who did not have the "great consideration, reflection and resistance necessary to resist seduction."[94] The *London Dispatch* repudiated the Whigs for pinning the blame for illegitimacy on women, "the confessedly weaker in mind," while an "Englishwoman" wrote to *Cobbett's Political Register* that the bastardy clause would be futile in dissuading "feeble and oppressed" women from "guilty passion."[95]

The chivalrous image of manhood, which had been dominant in radicalism since Queen Caroline, acquired a further boost in the anti–Poor Law campaign. At a meeting of the Chartist Convention in 1838, the Rev. Maberley evoked cheers when he reminded the audience of his defense of Caroline and proclaimed, "No man should ill-use a woman."[96] Radicals had to denounce seducers of poor girls as irresponsible libertines if they were to capitalize on the affair, but such denunciations further damaged the credibility of Owenite ideas of free love. Samuel Roberts celebrated the old Poor Law as "less indulgent to the powerful assailant, than to the frail, feeble, confiding victim," and he denounced the bastardy clauses for allowing thousands of agricultural laborers, "savage Irishmen," policemen, and soldiers "to corrupt and ruin our young female population."[97] Radicals described the bastardy clause as an "insult to manhood," contrasting the "gross and brutal libertine" with the honorable, controlled, manly working man.[98]

Yet radicals also evaded the fact that most illegitimate children were fathered by working-class men. These men were not necessarily the manipulative "vile seducers" of rhetoric, but often had planned to marry their sweethearts and then had lost their jobs. However, others simply did not want to marry women they impregnated, and rape was by no means uncommon in courtship.[99] Instead of confronting these issues directly, radicals preferred to blame seduction on aristocratic libertines. Drawing from the stereotypes of melodrama, the *Pioneer* declared, "If a faithful register were kept of seductions, and of the fathers of natural children, the great majority would be found to belong to the aristocracy," although it went on to blame as well "the small fry who serve them, or imitate them in their profligacy."[100] Seduction thus became a metaphor for class exploitation rather than a real issue in radical politics.[101] Peter Bussey made the connections clear at a large Bradford anti–Poor Law meeting when he declared,

> There is a set of young boobies in this country, who are connected with the aristocracy, and who are regular plunderers of the

people. . . . They would destroy your lives; but you are useful in laboring for them . . . and they are in the habit of seducing the daughters of poor men, and I have formed an opinion that the bastardy clauses have been introduced into this act, in order to protect, and to screen the despicable aristocrat in all his wicked intrigues (hear hear).[102]

However much it distorted reality, such rhetoric was quite effective, both in stirring up working people confused and disturbed by the sexual crisis and pinning the blame on a political rather than a personal cause, and in manipulating the dominant morality for political ends. In 1844 the bastardy clauses were amended to make it easier for poor unmarried mothers to claim maintenance. Yet in the process, radical critiques of sexuality and marriage had been lost.

Conclusion

The 1820s began with radicals promulgating birth control information and challenging patriarchal tyranny. Yet their efforts seemed to do nothing to solve the sexual crisis between men and women, for labor mobility and unemployment increasingly compelled men to desert wives and pregnant sweethearts and intensified marital conflict. Furthermore, the imposition of the New Poor Law forced working-class people on the defensive, impelling them to uphold conventional morality in order to combat attacks on their integrity as parents and spouses. The portrayal of unmarried mothers as weak and passive paralleled the way in which upper-class paternalists such as Tory radical Richard Oastler saw working people. Following the tenets of the old moral economy, they believed they had an obligation to help the needy, but they tended to regard the poor as children who were not ready to exercise political rights. However, working people did not simply accept this melodramatic depiction of themselves. They wanted to be heroes of their own dramas, and working men demanded universal suffrage as the only way to defeat the 1834 act. Anti–Poor Law associations in the north and in London were split over this issue by 1838, as working-class men stormed into meetings chaired by gentlemen, demanding that they resolve in favor of universal suffrage and starting fistfights if their demands were rejected.[103]

Although the anti–Poor Law movement necessarily cut off any public exploration of alternative moralities, it did contribute to innovative approaches to the working-class movement as a whole. The anti–Poor Law agitation revived the earlier tradition of mobilizing whole communities and demonstrated the contribution women could make to the working-class movement. Working men needed the vote, they argued, to protect the rights of their families; they needed to vote on behalf of a working class composed not only of skilled men but also of pauperized women and children. They began to incorporate domesticity into their rhetoric, to appeal to middle-class public opinion and also to gain working women's support by promising that their husbands would behave better. Personal lives remained highly political, and politics rather personal.

11 Equality or Domesticity
The Dilemma for Labor

During the good times of the early 1820s, trade unionists were able to organize to recoup some of the losses endured during the years following the Napoleonic wars, and they militantly defied their masters. But after 1825, masters took advantage of a depression in trade to undercut the power of skilled artisans.[1] They began to defeat artisans' strikes by introducing sweating, transferring from factories into workshops the principle of dividing up skilled processes into simple tasks that could be performed repetitively by low-paid, unskilled workers such as women and children.[2] In cotton manufacturing, the perfection of the power loom brought increasing numbers of young women into factories, slowly choking the handloom weavers' livelihood, and spinning masters intensified their campaign to replace militant male cotton spinners with docile females.

Workers began to realize that simply striking to defend the privileges of skilled male artisans would no longer succeed. They began to develop wide-ranging analyses of the labor market and economy which in turn led to new strategies for mobilizing workers, bettering their conditions, and combating laissez-faire economics. The issue of female workers became a catalyst in many of these debates. On the one hand, some advocated organizing the skilled and unskilled men and women together, or even supporting autonomous female unions. London laundresses clamored for a shilling more a week, and thousands of proud powerloom weavers crowded into a Glasgow hall to receive their trade membership cards. But another, more popular option was to win over public opinion to force the state to regulate the work of women and children. Male trade unionists began to demand wages high enough that they could keep their wives at home, arguing that factories and workshops contaminated women.

Were male workers who demanded the breadwinner wage genuinely motivated by concern for women and children, or were they seeking their own self-interest? Jane Humphries argues that when men tried to exclude women from the workplace on the basis of the breadwinner wage, they were following a strategy meant to benefit working-class families, not just skilled men.[3] Heidi Hartmann, however, declares that the breadwinner wage was just an excuse for men both to monopolize skilled status in the workplace and to dominate their wives at home.[4] While Sonya Rose acknowledges that higher wages for men may have benefited their families, she demonstrates that the breadwinner wage continued to justify exclusionary strikes against women workers throughout the century.[5] To understand why the working-class movement chose to demand the breadwinner wage instead of organizing women, these alternative strategies must be understood in the context of the social, economic, and political turmoil of the 1820s and 1830s.

London Artisans and the Debates over Women Workers

The breadwinner wage was not an artisan tradition.[6] Previously, artisans had occasionally complained that they did not earn enough to support their families, but they had usually expected their wives to contribute earnings to the household. An artisan's status had rested on his place in the fraternity of skilled men rather than on his ability to keep a wife at home. When artisans struck against women in their trades, they did not depict them as frail females in need of protection, but insulted them as whores. Even in the 1820s the fraternal masculine ethos of heavy drinking and loyalty to mates taking precedence over responsibility to families persisted in the pages of new labor periodicals. For instance, when a shoemaker's wife blamed on a strike her husband's violence against her, the *Trades' Newspaper* insisted that his trade union activity had nothing to do with the beating, but the paper failed to reprimand his action. Similarly, other newspapers criticized the hatters' society for giving a man a ticket to go on tramp on the eve of his wife's lying-in. In response, the *Trades' Newspaper* indignantly asked whether trade societies were expected to compel men to support their wives.[7]

During the 1820s, however, traditional trade union techniques faltered as strikes failed to keep out women workers. In response, artisans intensified their efforts to coalesce into a larger trade union movement, trying to overcome the splits and dissensions of earlier attempts by introducing a new sense of respectability and discipline. The shipwright John Gast advocated unity and discipline among trade unionists. He told workmen,

The antidote [to misery] is in your own hands. Throw away your sottings, your pipes at improper times, your jealousies and divisions, your underselling of labor—let all the useful and valuable members of every trade, who wish to appear respectable, unite with each other, and be in friendship with all other trades.[8]

Artisans also began to incorporate domesticity as a key element in their new respectability. Trade unionists turned to the sphere of public debate, trying to develop a rhetoric to combat laissez-faire ideology in their new periodicals. By the mid-twenties, trade unionists began to link the exclusion of women from the labor market with the breadwinner wage. They argued that married women's work harmed domestic life, contaminated female morality, undercut male wages, and prevented men from earning enough to keep their wives at home. This rhetoric seemed less selfish and more convincing than misogynist insults against women workers. For instance, in 1825 a "Laborer" wrote to the *Trades' Newspaper* that women and children should be entirely withdrawn from the labor market, a plan which would be "highly congenial to the feelings and habits of Englishmen, as conducive to domestic comfort and kindly affections, as tending to establish the authority of fathers, and as making each man responsible for the comfort, respectability, and the education of his family."[9] Of course, this plan would also prevent the erosion of the skills and wages of working men.

There were two problems with this proposal. First, what was the exact meaning of domesticity? Many believed that the total withdrawal of women and children from the labor market was impractical, given that their earnings were essential for family support. In another letter to the *Trades' Newspaper*, a silk weaver signing himself "H. C." devalued the skill of women weavers and stressed that of men. But, he admitted, he could not call for the prohibition of women's work altogether, for the "earnings of women are almost indispensible to the maintenance of a family." Instead he called for women to be restricted to warping and winding at home, for they would be better "employed in their proper place, attending to their domestic affairs." "H. C.," therefore, wished to reconstitute a family economy in which wives and children could earn wages at home under patriarchal supervision.[10] Even Francis Place, so adamant about the exclusion of women from trades, would allow "light labor as can be done at home" for women—the very homework which undercut workshop labor in trades such as tailoring and shoemaking.[11] This tactic preserved the availability of women as low-paid workers and in fact would intensify the problem of sweating and decrease household earnings.

Second, how could trade unionists actually remove women and children from the workplace? While trade unionists such as John Gast and Francis Place agreed on the value of domesticity for artisans' respectability, they offered competing solutions to the problem of the labor market.[12] Francis Place and his followers emulated classical political economy in believing that "the main factors adversely affecting labor were the product of market imperfections" such as restrictions on trade unions and protectionism.[13] Instead of attempting to maintain wage levels through state intervention, working men ought to obey the iron law of wages and reduce the labor supply. They should simply refuse to work with women, striking until they were removed. However, many trade unionists had tried this technique and failed, and they also suspected Place's Malthusianism.[14]

John Gast advocated a dual technique: first, union of the trades to avoid sectionalism, increase their power, and promote respectability, and, second, legislation to keep up wages and protect their property in skill.[15] This was not the old-fashioned appeal to paternalist protective legislation for particular trades, as in the weavers' petitions at the beginning of the century, but a broader conception of the relation of labor to the state. Trade unionists believed that they should have the right to be represented in the state, and that the state should protect the rights of labor against exploitative capitalism.[16] Gast's philosophy resembled that of the factory movement, which demanded legislative restriction of the work of women and children.

While the factory movement obviously had little direct relevance to London artisans, the most radical economic theory of the time, Owenism, gained increasing support among them in the 1820s.[17] Where Place wished to reform artisan culture, the Owenites planned to revolutionize it, envisioning a philosophical transformation of competitive misery into cooperative harmony. They believed that working people's misery was caused, not by an oversupply of labor, but, rather, by distortions in the mechanisms of exchange which denied them the true worth of their labor.[18] Therefore, the Owenites said, instead of trying to keep up their position by excluding the unskilled or women, trade unionists should draw them all into consolidated unions. The ultimate goal was to form labor cooperatives where workers would control their own means of production. As part of this project, the Owenites encouraged women to defend the value of their own labor. As "A Bondswoman" wrote to the Owenite *Pioneer*, "Look at the value that is set on woman's labour, whether it be skilful, whether it be laborious, so that woman can do it. The contemptible expression is, it is made by woman, and therefore cheap."[19] The Owenites encouraged women to organize their own unions, both independently and in association with men. "Lodges of lace-makers, strawbonnet makers, shoebinders, laundresses, milliners, glass cutters, stockingers, and glovemakers" joined the Grand National Consolidated Trades Union, and female shoemakers, weavers, washerwomen, and card-setters all went on strike in 1833–1834.[20]

But artisan traditions and Owenite feminism clashed in the tailors' strike of 1834. A central problem for tailors in the early 1830s was competition from cheap female labor, which employers used to introduce home work and other sweated methods. In 1827 and 1830, strikes by tailors to exclude women failed. Owenism appealed to tailors facing increased sweating and degeneration of their trade, for its cooperative vision resembled workshop democracy and its labor theory of value promised to redeem their damaged property in skill. The tailors affiliated with the Grand National Consolidated Trades Union and hoped labor exchanges would overcome the problem of sweating. Owenism also appealed to the tailoresses, who faced pay below subsistence. However, the trade was divided between those who followed the Owenite strategy of uniting the skilled and the unskilled, men and women, and those who wished to use the union's power to return to the trade's elite traditions. In 1834 the conservatives won, and, as Barbara Taylor observes in her pathbreaking work, their strike for higher wages and against piecework and homework only thinly veiled an attack on tailoresses in the trade.[21]

This strike exposed tensions over artisan misogyny and sectionalism that had been festering in journeyman culture for decades. Tailors had long founded their communities on an exclusivist basis, distinguishing between the honorable Flints, who were unionized, highly skilled men, and dishonorable Dungs, who worked in unorganized, sweated conditions for the mass market. Although they tried to overcome the divisions among men, the tailors refused to incorporate women into the unions, leaving themselves vulnerable to female strikebreakers. The tailors had structured their communities around the workshop and pub rather than the family, and this strike was itself an effort to retain the barriers between the two by prohibiting homework.

In Manchester, the behavior of striking tailors a few months later continued the artisan misogynist tradition. The men not only attacked strikebreaking men but also harassed and assaulted young tailoresses, whom they perceived as rivals. Fanny Wainwright, an eighteen-year-old tailoress, testified that the tailors "pointed out to her all the unfortunate girls on the street, and said that when they [the turnouts] went to work she would have to go on the town for a living. They said if they ever caught her in the dark they would squeeze her."[22] The *Manchester Guardian*, admittedly hostile to the strike, reported that a striking tailor had not only quit his employment but deserted his wife and children.[23]

But the Owenites had given the women on the other side of the barrier a new voice in which to protest this heritage of misogyny. They repudiated the old artisan strategy of bonding through drinking and keeping up their own positions at the expense of women and children. The *Pioneer* blamed drunkenness on "lordly husbands, whose corrupt taste for male associations, to the exclusion of women, has produced a depravity of habit."[24] A tailoress alleged that some of the tailors allowed women's work only because "instead of working themselves, they can loiter away half the week in a pot-house, while the poor woman sits slaving at home, and gets only scorn and abuse for her devotedness."[25] If women organized themselves to "resist such authority, and claim the privilege of a fair reward for their labor" their husbands accused them of "high treason."[26]

Despite this opposition, Owenite tailoresses asserted their right to work and even to unionize. One woman asked, "What is to become of the numerous women now working at the business . . . surely the men might think of a better method of benefitting themselves than that of driving so many industrious women out of employment. Surely, while they loudly complain of oppression, they will not turn oppressors themselves."[27] They compared misogynist unions to aristocratic oppressors: "Speak of any project which shall diminish the authority of the male, or give him an equal, where once he found an inferior, and then the spirit of Toryism awakes that has long been dormant. All men are Tories by nature. Even the unionists themselves, who rail against tyrants and oppressors, have the blood of the aristocrat flowing in their veins."[28]

Some male tailors feared that their domestic patriarchal authority would be undermined if they acknowledged the women's claims to be members of the trade. One wrote to the *Pioneer*, "None but lazy, gossiping, drunken wives will wish to go to meetings."[29] Such men faced not only the protests of women in the *Pioneer* but attacks by newspapers which accused the tailors of trying to deprive poor working girls of their bread. The *Manchester Guardian* defended the right of women to work, portraying them as more skilled at making "light waistcoats" than the men, and attacking the tailors for keeping women from using their "ability of earning their livelihood by the exercise of their industry," leaving them no alternative but to go "on the town or starve."[30]

To defend themselves against accusations of misogyny, the tailors adopted a new tactic: appealing to the rhetoric of domesticity. They claimed they were sympathetic to the tailoresses, but insinuated that "the terms under which they obtain employment are of a nature too gross for the public ear." They took over the language of the "natural family" from the middle class, demanding, "Have not women been unfairly driven from their proper sphere in the social scale, unfeelingly torn from the maternal duties of a parent, and unjustly encouraged to compete with men in ruining the money value of labor?"[31] Despite such clever rhetoric, the strike failed. It was perhaps a lingering resentment of the tailors' traditional exclusivism that finally pushed the other trades in the Consolidated Union to refuse them the financial support essential to prevent collapse of the strike.[32] Nonetheless, the tailors had set a precedent in the rhetorical war of domesticity.

Adoption of the rhetoric of domesticity was a key aspect of the effort to transform the old artisan culture into a new, respectable trade union movement. However, the tailors' strike also revealed the defensive nature and the limitations of this transformation. Artisans' efforts to retain their position by striking against women had been defeated. Their claims that the government should protect their property in skill had fallen on deaf ears. But the Owenite alternative of gaining greater trade union strength by organizing women and the unskilled posed too great a challenge to masculine artisan pride. Defeated industrially, artisans turned to the sphere of public debate and politics. Whereas the earlier tradition of artisans' strikes could not contend with laissez-faire ideology and bourgeois morality, the new rhetoric of domesticity deflected attention from the weakness of the artisan position toward the problems of female morality and the home. Artisans began to shift their archetype of masculinity away from the fraternal artisan to the patriarchal breadwinner, turning from a failed quest for industrial power to a new demand for political rights.

Women and Unions in the Factory Districts

Textile workers' traditional patriarchal cooperation with women began to fray at the edges as masters introduced technology that enabled female and child workers to supplant skilled men. On the defensive, textile workers had to develop new strategies to cope with the increased presence of female workers. As did artisans, they had two options: to organize women, or to demand domesticity. However, unlike the tailors, they could not simply ignore or denounce female workers. Since females composed over half of the work force in many factories, trade union activists had to devise ways of simultaneously appealing to women and protecting the position of men.

Debates on women factory workers in northern trade union journals reveal many of the contradictions and divisions evolving within textile culture. In the early 1830s, the cotton spinner John Doherty tried to broaden his vision of trade union tactics into a wider strategy of reforming working-class culture through a "National Regeneration Society." Influenced by Owen, he wished to bring together middle-class reformers, Tory radicals, and trade unionists to improve education and teach temperance and thrift.[33] Women were a key element in this program, although Doherty's appeals to them were always rather contradictory. He began to argue, on the one hand, that women had to be regarded as equals, and, on the other, that men should protect and take care of women in the home. In his journal, *Herald of the Rights of Industry*, Doherty advocated that men should earn enough to keep their wives out of "these artificial hells" of the factories, but in the same breath he opposed "the destructive principle of reckoning the labor of women of inferior value, because they have learnt to live more temperately and cheaply than men."[34]

Similarly, in Glasgow trade unionists debated ways their movement could respond to the increased number of factory females. While some men denounced them as immoral, others recognized the necessity of reforming working-class sexual politics. In 1830, John Aird claimed in the Glasgow *Herald to the Trades' Advocate* that "one great cause of crime, and consequent misery, is the unnatural and degrading manner in which females are huddled together in factories, where their minds are debauched before they can distinguish right from wrong, and their surplus earnings only emboldens [*sic*] them, unblushingly, to perform actions abhorrent to all but a prostitute." However, Aird's letter excited a storm of protest; his own Tradeston Temperance Society disapproved of his sentiments, and another operative defended factory girls' morality and their right to work.[35]

These tensions among textile workers were also apparent in their industrial strategies. On the one hand, workers in the powerloom weaving industry moved from the strategy of patriarchal cooperation with women, in which women supported male workers, to a new strategy of female autonomy supported by men. On the other, cotton spinners and calico printers intensified the patriarchal element of their organization by fighting female competition, but managed nonetheless to draw on women workers' aid. Both strategies drew on community support. Unlike artisans' trade unions, textile workers' had been based on the neighborhood, including women and children, rather than the workshop. Trade unionists held up community as an alternative principle to the bourgeois press's notion of free competition in trade. As an editorial in the radical Owenite-influenced *Reid's Glasgow Magazine* declared in 1834, the "nob," or strikebreaker, is "a miscreant, who tramples on all the laws of social obligation, who has no participation in the indignant feelings of the half-starved and half-clothed class to which he belongs, and, in short, who has no humanity or sympathy but for himself." Sometimes this combat took literal form: as the magazine continued, the nob "can have no claim to either sympathy or pity, when he comes to meet his punishment at the hands of the aggrieved."[36]

But, as we shall see from strikes of calico printers, tenters, spinners, and powerloom weavers, the early 1830s witnessed heightened tensions over shifting community boundaries. Skilled workmen such as tenters and spinners fought to retain their status, combating incursions of handloom weavers and poor women workers. But even while these men used misogynist rhetoric against rival female workers, they depended on their female neighbors for support. Meanwhile, women workers drew so much sustenance for survival from their community roots that they were unwilling to challenge their male neighbors' sexual discrimination. Their loyalty to their community outweighed any loyalty to other women per se: women workers sometimes defended men from their communities who were fighting against other women workers. However, poor women workers shut out from the communities of skilled textile workers formed their own communities, however marginal and impoverished. While textile workers struggled to recreate their traditions of patriarchal cooperation under changing circumstances, new forms of female organization sprang up in the interstices.

The calico printers responded to the challenges of the early 1830s in two ways: first by resisting women's work, then by reconstituting patriarchal cooperation with women. Calico printing was organized as a traditional masculine elite artisanal trade, demanding the high initiation fee of five or seven guineas for apprentices. Like mule spinners, calico printers employed women and children in subsidiary tasks such as penciling (coloring in the pattern) and tearing, spreading the color on a sieve for the printer's block. However, Scottish workers, who had lost control over their trade, blamed the presence of women workers for the fact that by 1831 their wages in general were much lower than in Lancashire.[37] Yet when they complained, the *Glasgow Courier* accused them of "endeavour[ing] to throw out of employment a number of industrious, unprotected, and virtuous females, in order that they, the lords of creation, may enjoy an exclusive monopoly of a particular description of work."[38] Publicly, the printers adopted a moralistic rhetoric to combat this laissez-faire argument, accusing the females of "audacity" and lack of modesty in entering men's workshops, and professing to fear that they would acquire men's habits—a somewhat disingenuous assertion, given the calico printers' long tradition of sharing their whisky "footings" with the women of their villages and workshops.[39]

Eventually, sexual cooperation proved more effective than patriarchal rhetoric. By 1833, masters in calico-printing factories near Glasgow were determined to break the union and introduce women and children, as well as impoverished handloom weavers, as "grounders" replacing men. But they had not counted on a fierce neighborhood solidarity that crossed occupational boundaries. When a strike broke out, women workers of the neighborhood vigorously supported the male calico printers. As the nobs attempted to go to work in Kelvindock, a suburb of Glasgow, the women powerloom weavers of a nearby factory and the striking male calico printers, who all lived in Botany Row (known locally as Reform Row) joined forces to stone the new hands, both male and female. Local young women refused to cook for strikebreaking calico printers.[40] This solidarity seems to have resulted from a wider community sense rather than tight kinship relations, for—with a few exceptions—female powerloom weavers were the daughters of agricultural workers rather than relatives of calico printers.[41] However, it should be noted that the women, while vigorously active in insulting the "nobs," did try to restrain the extreme violence of the male teenage tearers, who severely beat some of the young women strikebreakers and called them "whores."[42] Eventually, the old calico printers went back to work. Some even married the female grounders who had undercut them, and their offspring became tearers. The family labor system was reconstituted, and patriarchal cooperation with women prevailed.[43]

In the powerloom industry, Scottish tenters (powerloom mechanics) realized they could succeed in forming unions only if they enlisted the support of the far more numerous female powerloom weavers as unofficial auxiliaries. The most dramatic evidence of this solidarity between women powerloom weavers and the more skilled tenters comes from 1830. James Hewit, a handloom weaver, took a job as a tenter at Mr. Broughton's powerloom factory because his earnings would increase from six to eighteen shillings per week. However, the female powerloom weavers objected to Hewit's employment because he had accepted two shillings less than the union rate. One dark December afternoon a few days after Hewit started work, the women weavers suddenly put out the gas lights on the factory floor. Shrouded in gloom, they emerged from behind their massive power looms, jeering menacingly, to force Hewit into a dark passage where Mary Moorrie struck him with her "loom semple."[44] Just in time, the manager rushed in to rescue him and promptly fired Janet Cain and Sarah Quin as ringleaders. But Cain just "shook her fist in [Hewit's] face and called him all the old buggers she could think of—said it was he who was the cause of this and if God spared her she would be revenged on him." That evening, Hewit tried to slip out of the mill, but after a crowd of women again surrounded him, Janet Cain attacked him "as bold as any pugilist." He ran off, but stumbled and fell in a dark alley. Stunned and fearful, he crawled into a spirit cellar to escape the women. But Cain and Quin followed him in and seized him by the hair, and Cain stabbed him in the eye with her powerloom hook. Tellingly, Quin's alibi for the stabbing—that she had earlier left her powerloom hook at the engraver's to have it inscribed with her name—suggests her consciousness of herself as a skilled worker owning the tools of her trade. In supporting male workers, then, these young women emulated traditional violent tactics to defend their own craft pride.[45]

Perhaps inspired by Owenism and the factory reform movement, by 1833 the male tenters and the female powerloom weavers had decided they needed more rational and disciplined forms of union organization. According to a manager of a Glasgow powerloom factory, the overseers and tenters "countenanced" the formation of the West of Scotland Female Power Loom Weavers Association to enable themselves to go on strike. But the female union was run entirely by women, organized for mutual protection "against the tyranny of the overseers and against any wage cuts by the masters." Its first meeting attracted a thousand "well dressed females"; according to the Owenite William Campbell, six thousand women belonged to the association.[46]

The Glasgow women's organization had an important impact on trade unionism as a whole in the early 1830s, for they tried to prove that workers in overstocked trades, perceived as unskilled, could organize as well as traditional artisans could. By organizing and cooperating with other workers rather than excluding them from access to skill and status, these women were able to form unions. They inspired the notoriously low-paid women of the country mills to organize to resist wage cuts by the masters.[47] Even male handloom weavers tried to emulate them, overcoming their despair at the overstocking of their trade to ask, "Would any man say women were a scarcer commodity than even the weavers?" But after a few weeks the handloom weavers realized that even if they organized to subsidize wages in hard times they could never hold their own against steam looms.[48]

The Glasgow association inspired the Aberdeen powerloom and spinning women to form a union in 1834. Aberdeen manufacturers put out spinning and weaving to women and men, but as they built factories masters contrived to employ only women as spinners and powerloom weavers. They modified the spinning machines so that women could work them and trained them for the several years it took to make a good spinner. Despite the potential for gender antagonism, Aberdeen textile workers seem to have cooperated in 1834, perhaps because factory girls generally married handloom weavers.[49] In 1834, however, the female factory operatives struck at the Broadford mills, which in turn led male and female operatives at a calico printfields to organize together; indeed, all the trades in the town were "determined to stand out until every complaint shall be redressed."[50]

Women's labor consciousness owed more to the proletarianized experience of the factories than to the traditions of artisanal independence. The Aberdeen women complained bitterly of the harassment they experienced at the hands of overseers for such minor infractions as reading, talking, singing, or sitting down, and even for faults in the machinery over which they had no control.[51] They defended themselves against the clergy's attacks on their morality, declaring that overseers and clergy should remember that "some of the women within the gates of Broadford are far superior to you in the point of respectability and moral worth."[52] Over the next few decades, female powerloom weavers continued to protest unjust fines, bullying overlookers, and sexual harassment.[53]

Yet female powerloom weavers also developed pride in their skill. Jessie Campbell, an elderly spinster, remembered years of unending toil at the looms, but she also boasted that it had been a difficult trade to learn, especially as fancy work replaced the plain work of early years.[54] Factory girls celebrated their respectability and depicted themselves as hard workers who supported their families. For instance, in one ballad "The Factory Maid" exhibited pride in her skill and self-reliance, as well as a fierce class antagonism:

> The rich haughty noble may boast of her grandeur
> While wantonly wasting the short fleeting hours;
> But vain her attainments and light gaudy splendour
> If dignified labor calls forth her powers.
> The factory maid on her own power relying,
> And knowing that labor can never degrade
> Delights in her duty although self-denying
> Thus labor exalteth the Factory maid.
>
> The low servile menial, while aping her betters,
> Surveys all around her with looks of disdain,
> The factory maid would scorn her vile fetters
> And spurn at the deep galling yoke of the chain.
> The factory maid, all tyranny scorning,
> To stand for her rights she's never afraid—
> Through high independence her mind is adorning,
> Yet modesty claims the sweet factory Maid.[55]

Organized women also declared, like men, that they needed "a fair day's wage for a fair day's work," to support themselves and their "widowed mothers and orphaned families," in the words of an operative powerloom weaver in 1840.[56] Another song, "The Rambling Factory Girl's Return," promises, "With industrious hands I hard will work, / My mother to maintain."[57] Similarly, the Paisley female powerloom weavers who struck in

1842 declared that although a number of them were widows with children to support or young women with parents dependent on them, they earned only two and a half to four and a half shillings for eleven hours of work per day, six days a week.[58] While the female powerloom weavers were certainly unusual among women in their sense of skill and solidarity, they represented a valid alternative strategy of organizing, based, not on exclusion, but on cooperation and inclusion.

The cotton spinners stressed the patriarchal aspects of the textile tradition much more than the female weavers did, and they passed up some opportunities to incorporate women into their struggle. For instance, in 1824 the *Manchester Guardian* attacked as monopolizers cotton spinners who struck against the introduction of female spinners. In response, the men acknowledged women's right to work but attacked their morality when they invaded the turf of adult men. "We do not stand opposed to women working," the union stated, "but we do enter our protest against the principle on which they are employed." They alleged that girls in the cotton mills had only themselves to support, whereas cotton spinners had to feed their families. Moreover, they described the "character and conduct of females in a cotton mill . . . as disgusting and appalling." Of course, male spinners did not object to having female piecers work for them; indeed, they often employed their own wives or daughters. Rather, attacks on female workers' sexual reputations transparently reflected male hostility to their potential independence. The cotton spinners ended their plea with heightened rhetoric: "In this unnatural and unwholesome state of things, the reins of government are broken, and the excited feelings of youth and inexperience let loose upon the world, a prey too often to pride, vice and infamy."[59]

Five years later, John Doherty used similar misogynist rhetoric in an 1829 Manchester strike against changes in technology which led to the employment of female spinners. Doherty protested to a factory owner that "if he could not find it in his heart to employ, and pay men for doing his work, he should look out for women whose morals are already corrupted, instead of those whose lives are as yet pure and spotless."[60] Yet Doherty also attempted to develop a more sophisticated strategy for the cotton spinners, gathering British cotton spinners at the Isle of Man in 1829 to form into a powerful consolidated union. In the minutes of that meeting, the spinners vowed to follow their traditional strategy of tightly controlling the labor supply by training only male relatives of spinners to the trade and prohibiting female spinners from joining the union, but they did suggest that female spinners form their own union.[61]

After strikes in 1829 and 1830 failed and the spinners' consolidated trade union collapsed, unions in Lancashire faltered. Factory masters encouraged Richard Roberts to perfect his self-acting mule, on which they hoped to employ women and thereby to hamper male spinners' union organization.[62] It was at this time that Doherty began to branch out to his "National Regeneration Society" and to ally with the factory movement. In the pages of his various labor periodicals, he shifted away from misogynist rhetoric toward a display of consideration and sympathy for women workers. In the *Poor Man's Advocate* in 1832, he published letters expressing women workers' complaints about unfair fines and sexual harassment in specific mills.[63] In 1834 in *Herald of the Rights of Industry*, he editorialized against the "dastardly stratagem of running women against men" and advocated acknowledgment of the "natural equality of women; include them in all your schemes of improvement. . . . Treat them as equals, and you will find them the strongest part of your force."[64]

The softening of Doherty's misogyny was apparently more of a rhetorical strategy than a personal change of heart. His own wife complained bitterly that he spent his time drinking with his trade union mates, and several times she charged him with assault.[65] Nonetheless, cooperation with female workers did characterize Lancashire spinners' strikes. In 1830, as Marc Steinberg observes, when exclusionary efforts failed the men "sought an accommodation" with female spinners. They struck in "sympathy for striking female spinners who were demanding that they be paid in accord with the male piece rates (prompted by male pressure)."[66] In an 1834 strike of cotton spinners in Oldham, females came out of their houses to insult strikebreaking workmen, and, in Salford, piecers and scavengers refused to work with "nobs." In Manchester, factory hand Phoebe Sherry was arrested for assaulting a woman carrying dinner to a strikebreaking spinner.[67]

Lancashire employers responded to these strikes by doubling the size of the mule spinning machinery to increase productivity, instead of substituting cheaper women for men. There has been a great deal of historiographical debate as to why male mule spinners were able to retain their dominant position in Lancashire but not, as we shall see, Glasgow. In Lancashire, as William Lazonick has pointed out, by delegating the supervising and recruiting of piecers to the male mule spinners, employers maintained a tenuous labor peace.[68] In the process, as Mary Freifeld has argued, women lost the opportunity to transfer mule spinning skills from one female worker to another. Even if employers had wanted to hire women, it would have been difficult for them to do so, then, for by the 1840s skilled female spinners had become scarce in Lancashire.[69] But their strategy of patriarchal cooperation with women may have also contributed to the success of Lancashire male spinners in retaining their dominant position in the industry despite the weakness of their union in the 1830s.

The outcome of the Glasgow cotton spinners' struggles in the 1830s was less harmonious—and also challenges some of these arguments about female skill and union strength. The Scottish masters faced a much stronger male mule spinners' union than the Lancashire spinners'. They attempted to fight back by hiring skilled female spinners. Instead of cooperating with the women, the Glasgow spinners attacked them, masking their misogyny with patriarchal, domestic rhetoric. The intensity of their conflict with employers led to a tragic outcome that was crucial for the history of the working-class movement as a whole.

Like the calico printers, the cotton spinners had to cope with the splits in communities between elite mule spinners and their female and child assistants, on the one hand, and marginal women workers and handloom weavers, on the other.[70] But unlike the tenters, they put most emphasis on the patriarchal aspects of textile tradition and less on cooperation with women. The Glasgow union was much stronger that Lancashire's because of its ability to exclude, not only all women, but also men from other, less organized districts. The minutes of the 1829 meeting at the Isle of Man reveal that the Glasgow leaders were much less amenable to cooperating with other unions than their Lancashire counterparts were. As they had in the 1820s, again they developed a dual strategy of public respectability and private violence. The spinners not only fomented unrest with mobs of young women and men but employed terrorist techniques such as vitriol throwing and even shootings.[71] In private meetings, the exclusivist Glasgow men justified violence "by saying that the Church and State were kept up by the fear of Hell and that fear was a most efficient way of accelerating the purposes of the association." But the Renfrewshire men (from Paisley, noted for its moderation) "reprobated the conduct of the Glasgow spinners in using violence . . . as worse than savages or barbarians."[72]

By the 1830s, many of the leaders of the cotton spinners were trying to present themselves as respectable members of the community, often heavily involved in religious activities and temperance.[73] As part of this new respectability, the cotton spinners developed a more sophisticated rhetoric of domesticity. While some male spinners were somewhat sympathetic to women workers, others cloaked misogyny with moralism. On the one hand, a "cotton spinner" wrote to the trade press suggesting that better education would make women "agreeable, useful, and intelligent companions and helpmeets for man" instead of "narrow-sighted [wives who destroy] the peace and happiness of those connected with them." Sympathetically describing factory girls as "worn out and exhausted with incessant fatigue," he saw the solution as enabling men to keep wives and children at home rather than organizing women.[74] On the other hand, cotton spinner William Smith declared to Sadler's select committee on the factory system that when masters employed females to replace striking men, the result was that women workers learned improper morals instead of domestic skills.[75] In the 1833 parliamentary report, operative spinners reiterated that female spinners were immoral and undomestic. Thomas Steele, a spinner, said factory girls were ignorant and bad wives. He had "known instances of their paying other females to take care of their children, they themselves preferring rather to work in the mill than nurse them."[76] Curiously, James M'Nish cited a rape by a male spinner of his ten-year-old piecer to support his claim that factory work for female spinners "render[s] them vicious and dissolute."[77]

In a strike against women spinners at Dennistoun's mill in Calton, Glasgow, in June 1833, the male cotton spinners alternated several, often contradictory, tactics against female spinners, demanding equal pay, citing domestic ideology, and then employing violent harassment.[78] Unlike the tenters, who worked alongside the female powerloom weavers rather than over them, the cotton spinners were accustomed to deriving their pride from their patriarchal position as supervisors of female and child labor. Although some female spinners had joined the female powerloom weavers union, the male cotton spinners could not conceive of the female spinners as comrades, but only as the enemy. As we have seen above, they publicly claimed female spinners belonged in the home; covertly, they used violence to try to drive them out of work. The fact that only when these tactics failed did they demand equal pay for women clearly indicates that egalitarianism was not their goal.[79] The company was eventually forced to compromise and pay the women equal rates, although they continued to insist that the women were not as productive.[80] However, the men's violence against the women continued. In September, a woman named Mary M'Shaffery was injured by having vitriol thrown upon her; her assailants had probably mistaken her for one of the female spinners. The union indirectly admitted its guilt in planning this attack by settling an annuity on her, explaining that she was injured by mistake "on account of a public concern of the combination."[81]

Members of two communities competed for work in the Charles Street area, where Dennistoun's factory was located. Charles Street was inhabited by poor handloom weavers and lower-level cotton workers such as piecers and winders, as well as some powerloom weavers.[82] Many women living there supported themselves and/or their families—women headed 36 percent of the households in Charles Street in 1841, compared to 27 percent for Glasgow as a whole.[83] David Sloan, the manager of Dennistoun's mill, testified that many of the women in the mill had illegitimate children, which may have motivated them to risk their safety for high wages as female spinners. Of the four female spinners who withstood the harassment, three were in their thirties: a thirty-four-year-old widow with four children, and a pair of sisters, Catherine Macdonald and "Big Sally"; and one was a teenager, who lived with her father.[84] None of these women earned enough to rent a room on their own; Catherine and her daughter, for instance, shared a room with a handloom weaver and his wife. The employers claimed, however, that most female spinners earned eighteen shillings a week on light mules, one-thirteenth less than men's earnings, but still more than double the average wage for women in the textile industry.[85]

The unionized male spinners did not live on Charles Street, but crowds of young male spinners and piecers collected at the end of the street to watch for nobs going into Dennistoun's mill.[86] Sally Macdonald testified that when she and Mary went to a drink shop to share a gill of whisky, a group of teenage male piecers and unemployed spinners came in and "began jawing" her about "nobbing," and one especially hostile lad struck Sally on the head with his fist, insulting her as a "damned nobbing whore."[87]

The underemployment of young men under twenty-one in the cotton mills may have intensified antagonism toward women workers. In 1833, roughly equal numbers of children were employed in twenty-nine cotton mills in and around Glasgow: 941 boys and 1,014 girls between the ages of nine and fourteen. Of those between the ages of fourteen and eighteen, 480 boys and 905 girls were employed. The difference became especially acute in the eighteen- to twenty-one-year-old range, with only 139 men to 563 women. After that age the proportions reversed, with 924 adult men to 387 women.[88] This resulted from the system of piecers: adult male spinners preferred to employ girls, both because they were easier to discipline and because they could therefore restrict the number of adult male spinners.[89]

After the 1833 strike, the cotton industry enjoyed peace and prosperity for a few years as more work became available for men. Mr. P. M'Naughten, a Glasgow mill owner, said that the employment of females in the mills had been increasing, but that the men did not mind, because most of the places were filled by "their own relatives and they make good wages." Nonetheless, he said that they did not earn as much as men, because they were not as good workers.[90] However, another employer claimed that one woman could handle enough spindles to earn thirty shillings a week.[91] James M'Nish, the operative spinner and unionist leader mentioned earlier, countered him on moral and industrial grounds, proclaiming, "They [the spinners] are not fond of seeing women at such a severe employment," and describing the women as being inferior workers.[92]

In 1837, turmoil erupted once again as the masters of Glasgow area mills announced a reduction in piece rates, possibly in an attempt to smash the union.[93] The spinners mounted a huge strike beginning in April, and they were joined by many other trades. Eight to ten thousand women and girls were thrown out of work, for each spinner gave employment to four to fourteen women and girls.[94] As in earlier strikes, women and children who worked as piecers joined the riotous crowds outside the mills, jeering, threatening, and hurling fishheads at nobs.[95] But the cotton spinners preferred to stress the more organized, respectable aspects of their strike. Only women and boys rioted, they claimed, although it is quite likely that the male spinners directed this activity from a distance.[96]

Despite the violence of the strike, the spinners managed to turn their reputation for misogyny into a chivalrous defense of women. The most violent incident occurred when John Smith, a nob spinner, was shot and killed in the street in July 1837. Several spinners were convicted of his murder, which the prosecutor, despite dubious evidence of their guilt, characterized as a conspiracy connected with the strike.[97] The organized spinners both denied their responsibility for the shooting and pointed out that Smith was of "notoriously bad character," having been tried for raping his child piecer some years before. The radical trades newspaper the *Monthly Liberator* claimed that "Smith had either fallen victim to a just revenge from the relative of some of those unfortunate children who he had abused, or was assassinated at the request of the masters."[98] Publicly, the cotton spinners tended to allude more indirectly to Smith's character, but given the Victorian propensity toward indirection in such matters, these hints were probably enough.[99] Privately, Charles Hassan, a union spinner, testified that Smith had confessed to him that he had raped a piecer "in a fit of drink" and added that Smith had been suspected of other similar attacks. But Hassan went on to say that "whatever may be the pretence of some of the members of the Trade as Smith being shot for these offenses the Declarant is perfectly sensible and certain that nothing of the kind was the case for the Spinners Association care not what he did if he had been a good member and acted like the rest of them."[100] More plausibly, spinners who clung to the old plebeian violent misogyny hated Smith as a nob, while other working men also wished to punish his violation of the new respectable discipline; and respectable revenge proved more useful in the public relations wars.

Although women's work was not initially an issue in the strike, the cotton spinners sought to justify their actions with the rhetoric of domesticity. They imported the Rev. J. R. Stephens from Yorkshire, and he escalated the rhetoric and cemented the association of violence with patriarchy, proclaiming at a mass meeting, "If you will insist on violating God's law by compelling women and children to labor when God in his book said man shall feed his wife and child by the sweat of his brow . . . we shall wrap with one awful sheet of devouring flame, which no army can resist, the manufactures of the cotton tyrants, and the palaces of those who raised them by murder and rapine."[101]

However, the strike failed, and the trial for conspiracy succeeded in smashing the union. While men continued to be employed as spinners, especially on the finer grades, piecers were even more likely to be women, and employers intensified the pace of work. Eventually, "enlarged machines and self-acting mules . . . worked by youths and women" were introduced.[102] Trade unionists decided that industrial power was not enough; political power had to be sought. They redoubled their long-term demands for state interference in the work of women and children.

The Factory Movement

In the early 1830s, the campaign for the factory acts emerged as a mass movement in Glasgow and Lancashire. Those in favor of legislative restriction on women's and children's work formed an uneasy and shifting coalition with Tory radicals and sanitary reformers, negotiating the meanings of domesticity in different rhetorical traditions.[103] They all argued that children's—and, increasingly, that women's—work harmed the domestic lives of factory operatives. While trade unionists were genuinely distressed by their children's working conditions, their domestic rhetoric also enabled them to combat laissez-faire ideology and protect adult workers as well. The radical *Monthly Liberator* made clear that it was in the interests of skilled male factory operatives to support factory legislation, for "a greedy insatiable monster is at your heels. . . . 'Mechanical Improvement' . . . [and] the blood of tender infants and youths drips from his crocodile jaws."[104]

The rhetoric of domesticity enabled factory reformers to point out the contradictions between middle-class morality and the theories of political economy—the Achilles' heel of that discipline. Political economists were moving away from their earlier concern with general social issues toward purely economic considerations.[105] They tried to argue that the work of women and children was outside the domain of government, for it benefited industry and families. Scottish member of Parliament Kirkman Finlay opposed the Ten Hours Bill of 1833 on similar grounds, arguing that even respectable tradesmen sent their children to factories to earn money for the family.[106] R. H. Greg, an economist, defended the morality of factory girls, pointing out that they preferred the mills to service, and lauded the "contribution to the national wealth" made by low-waged women substituting for men.[107]

Yet many political economists had to admit that women's work violated the principles of middle-class morality, and their advocacy of education and self-improvement was hardly a solution to these problems.[108] Nassau Senior argued against factory legislation, claiming that in textile districts men could benefit from the labor of their wives and children, but he admitted that women and children working could cause moral and domestic inconvenience.[109] W. R. Greg, a mill owner, also opposed any further regulation of the factory system, and he, too, nonetheless depicted the deleterious effects of women's work on family life.[110] Other political economists moved toward advocacy of the factory acts, on sanitary and moral grounds. In 1832, John Stuart Mill went so far as to propose in the *Examiner* that "females of any age" should eventually be excluded from manufactories.[111] Dr. James Kay-Shuttleworth wrote of the insanitary conditions of Manchester factory people in 1832, attributing much domestic discomfort and unhealthiness to mill girls' lack of training in cleaning and cooking, and their willingness to go out to work and "abandon" their infants to "the care of a hireling or neighbor."[112] R. H. Greg, echoing much of the medical testimony to the factory commissioners, wrote of the "injurious influence which the weakened and vitiated constitution of the [factory] women has on their children" and advised that no mothers be allowed to work in factories or any other occupation that would take them away from their children.[113] The *Scots Times* supported the factory acts because "excessive labor and low wages render the operatives" not only "ignorant, reckless, wretched and immoral" but vulnerable to cholera, which could spread to the city's more prosperous citizens.[114] Thus, most sanitary and social reformers tended to treat the factory populations as objects of scientific and state intervention rather than as subjects in their own right.[115]

Tory radicals, in contrast, made more direct alliances with working people. Working-class factory reformers were able to gain Tory support by portraying the destruction wreaked by mill work on proletarian family life, claiming that the benefits of domesticity were a right that should be enjoyed by rich and poor alike. When Richard Oastler, an Evangelical originally active in the anti-slavery movement, was finally confronted with factory conditions, he turned his energies to the cause of the "white slaves" of England. He was a powerful orator whose chief gift, according to his biographer, was for "identifying himself with his hearers, enabling him to enunciate and give back to them their own unformulated aspirations."[116] Oastler and other Tory radicals told the classic pastoral narrative of the golden age of cottage industry and village life, where due subordination to "altar and throne" had preserved virtue, a way of life that was destroyed by the factory system, which forced children to support their parents and drove mill girls into prostitution.[117] In 1835 he wrote that it was not enough for the manufacturers that poor men must send their little children to the mills; the wife must go too, "domestic comforts must be abandoned, parental and filial joys must be forgotten . . . deprived . . . of all the endearing comforts of home; what wonder that they should turn thieves, drunkards and prostitutes!"[118] Another Evangelical clergyman in the movement, the Rev. G. S. Bull, attacked the factory system for destroying women's domestic skills, inspiring "impudence" in factory girls, and leading them into prostitution.[119]

Oastler and Bull's rhetoric appealed to the patriarchal sentiments of many working men, especially the religious. In a parliamentary inquiry William Kershaw, a Yorkshire Sunday school teacher and unemployed weaver, testified that "impudence and immorality of every description" increasingly characterized his own factory-working daughters.[120] Mathew Crabtree was horrified by pregnancies among unmarried factory girls and complained of their indecent language.[121] John Hannam of Leeds alleged that the reason why factory girls did not have more illegitimate children was that they read books about abortion, a claim also made by a doctor, James Blundell.[122] However, these lurid tales of books about abortion were generally not corroborated and seem unlikely, given that other witnesses to the inquiry complained that factory girls had little opportunity for schooling. Rather, religious and moralistic factory workers were confusing use of rude language with actual "immoral" behavior; as one Dundee doctor pointed out, factory workers "have not time to engage in dissipated courses."[123]

Radicals sometimes used melodramatic rhetoric to deflect accusations of immorality away from working-class women. At a Glasgow public meeting on the factory system, the radical Mr. McAulay countered one speaker who claimed that most of the city's prostitutes and felons came from the factories, declaring, "Factory Lords acted as pimps for young and beautiful girls . . . while they were doomed to labor within the gates of the bastile factories, the blame attached not to themselves, but to those that had not emancipated them earlier."[124]

Radicals, working men, conservative male trade unionists, and Tory radicals alike colluded in depicting factory women as passive victims rather than active agents capable of organizing themselves. Although this picture ran counter to the actual activities of women unionists, it enabled trade unionists to refute the laissez-faire theory that the government had no business interfering with adult workers. A letter to the *Herald to the Trades' Advocate* urged skilled male factory operatives to support the factory acts:

> This is a matter in which a great number of persons are deeply interested, who on account of their tender age and their sex cannot

state and defend their own case, and who, in fact, have no clear conception of any of the mental and moral evils which the present system brings upon them; although they are fully alive to what they
have to endure, in the way of physical and bodily suffering and
inconvenience.[125]

In fact, although some women worried about how they could earn enough
money for food if their hours were shortened, many others, including the
organized Glasgow female powerloom weavers, did support the factory
movement, and Oldham women not only rioted but helped spread secret information through female friendly society meetings in 1834.[126] Yet
women and children factory operatives continued to be depicted as mere
suffering bodies. In Glasgow, operative cotton spinners campaigning for
the Ten Hours Bill marched with a "stunted and sickly Factory Girl"
who held a banner inscribed, "The Christian Slaves of England."[127] The
strongly patriarchal character of the movement may account for the fact
that women did take a less prominent part in the factory acts agitation of
the early 1830s than in other movements of the time.[128]

Conclusion

Why, then, did domestic rhetoric prevail over more egalitarian strategies?
For one thing, sexual tensions within working-class communities at this
time eliminated the possibility of radical change in gender relations. Even
as they adopted Owenite cooperation, artisans clung to fraternal male
bonding and excluded women from their unions. While powerloom weavers built on the textile tradition of sexual cooperation to form women's
unions, cotton spinners would not give up their patriarchal privilege in the
factory. Although they accepted females and children as auxiliaries, they
could not stomach the thought of women as independent workers and trade
unionists.

Yet the main reason domesticity prevailed over egalitarianism was its
rhetorical power. First, domesticity in fact enabled radicals to address some
of those sexual tensions. In demanding the breadwinner wage, trade unions
tried to appeal to women, claiming their lives would be easier if they were
sheltered in the home instead of toiling in mills or sweatshops. They promised to replace the hard-drinking artisan who neglected his family with a
respectable patriarch who brought home the bacon.

Domesticity was especially useful in political struggles with the state.
By the mid-1820s, with the failure of strikes and apprenticeship legislation,
trade unionists were on the defensive against laissez-faire ideology. Political economists repeatedly argued that male trade unionists selfishly excluded women from their occupations in order to perpetuate artisans' mo-

nopolies. They lauded the work of women and children as virtuous and beneficial to industries and families. Thus, middle-class reforms did not impose the ideal of domesticity from above on working-class homes. Instead, trade unionists cleverly exploited the contradictions between bourgeois morality and theories of political economy. They drew upon domesticity to demand the breadwinner wage for themselves, claiming that they needed higher wages and the legislative exclusion of women and children in order to protect their families from the immorality of factories and workshops.

By espousing domesticity, trade unionists gained the support of Tory radicals, who were able to reject the image of the poor as an unregenerate, immoral mass in favor of a new vision of a nation united by the ideals of paternalism, one happy family of head, heart, and hands.[129] Despite the contemporaneous organizations of women workers, male unionists colluded in depicting female factory workers as passive victims, although they eventually objected when Tory radicals treated the men themselves as helpless children who needed assistance from above. Bull, for instance, attacked workers as drunken and immoral.[130] Oastler had proclaimed that the vanishing of "parental control" led to excessive drinking, idleness, strikes, and defiance of the magistracy.[131] Eventually, trade unionists tired of Tory radicals' paternalism and turned to Chartism to demand political rights for themselves, yet they continued to apply the rhetoric of domesticity to restrict women workers. As radicals tried to mobilize their communities to challenge a recalcitrant state, then, the tensions between egalitarianism and domesticity persisted.

12   Chartism
Domesticity and Politics

In 1837 and 1838 radicals began to rally working-class people to demand the "People's Charter": a call for universal manhood suffrage, annual Parliaments, the ballot, and other political reforms.[1] Like the Painites of the 1790s, the Chartists believed that citizenship was a "universal political right of every human being" rather than a privilege of property, and a few women took this philosophy to justify female suffrage.[2] Furthermore, Chartism was a mass movement, in which working men *and* women drew upon their plebeian heritage of community mobilization to meet on moonlit moors, petition Parliament, and riot for their rights.

Yet this wider vision of the working class ultimately narrowed. Most Chartist women defined themselves as wives and mothers, auxiliaries to their husbands and fathers, and eventually retreated from activism.[3] Chartist men pushed to exclude women from the factory system and even hoped to "protect" them from wage labor altogether. By the late 1840s, they seemed to understand working-class consciousness as representing the political and economic concerns only of skilled men.[4] Why did Chartism lose its egalitarian potential and adopt a restrictive rhetoric of domesticity? The answer lies in the fact that domesticity helped Chartists address two tasks: first, to resolve sexual antagonism among working people; and, second, to refute claims that working people were immoral, undeserving of both family life and political rights.

Chartists tried to create a positive class identity for working people, uniting diverse elements into an "imagined community" through political organization and rhetoric.[5] They wished to draw upon working people's heritage of tumultuous community action but also strove to overcome the indiscipline and sexual antagonism that had plagued plebeian cultures. Since the Chartists lacked political power, they had to mobilize the power of numbers, appealing to women as well as men. Chartism therefore built on the experiences of the anti–Poor Law and factory struggles to define working-class interests as encompassing those of impoverished mothers and wan factory girls as well as proud artisans. Chartists tried to transform the old masculine plebeian public of beershops and workshops into a more integrated, disciplined public sphere.[6] They organized female powerloom weavers of Lancashire, Glasgow housewives, and London schoolteachers alongside male cotton spinners, handloom weavers, and shoemakers, inviting them all to mass meetings and genteel soirees.[7] This was very different from the middle-class public sphere, where men associated together to discuss politics and economics, relegating family issues to the private realm.

Yet, with few exceptions, Chartists were not willing or able to articulate the practice of organizing women along with men into a principle of gender equality. A possible precedent, Owenite feminism, had seemed to divide the working class at a time when unity was needed, for it exposed the festering sore of sexual antagonism and demanded concessions men were not willing to make. Working men instead often defined their fight for the vote as a struggle for manhood, using highly gendered language that would make egalitarianism impossible to consider.

The most important reason why Chartists turned to domesticity, however, has to do with the movement's second, and crucial, task: to defend working people against attacks on their family morality and to assert that they deserved political rights. For instance, some opponents of a wider suffrage denied working men the vote by claiming that they were not good husbands and fathers. In the conservative *Blackwood's Edinburgh Magazine*, Archibald Alison, the sheriff of Glasgow, contrasted the middle-class man's "self-denial" in supporting his family with the "sensual indulgence" of excessive drinking, bastardy, and desertion of wives allegedly prevalent among working men.[8] Chartist men, in response, blamed capitalism and governmental oppression for the misery of their families, and they manipulated the ideology of separate spheres to claim that domesticity was a privilege all, not just the middle class, should enjoy. Domesticity provided a way of both defending working-class families and appealing to women without threatening men.

Manhood, Domesticity, and Melodrama

Chartists often spoke of domesticity in melodramatic terms, for melodrama provided a vision of a golden past spoiled by aristocratic exploitation and reclaimed by heroic working-class manhood. It spoke to working people's experience of domestic misery and promised to cure it, and it enabled working men and women to stretch and debate domesticity to define political identities for themselves. Chartist rhetoric did not create a consistent, coherent political philosophy, but mingled Painite radicalism, constitutionalism, and Owenite socialism with Scripture and dialect literature. Similarly, Chartists used the rhetoric of domesticity to serve several functions and convey several meanings.[9]

Chartist domesticity echoed middle-class moralists but twisted their sentimentality into melodramatic tropes. In Evangelical narratives, individual sin, especially feminine indiscipline, poisoned the happy home.[10] But melodrama blamed familial disruption on an outside villain—the aristocratic libertine.[11] Gerald Massey, a Chartist working-class poet, encapsulated the domestic melodramatic narrative neatly in verse:

> Our Fathers are Praying for Pauper Pay
> Our Mothers with Death's Kiss are white;
> Our Sons are the Rich Man's Serfs by day,
> And our Daughters his Slaves by night.[12]

But, as Massey proclaimed in another poem, "The Chivalry of Labor," "We'll win the golden age again."[13]

Melodramatic domesticity appealed to working people whose families were disrupted by industrialization, urbanization, and unemployment. The vision of the golden age enabled Chartist orators to condense the disparate family experiences of artisans, factory workers, and laborers into one potent narrative of a past golden age, present domestic misery, a wicked villain, rescue by heroic Chartist manhood, and a future of domesticity brought about through manhood suffrage.[14] For many textile workers, domesticity originally meant domestic industry, when families worked together under one roof. In an era of factory labor, it had become a nostalgic vision of independence.[15] For London artisans, however, domesticity meant that a man deserved a breadwinner wage.[16] The vague, symbolic narrative of melodrama enabled Chartists to evoke a vision of domesticity that attracted all these disparate workers.

By using even fragmentary melodramatic motifs in their speeches, Chartists increased the emotional power and accessibility of their rhetoric.[17] For instance, individual Chartists disagreed on whether economic, ideological, or political oppression was more important. But if orators wove their political analyses into a melodramatic narrative, audiences could simply identify the upper-class villain as the enemy. One Chartist speaker attributed working people's woes to mill owners, asking a meeting, "Who are compelling women and tender babes to procure the means of subsistence in the cotton factories—to be nipt in the bud, to be sacrificed at the shrine of Moloch? They are the rich, the capitalists."[18] George Harney blamed Malthusianism: "A pretended philosophy . . . [that] crushes, through the bitter privations it inflicts upon us, the energies of our manhood, making our hearths desolate, our homes wretched, inflicting upon our heart's companions an eternal round of sorrow and despair."[19] And Scottish Chartist Mr. MacFarlane pointed the finger at Toryism: "Toryism just means ignorant children in rags, a drunken husband, and an unhappy wife."[20]

Melodramatic narratives gave working people "a moral purpose and a sense of agency"—in other words, a political identity.[21] The Tory paternalists used melodrama to express the melancholy of a lost paternalist past, but working men wanted to be the heroes of their own dramas, not impotent victims. To the pathos of melodrama's images of broken homes, they added a new vision of domesticity redeemed by working-class manhood. Chartist Thomas Ainge Devyr firmly believed melodramatic romances would inspire men to chivalrous deeds against aristocratic tyrants in order to win "woman's smile."[22] In using melodrama to portray manhood in opposition to childhood, Chartists also repudiated the paternalism of Tory radical leaders such as Richard Oastler.

While melodrama provided a tragic vision of the past and a promise of heroic rescue, Chartists also discussed domesticity as a hopeful dream of future family life. They tried to create a new ideal of working-class manhood, in part to attract women alienated from the masculinity of previous trade union movements. For instance, when a southern orator proclaimed at a Newcastle meeting, "If I had a wife I would fight for her, I would die for her," a working-class woman in the audience muttered to her neighbor, "He disen't [*sic*] say he would work for her."[23] By promising women that Chartism would transform their husbands from drunken louts into responsible breadwinners, radicals overcame women's suspicion of the movement. For instance, Mr. Macfarlane of Glasgow proclaimed, "Instead of the old Tory system of the husband coming home drunk to his family, we will have him sober, contented, and happy."[24] Two years later, the Scottish *Chartist Circular* detected that the promise of domesticity was being fulfilled: "our fair countrywomen . . . acknowledged the change for the better in the 'guidman,' as he comes home on the Saturday evening to read his *Circular*, and watches over the interests of his family."[25]

Chartists desired women's support because they feared that if women remained uneducated they would deter their husbands from participating in politics or would even drag down the movement. The East London Mental Improvement Association declared that "in the absence of knowledge [wives] are the most formidable obstacles to a man's patriotic exertions, as, imbued with it, they will prove his greatest auxiliaries."[26] Apparently wives often saw Chartist meetings as just another excuse for men to go to the pub.[27] A fictitious Stockport couple in a Chartist magazine "spent a very fractious and uncomfortable life, since that plaguey Charter, as Betsy termed it, came up."[28]

In Chartists' promise to transform the old marital misery into happy domesticity, temperance played a major role, for it was crucial to solving the problems of working-class marriage. Looking at temperance in this way makes it clear that it was not an emulation of false middle-class ideals of respectability but a practical response to the ravages alcoholism made on the ability of men to be good husbands and good Chartists.[29] This was a change from the old trade-union response to accusations of domestic mistreatment: that a working man's private life was not a political issue.[30] While plebeian ballads told the wives of drunken husbands to "whack them with a rolling pin" or admonished them to forgive, temperance Chartists sympathized with the women's plight and promised a solution. The complaints women had been making for decades finally acquired a political context: the taxes the government extracted for liquor and the demoralization of the working-class cause.[31] Robert Lowery declared, "I hate a pot-house politician, who, to satisfy his own desires, robs his wife and family of those comforts he ought to administer to them; such are not the men on whom we must depend."[32] A writer observed in the Chartist *Lifeboat* that drunken men who were brutal to their wives did not deserve the name of Chartist.[33]

The precise nature of Chartist manhood, however, became entangled in Chartist debates over whether "physical force" or "moral force" would be most effective in obtaining the vote. Should the Chartist patriarch protect his family by instructing them at home, or by fighting in the streets to defend them? The mainstream majority of the movement were willing to consider physical force as the ultimate resistance to state repression, and in the first two years of Chartism some, especially in Lancashire, in fact engaged in arming and drilling.[34] Their motto was "peaceably if we can, forcibly if we must." Moral-force Chartists demanded that the movement utterly repudiate any possibility of violence and rely totally on persuading middle-class allies and Parliament that they were respectable enough to deserve the vote. Although the older historiography viewed physical-force Chartists as "irrational," degraded, and deskilled factory workers who discredited Chartism by their threats of violence,[35] more recent historians have pointed out that the divisions could not be broken down sociologically on occupational lines. Physical-force Chartists considered violence as a last resort and preferred to concentrate on building communities through moral reform.[36] Nonetheless, the physical-moral division *was* a major focus of debate in the first two years of Chartism, especially in Scotland.[37]

There, intense controversy broke out when the Reverend Patrick Brewster of Paisley insisted that his fellow Chartists follow him in repudiating physical force, only to be defeated as a delegate to the 1839 convention and defied by Paisley workers who armed themselves.[38]

While both sides agreed on the prevalence of domestic misery among working people, and the necessity of gaining the vote in order to ameliorate it, they differed in their visions of the source of masculine authority. The moral-force Chartists never gained the adherence of more than a minority, partially because in order to gain middle-class support they regarded suffrage not as a right but as a privilege that had to be earned by proving moral virtue. The moral-force London Working Men's Association admitted as members only those men who "possess the attributes and characters of *men*; and little worthy of the name are those who . . . forgetful of their duties as fathers, husbands, and brothers . . . drown their intellect amid the drunken revelry of the pot house."[39] William Lovett's vision was closer to the middle-class sentimental ideal of domesticity, for he blamed working people for their own familial misery. His notion of masculinity was middle-class as well, for he stressed a masculinity based on rationality and self-control, rather than the "pugilistic skill" on which many working-class men still based their honor.[40]

Not surprisingly, Lovett's opponents complained that he was too beholden to middle-class men such as Edward Swaine, an anti–Corn Law activist who told working-class men, "If you are careless of personal decency and domestic comfort, you cannot be believed, if you profess concern about national improvement."[41] Mainstream Chartists argued that they did not want to wait to persuade the middle class that they deserved the vote. The only power working men had, they argued, was that of numbers—and without the vote, they could exercise that power only by threatening physical force as a last resort if moral force failed. They scorned the moral-force men as toadies to the middle class. Physical-force men vaunted the vigorous, even violent, manhood that had its roots in pugilist and pub culture.[42] They took over meetings of the Anti–Corn Law League by force of fisticuffs to declare that the Charter was the first political priority, to be taken up before any other cause.[43]

The physical-force *London Democrat* often referred to the "manly virtues" of working men and opposed the *Charter* newspaper because its "dandy cockney politician" editor did "not represent the straightforward, manly political sentiments of the working men of this country."[44] They insulted their moral-force opponents with such epithets as "old women" and "kitchen maids."[45] As David Goodway writes, "By 1839, the capital was firmly physical force," with the militant London Democratic Association claiming far more adherents than Lovett's London Working Men's Association.[46] The London Democratic Association allied itself with the physical-force movement of the north, which was rooted in the anti–Poor Law and factory system struggles. Physical-force Chartists eschewed Lovett's sentimental, self-blaming domesticity, espousing instead a melodramatic and biblical narrative that blamed familial misery on the forces of evil—capitalism, the New Poor Law, and the aristocracy. When Lovett and his colleagues later repudiated the "foolish displays and gaudy trappings" of early Chartism, Trowbridge Chartists wrote that this "passionate invective . . . first aroused [many working men] to a sense of their degradation, their rights, and their strength."[47]

Working men often felt that oppression had robbed them of their masculinity. They were especially enraged at their loss of control over women, as the Rev. J. R. Stephens made clear when he proclaimed to a meeting, "God cursed woman as well as man . . . that she should be in subjection to her own husband, her desire should be unto her husband, and he should rule over her (hear hear) and not the millowners (tremendous cheering) nor the coal pit masters (continuous cheering)—not the Poor Law Commissioners."[48] Stalybridge Chartist Mr. Deegan echoed this sentiment when he argued that English men wanted their wives and children in happy cottages, not "polluted by lickspittles" in the mines and factories.[49] Stephens explicitly linked physical force to familial issues when he proclaimed, "If society cannot be renovated . . . [so that] every industrious, virtuous man should have a home, and the blessings of home . . . then, I say, 'Cry havoc, and let slip the dogs of war!' (Loud cheers) Revolution by force—revolution by blood!"[50]

The favorite slogan of Stephens's followers was "For child and wife, / We will war to the knife!"[51] Their claim was that they wished to exclude women from the workplace in order to protect and support them.[52] This tactic had, of course, long been an issue in the northern factory movement, but the problem of women's work affected London as well. Silk weavers, hatters, shoemakers, and tailors were disproportionately involved in Chartism, and all were trades whose unions had had to cope with the threat of undercutting by cheap female labor.[53] Yet Stephens's supporters were not simply motivated by a desire to regain patriarchal authority. Rather, they were following a new rhetorical strategy which united their diverse experiences and transformed sexual antagonism into chivalry. As a result, they gained the support of many women in their communities. Despite its belligerent masculinity, the London Democratic Association was rooted in a Painite radicalism which opened up possibilities for women's independent participation. It was allied with the London Female Democratic Association, whose women declared, "We assert in accordance with the rights of all, and acknowledging the sovereignty of the people as our right, as free women (or women determined to be free) to rule ourselves."[54]

Women's Activism in the Chartist Movement

In the north, women continued their tradition of supporting community uprisings as Lancashire workers in many localities made pikes and even bought revolvers in expectation that the government would use violence to repress a planned general strike.[55] Lancashire women purchased pikes for their men, and one young mother, a framework knitter, was arrested for marching in a Chartist demonstration carrying a revolver and ammunition.[56] In Dunfermline, Scotland, a Mrs. Collie incited a physical-force meeting to defy the government: she sang,

> The time draws nigh, and is at hand,
> When females will with courage stand!
> Each heart united will decree,
> We'll have our rights, we will be free!
> We'll sever ne'er, but steadfast be!
> We'll die to have our liberty![57]

The men of Dunfermline believed that women could defy the government: the government had imprisoned three hundred men, but they would never dare to jail hundreds of females.[58] Sketching the dire consequences of an insurrection in Birmingham or Glasgow, Alexander Somerville anticipated fierce participation by women: in his imagined scenario, the wife of a "fustian-jacketed pikeman" who was wrestling with a policeman sprang to her husband's aid "like a tigress." Admonishing her neighbor Peggy to "break their heads with the axe, or the poker, or the tongs," she "laid on the shoulder of a policeman most prodigiously, with a sawyer's handspoke." For the rather moderate Somerville, however, such female ferocity was just another reason to avoid violence.[59] The violence of physical-force Chartism, however, was more often rhetorical than real, intimidating opponents and inciting the fervor of its adherents with a "language of menace."[60]

In late 1839, the failure of the planned general strike and insurrectionary plots turned the movement in a new direction. Despairing of revolutionary tactics, Chartists renewed their interest in temperance, education, and radical religion.[61] That move also enabled them to gain greater female support, for only the most militant women would risk their family's safety by advocating arming. Chartists did not need women's support only in the home. They also needed women in mass demonstrations; gathering signatures on petitions; striking; and exclusive dealing, that is, boycotting shop-keepers who refused to support Chartists.

Yet male Chartists expressed ambivalence about women's activities. In 1839 the radical *Scottish Patriot* lauded the new Gorbals Female Univer-sal Suffrage organization for supporting their brothers and husbands, but noted, "We lament the necessity that exists for drawing the female mind from employment more congenial to the close and retiring habits of the women of this country, than the arena of politics."[62] A Leeds speaker de-clared that women must "take the part of men" in the Chartist struggle, but also hoped they would remain delicate and domestic.[63] They preferred females to act as decorative symbols of working-class virtue. When mili-tant Chartist Mary Anne Walker spoke at length before a mixed meeting, the *Northern Star* reporter rhapsodized about her "very graceful bust" before alluding to her political views.[64] In Scotland, one Dunfermline radi-cal, "observing many women present at a political meeting, grumbled, "A lecture on domestic economy would perhaps be more suitable for them." In response, the militant women there formed their own association.[65] Yet Chartist men usually defined women's role initially in subordinate terms and in many areas they controlled women's meetings tightly, taking up the time with long speeches by male visitors.

Nonethless, Chartist women organized themselves, even if only as sup-portive auxiliaries. Women formed over a hundred and fifty flourishing female Chartist associations in England, and at least twenty-three in Scot-land.[66] They extended the activist tradition of women in textile commu-nities into Chartism. Women were particularly involved in Chartism in "centres of decaying industry," such as Lancashire handloom weaving communities, and in industrial towns such as Stockport, where there were high concentrations of women workers.[67] In Bradford, center of the woolen industry, the Female Radical Association was a "quasi-autonomous group of five branches with six hundred members."[68] In Scotland, female Chartist associations flourished in the textile districts of Aberdeen and in the fac-tory villages of Bridgeton, Calton, Mile End, and the Gorbals, near Glas-gow.[69] Although we know the occupations of only a few Glasgow female Chartists, Robert Duncan states that most female Chartists in Aberdeen were mill workers.[70] In 1839, the largest contributions to the Chartist De-fense Fund by factories in Bridgeton came from the women of Stephen's Factory and Humphrey's Mill.[71] The more articulate women in Chartist meetings, however, probably came from politically active artisan families.[72]

Chartist women fashioned a political identity for themselves as moth-ers, workers, and activists which differed in important ways both from the middle-class ideal of domesticity and from male Chartists' notions of women's role.[73] They developed what I would call a "militant domesticity," justifying their actions in stepping outside the home by defining the responsibilities of motherhood not just as nurturing children in the home but as laboring to feed them and organizing to better their lives.[74] Mrs. Lapworth, a Birmingham reformer, compared the hunger she suffered after childbirth with the luxury of "hundreds around her, of her own sex, who had never labored, and did not know how to labor, and were enjoying all the comforts of life."[75] The female Chartists of Manchester maintained "we have a right to struggle to gain for ourselves, our husbands, brothers and children, suitable houses, proper clothing and good food."[76]

Women's own addresses differed subtly from the flowery rhetoric of the Chartist men who objected to female factory labor. For instance, Ashton's Rev. J. R. Stephens presented a lurid picture of female mill workers who "don't care whether their children live or not—when they don't care whether they have husbands or not."[77] Stephens was admittedly extremely popular among Chartist women and counterbalanced his criticism of mill workers by blaming their faults on the system. Yet when the Ashton female Chartists wrote their own address in the same month, they presented themselves as griefstricken, rather than indifferent, at the "desolat[ion]" of their homes. Instead of depicting factory girls as immoral, they declared that "our daughters, are considered, by haughty and iniquitous capitalists, as only created to satisfy their wicked desires." And, in contrast to Stephens's patriarchalism, they demanded the franchise for themselves as well as for men.[78]

In contrast to Lovett's paternalist view of marriage, an anonymous author in the *National Association Gazette* declared, "Woman stands in the same relationship to a man, as the subject of a despotic government to his monarch."[79] Some Scottish women called for their sisters to "enlarge their thoughts beyond the domestic circle."[80] Other Chartists claimed that factory labor deprived women of the education that would enable them to be active beyond "the dull round of their household duties."[81]

As they became more deeply involved in Chartism, some women changed their political identities from passive spectators to outspoken activists. Since it was more difficult for women to claim a public political role, most Chartist women initially defined themselves as auxiliaries in the struggle for the rights of their husbands and brothers. It must be acknowledged, however, that the women's stress on domesticity was in part a rhetorical gesture to answer vitriolic attacks made on their activities by the middle-class press.[82] The Scottish Chartist women of Glasgow initially spoke with great hesitance and modesty, but they soon became more militant, defining themselves as heroines and not just as victims. They "improved their habits of thought" by reading and by writing essays on various topics.[83] Their spokeswoman Agnes Muir at first apologized for her oratorical inadequacies, but soon refuted the notion that it was indelicate for a "starving woman to say she is in want." She cited a long list of heroines for Chartist women to take as precedents.[84] A Miss M'Kay went even further when she declared, "I offer no apology for appearing before you this evening, nor do I require to prove to you that the sex to which I belong has rights, and that these rights have been unlawfully taken from us as from the other sex." [85] The women of Dunfermline defended themselves against criticism for organizing a meeting by declaring that "until woman becomes an independent creature, not the subservient slave of man, but a fit companion and assistant in all his undertakings," the Constitution could never be reformed.[86]

A few women demanded the vote for themselves on the basis of natural rights, and a few men supported them.[87] A "plain working woman" of Glasgow, a weaver, argued in 1838 that women could reason as well as men and therefore deserved the vote.[88] The *National Association Gazette* accused opponents of female suffrage of hypocrisy for "contradicting the Chartist profession of universal justice."[89] After all, according to Chartist logic there was no reason women should not have the vote. Because working men lacked property and, often, households, Chartists could not demand the vote on the Lockean basis of the male householder, but instead resorted to the Painite tradition of the inherent individual right to representation. For instance, Ashton women argued, "intelligence [being] the necessary qualification for voting," women should "enjoy the elective franchise along with our kinsmen."[90] But female suffrage was difficult to reconcile with domesticity. For instance, R. J. Richardson in his pamphlet *The Rights of Women* used a Painite language of rights and citizenship to show that women, because they were subjected to the laws of the state, paid taxes, and worked, should participate in political affairs. Yet Richardson also proclaimed that women were formed to "temper man" and should "return to [their] domestic circles and cultivate [their] finer feelings for the benefit of their offspring."[91] He attempted to resolve these contradictions by advocating suffrage only for single women and widows; married women were to be represented by their husbands. However, radicals were somewhat uncomfortable with the notion of independent political spinsters. At a Southwark reform meeting, D. W. Harvey, a radical publisher and member of Parliament, admitted that spinsters who kept shops and acted as churchwardens logically deserved the vote. But he then elicited laughter from the audience, jovially dismissing women's claims and ridiculing their independence by alluding to the punishment of female scolds in the stocks.[92] Only the Owenites consistently supported female suffrage.[93] When an Owenite tried to raise the question of female suffrage at an 1842 meeting in Shoreditch, a poor East End district, he was laughed down by the audience.[94] These arguments continued through 1846 and 1847, as Owenites supported female suffrage but the majority opposed it as creating "domestic unhappiness."[95]

Yet opponents of universal manhood suffrage used the argument for women's votes as a reductio ad absurdum; if everyone had the inherent natural right to vote, they asked scornfully, why not women? Commenting on the 1842 debates in the House of Commons over Sharman Crawford's motion to extend the suffrage, the *Times* noted, "Were they consistent with themselves, they must at least give the franchise to women."[96] Chartists could only answer lamely that it was "paltry twaddle" to argue that working men should be denied the vote unless women were included as well.[97] By subsuming women under their husbands, the rationale for universal suffrage as a natural right was lost.

One alternative was household suffrage, descended from eighteenth-century versions of civic humanism that defined the citizen as the property-owning heads of households.[98] Advocates of household suffrage believed that the role of male head of household proved a man's stability and responsibility, even without property. *Northern Star* editorials denounced household suffrage because it would subsume radical sons' views under conservative fathers' votes, but they did not see any contradiction in excluding wives from the vote in order to "preserve harmony" in the family.[99] Feargus O'Connor, for instance, on this ground opposed the vote for any woman, thundering that "it would lead to family dissensions."[100]

Conclusion

The Chartists adopted the rhetoric of domesticity, in part, to address this problem of "family dissensions." By promising women better husbands, who would actually bring home the bacon rather than drinking up their wages at the pub, Chartists gained women's support for the movement. At the same time, men believed domesticity would give them back their masculine self-respect through the breadwinner wage, and hoped the vote would help them attain that wage. Yet the image of the delicate wife sheltering at home while her brave husband strove forth into the world to protect her was always an ideal rather than a reality for working people—and for the movement. Chartists did not only need women's passive support at home, they needed their active participation in the movement, which had grown out of traditions of community mobilization where women workers struggled alongside men.

As Chartism matured, it became more and more difficult to balance egalitarianism and domesticity, to draw upon the strength of women's activism while depicting them as helpless creatures in need of male protection. Like the radicals of the 1790s, Chartist men could not accept the full implications of Painite egalitarianism because their notion of citizenship was so bound up with masculinity.

13 Chartism and the Problem of Women Workers

The contradiction between Chartist egalitarianism and domesticity became particularly acute as women workers gained prominence as a public issue in the early 1840s. On the one hand, Chartists needed to appeal to women workers in order to mobilize northern communities, where women composed over half the labor force in the cotton industry.[1] On the other hand, male Chartists demanded the vote in order to protect females from the contamination of factories and mines. As Chartists tried to sway parliamentary opinion to grant both the suffrage and factory regulation, they found that domesticity was a clever tactic, but also a dangerous gamble.

Labor was an essential component of the Chartist notion of suffrage. To avoid the contradiction between Painite egalitarianism, which would mean female suffrage, and their masculine notion of citizenship, Chartist men rewrote the constitutionalist tradition, simply replacing property in a household, land, or business with property in skill as the qualification for the vote.[2] To be sure, this was not enough to exclude women. R. J. Richardson included among his arguments for female suffrage the fact that "woman contributes directly and indirectly to the wealth and resources of this nation by her labor and skill."[3] However, he contorted his argument by claiming that, on the one hand, women should have the vote because they labored, but, on the other hand, they should use the vote to change society so that they would not have to work and could remain dependent on their husbands and fathers.

The majority of male Chartists who did not believe women should vote simply assumed that skill was a masculine monopoly. As Clive Behagg writes, the Chartist democratic ideal derived from the artisanal experience of collective democracy in the workplace—working as a team and expressing pride and honor in skill.[4] Yet the artisan ethos was democratic in only the most limited sense, for it had always been based on the exclusion of the less skilled, whether the unapprenticed, women, or Irish. And even as working men claimed that their skill qualified them to vote, they also complained that mechanization and the sweating system had robbed them of their skill and that they needed the vote to reclaim it. Since the replacement of women by men was often identified as the cause of deskilling, the exclusion of women from the work force became a necessary condition for male citizenship. R. J. Richardson lectured women who were assisting their husbands and fathers "in printing the most difficult patterns" on calico in Dumbartonshire, Scotland: "This is the work of men, and you ought not to perform it; your places are in your homes."[5]

Men hoped to derive pride and independence from their work, but women labored in order to survive, experiencing work as an alienated cash-nexus. The Newcastle women declared that "because the husband's earnings could not support his family, the wife has been compelled to leave her home neglected and, with her infant children, work at a soul and body degrading toil."[6] The Manchester Chartist women bemoaned that "we can scarcely get sufficient to keep body and soul together, for working twelve or thirteen hours per day."[7] Similarly, although the Birmingham Chartist women agreed with male speakers that a woman's place is in the home, they also protested against the heavy taxes taken out of their own wages and the stress of laboring hard for a pittance inadequate to support their families.[8] Yet even as these women lamented the hardships of wage labor, they expressed their willingness to fight for their families by organizing and striking in public.

Chartist men, however, found it very difficult to acknowledge the long-standing organizing traditions of women workers.[9] Forgetting the precedent of Owenite female unions only five years before, in 1839 the radical *Weekly Dispatch* detailed the plight of the poor needlewomen but assumed that "they cannot call public meetings, form committees, and join unions like men." To be sure, the newspaper suggested that women organize within their individual workplaces, but it could not conceive of them as public political actors.[10] By 1842, the *English Chartist Circular* denounced "a conspiracy" against poor needlewomen to keep down their wages, but stated that only a change in political representation could ameliorate their condition. When male Chartists addressed London "Sisters in Bondage," they first commiserated with their long hours of toil and scanty pay and then proclaimed, "We would fain see you the presiding divinities of a happy home."[11] These men seemed to think of women workers as frail victims who needed chivalrous protectors because they could not organize themselves. In contrast, when Mary Anne Walker, a London Chartist, addressed a large mixed meeting, she painted a touching picture of the plight of sweated needlewomen, but instead of advocating their return to the home, as did male Chartists, she simply declared that "these poor creatures should have fair remuneration for their labor."[12]

When women did organize, the Chartists often ignored them. In 1838 the female glassworkers of Cookson's Plate Glass factory in Newcastle mounted a militant strike over a change in their payment schedule and the dismissal of a sympathetic Chartist overseer. Taking advantage of this industrial unrest, the Chartists called a public meeting in Newcastle and extended an invitation to the striking women.[13] But as they looked out over the sea of angry female faces, the Chartist speakers did not allude to the women's grievances. Instead, the women's struggle seemed invisible, for the male orators proclaimed that the Charter would bring a day when "the working man should not be looked upon as a mere tool of the capitalists," and they celebrated the "manly conduct" of trade union men.[14] It is not surprising that when the Newcastle female Chartists addressed their fellow countrywomen they defined themselves as auxiliaries in the struggle of their male relations; perhaps they could not have been heard if they had defined themselves as trade unionists.

In Lancashire, however, Chartists and male powerloom weavers were forced to acknowledge female workers if they were to organize themselves, for 58 percent of the adult workers in the trade were women.[15] In the 1840 strike of powerloom weavers in Stockport, Lancashire, Chartists and trade unions faced a delicate balancing act between their feeling that female labor unfairly competed with men and their recognition that female workers were essential to the success of their cause. The manufacturer Bradshaw provoked the strike by reducing wages at a factory where he employed only female operatives. In response, the women struck, perhaps inspired by a turnout of female throstle spinners in Stockport several months earlier.[16] A larger issue soon erupted: Bradshaw's refusal to employ men.

The local Chartists, who were very involved in the strike, were rather ambivalent about this issue. On the one hand, Chartists had to persuade the women that to strike against Bradshaw's for not employing men would not endanger their own jobs. Thomas Leonard, for instance, declared that it was not that men wanted to take female places at the mills, but that they wanted to protect women from lusty overseers. A Mr. Clark proclaimed, "There were females in Mr. Lord's mill who were a pride to the town."[17] In a related strike at Manchester, Chartist Peter McDouall told the weavers that "the women were the better men." They must all "unite like men and women, who knew their rights, and dared obtain them."[18] Women responded enthusiastically to these calls, composing the largest part of a strikers' procession through Stockport and also marching on their own. An anonymous female weaver made a "powerful" Chartist and unionist speech at one strike meeting, according to the *Northern Star*, but she did not mention domestic issues. Fifteen women were arrested and charged with intimidating strikebreakers, and several were imprisoned for nine to twelve months.[19]

On the other hand, Chartists found factory work a degraded occupation for men such as Richard Pilling, a Chartist who had been forced to leave his handloom for the factory that very year, only to be blacklisted for union organization.[20] In his speeches for the strike, Pilling yearningly evoked the golden age of handloom weaving, when families were able to work together. At the same time, Mr. Campbell declared, "It was a melancholy fact, that women now do men's work in the factory, and their husbands stop at home."[21] By raising the question of domesticity, Chartists could appeal both to men anxious about employment and to mothers exhausted by the combination of factory labor with domestic chores. Mr. Leech, a Chartist, knew how to evoke the specific experience of married women: he asked at a meeting for a Manchester strike later that year, "Was it not enough for mothers to leave their infants at home, at five thirty in the morning, and to be exposed to the insolence of some domineering wretch, with only a half hour for breakfast, an hour for dinner, for eleven shillings?"[22] This line could appeal to married women such as Mrs. Wrigley, who left the factory after having worked there for thirty years. She demanded of workers, "Women! will you stand by the rights of men for your own benefit. ('We will.') Men! Will you stand by and protect the women? ('Like glue': laughter)." She spoke from her own experience when she proclaimed, "We are wives—not slaves!"[23]

Married women working was a sign of bad times. When wages were high, in the mid-1830s, many cotton factory worker families relied on the income of the father and the older children, but by 1840, when wages had declined and unemployment hit, all members of the family were forced to go out to work.[24] Domestic comfort was a marker of class division and exploitation, for after the strike was defeated, the men complained bitterly than the masters offered to make up for the lost wages by employing their wives and children. As the *Northern Star* proclaimed, this proved the "infernal rapacity which robs the unprotected workman of his hire to provide the extravagant expenses of mansions and carriages and parks and grounds, and splendid buildings and costly w——s for the cotton lords."[25]

Chartism and the Factory Acts

Despite the cooperation of men and women in Stockport and other strikes, Chartists soon began to emphasize the strategy of calling for the exclusion of women from the work force through pressure on the state to pass factory legislation. They pushed the factory movement to move away from its tactic of uniting men and women on the demand for a limitation of hours for children (and, by extension, for all workers), to a demand for excluding women from the workplace altogether.[26] The Chartists continued the factory movement tactic of turning middle-class domestic ideology against itself, exposing the contradictions between the doctrines of political economy and separate spheres. Whereas the factory movement was led by paternalists, Chartists linked the demand to exclude women with their own demands for political rights. Furthermore, they extended political rights to encompass patriarchal privileges: the right to a masculine monopoly on occupations, and the right of men to women's domestic services. Robert Blakey wrote, "I see no reason why working men, whose labor creates every necessary and luxury of life, should be denied the pleasures and comforts of home."[27]

In the short run, manipulating the notion of domesticity was a powerful tool to claim concessions from the government. Yet the Chartists' persuasive power came not only from their domestic rhetoric but from the threat of a united working-class movement—the thousands of men *and* women ready to take to the streets. However, instead of organizing women, Chartists wanted to use their power to protect women from the evils of waged work. They also denigrated the very females they sought to protect, in the process bolstering their own status as male citizens, skilled workers, and breadwinners.

The issue of domesticity allowed working-class morality to return to the center of political debate. To press for the factory acts, Chartists claimed that women working undermined male workers' manhood and demoralized communities. Chartist journals began to merge the old melodramatic narrative of domestic misery caused by industrial evil with the sentimental and sanitary reformers' versions of domesticity, which blamed family unhappiness on women workers themselves. They monotonously complained that factory work made girls insubordinate, selfish, and immoral and that it deprived working men of "virtuous wives" skilled in housewifery.[28] The Scottish *Chartist Circular* argued that factories "degraded and contaminated" female workers, while the *English Chartist Circular* went even further, claiming that "wives and daughters are made to perpetuate the contamination of the laboring classes."[29]

The language of "contamination" was odd for working-class journals to use to describe their own class. Rather than pinning the blame for factory misery on the employment relationship, it displaced it onto women's work, depicting factory girls as creatures alien to the working-class community. Dropping the melodramatic trope that portrayed "fallen" factory girls as innocent victims of scheming "millocrats," the domestic line blamed women operatives themselves for going out to work and being too independent. This rhetoric contrasted with women workers' own more prosaic complaints. When Sheriff Archibald Alison of Glasgow claimed that factory girls inevitably became prostitutes, due to the "great sexual depravity" among urban workers, and claimed that three-quarters of the female factory workers lost their virginity before the age of twenty, factory women indignantly defended their morality.[30] An operative powerloom weaver admitted that when wages were cut in 1837, "a great number of our destitute factory girls were driven by poverty into a state of prostitution," but that if they were paid a fair wage, "the virtue of our factory girls would yet triumph over the cruel statements made by Sheriff Alison against our character, and make it sink into oblivion."[31] The Paisley women weavers similarly declared that they had a "most respectable character for industry and modesty."[32]

When Engels, speaking from the working men's perspective, commented that the factory system "virtually turned [men] into eunuchs" by forcing them to do housework, since only their wives could find work in factories, he simply echoed Chartists' complaints—but, unlike Engels, the Chartists rarely questioned the naturalness of the gender order.[33] Chartist Thomas Wheeler described factory women's husbands as "that crowd of women-men, inverting the order of Nature, and performing a mother's duties."[34] In 1842 William Dodd observed "It is quite pitiable to see these poor men taking care of the house and children, and busily engaging in washing, baking, nursing, and preparing the humble repast for the wife, who is wearing her life away in the factory."[35]

Many Chartists had criticized married women's factory work by focusing on the hardship it involved for the women themselves, who had to feed their children and keep house, in addition to working for twelve to fourteen hours a day in the mill.[36] Lancashire married female factory operatives declared they were being treated "worse than their master's horses," and that they were not even able to bring up their children properly.[37] The Aberdeen Chartist women, most of whom worked in mills, lamented in 1839, "We find ourselves outworn by toil in keeping our offspring from a premature grave."[38]

In contrast, advocates of the exclusion of women focused on the hardships married women's work inflicted on their husbands: cranky wives, noisy children, the bustle of washing and cooking going on around them after their day's work was done. Radical journals repeatedly quoted Joseph Corbett, who had testified before the commissioners on women's and children's work, "After the close of a hard day's work, [my mother sat] up nearly all night for several nights together washing and mending of clothes." Yet he stressed, not her hard labor, but the disturbance housework caused his father: "My father could have no comfort here . . . and sought refuge in an alehouse."[39] Corbett was echoing middle-class observers such as the vicar of Leeds, who blamed working wives for men's resort to the alehouse.[40] This represented a turn away from Chartist temperance activists' efforts to get men to take the blame for the domestic misery caused by their drinking. Another group blaming women workers for men's discomfort was a short-time delegation who told Sir Robert Peel that female factory workers were so debased and ignorant of housework that middle-class people would not employ them as servants. "Yet those who are thus considered unfit even to fulfill the office of menial to the rich, are the only parties whom, ordinarily, the male factory worker has a chance of obtaining a wife."[41]

However, various strands of the movement espoused subtly different versions of domesticity. The cotton spinners and powerloom weavers seem to have been most concerned with reducing the hours *all* labored; even though they found the factory system oppressive, the total abolition of female and child labor would not have been practicable for them.[42] To the handloom weavers and other artisans of the woolen and worsted districts of the West Riding, radicals depicted factory labor even for men as degrading, robbing them of their independence.[43] One Chartist essay claimed, "It is a system that drags men out of their proper sphere and drags them into the most unnatural, the most unmanly ways of gaining a livelihood."[44] Their nostalgia for the domestic system of production enabled short-time advocates to join forces with paternalists to clamor for the return of a golden age of family harmony. In fact, although these men fought for the total exclusion of women from the factories, they often assumed that women should still engage in subsidiary productive labor within the home.[45]

Despite their Chartism, advocates for factory regulation played into the hands of conservatives concerned with social disorder. On the one hand, Chartists saw working-class domestic misery as a symptom of the ravages of industrialism, and their organizations worked to overcome it through moral education and political action. On the other, outside observers could divert attention away from the roots of working-class misery by blaming it all on women's labor and depicting working-class people as degraded, passive, and immoral rather than as people determined to better themselves. For instance, Ralph Grindrod claimed that factory girls' lack of domesticity was "the one great and universally prevailing cause of distress and crime among the working classes."[46]

In January 1842, the Chartist-influenced West Riding Short-Time Commet with Peel and Lord Ashley to demand the gradual withdrawal of all females from factories. By stressing the immorality of female factory work and calling for its total abolition, Chartists allowed the governing classes to see their movement as a symptom of the degradation of womanhood, to be solved by protecting women rather than by giving rights to men. They played into paternalists' hands by declaring that the "domestic unhappiness" caused by the factory system's "inversion of the order of nature" was "fraught with danger to the State. Disaffection and discontent must be engendered among parties so situated."[47]

Their prediction came true in August of that year, when the "Plug Plot" riots and strikes erupted in the factory districts of Lancashire and Yorkshire.[48] Inspired by striking coal miners and angered by 25 percent wage cuts, Lancashire cotton operatives marched from factory to factory, encouraging other workers to "turn out" and removing the plugs from steam boilers to ensure that mills would shut down. Chartists had been actively organizing in the area, but national leaders counseled peaceful, patient organization rather than resort to physical force. When the disturbances broke out, they blamed local middle-class Anti–Corn Law leaders for provoking the people into rioting over food.[49]

However, although the strikes sparked chaotic demonstrations, they were not spontaneous outbreaks of misery and frustration. Cotton factory operatives faced the failure of conventional strikes to remedy repeated deep wage cuts and widespread unemployment. Local Chartists such as Richard Pilling, the former handloom weaver who had been active in the 1840 Stockport powerloom weavers' strike, turned their energies into demanding the Charter.[50] Indeed, while the more skilled artisans and cotton operatives wanted to restrict their demands to the question of wages, many poorer operatives now saw striking for wages as hopeless, and an uprising for the Charter their only alternative.[51] Chartist orators whipped them into a fervor with an apocalyptic, melodramatic vision:

> Your taskmasters tremble at your energy, and expecting masses eagerly watch this the great crisis of our cause. Labour must no longer be the common prey of masters and rulers . . . his cottage is empty, his back thinly clad, his children breadless, himself hopeless, . . . that undue riches, luxury, and gorgeous plenty might be heaped on the palaces of the taskmaster.[52]

The strikers intended to demonstrate massed power through both peaceful and violent protests that were deeply rooted in community traditions of political and industrial action. Women joined, as they always had, in the strikes and demonstrations. On 8 August, male and female powerloom weavers of Bayley's Mill in Stalybridge marched to Ashton and Hyde, carrying a red cap of liberty on a pole in a gesture reminiscent of earlier radicalism.[53] One-third of the crowd of five thousand were female, according to the *Manchester Guardian*.[54] On a later march from Rochdale to Todmorden, "Girls, not more than twelve or fourteen, wearing heavy clogs, went along with this party, at a distance of at least twenty-one miles, without the least refreshment. It was distressing to see them coming down Yorkshire Street, haggard, tired and lame."[55]

Many speakers reminded the crowds that they were approaching the anniversary of the Peterloo massacre.[56] On 9 August an orderly procession marched down Ancoats Street, Manchester, to turn out the mills, led by "a large number of young women, decently dressed," just as women had led the march to Manchester in 1819.[57] But the marches also drew on the textile trade union tradition of organized violence. While male delegates from the powerloom factory met on 10 August in Manchester, a "number of females assembled to stop Kennedy's mill," along with many boys, and they stoned the factory when its employers refused to shut it down.[58] Three days later in Preston, male and female weavers mounted a violent assault on another factory: "Women [brought] stones in the brats and aprons, and lay them down in the street for the use of the mob."[59] As Chartist Frederick Augustus Taylor declared at a Manchester meeting on 17 August, "the men must use the sword, and the women will know where to direct them."[60]

Women spoke of a variety of concerns as impelling their actions. Hunger motivated many, such as Deborah Finchett, who incited a food riot in Deansgate, the center of Manchester.[61] One woman shouted to the soldiers who confronted her, "We didn't come for bayonets, we came for bread!"[62] Religious rhetoric empowered the only two women who spoke at mixed public meetings. At a large outdoor meeting in Cronkeyshaw, a Methodist woman climbed up on a wagon, took off her spectacles and bonnet, and "exhorted the people to stand firm like the Israelites of old, and drive out the pharaoh and his multitudes."[63] Another woman was concerned with marital harmony: she "advised poor men to shun the ale-house and look to their wives and families."[64] Women occasionally held their own meetings, although they seem to have been informal. Yet women also expressed their consciousness of themselves as workers. In one Ashton meeting, the women resolved that "they [would] neither go to work themselves, nor allow their husbands to do so, until they get their price as agreed upon."[65] At a Macclesfield meeting of women, the female speakers addressed each other as "sister operatives" and "sister slaves," but declared that their husbands should earn enough so that their wives would not have to break their health by toiling in the factories.[66]

However, women's voices were heard publicly only in discourses outside

formal politics. Women were not necessarily remaining silent because formal organization made them feel awkward, for, only two years earlier,
Stockport female strikers had made impassioned political speeches at mixed
meetings. Rather, Chartists had newly defined political and economic leadership as a male monopoly. As Chartists and trade unionists began to har-
ness the energy of the strike, organizing a formal meeting of delegates in
Manchester to articulate their demands, they ignored previous precedents
of Lancashire strikes and prohibited women from attending the meeting.
Men were determined to define themselves as protectors of passive female
factory girls who could not act for themselves, despite evidence to the contrary in the streets all around them. Richard Marsden wrote to the *Northern Star* celebrating the "brave working men" who led the strikes, but the
rest of his speech made it apparent that the majority of the striking weavers
were females and the examples of oppression to workers were those of
overseers unjustly abating girl workers.[67] The organized powerloom weavers of Manchester declared that they "deem[ed] it a most unpardonable
injustice, on the part of a great number of factory masters, that they refuse
to give employment to *men* in their factories, but in their stead employ
women, over whom they can tyrannise with impunity."[68] Activists addressed the people as if they were all male: instead of the earlier "Ladies
and gentlemen" or "Men and Women," they spoke to "Brothers," declaring that "the blood of your brothers has been shed while lawfully agitating
for their rights" and ignoring the fact that at least one female had been
killed and many arrested.[69]

While the Chartists downplayed women's role in the struggle, the spectacle of striking and rioting women horrified middle- and upper-class
observers. One author, possibly Samuel Smiles, claimed that "public meetings of female operatives" were an "ominous feature of the late disturbances." He emphasized women's participation much more than the *Northern Star* had, alleging that "women were, in many instances, the directors
of the strikes." So long as women worked in factories, he warned, "the
population of the manufacturing towns will be uneducated, turbulent and
discontented."[70] The Commissioners on Women and Children in the Factories declared, "The girls of some of our manufacturing districts are . . .
wearing the garb of women, but actuated by the worst passions of men, in
every riot and outbreak the women are the leaders and exciters of the
young men to violence."[71] Lord Ashley told the Short-Time Central Committee, supporting their goals, that "when the women of a country become
brutalized, the country is without hope."[72]

When the government put Feargus O'Connor and fifty-eight other
Chartists and trade unionists on trial for seditious conspiracy to riot, the

defendants manipulated middle-class fears by blaming the events on the factory system's disruption of the family. In his successful defense speech Richard Pilling presented himself as a simple man driven to action by familial tragedy, but his rhetoric was a sophisticated melodramatic construction: "I have seen husbands carrying their children to the mill to be suckled by their mothers, and carrying their wives breakfast to them. . . . In consequence of females being employed under these circumstances, the overlookers, managers, and other tools, take the most scandalous liberties with them."[73] Indeed, the Chartists' lawyer Dundas attempted to explain away their radical apocalyptic language as "poetical rhetoric" rather than sedition.[74] The jury acquitted them on most counts, and the government took a more conciliatory approach and pushed for factory acts limiting the work of women and children.[75] In 1843 the work of women was banned in underground mining, and in 1844 an act was passed limiting the work of women and children in factories to twelve hours per day.

Such success gave added momentum to the factory movement, which mounted a campaign for a Ten Hours Bill from 1845 through 1847. The dominance of this movement in Lancashire and Glasgow textile districts enabled women to continue to participate in politics, but the cult of domesticity still complicated their position. The Ten Hours campaign resurrected the traditional sexual cooperation of textile communities in Lancashire and Glasgow, calling for restrictions on women's work rather than its abolition. The leaders of the movement encouraged women to join, and they responded vigorously, attending meetings in large numbers.[76] The *Ten Hours' Advocate* of 1846–1847 contained articles on knitting and other topics of interest to women, and in its vision of domesticity it stressed women's points of view as well as men's.

Although this approach meant women workers were much more active than they had been in the factory movement of the early 1830s, their support for shorter hours was ambivalent. Married women welcomed the opportunity to spend more time at home, but single women were more concerned about having less pay. In response, a worker calling herself "Elizabeth" scolded her fellow female workers for worrying about money, pointing out that shorter hours would leave them time for education.[77] Women workers thought, too, that shorter hours should be enjoyed by all workers, including men, not just females and children.[78]

Yet the *Ten Hours' Advocate* also revealed the continuing tensions between factory men and women. The journal criticized a Bradford clergyman's Society for Bettering the Condition of the Female Factory Operatives for placing the blame for domestic misery on the immorality of factory girls. Instead, it argued that "corruption begins on the side of the male" and that the society should realize that working long hours prevented men from enjoying domestic life. At the same time, the *Ten Hours' Advocate* continued to publish articles and letters disapproving of women's work on the grounds that it distracted mothers and made young girls too independent. One editorial blamed the rich for forcing poor females to "wade through wet and snow" to work long hours in the factories, "an awful sacrifice of grace, truth and purity, in the shape of dear woman."[79] As Robert Gray notes, however, "Short-time committees militantly resisted the very course of action—substitution of adult men to work longer hours"— that was required if women's work were to be restricted. Once the Ten Hours Act passed in 1847, male trade unionists began to lobby and strike for shorter hours for working men as well as women.[80]

Male trade unionists also attempted to limit, control, and even belittle women's strikes in Scotland and the north in the mid to late 1840s.[81] When Bradford female powerloom weavers struck in 1845, their treasurer, a Miss Ruthwell, declared that "while she had a tongue to proclaim the wrongs of sisters in slavery; while a drop of British blood flowed in her veins she would strive for the emancipation of her class."[82] Ignoring the fiery power of her rhetoric, the men claimed that only "mere chance" could explain the success of such inexperienced, female trade unionists.[83] In 1849, although working men admonished the female powerloom weavers of Glasgow, who were striking over wages, to "return at once to their work, and trust to the generosity of good sense of their employers," the vast majority of the women vowed to continue the strike.[84] Yet by the great Preston strike of 1853–1854, activist women called for married women to leave the work force, a strategy which would diminish women's interest in trade unionism.[85] While textile unions continued to need women's support, they only grudgingly accepted women in the work force. Sexual cooperation remained important, but it lost its egalitarian potential as patriarchalism took firm hold.

The Decline of Chartism

Despite the success of the working-class movement in gaining state regulation of women and children's work, the factory acts took the wind out of Chartist sails.[86] Stedman Jones argues that Chartist rhetoric about the state seemed irrelevant to working people when the government had modified the principles of political economy to pass the factory acts, sanitary reform, and banking regulation. As a result, the movement retreated, declined, and eventually failed.[87] However, as Saville points out, few of these reforms actually made an impact on working people's lives until decades later, which undercuts the theory that they contributed to the decline of Chartism.[88] The one set of exceptions were the factory and mines acts, which soon ameliorated the worst hardships of industrial labor for women and children. This fact suggests that domesticity played a key role in moderating the appeal of Chartism.

Domesticity ultimately contributed to a narrow notion of working-class politics far removed from Chartism's roots in community mobilization. Although it was in part women's activism that had frightened the government into passing the factory acts, the Plug Riots had also frightened the Chartists themselves. Many Chartists retreated into the self-improvement of cooperation, the Land Plan, Chartist churches, temperance, and agitation over issues of foreign politics.[89] In general, the movement focused on a more "rational" form of national organization, slighting community-based populism.[90] But in doing so, they lost support to the movement for the Ten Hours Bill, which dominated northern areas. In Glasgow and Manchester, one wing of the movement moved to a closer rapprochement with the middle class, while the majority focused on the factory movement.[91]

By the mid-1840s, as Dorothy Thompson notes, the formal organization Chartism had adopted was encouraging women to retreat out of politics back into domesticity.[92] However, it was not only that women found the style of 1840s Chartism less welcoming than it had been earlier; rather, male Chartists actively pushed women out of the movement, and a few women protested. When Mary Anne Walker, inspired by the women of the Plug riots, addressed a meeting to found a female London Chartist Association in 1842 a male speaker put down the whole idea of women's participation in politics. Mr. Cohen "put it to the mothers present, whether they did not find themselves more happy in the peacefulness and usefulness of the domestic hearth, than in coming forth and aspiring after political rights."[93] While other men at that meeting supported the formation of a female Chartist association, the 1843 rules of the National Chartist Association used the word "males" instead of "persons," making clear that Chartism defined only men as political agents. A woman using the pseudonym "Vita" wrote to protest that women might as well "withdraw from a movement from which an improvement of their status was not to be expected."[94]

In London, many Chartist men retreated to the masculine world of smoky meetings in pubs and militant confrontations with the police.[95] Rejecting temperance propaganda, the stonemasons who carried the people's petition to the House of Commons objected to the "hired policemen [who] are constituted masters of ceremony at all popular amusements" and noted resentfully that they could not even hire a piano in a pub.[96] The costermongers, who were known for beating their wives, espoused Chartism because they hated the police.[97]

In 1848, the Chartist movement tried a last, spectacular, but futile move to revive its fortunes. Inspired by the European revolutions of that year, and the campaigns of Feargus O'Connor for a parliamentary seat in Nottingham, Chartists revived talk of physical force and envisioned an uprising. By this time, physical force had been detached from its roots in the united action of communities and had become an all-male affair. The large demonstrations Chartists thought would intimidate Parliament into granting them manhood suffrage failed, undermined by lack of enthusiasm and suppressed by efficient state coercion.[98]

By focusing on procedural rules, foreign politics, and confrontations with the state, Chartists slighted the issues of more immediate concern to women. For instance, George Mudie depicted an Amazon leader haranguing the crowds, expressing her disgust with Chartist speeches at the disastrous Forfar, Scotland, march of 1848:

> Care I a straw for France's peers,
> Quo' Meg or Britain's Commons?
> I'm ae day's rations in arrears,
> An' fain for talk o' na man's!
> Still making speeches, wanting cheers?
> Such conduct's like a showman's.
> Faith, if we need to pu' your years
> The task shall be a woman's
> I swear this day.[99]

Conclusion

The Chartist movement was an attempt to create class consciousness as a rational community, both real and imagined, that could draw on traditions of sexual cooperation but at the same time transform the flaws of plebeian society into a united movement. It failed partially because of state repression and parliamentary recalcitrance. But it also failed because the movement could not reconcile its egalitarian ideals with its commitment to working-class patriarchy.

To be sure, domesticity enabled Chartists to address some of the real problems of marital violence and sexual antagonism within working-class communities. In any case, the defensive politics of the 1830s and 1840s may have forced working-class radicals to draw upon the melodramatic rhetoric of domesticity. By the 1840s, the working-class movements of Chartism and the Ten Hours Bill had induced Parliament and industrialists to moderate the strict tenets of political economy and admit that the state must regulate the work of women and children. Yet these concessions came only after working men *and* women took to the streets, raising the spectacle of communities in insurrection.

Nonetheless, in order to bolster working men's claims to citizenship Chartists abandoned the textile trades' tradition of patriarchal cooperation with women and replaced it with the doctrine of separate spheres. By manipulating the ideology of separate spheres for their own ends, the Chartists claimed the privileges of domesticity for their wives and demanded entry into the public sphere for working men. Yet the factory acts undercut the Chartist argument that working men needed the vote in order to protect women and children, for Parliament took on that task while denying working men the franchise. Working-class women, Parliament agreed, should be sheltered in the home; yet it shut the door on working men's claims for political power. The Chartists thus bequeathed to later movements a narrow vision of class, promoting skilled working men organizing for their own political rights, occupational privileges, and patriarchal power. Domesticity had promised to open up working-class family life, but instead it imposed a new rigidity.

14   A Difficult Ideal

*Domesticity in Popular Culture
and Practice*

In the 1790s, a poem by the radical Alexander Wilson, "Watty and Meg," had advised husbands to threaten to leave wives who complained about their drinking. Several decades later, radical temperance advocate John Mitchell took a different tack: in his "Cautious Tam," a shoemaker's wife cures her husband's alcoholism by warning she'll leave him to save herself.[1] Radicals, Methodists, temperance advocates, and trade unionists alike promulgated a new notion of manhood that repudiated the heavy-drinking bachelor misogyny of plebeian culture and instead promoted chivalry and responsibility.

A new ideal of womanhood also accompanied domesticity. Whereas plebeian popular culture had represented the wife either as an industrious partner or as a powerful virago, under the new notion of separate spheres she was expected to be passive, protected by her husband and sheltering in the home. Whatever its political efficacy, many working people no doubt welcomed the new domesticity because it promised to heal the wounds of sexual antagonism within working-class marriage by bringing men self-respect and women greater security. Was this promise fulfilled? Radicals hoped that domesticity would bring husbands and wives closer together, as the paterfamilias educated his wife in politics instead of spending his wages at the pub. Yet they found that domesticity clashed both with their egalitarian ideals and with the reality of their lives. For ordinary working people, male breadwinning became central to working-class respectability, yet few men could earn enough to do without their wives' wages, and the resultant conflict between image and reality could put great strain on marriages.[2] Even when husbands could support their families, working people had to negotiate ways to put the principles of domesticity into practice.

Although domesticity promised a romantic union very different from the prosaic partnerships or bitter struggles of plebeian popular literature's portrayals of marriage, its emphasis on separate spheres may have pushed husbands and wives further apart. The responsible husband brought home the bacon, but he found political fulfillment in the public world of trade unions and Mechanics' Institutes. Immured in the home, distant from the world of work, wives were valued less for their sage advice than for their domestic skills.

While the new ideal certainly advocated increased respect for women, it continued to embody patriarchal assumptions. Men and women were supposed to be complementary opposites—yet men were still to rule gently and women to submit for the sake of love. Methodist Adam Clarke declared, "The authority of the man over the woman is founded on his love for her. . . . Superior strength gives the man domination, affection and subjection entitle the woman to love and protection."[3] Although the domestic ideal promised greater harmony, its stress on male dominance and female dependence contained within it the seeds of continuing family violence.

Chartists and Marriage

While Chartists used the rhetoric of domesticity to wrest concessions from the state, they also genuinely hoped to improve working people's personal relations. Chartists believed marriage should be the happiest aspect of working-class people's lives.[4] They envisioned a ideal of manhood that could change women's lives for the better.

Temperance advocates directly addressed the problem of unequal resources within working-class marriage.[5] Chartist T. B. Smith wrote that "destructive selfishness" tainted working men's homes. "Look at the tattered gowns of your wives, at the frockless and shoeless children who are crawling on the floor, at the almost coalless grate, and the nearly breadless cupboard, and then look at the well-filled tobacco pouch, and the flowing pint, and blush for your own delinquencies." In many trades and times wages were so close to subsistence that even very moderate drinking and smoking could deprive wives and children of food. Smith promised a redistribution of income within the working-class home, pointing out to husbands that one who gave up his pint a night and tobacco could "buy your wife two gowns, a bonnet, shoes, shawl, stockings, and petticoat, and same for children as well as a pig and extra coals."[6]

Chartists and radical temperance advocates did not only demand the breadwinner wage from employers; they also demanded that men bring home their wages to their wives instead of forcing them to work. Men such as the shoemaker and temperance poet John O'Neill scorned workmates who relied on their wives' earnings for subsistence and spent their own on drink.[7] Charles Manby Smith, a printer, described such a man as "an idle, boozing, shammocking scamp."[8] However, some Chartist leaders themselves had to rely on their wives' labor. R. J. Richardson could not get work as a carpenter after he was injured, so he busied himself with Chartist activities while his wife ran their newspaper shop. Similarly, Mary Lovett ran a bookshop with her husband, although Lovett kept control of the business even when he was away, writing home letters of instruction.[9]

Chartist and other radical men repudiated wife-beaters as "tyrants and tormenters."[10] Yet they recognized that domestic violence continued to be a problem in working-class communities. John Watkins attributed its prevalence to the hardships of unemployment and want: "How many take that vengeance on themselves, or their wives and children, which they should take on their tyrants!"[11] Similarly, Ernest Jones's 1852 tale of "Women's Wrongs" depicted a respectable working man driven to drink and wife-beating when his employer reduced his wages. After his wife taunted him by saying, "I thought I married one who had the arms of a workman, and the heart of a man," he degenerated into theft and murdered his employer.[12] These Chartists, however, attributed domestic violence solely to exterior factors, such as capitalism, instead of questioning the power relations inherent in working-class marriage. Another Chartist, John Jacob Bezer, remembered his radical master beating his wife with enthusiasm, "like many radicals of the present day, who can prate against tyranny wholesale and for exportation, and yet retail it out with all their hearts and souls, whenever they have an opportunity."[13]

By blaming domestic disturbances in the factory districts on women's work, most Chartists and factory advocates precluded any exploration of creative domestic divisions of labor. A notable exception was Mary Leman Gillies, who protested that men in the factory districts, who worked shorter hours than their wives, spent their time "smoking, drinking, and lounging about." They treated their wives like "drudges," expecting them to spend their day of rest cleaning and cooking while they never lifted a finger themselves—only raised their fists against their wives. Instead, she argued, under- or unemployed laboring men ought to assist their wives in domestic labor.[14] But this argument was rarely heard. Even the socialist Catherine Barmby blamed women for working men's brutality: "It is because woman does not truly appreciate her mission in domestic life."[15] An admonitory tale in the *Ten Hours' Advocate* blamed a slovenly wife for domestic unhappiness: "honest, hard-working, good-tempered," and sober cotton spinner Joseph Edwards married Elizabeth Green and installed her in a tidy home, but her lazy, dirty habits drove him to drink, and drink caused his accidental death.[16]

Chartist men believed husbands should act as breadwinners, protectors, and instructors of their wives. William Lovett emphasized husbands' duty to instruct their wives in political affairs, so that they would not be, as he said, "mere domestic drudges, and ignorant slaves of our passions," but instead, "our equal companions in knowledge and happiness."[17] However, this was not an egalitarian vision. The paterfamilias was to impart his greater wisdom to his wife at home to increase the happiness of the domestic circle, not to prepare women for an independent political role. Nor did male Chartists believe women should work outside the home. Thomas Martin Wheeler depicted the perfect Chartist wife in his melodramatic serialized novel, *Sunshine and Shadows*: well-versed in the domestic arts, Mary Morton attended Chartist meetings but never spoke in public. She comprehended politics "by instinct" and discussed them only "in the domestic circle."[18] The first few years of her marriage to a radical printer were blissful, blessed by a young son, and their home became a "pleasant retreat from the cares of business," where Arthur instructed Mary in "intellectual attainments."[19]

Chartist men put stress on the education of women because many political men felt frustrated by their wives' seeming indifference or ignorance concerning politics. A misogynist view of wives as a drag on the movement lurked behind the idealization of domesticity. Lovett wrote, in rather chilling terms that cast a shadow over his sentimental eulogy of domesticity,

> Women, by laws unjust, in bondage bound,
> Will e'er some fetters forge to enslave mankind.
> She, of just power bereft, of right withheld;
> Claimed as man's property, his pet, or slave;
> Her creed submission, though her heart rebel;
> So warped her nature from its purpose true,
> So placed by lordly man beneath his throne,
> Is she not formed by him his peace to mar;
> His children's minds often to mould awry;
> Despite his efforts, and the teachers' skill,
> And plant sharp thorns where flowers should ever bloom?[20]

Conversely, women found themselves frustrated by their lack of education, which could shut them out of men's conversations. "Sophia," a correspondent to the *English Chartist Circular*, evoked the mutual frustration of men and women at women's lack of education: "We listen to the theories and arguments of our brothers, as so much Greek or high Dutch, unable to comprehend, much less suggest one single idea. They, in their turn, despise the frivolity of the gay and smart wife, and equally abominate the society of the mere household drudge." But "Sophia" also pointed out that, despite Chartist rhetoric, "man has never sought to render *us* intellectual companions." When women educate themselves, she said, we "must convince our husbands that in doing so we do not neglect their domestic comfort."[21]

The Chartist movement experienced a continual tension between its advocacy of domesticated manhood and the necessity to build on the masculine trade organizations and the solidarity of pub culture. In a world divided by the middle class into public and private, the home was the private, and powerless sphere. Working men therefore resisted efforts to push them out of their pubs and clubs back into the home. But as they improved themselves and the world, their wives languished, alone and uninstructed, at home. Political activism, as always, put great stress on marriages. In Wheeler's novel, Arthur flung himself into Chartist activities to redeem the misery of working people's lives, but "if he was a better citizen, he was no longer so affectionate an husband."[22] The *Ten Hours' Advocate* advised husbands to spend evenings at home with their wives, but of course the self-improving working man often went out at night to meetings and Mechanics' Institutes.[23] The journal recounted a touching story of an honorable, sober mechanic who gave his wife his wages, but rarely his company. Instead, he attended the Mechanics' Institute in the evening to read newspapers. Never did he consider that his lonely young wife would enjoy his company and deserved enlightenment herself. Eventually, she pined away and died of loneliness.[24]

Radicals involved in Chartism, temperance, and the Ten Hours movement alike thus promulgated an ideal of marriage that may have brought women easier lives. But unlike the Owenites, who identified wife-beating and the unequal distribution of resources within marriage as direct consequences of marital inequality and women's dependence, the Chartists promulgated a patriarchal ideal of marriage which confined women to a limited sphere.

Domesticity in Popular Culture and Practice

Chartist notions of domesticity were closely congruent with the picture of marriage presented in popular culture. While earlier songs had admonished husbands to listen to their wives' wise advice, later versions advised men to shelter their women from the hardships of life. "The Way to Live Happy Together" proclaims,

> Woman was formed to please man,
> And man to love and protect them,

And shield them from the frowns of the world,
Through the smooth paths of life to direct them.[25]

Moving away from the old plebeian misogyny, songs of the 1830s and 1840s advised men to "Think of Your Poor Wife at Home."[26]

Although the ideal of domesticity seemed devoid of power relations, with each partner sovereign in his or her sphere, there was certainly room for power struggles in the new model marriage. Indeed, the tradition of the "struggle for the breeches" continued to be a popular motif in street literature (see Figure 10).[27] Working-class couples had to negotiate between old habits, new expectations, and the exigencies of family survival. Sometimes they may have developed new, positive patterns, for separate spheres very likely brought greater harmony and affection to the marriages of many working people. But for others, marriage degenerated into violent conflict.

Very few working men could live up to the domestic ideal, but they were ashamed to depend on their wives' labor. In 1826 Charles Manby Smith ran into a friend of his, an unemployed printer who soon took his leave, explaining, "I must be after wishing you goodnight now, for the old 'oman will be coming home. She goes out a charring in the day (God help me! I never thought to have let her.)"[28] In 1849 Henry Mayhew noted, "The more respectable portion of the carpenters and joiners 'will not allow' their wives to do any other work than attend to their domestic and family duties, though some few of the wives of the better class of workmen take in washing or keep small 'general shops.' "[29] Women's work remained necessary, not only for survival, but to enable families to attain a higher level of respectability. In 1844, John Overs described a carpenter's ambition as "soaring no higher than the establishment of his wife in some light business, and the better education of his children."[30]

The wives of tailors and hatters found it increasingly necessary to assist them as these trades degenerated into sweated labor carried out in the home. Many trades that depended on the vagaries of fashion, including tailoring and hatting, provided a decent wage only in the "season" and then required debilitatingly long hours of work.[31] A tailor told Mayhew that, "owing to the reduction of prices, many wives who formerly attended solely to their domestic duties and their family are now obliged to labor with the husband, and still the earnings of the two are less than he alone formerly obtained."[32] Even though husband and wife worked side by side, the women, like those working in factories, still had the double load of waged work and housework. A tailor who lost his position in the "honorable" West End of the trade lamented that his wife "slaves night and day, as I do: and very often she has less rest than myself, for she has to stop up

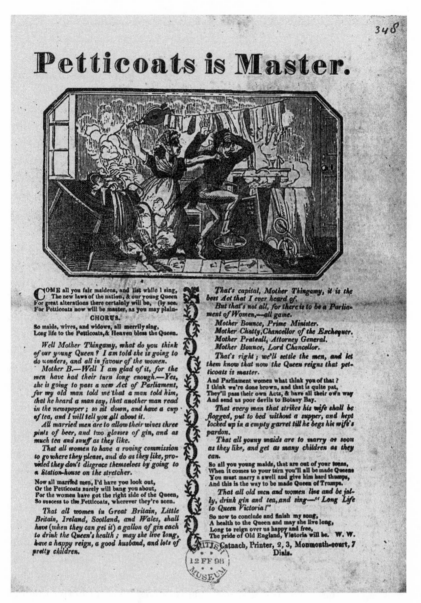

Figure 10.   Petticoats Is Master. LR.271.a.2, f. 348. By permission of the British Library.

after I have gone to bed to attend to her domestic duties."[33] Shoemakers had always drawn upon the assistance of their wives, but with sweated labor, whole families worked long hours to earn less than a living wage.[34] Similarly, because laborers' work was seasonal and irregular, they had to depend on their wives' wages in slack periods. In Kensington, for instances, the wives of builders and brickmakers labored in laundries when their men were unemployed.[35]

Although the factory districts were known for the prevalence of working women, in the 1820s the elite cotton spinners had pioneered the practice of the domestic wage. Among better-off Scottish textile families, the "eldest female" stayed at home, her "sole employment consist[ing] in making purchases, and attending to the household duties." Yet only families with several teenage or adult wage-earners could afford the luxury of such a homemaker.[36] Even in the late 1840s, when times improved, the wives of less skilled men had to work in the factories.[37] The division between male textile workers with a wife at home and those whose wife had to work may have been one of the lines between the two cultures that existed in factory towns in the 1840s and 1850s. In the one, couples retained the rough, crude vitality of the old culture, socializing in a larger community setting, drinking and fighting together in public; in the other, a few disciplined men tried to pull themselves out of poverty, saving the money they would otherwise drown in drink by spending their evenings at home with their wives—or improving themselves at Mechanics' Institutes.[38]

However, these divisions between rough and respectable were always tenuous. When unemployment struck, even the elite cotton spinners had to send their wives to work. For instance, a Glasgow Irish cotton spinner remembered that his wife, whom he described as "soother of my sorrows, and helper of my joys," had to go out to work after a strike.[39] Employers often demanded that their male workers bring their wives to work as weavers.[40] And wives' work was most necessary when the children were too small to go out to work themselves. By mid-century, between a quarter and a third of married women in factory towns were employed.[41]

Despite the power of the domestic ideal, the reality of textile workers' lives could modify its patriarchal strictures. On the one hand, women's work in the factories could potentially bring them more power in marriage. Rather than posing as the twining vine of the domestic ideal, factory women, accustomed to earning a living at a young age, could be quite independent. Ben Brierly recalled that the women in his textile industry neighborhood near Manchester went on walking holidays together without their husbands, "as they do not care for their company."[42] When there was domestic conflict, factory work gave wives an alternative—albeit a minimal one—to dependence on a hostile husband. Ellen Johnston, a factory girl who wrote poetry, spun a rhyme about a shoemaker who refuses to support his scolding wife:

In a wee Verdant factory she toiled for her bread,
For her manie, he swore by his rosit-end thread,

He wad ne'er sew a shae [shoe] sic a limmer [prostitute or rascal] to feed,
As his gossiping, trolloping wife.[43]

John O'Neil, a former handloom weaver who worked in a powerloom factory along with his daughter, noted, "Being paid by piece rate meant that there was equal pay for equal work. It led to an independent female attitude and a contempt for domestic service which was often misunderstood."[44] In Haworth, Yorkshire, where women worked in the mills, husbands helped clean house exteriors and windows on Friday nights.[45] In Manchester, Angus Reach observed "two or three lords of creation usefully employed in blackleading their stoves" during the ritual Saturday cleaning.[46] Yet even among powerloom weavers, where men and women worked in factories at nearly equal wage rates, wives retained primary responsibility for housework and child care.[47]

Working people regarded husbands who helped with the household chores as unmanly. A man who helped his wife with the housework was considered a "molly," an effeminate, even homosexual man. As a result, by the late nineteenth century working-class men were avoiding any participation in housework.[48] Thomas Wright, an engineer, scornfully declared that only "mollicot" men with "termagant" wives helped with the dinner preparations and housework on Saturday afternoons.[49]

Popular culture presented housework as a skill specific to women and ridiculed the inability of men to appreciate or carry out feminine tasks. Modifying an ancient tradition of stories in which farmers claim they can carry out household chores better than their wives, only to botch the milking and spinning, urban ballads updated the household division of labor. "The Molly Coddle" and "The Dandy Man" both mocked an effeminate man who "reverses nature's plan" by claiming he is much better than women at cooking, laundry, marketing, and cleaning, only to boil the cat instead of the beef when he tries to make Christmas dinner.[50] Songs depicted men who helped with the housework as being dominated by their wives:

> A tyrant is my wife,
> Her temper's far from mild,
> Each day she causes strife,
> And makes me nurse the child.[51]

A song from the bloomer era fantasized that if women wore breeches they would turn the tables:

> Their husbands they will wop and squander all their riches,
> Make them nurse the kids and wash their shirt and breeches,

If the men should say a word they'll be such jolly rows, sir
Their wives will make them sweat and beat them with the trousers.[52]

These songs try to promote the naturalness of the domestic division of labor by portraying any variation as totally ridiculous; yet they also poke gentle fun at unrealistic expectations that every husband will be a responsible patriarch and every wife a sweet, submissive housewife.

The ideal of domesticity and, by the 1850s, an increase in prosperity raised the standards of housework women had to reach. Most factory women in 1832 did very little domestic work. Families lived in cramped rooms with little furniture to clean and no time to do so; they ate bread or potatoes out of a common pot or went to the beerhouse; they bought cheap ready-made clothing; and older children or neighbors looked after the younger children.[53] When standards of living rose, women had to wash more clothing by hand; cook and serve food on separate dishes, which then had to be cleaned; beat carpets; and dust and polish knick-knacks. In Manchester, for instance, working people crowded their front rooms with "a row of smoke-browned little china and stone-ware ornaments," a cupboard full of "a shining assortment of plates and dishes," and a "glaringly painted and highly glazed tea-tray."[54] In London, many artisans' wives were exposed to middle-class domestic luxury when they worked as servants before marriage, and the subsequent reality of their cramped working-class home disappointed them, according to working man John Overs. He described such a wife "cooped up in a single room, full of loop'd and window'd wretchedness, where by contrasting her former profusion with her present penury, she takes to fretting, gossiping, and gin."[55]

It was clearly the husband's duty to earn money, the wife's to provide domestic services; each retained responsibility for and control over their separate sphere. But in the 1830s and 1840s, working-class couples were just beginning to negotiate this marital contract, tussling over the terms of the household budget. When working men won higher wages to feed their families, their wives' portion was not always increased.[56] In the 1830s and 1840s there seemed to be no definite pattern as to whether the husband handed all or some part of his wages to his wife. Both husbands and wives felt they had a right to this money—he because he had worked for it, she because she needed it for the household and children.

For instance, northern skilled worker William Marcroft and his wife negotiated for a long time over the best mode of controlling household expenses. At first he gave her a sovereign at a time and trusted her to spend it wisely, but, finding that they spent too much on entertaining visitors, he "contract[ed]" in his terms with his wife that she would account to him for every penny she spent. However, this caused "too many tears," along with ridicule from a neighbor woman, who commented, "If my husband could not trust me with his wage, he should spend it hisself!" So Marcroft changed the "contract" to give his wife nineteen shillings a week, out of which she was to find food, the children's clothing, the rent, and so on—quite a meager amount for a skilled working man. He retained the rest of his earnings for his own clothes, extra expenses such as doctors' bills, and savings. He also agreed to not interfere in the choice of meals or to expect domestic services on washing or cleaning days.[57]

Similarly, before Charles Manby Smith's second wife, a charwoman, agreed to marry him, she insisted he write a contract allowing her sixteen shillings a week household money.[58] In this way women tried to carve out an autonomous sphere within the household for themselves, to introduce some regularity into and gain control over their work. Thomas Carter, a tailor, wrote, "I have always thought it to be far more within my proper sphere of action to aim at providing what might buy food, or other necessaries, than to be giving orders about either dinner or any other meals. As a natural consequence, I have ever found, from both mother and wife, an unwearied attention to my personal comfort."[59]

By the late nineteenth century, London husbands seem to have given their wives a "wage" for the household out of their own earnings, reserving some for their own amusement, whereas in the north, husbands gave their whole wage packets to their wives, who returned "pocket money" to them.[60] But in either case, the popularity of songs such as "Eighteen Shillings a Week" suggests that many husbands expected their wives to account for expenditures. In this genre, a wife lists the entire household budget, penny by penny, to show what a good manager she is—and what proportion of the household budget went on luxuries for the husband, such as baked sheep's head, capers, tobacco, ginger pop, and, of course, drink. As "A Hint to Husbands" concludes, "No person knows how much money is wanted in housekeeping, but those who have to lay it out," and even a few shillings spent at the alehouse keeps the household short.[61]

The Chartist ideal of marriage had promised intellectual companionship and romance, but working men actually rated housewifery more highly. They wanted to keep their wives at home not only to protect them but, more important, because they needed their domestic services. Tailor Thomas Carter learned that "my domestic happiness did not depend on my having what is quaintly called a 'bookish' woman for my wife, but that it would be greatly dependent upon my choosing one of plain good sense and thoroughly domestic habits."[62] Skilled textile worker William Marcroft not only sought a wife who would regard her husband as "the altar of her worship," but he required her to rise an hour earlier than her husband to prepare his breakfast.[63] Charles Manby Smith's father advised him around 1835 that a wife's "capabilities and aptitude to create domestic comfort are far beyond a sackfull of gold."[64] Chartist Ernest Jones described a laborer who regarded his wife "merely as a servant without wages, whom he found convenient to prepare his meals, and make and share his bed." Nonetheless, "they bore the character of a happy couple in their court . . . because Haspen *did not beat her*."[65]

Even in happy marriages, wives' concentration on domestic duties and husbands' on public responsibilities meant that spouses had less and less in common. Charles Manby Smith's father reminded his "new daughter that her husband has a thousand elements of disturbance in his daily avocations to which the wife is an utter stranger; and it will be her privilege . . . to make his fireside the most attractive place . . . for the calm repose of a[n] . . . excited mind."[66] Manby Smith, a compositor, added, "That share which a father is morally bound to take in the nurture and raising of his offspring is not infrequently repudiated altogether by the working man of London, who conceives . . . that if he undertakes and performs the duty of providing food, shelter, and raiment for his family, no more ought to be required of him."[67] While the ideology of domesticity encouraged men to stay at home rather than go to the alehouse, the breadwinner wage enabled husbands to enjoy the new working-class public sphere. Wives' complaints that their husbands spent all their time and money away from home continued. Most men continued to frequent pubs, and even those who went out to respectable Mechanics' Institutes or working men's clubs left their wives at home. The difference was that wives now rarely had their own wages to fall back on.

The Continuing Problem of Wife-beating

Songs of the old plebeian tradition celebrated wife-beating cobblers, but one Lancashire dialect poem by Thomas Brierly, "God Bless these Poor Wimmen that's Childer" (have children) suggested,

> If t' maddest un' vilest o' men
> Wurn [were] just made i' [into] wimmen a fortneet [fortnight]
> They'd never beat wimmen again.[68]

As the songs suggest, domestic violence continued to plague working-class communities. In nine months during 1835 and 1836, eighty-one cases of domestic violence came before the police court in the Gorbals district of Glasgow—approximately two cases a week.[69] For London, Nancy Tomes estimated that "ten to twenty men would be convicted of common assaults on women" per year in the average mid-nineteenth-century working-class neighborhood. Despite the popular repudiation of wife-beating, neighbors rarely interfered in cases of domestic violence unless they feared that death or serious injury would result.[70]

The old ideal of patriarchal partnership, which had brought relative domestic harmony to textile workers, deteriorated as unemployment became chronic. As Tables 5 and 6 demonstrate, the proportion of weavers among wife-beaters began increasing in the 1820s and 1830s. In 1829 police court reporter John Brownlie noted that five thousand weavers were starving in Calton, the textile district of Glasgow. On one day in August, thirty-five cases of drunken weavers came before the police court there, which Brownlie explained as a result of drinking on an empty stomach: "Their brains become heated, and . . . they become enraged and ungovernable, often carrying destruction against the poor wives and children."[71] One weaver publicly whipped his wife for drinking with her neighbors, defending himself by asking, "Is it all at all like a waver's [*sic*] wife to go on the rig in them hard times?"[72] The Glasgow *Thistle* reported in 1830 that a "poor, dirty, cat-witted weaver" turned his wife out at midnight because "she had no regard for him and did everything contrary to his interests."[73] In 1831, when the wife of an unemployed weaver admonished him for getting drunk "at a time when wages were so low," in retaliation he assaulted her.[74] To be sure, the new chivalrous ideal of manhood may have had some impact on artisans, for their percentage among men accused of wife-beating declined in Glasgow from 36.5 in the period before 1825 to 29.4 in the early 1830s, and in Lancashire from 28.2 in the period before 1821 to 22.3 in the period from 1821 through 1835. However, they still remained overrepresented in cases of domestic violence, for they accounted for 18.9 percent of the occupied population in Glasgow in 1831 and 15 percent in Lancashire.[75]

Among those men who aspired to the breadwinner ideal, failure to succeed could trigger violence. When a Glasgow tailor's wife told him to go look for work, he threatened to murder her.[76] In London, John Frederick Jordan told the police constable who found him attempting to murder his wife, "It was all very well when he worked for her, but when she had a little money left to her, she despised him."[77] At his trial for shooting his wife in her greengrocer's shop, carman James Rogers explained why he became so angry when she left him to maintain herself, declaring to the court, "I think it is a man's duty, and as much as a man can do" to support his wife.[78] Abraham Moss asked his estranged wife Phoebe, whom he had stabbed, "Did not I bring up the children for thirty-one years, and provide for you in respectability, and with hard work and honesty?" She retorted, "I . . . stood in frost and snow with fruit to support my children—I supported them."[79]

The problem of alcohol continued to haunt working-class families and to exacerbate domestic violence. A coal-lumper's wife told Mayhew, "I have had many a bitter bruise for the last fifteen years, and all through drink."[80] Glasgow city missionaries found wife-beating to be widespread in the early 1850s, noting that "these poor decent women . . . said they could not live with their husbands; that rather than be murdered by them, they were thinking of separating from them," for their husbands "drink their own and their children's bread."[81] Wives sometimes drank too, and the consequences were much worse for them. In Scotland, drunken wives could be imprisoned by their husbands or relatives. In 1840, the radical *True Scotsman* noted that eight women were currently confined in the Greenock jail near Glasgow for this reason. The journal attacked the hypocrisy of their husbands: "What folly, what imbecility, what blindness for a husband to mourn over a drinking wife, when he swallows from day to day his moderate glass in her face."[82] Men could excuse their own violence by claiming that their wives drank. John Wilson, a bootcloser, beat his wife with a candlestick when she refused to give him his drinking money, and then claimed she had been drinking herself. She indignantly told the court, "I am not in the habit of getting drunk. I have the misfortune to be married to a drunken husband," and a policeman corroborated her reputation for sobriety.[83]

Hard times intensified conflicts over money. Mayhew reported that East End dockworkers, forced to spend most of their wages at houses of call in order to obtain work from the publicans, usually came home to their wives with only their drunkenness and two or three shillings to show for a week's work.[84] For instance, when docker Michael McCarthy gave five shillings to his common-law wife, she scornfully commented, "We are very rich—we owe three shillings for rent, and what are we to do with this small trifle?" Enraged, he demanded it back, but she retorted, "No I won't give it to you, it don't belong to you." He stabbed her to death, and in court excused himself by saying he had needed the money to pay debts. Similarly, David Anderson blinded his wife in one eye after they quarreled in the pub about his wages, for, as she testified, "I wanted him to give me all the money, and he wanted to keep it."[85] A Glasgow weaver threw his wife onto the fire, excusing himself by claiming she had taken half a crown from his pocket on rent day, but the neighbors testified that "she was industrious, and wrought for herself, and did everything for her husband besides."[86]

Yet failure—whether caused by drinking or unemployment—to live up to the domestic ideal cannot fully explain the persistence of wife-beating in working-class communities. Rather, the new marital ideal still contained the seeds of violence within a shell of chivalry. However bound up in romance, the relationship was still one of domination and dependence. In nineteenth-century popular theater, trivial, often ridiculous domestic quarrels between man and wife entertained audiences for farces, but at the end, "The husband's marital superiority, an essential aspect of Victorian drama, is asserted or reasserted at the end of many a play in which the wife has too long had her own way."[87] On a more sinister note, the song "I Should Dearly Like to Marry" lists the ideal wife as loving, patient, and a good cook and mother, but concludes,

> She must always be good tempered, but never on me frown
> And thank me very kindly,
> If I chance to knock her down
> . . .
> And if I beat her with the poker,
> She must never say a word.[88]

Receiving a husband's entire wage packet may have given a wife control over spending, but when there was not enough money, it was a burdensome responsibility. Husbands often beat wives who could not stretch the wage far enough.[89] Some men regarded a wife's failure to do the housework or even to cook a meal to his exact specifications, as justification for a beating or separation.[90] William Tacey, a London coalporter, refused to support his wife because she did not provide his breakfast and a clean shirt on Sunday morning.[91] Another working man, arriving home drunk and hungry, threw his wife down the stairs because she had not cooked his midday meal.[92] Charles McKay, a Glasgow hamcurer, stabbed his wife when she did not have breakfast ready for him.[93]

Women often found themselves blamed for the violence they endured.[94] A magistrate told one wife that she could avoid beatings if she would only provide "a comfortable home, a clean hearth, and a cheerful face when he returns home from his labors," although he also counseled the husband to treat his wife better.[95] The ideology of domesticity, the reality of dependence, and the fear of retaliation may also account for the tendency of battered wives during the 1830s and 1840s to blame themselves for their husbands' violence. At her husband's trial, Ellen Mason tried to excuse him by testifying, "I rather provoked him, and was quite as much at fault as he was."[96] The wife of a bonnet-box maker claimed her husband hit her only because she spent their money on drink.[97] A Glasgow barber's wife treated with extreme and repeated cruelty by her husband "appeared to be a much uncomplaining creature, who had often interceded for her husband after he abused her."[98] A Mrs. Lockhart, who bore eleven children to her husband, declared at his trial for throwing her on a fire "that she was never much beaten by him," but a neighbor testified that Mrs. Lockhart had told her "she durst not, and could not tell truth about this."[99] Bridget Barrett, whose husband's brutality put her in the hospital for months, testified, "I know he did not intend to injure me—I wish to grant his pardon as much as possible—I have a child five years old [she was also pregnant] and we are dependent on him."[100] Ellen Donovan at first told the court, "Perhaps it was my fault as much as his . . . I do not wish to hurt him—I only want peace and quiet and a maintenance." Later in the trial, remembering his violence toward her when she was pregnant, she proclaimed, "He is a great murderer, and I should like him punished," but admitted that she had given him in charge only at the urging of her female neighbors.[101]

Conclusion

Chartists had held out the promise of domesticity as a utopian ending to the melodrama of working-class struggle. Despite the widespread acceptance of this ideal, its promise was not fulfilled in the 1840s and 1850s for most working people. Most working men simply did not earn a breadwinner wage, and low earnings and unemployment often necessitated their wives' entry into the labor force. And however much radical men may have disapproved of it, wife-beating was not an aberration, but a consequence of the domestic ideal. There was an inherent contradiction in the notion of separate spheres: husbands and wives were supposed to be equal but different, complementary in their own realms, yet husbands dominated the powerful public realm and wives retained respect only if they were submissive. The sentimental ideology of separate spheres promised protection for women, but the struggle for the breeches had given them a rhetoric of defiance. That defiance remained unheard, however, because domesticity kept women dependent and powerless.[102]

15   Conclusion

Gender profoundly shaped the making of the British working class, but what effect it would have was an open question until the 1840s. Was class consciousness demonstrated in male and female textile workers exhorting crowds of women and men on moonlit moors, urging them to strike for the good of their families? Or was it shown by respectable delegations of skilled working men asking cabinet ministers to prohibit female factory labor? Was working-class consciousness based on a vision of equality and community in the family as well as in the workplace, or on a defense of the rights of skilled men who believed they should be able to keep their wives at home? Although the version based on community never completely disappeared, what predominated in the second half of the nineteenth century was a concept of working-class consciousness in which politics was for men alone and domesticity for women. By tracing the roots of this conservative, gendered vision, debates on the nature of the late-nineteenth-century working class can be illuminated. The working-class movement did not simply reject the "feminine" in favor of a "masculine" version of class and a middle-class notion of domesticity; rather, radicals struggled for decades to define masculinity and to solve a persistent sexual crisis.

The roots of the working-class movement of the 1830s and 1840s lay in the radicalism of the 1790s, when middle-class and plebeian men demanded political enfranchisement. The alliance of the two groups was always tenuous, not only because of economic conflicts of interests but because middle-class radicalism, derived from the traditions of civic humanism, was based on a notion of masculinity that was unavailable to working men. The middle class believed they deserved political rights, that is, the right to act in the public sphere, because they were propertied heads of household who kept their wives at home in the private sphere. This ideal was simply un-

264

attainable for working men, who had to find another way to define themselves as citizens.

Plebeian radicals could reject the tradition of civic humanism and its narrow definition of citizenship in favor of Painite radicalism, claiming the inherent political rights of every human being. They developed their own indigenous plebeian public sphere, rooted in eighteenth-century artisan culture and branching out into a masculine, libertine ultra-radicalism. However, such a version of politics had severe limitations for working people. First, ordinary plebeians were much more interested in issues of survival, such as wages and food than with abstract constitutional concerns. Second, radicals had to gain mass support by drawing on community strength, not just relying on elite organized artisans but enlisting unskilled workers, women, and families. Once radicals began to address the issues critical to working-class survival, they drew in large numbers of women as well as men to activism.

In order to mobilize working men and women, radicals needed to offer a resolution to the problems of marital misery and sexual competition in the work force. Nineteenth-century radicals and twentieth-century historians and sociologists alike believed that industrialization had destroyed a golden age of family harmony. Before industrialization, they claimed, fathers had lovingly supervised the work of wives and children. Now, men were emasculated and women were forced into satanic mills. What is wrong with this picture is not the focus on family disruption, for that was a burning issue of the time, but the presumption of an earlier harmony. The industrial revolution exacerbated but did not create chronic sexual conflict, which was endemic to an economy where women's labor was necessary yet undervalued. Male artisans often spent much of their wages on drinking with their workmates, leaving little for their families, and they might erupt in rage if their wives questioned these priorities. Women resented the scanty sums they received to feed their children, and the necessity of earning wages they did not control. Wife-beating was common, especially among artisans. The family lives of textile workers were more cooperative, out of necessity, but domestic violence was still endemic in their communities.

Rapidly changing and conflicting gender ideals increased plebeian confusion. Moralists held out as the feminine ideal the image of the middle-class lady secluded in her home, tending her family, yet they expected poor women to work, often at heavy labor, to support their families. In turn, strong women who assertively carried out these responsibilities could be ridiculed as termagants who tried to wear the breeches. Working men could not live up to the ideal of a patriarch, supporting his family and running his own workshop, but they did not know whether they should instead be belligerent artisans whose first loyalty was to their mates rather than their families, or self-improving Methodists who shut themselves off from neighborhood companions. A man might go to chapel where the elders would rebuke him for drinking and fighting, yet if he mended his ways he would find his workmates teasing him as a "molly" for refusing to go to the pub.

Shifts in the gender division of labor exacerbated these tensions, as employers continually sought to substitute cheaper female and child labor for skilled men, whether in sweated workshops or in factories. Artisans in traditional apprenticed trades had long fought against female incursion, casting insults at women workers in order to preserve the status, honor, and wages of masculine workplaces. But artisans did not provide the only model for behavior within plebeian culture. While skilled male factory operatives adopted the conspiratorial methods of artisanal trade unions, to support their strikes they also drew upon loose, wide kinship and community networks that included women and children. They gained female support even when striking against women, by presenting themselves as defenders of women and children and accepting female labor as long as it was in auxiliary positions. Yet both artisans and textile workers often directed their efforts at excluding other workers, whether they were the unskilled, single women, or outsiders to the community.

To build a strong movement, radicals had to overcome these divisions and heal the wounds of family breakdown and sexual competition. In the late 1820s and early 1830s, working people were forced onto the defensive as the pace of industrial change accelerated and skilled men's strikes began to fail. One possible response was to try to bridge gaps among working people, organizing the skilled and unskilled, men and women together. Owenite socialists theorized this strategy, but textile communities pioneered it as they developed a practice of sexual cooperation which grew a little more egalitarian as female powerloom weavers organized autonomous unions and acted as the vanguard of unionization in Aberdeen and Glasgow.

Owenite socialists also addressed marital misery more directly, by criticizing the notion of marriage as a property relation and denouncing wifebeating. However, this sexual radicalism frightened many women, who feared sexual vulnerability in hard economic times. Male trade unionists sometimes reacted with hostility to the prospect of welcoming women into their fraternal bonds. Nonetheless, a new strategy was needed, for the old one of misogynist strikes against women workers was failing. Male trade unionists thus began, on the one hand, to reform artisan culture into sober respectability, and, on the other, to demand a breadwinner wage from employers and the state. The breadwinner wage was *not* an artisan tradition; it was a rhetorical ploy to gain public sympathy by presenting trade unionists as chivalrous protectors of women and children rather than selfish monopolizers of needed work.

Working people did not acquire a cohesive identity as a class until the early 1830s. And this working-class consciousness would not fit the Marxist mold, for it was based on politics rather than on an analysis of the economic system. Why, then, term it *class* consciousness, instead of *populism*, as Patrick Joyce has suggested?[1] First, in the 1830s, by refusing to include working men in the 1832 Reform Act, by passing the New Poor Law, and by refusing to enact effective factory reform Parliament defined the working class as distinct, separate, and inferior.[2] It is not surprisingly that, in turn, in the 1830s and 1840s Chartists expressed a distinct class antagonism.

Second, the Chartist movement deliberately attempted to *create* a working-class consciousness. They could not simply express and articulate the common experiences and culture of working people, for plebeians worked under many different conditions of skill and ownership of the means of production, and their cultures were divided by religion, region, and ethnicity. Instead, Chartists drew upon some ingredients of plebeian culture while rejecting many others. By basing their movement on the vote, Chartists transcended trade union rivalries and drew different occupational communities together. More overtly, Chartists tried to draw women into the movement by offering to transform the old plebeian culture into a reformed working-class culture; they promised that the "struggle for the breeches" would die, that drunken, violent artisans would become sober, responsible husbands. Many women responded with enthusiasm to these policies, drawing upon their earlier activist traditions to form dozens of female Chartist associations.

But the Chartists ultimately turned in a more conservative direction. Their task was not only to organize a working-class culture but to create a political rhetoric to defend it. They abandoned sexual radicalism when the working-class family came under attack. Instead, Chartists and leaders of the New Poor Law and factory movements drew on a powerful melodramatic rhetoric of family breakdown. In order to manipulate middle-class ideology, they demanded that they be granted the vote so that they could protect their families; by obtaining the breadwinner wage for working men, they would be able to exclude women and children from factories and mines. In this they partially succeeded when Parliament passed the factory and mines acts of 1843–1844 and the Ten Hours Act of 1847.

Previously, the practice of separate spheres had been a middle-class privilege, as moralists refused to admit working men into the public sphere or grant them the breadwinner wage, arguing that factory women and children's work was necessary to the economy and that working men should not marry if they could not support a family. In fact, by demanding the limitation of women's work, Chartists may have influenced middle-class moralists to articulate more clearly what they had long assumed. Sarah Stickney Ellis, for instance, insisted that it was "not genteel" for ladies to work.[3] The specter of the enraged factory women of the Plug Plot riots, however, frightened many parliamentarians and factory owners into accepting the notion that the state should protect women and children in the workplace and that working men should be able to keep their wives at home. The ideology of the breadwinner wage was therefore the outcome of bitter political and trade union struggles, a rhetorical strategy rather than an outgrowth of plebeian traditions.

By demanding the vote, the Chartists also impelled middle-class politicians increasingly to emphasize domesticity as a qualification for suffrage. The debates over the 1832 Reform Act hardly mentioned domestic virtues, instead stressing the probity of middle-class masculine public opinion—the public half of separate spheres.[4] Once the Chartists came onto the scene, however, opponents of working-class suffrage depicted middle-class men as responsible, respectable fathers and citizens, unlike the undisciplined working men.[5] And the passage of the factory acts undercut Chartist claims that they needed the franchise to protect women and children.

Accepting domesticity also led to a narrower conception of the vote. Although Chartists originally based their notion of the vote on Painite equality, they could not accept female suffrage as its logical consequence. Instead, they substituted a more restrictive justification for the vote as property in skill and respectability. Opponents of working-class suffrage continued to depict working men as drunken louts devoid of "decency and morality." In response, while working men struggled to retain the notion of the vote as a basic human right, for strategic reasons they argued that skilled working men were respectable enough to deserve the franchise, unlike the "residuum" or women. From this assertion it was a logical progression to compromise on household suffrage. While the remaining Chartists and most trade unionists resolutely supported manhood suffrage in the 1850s and 1860s, Feargus O'Connor, and also the Glasgow Trades Council, espoused household suffrage in order to ally with middle-class Parliamentary Radicals.[6] For instance, advocates such as Richard Cobden had argued, "I ask, what danger is there giving the franchise to householders? They are the fathers of families; they constitute the laborious and industrious population."[7] These arguments contributed to the Reform Act of 1867, which enfranchised skilled urban working men.[8]

But the paradigm of household suffrage also meant that any additional groups that desired the vote had to prove they had attained the status of respectable manhood, which made the attainment of universal suffrage excruciatingly slow for men and, for women, almost impossible. In turn, by conceding the principle of the breadwinner wage and household suffrage, accepting that the worker shared a common manhood with the gentleman, Liberals and Tories tried to insist that they were all part of "the People" rather than locked into antagonistic classes. Of course, various versions of this manhood persisted, ranging from the upright Liberal nonconformist patriarch to the jovial, hard-drinking Tory patriot.[9] At the same time this rhetorical ploy often failed to overcome the very real differences in experience between working-, middle-, and upper-class Britons, differences which persisted in intruding into politics and eventually produced the Labor Party.

Domesticity also softened class conflict on the industrial level.[10] As Sonya Rose notes of the late nineteenth century, employers generally accepted the principle of the gender division of labor in order to ensure labor peace, and because they themselves regarded it as natural. With some significant exceptions, such as the Kidderminster carpet weavers, employers kept women in auxiliary jobs and accepted (in Lancashire) the position of male mule spinners. Sonya Rose and Patrick Joyce both point out that employers preserved the dominance of the male worker at the factory and in the home as an essential ingredient in their recipe for controlling textile communities through paternalism.[11] In textile trade unions, men continued the traditional strategy of cooperation with women, but they intensified patriarchal control over female workers. Generally the trade union movement tried to keep women, children, and the unskilled out of male crafts, through negotiations and legislation if possible, through strikes if those tactics failed. When Whig reformers accepted their demands, justifying the regulation of women's and children's work as a problem of social morality rather than economics, they protected "political economy from the criticisms of its methodology and its doctrines on industrialization."[12] Trade unionists moved away from trying to organize all workers together on the grounds of class conflict, instead accepting the principle of political economy that control over the labor supply was the only way to improve their position. This trade union strategy perpetuated the permanent availability of a pool of low-paid, female labor that employers could use to undercut male wages. To be sure, the argument that the working class became deferential by the 1850s has been overstated, but the acceptance of domesticity significantly narrowed the terrain of class conflict.[13]

By the 1870s, as class conflict in the political sense diminished, the working class became more homogeneous, in the sociological sense of a stratum of people sharing experiences of work, culture, and community.[14]

Acceptance of the ideal of separate spheres was a crucial factor in this process. Working-class culture was characterized by insular communities; a leisure culture of music halls, betting, and drinking; moderate trade union activity; and a strict sexual division of labor both in the workplace and at home.[15] In Glasgow, for instance, the textile industry declined, outstripped by Lancashire, but the growing sectors of steel and shipbuilding employed Scottish male workers. Although these new opportunities lessened poverty, they increased divisions between men and women, as men worked in heavy industry and women either found jobs in the declining textile industry or stayed at home.[16] In her study of late-nineteenth-century London, Ellen Ross portrays homes and streets divided into distinct male and female worlds, husbands and wives with separate social lives and financial responsibilities. Conflict erupted on the border between masculine and feminine space, but the parameters of each world were strictly defined.[17] Working people, however, continued to find it difficult to live up to the ideal of separate spheres. Men were periodically unemployed, and their wages were often inadequate even in good times. Their wives therefore had to scrimp and save to make ends meet, taking in washing or lodgers to earn some money without losing face by going out to work. Despite Chartism's focus on temperance, in the second half of the nineteenth century heavy drinking was still consonant with respectability among skilled men.[18] Although there is some evidence that the incidence of wife-beating may have decreased in the late nineteenth century as men accepted the chivalrous ideal, domestic violence remained extremely common in working-class communities.[19]

Gareth Stedman Jones has attributed the conservatism of the late-nineteenth-century London working class to a "culture of consolation," a turning inward to family and personal life rather than outward to radical workplace organizations.[20] However, he assumes that only workplace issues had true political potential. The problem may have been, not working men's focus on the family, but the inability of working-class radicals to politicize family issues as had their predecessors in the Owenite, anti–Poor Law, and Chartist movements. Occasionally such issues as the contagious diseases acts or the white slavery scandal would stir working-class outrage, but their mobilization was still inscribed within a patriarchal, melodramatic rhetoric inherited from Chartism rather than integrated into a radical politics of class and sex.[21] Working-class public culture became ever more masculine, focused on exclusively male working-men's clubs, unions, and sporting organizations. As Ross McKibbin writes, politics were "based on male group solidarities—and therefore fractious, partial, and self-absorbed."[22]

Yet by the early twentieth century, Labor politics in some areas broadened to consider the welfare state and the needs of women and children.

Significantly, this took place earliest in Labor towns where women were skilled workers.[23] Textile communities thus revived their earlier tradition of sexual cooperation. Even in London, the impetus for reform moved, as Pat Thane has put it, from the "work-centered form of politics of the type of the older artisan radicalism to one based on neighborhood and community," which included women and middle-class supporters.[24] But large sectors of the Labor movement, such as the printers, continued to be extremely exclusivist, espousing a narrow notion of politics and trade unionism that pushed out not only women but the unskilled and, eventually, people of color.[25]

The narrative of this book has become, by the end, a tragedy rather than the melodrama of E. P. Thompson's story.[26] His stirring tales of compromising villains, soul-crushing political economics, and heroic radical artisans triumphing in the working-class movement of 1832, is richly textured, nuanced, and theoretically inspiring. But adding gender to the story casts a more sorrowful light. There was no golden age of family happiness; rather, there was a chronic sexual crisis. Working men and women struggled valiantly, together and apart, to overcome the sexual antagonism which plagued their communities. But the necessarily defensive nature of working-class politics in the hard years of the 1830s and 1840s blocked more radical solutions. However, an exterior villain cannot take all the blame. Although artisan culture transformed itself from drunken misogyny to respectable patriarchy, its exclusivism persisted. The fatal flaws of misogyny and patriarchy ultimately muted the radicalism of the British working class.

Appendix on 1841 Glasgow Census Sample

I compiled a database of 666 households from eight census districts in the 1841 Glasgow Census (on microfilm in the Local History Room, Mitchell Library, Glasgow). These census districts, numbers 156, 206, 44, 130, 157, 48, 25, and 93, comprised textile areas of Glasgow. All information on household composition and occupation from each household in these districts was entered into the database.

Notes

1. In Tom Leonard, ed., *Radical Renfrew: Poetry from the French Revolution to the First World War* (Edinburgh: Polygon, 1990), p. 30; cf. p. 8.

2. Neil Smelser, *Social Change in the Industrial Revolution* (London: Routledge and Kegan Paul, 1959). But, as Sonya Rose points out, Smelser's willingness to consider a connection between family change and political action remains a challenge for historians of the working class. Sonya O. Rose, *Limited Livelihoods: Gender and Class in Nineteenth-Century England* (Berkeley: University of California Press, 1992), p. 2. The first chapter of Rose's book is an excellent and useful consideration of many of the issues I am raising here.

3. For a critical assessment of Thompson's work, see Harvey J. Kaye and Keith McClelland, eds., *E. P. Thompson: Critical Perspectives* (Philadelphia: Temple University Press, 1990). For a theoretical consideration, see Ira Katznelson, "Working-Class Formation: Constructing Classes and Comparisons," in Ira Katznelson and Aristide Zohlberg, *Working-Class Formation: Nineteenth-Century Patterns in Western Europe and the United States* (Princeton: Princeton University Press, 1986), p. 16. Craig Calhoun has addressed Thompson's work directly: *The Question of Class Struggle: Social Foundations of Popular Radicalism During the Industrial Revolution* (Chicago: University of Chicago Press, 1982), ch. 7.

4. Joan Scott, *Gender and the Politics of History* (New York: Columbia University Press, 1988), p. 73.

5. E. P. Thompson, *The Making of the English Working Class* (New York: Vintage, 1966), p. 11.

6. Barbara Taylor, *Eve and the New Jerusalem: Socialism and Feminism in the Nineteenth Century* (New York: Pantheon, 1983).

7. Leonore Davidoff and Catherine Hall, *Family Fortunes: Men and*

Women of the English Middle Class 1780–1850 (London: Hutchinson, 1987); Scott, *Gender and the Politics of History*; Sally Alexander, "Women, Class and Sexual Difference in the 1830s and the 1840s: Some Reflections on the Writing of a Feminist History," *History Workshop Journal* 17 (1984): 125–49. A few notable studies of late-nineteenth-century gender and class are Judith Walkowitz, *City of Dreadful Delight: Narratives of Sexual Danger in Late Victorian London* (Chicago: University of Chicago Press, 1992); Rose, *Limited Livelihoods*; and Ellen Ross, *Love and Toil: Motherhood in Outcast London, 1870–1918* (New York: Oxford University Press, 1993).

8. Thomas Laqueur, "Orgasms, Generation and the Politics of Reproductive Biology," *Representations* 14 (1986): 2; Genevieve Lloyd, "Reason, Gender and Morality in the History of Philosophy," *Social Research* 50 (1983): 509.

9. Davidoff and Hall, *Family Fortunes*, ch. 3. Despite a prevailing belief in the "naturalness" of separate spheres, contradictions and tensions were hidden within this system, as Davidoff and Hall have pointed out. Cf. Mary Poovey, *Uneven Developments: The Ideological Work of Gender in Mid-Victorian England* (Chicago: University of Chicago Press, 1988), p. 4.

10. For an excellent example of a book that integrates different levels of class formation by contrasting the middle and the working class, paying attention to gender although it is not a primary lens of analysis, see Theodore Koditschek, *Class Formation and Urban Industrial Society: Bradford, 1750–1850* (Cambridge: Cambridge University Press, 1990).

11. Thompson, *Making*, p. 9.

12. Heidi Hartmann's formulation of a dual-systems approach to capitalism and patriarchy broke through the trap of trying to conform women's experience to Marxist categories: "Capitalism, Patriarchy, and Job Segregation by Sex," *Signs* 1 (1976): 137–69. More recent historians try an integrated approach, demonstrating how gender integrally structures capitalism and worker's responses. See Rose, *Limited Livelihoods*; Cynthia Cockburn, *Brothers: Male Dominance and Technological Change* (London: Pluto Press, 1983); Barbara Taylor and Anne Phillips, "Sex and Skill: Notes Toward a Feminist Economics," *Feminist Review* 6 (1980): 1–15.

13. E. P. Thompson, *Customs in Common: Studies in Traditional Popular Culture* (New York: New Press, 1991); see also Calhoun, *Question of Class Struggle*, pp. 149–83; Koditschek, *Class Formation*, pp. 450–83.

14. Thompson, *Making*, pp. 9–10; Thompson, *Customs in Common*, p. 64.

15. Thompson, *Customs in Common*, p. 73.

16. Thomas Laqueur, *Religion and Respectability: Sunday Schools and Working-Class Culture, 1780–1850* (New Haven: Yale University Press, 1976), p. 244.

17. Rose, *Limited Livelihoods*, p. 9; Joan Scott, "Gender: A Useful

Category of Historical Analysis," in her *Gender and the Politics of History*, p. 43; for examples, see Lynn Hunt, ed., *Eroticism and the Body Politic* (Baltimore: Johns Hopkins University Press, 1991). My discussion of wife-selling in ch. 5 will illuminate the point about Thompson's romanticism.

18. Thompson, *Making*, p. 9.

19. For economic determinism, see John Foster, *Class Struggles and the Industrial Revolution* (London: Weidenfeld and Nicolson, 1974).

20. Gareth Stedman Jones, *Languages of Class: Studies in English Working Class History 1832–1982* (Cambridge: Cambridge University Press, 1983), p. 102.

21. David Mayfield and Susan Thorne, "Social History and Its Discontents: Gareth Stedman Jones and the Politics of Language," *Social History* 17 (1992): 165–88; Marc W. Steinberg, "The Re-making of the English Working Class?" *Theory and Society* 20 (1991): 173–97; James Epstein, "Rethinking the Categories of Working-Class History," *Labour/Le Travailleur* 18 (1986): 202; Neville Kirk, "In Defense of Class: A Critique of Gareth Stedman Jones," *International Review of Social History* 32 (1987): 5.

22. Joan Scott, "On Language, Gender and Working-Class History," in *Gender and the Politics of History*, p. 53.

23. For a discussion of this problem, see Laura Lee Downs, "If Woman Is Just an Empty Category, Then Why Am I Afraid to Walk Alone at Night? Identity Politics Meets the Post-Modern Subject," and Reply by Joan Scott, *Comparative Studies in Society and History* 35 (1993): 415–51.

24. For discussion of Thompson's versus Marx's view, see Calhoun, *Question of Class Struggle*, p. 52; for the historiography, see, for example, J. L. Hammond and Barbara Hammond, *The Town Laborer* (London: Longman, 1978 [1917]), and their *The Skilled Labourer 1760–1832* (New York: Augustus M. Kelley, 1967); the classic work is Smelser, *Social Change*. See also Foster, *Class Struggles*; Michael Anderson, *Family Structure in Nineteenth Century Lancashire* (Cambridge: Cambridge University Press, 1971). For other discussions of artisans, see, among many other studies, Iorwerth Prothero, *Artisans and Politics in Early Nineteenth Century London* (London: Methuen, 1981); E. J. Hobsbawm and Joan Scott, "Political Shoemakers," in E. J. Hobsbawm, *Workers: Worlds of Labor* (New York: Pantheon Books, 1984), pp. 103–30; and John Rule, "The Property of Skill in the Period of Manufacture," in Patrick Joyce, ed., *The Historical Meanings of Work* (Cambridge: Cambridge University Press, 1987), pp. 99–118. For a critique of the romanticization of the artisan, see Jacques Rancière, *The Nights of Labor: The Workers' Dream in Nineteenth-Century France*, trans. John Drury (Philadelphia: Temple University Press, 1989).

25. In the last few decades the historiography of the industrial revolution has shifted away from the notion of a sudden technological transformation in history toward a view of gradual growth. See Raphael Samuel, "The Workshop of the World: Steam Power and Hand Technology in Mid-Victorian Britain," *History Workshop* 3 (1977): 6–72; Maxine Berg, *The Age of Manufactures: Industry, Innovation and Work in Britain, 1700–1820* (London: Fontana, 1985), pp. 15–20. But, more recently, Maxine Berg and Pat Hudson have pointed out that by ignoring women workers these studies distort the significance of changes in the cotton industry and in the work process of nonmechanized trades. Maxine Berg, "What Difference Did Women's Work Make to the Industrial Revolution?" *History Workshop Journal* 35 (1993): 22–44; and Maxine Berg and Pat Hudson, "Rehabilitating the Industrial Revolution," *Economic History Review* 45 (1992): 24–50.

26. Berg and Hudson, "Rehabilitating the Industrial Revolution," p. 36.

27. The gender division of labor was also an issue in other trades which I do not have space to explore. For a survey, see Sonya O. Rose, "Gender at Work: Sex, Class, and Industrial Capitalism," *History Workshop Journal* 21 (1986): 113–31. Case studies: for coal mining, see Angela V. John, *By the Sweat of Their Brow: Women Workers at Victorian Coal Mines* (London: Routledge and Kegan Paul, 1984); for the Birmingham metal trades, Berg, *The Age of Manufactures*, ch. 12; for hosiery, Sonya O. Rose, "Gender Segregation in the Transition to the Factory," *Feminist Studies* 13 (1987): 163–84, and Nancy Grey Osterud, "Gender Divisions and the Organization of Work in the Leicestershire Hosiery Industry," in Angela V. John, ed., *Unequal Opportunities: Women's Employment in England, 1800–1918* (Oxford: Basil Blackwell, 1986), pp. 45–70, and cf. the other essays there. For women's work and industrialization in general, the classic work is Ivy Pinchbeck, *Women Workers and the Industrial Revolution, 1750–1850* (London: Virago, 1981 [1930]).

28. As Maxine Berg suggests in *The Age of Manufactures*, p. 161.

29. For Scottish popular literature, see Leonard, ed., *Radical Renfrew*, p. 24; I. McGregor, *Collected Writings of Dougal Graham, Skellat Bellman at Glasgow* (Glasgow, 1883). Although I will not dwell on the problem of nationalism, I should point out that radical movements of the time were intrinsically involved in the struggle to define national heritages with respect to each other, avoiding both ethnic antagonism and domination by the metropolitan power. Roger Wells discusses the United Scotsmen, a parallel to the United Irishmen in the 1790s, in his *Insurrection: The British Experience* (Gloucester: Alan Sutton, 1986); see also Peter Beresford Ellis and Seumas Mac a'Ghobhaim, *The Scottish Insurrection of 1820* (London: Pluto Press, 1989).

30. William Lazonick, "Industrial Relations and Technical Change: The Case of the Self-Acting Mule," *Cambridge Journal of Economics* 3 (1979):

239–40; Mary Freifeld, "Technological Change and the 'Self-Acting' Mule: A Study of Skill and the Sexual Division of Labor," *Social History* 11 (1986): 319–43. Per Bolin-Hart, *Work, Family and the State: Child Labor and the Organization of Production in the British Cotton Industry, 1780–1920* (Lund, Sweden: Lund University Press, 1989), provides a useful overview and illuminates the Glasgow experience.

31. For the term *sexual crisis,* see Taylor, *Eve and the New Jerusalem,* p. 268.

32. John Gillis, *For Better, for Worse: British Marriages, 1600 to the Present* (Oxford: Oxford University Press, 1985), p. 110.

33. Iain MacCalman, *Radical Underworld: Prophets, Revolutionaries and Pornographers in London, 1795–1840* (Cambridge: Cambridge University Press, 1988), p. 28.

34. For plebeian culture, see Hans Medick, "Plebeian Culture in the Transition to Capitalism," in Raphael Samuel and Gareth Stedman Jones, eds., *Culture, Ideology and Politics* (London: Routledge and Kegan Paul, 1983), p. 91.

35. The term *social discourse* derives from Clifford Geertz, *The Interpretation of Cultures* (New York: Basic Books, 1973), pp. 5–12. For a discussion of the term *discourse* applied to workers' politics during the period 1800–1820, see John Smail, "New Languages for Capital and Labour: The Transformation of Discourse in the Early Years of the Industrial Revolution," *Social History* 12 (1987): 51. Smail applies the term *corporate discourse* to the clothiers in the woolen trade. I am building upon Smail's work to differentiate between social discourse and the more self-conscious, deliberate rhetoric formulated by activists for use in specific political contests.

36. Urban literacy was not universal but was relatively high in Glasgow, Lancashire, and London. Literacy in Scotland was somewhat higher than in England, as a result of the traditional system of parish and kirk schools; in 1833, a study found that 96 percent of Scottish mill workers could read, and free or very inexpensive schools were available in the industrial areas of Glasgow. However, many of these workers had had their childhood education interrupted by the necessity for them to go to work, and often they could read but not write. In England as a whole, between two-thirds and three-fourths of the working class could read if not write, and literacy was even higher in London. In plebeian Bethnal Green, for instance, 92.5 percent of the men and 83 percent of the women who married in 1815 signed their names in the marriage register: R. K. Webb, *The British Working-Class Reader* (London: George Allen and Unwin, 1955), p. 25. See Helen Corr, "An Exploration into Scottish Education," in W. Hamish Fraser and R. J. Morris, eds., *People and Society in Scotland.* Vol. 2: *1830–1914* (Edinburgh: John Donald, 1990), p. 292; Donald Withrington, "Schooling, Literacy and Society," in T. M. Devine and Rosalind Mitchison, eds., *People and Society in Scotland.* Vol. 1: *1760–1830* (Edin-

burgh: John Donald, 1988), p. 179; L. D. Schwarz, "Conditions of Life and Work in London, c. 1770–1820, with Special Reference to East London" D.Phil. diss., Oxford University, 1976, p. 340.

37. We know few of the London ballad-writers; those few seem to have been rather marginal figures down on their luck: Louis James, *The Print and the People* (Harmondsworth: Penguin, 1978), p. 23. Northern publishers plagiarized London songs but also printed the works of local ballad writers and "town spokesmen." Martha Vicinus, *Broadsides of the Industrial North* (Newcastle upon Tyne: Frank Graham, 1975), p. 2; also Martha Vicinus, *The Industrial Muse* (London: Croom Helm, 1974); Leonard, ed., *Radical Renfrew*, p. 24; McGregor, *Collected Writings of Dougal Graham*. For a good overview of earlier ballads and their social context, see Joy Wiltenburg, *Disorderly Women and Female Power in the Street Literature of Early Modern England and Germany* (Charlottesville: University Press of Virginia, 1992), esp. pp. 27–46. For a discussion of later nineteenth-century Lancashire street literature, see Patrick Joyce, *Visions of the People: Industrial England and the Question of Class 1840–1914* (Cambridge: Cambridge University Press, 1991), pp. 231–55.

38. Thompson, *Making*, ch. 11.

39. Davidoff and Hall, *Family Fortunes*, p. 191.

40. Jones, *Languages of Class*, pp. 90–95; Geoff Eley, "Edward Thompson, Social History and Political Culture: The Making of a Working-Class Public, 1780–1850," in Kaye and McClelland, *E. P. Thompson*, p. 29. For the 1832 Reform Act as defining the middle class, see Drohr Wahrman, "Virtual Representation: Parliamentary Reporting and the Languages of Class in the 1790s," *Past and Present* 136 (1992): 113.

41. Ernesto Laclau and Chantal Mouffe, *Hegemony and Socialist Strategy: Toward a Radical Democratic Politics* (London: Verso, 1985), p. 88; see also Pierre Bourdieu, "What Makes a Social Class?" *Berkeley Journal of Sociology* 32 (1987): 13.

42. See Benedict Anderson, *Imagined Communities* (London: Verso, 1983).

43. For rhetoric, see Terry Eagleton, *Literary Theory: An Introduction* (Minneapolis: University of Minnesota Press, 1983), p. 206; Mikhail Bakhtin, *The Dialogic Imagination*, trans. Michael Holquist (Austin: University of Texas Press, 1981), pp. 342, 353. V. N. Volosinov, *Marxism and the Philosophy of Language*, trans. Ladislav Matejka and I. R. Titunik (Cambridge: Harvard University Press, 1986), is thought to be in part by Bakhtin and presents a more social interpretation of language in context. See also John D. Schaeffer, "The Use and Misuse of Giambattista Vico: Rhetoric, Orality, and Theories of Discourse," in H. Aram Veeser, ed., *The New Historicism* (London: Routledge, 1989), p. 97; and Kenneth Burke, *A Rhetoric of Motives* (New York: Prentice Hall, 1950), pp. 43, 45, 86.

44. This analysis is similar to that in Jones, *Languages of Class*, p. 96, though with more stress on popular culture and emotion.

45. Most notably, Joan Scott, "Experience," in Judith Butler and Joan W. Scott, eds., *Feminists Theorize the Political* (New York: Routledge, 1992), pp. 22–40; Jones, *Languages of Class.* For overviews of this debate, see Gabrielle M. Spiegel, "History, Historicism and the Social Logic of the Text," *Speculum* 65 (1990): 59–86; and John E. Toews, "Intellectual History After the Linguistic Turn: The Autonomy of Meaning and the Irreducibility of Experience," *American Historical Review* 92 (1987): 879–907.

46. James Vernon stresses "the importance of the state's use of the law in structuring the shape of political languages by limiting the choice of discursive strategies" (i.e., through censorship and imprisonment of radicals). James Vernon, *Politics and the People: A Study in English Political Culture c. 1815–1867* (Cambridge: Cambridge University Press, 1993), p. 301. I owe thanks to James Vernon for allowing me to see a chapter of this work before publication. For a discussion of agency in this context, see Mayfield and Thorne, "Social History and Its Discontents," pp. 180–88; and David Mayfield and Susan Thorne, "Reply to the 'Poverty of Protest' and the Imaginary Discontent," *Social History* 18 (1993): 219–34.

47. Renato Rosaldo, "Celebrating Thompson's Heroes: Social Analysis in History and Anthropology," in Kaye and McClelland, *E. P. Thompson*, pp. 115–17.

48. William Sewell, "How Classes Are Made: Critical Reflections on E. P. Thompson's Theory of Working-Class Formation," in Kaye and McClelland, *E. P. Thompson*, p. 68.

CHAPTER TWO: SETTING THE STAGE

1. M. Dorothy George, *London Life in the Eighteenth Century* (Harmondsworth: Penguin, 1966 [1925]), p. 425.

2. As Maxine Berg suggests in her *The Age of Manufactures: Industry, Innovation and Work in Britain, 1700–1820* (London: Fontana, 1985), p. 161.

3. Alice Clark, *The Working Life of Women in the Seventeenth Century* (London: Virago, 1982 [1919]); Hans Medick, "The Proto-Industrial Family Economy: The Structural Function of Household and Family During the Transition from Peasant Society to Industrial Capitalism," *Social History* 3 (1976): 299. For criticisms of this view, see Chris Middleton, "Patriarchal Exploitation and the Rise of English Capitalism," in Eve Garmanikow et al., *Gender, Class and Work* (London: Heinemann, 1983), p. 25. For a critique of proto-industrialization theory, see Rab Houston and K. D. M. Snell, "Proto-industrialization? Cottage Industry, Social Change, and Industrial Revolution," *Historical Journal* 27 (1984): 473–92.

4. Judith Bennett, *Women in the Medieval English Countryside: Gender and Household in Brigstock Before the Plague* (New York: Oxford University Press, 1987), pp. 4–8.

5. Jane Mark-Lawson and Anne Witz, "From 'Family Labor' to 'Family Wage': The Case of Women's Labor in Nineteenth-Century Coalmining," *Social History* 13 (1988): pp. 158–59; Wally Seccombe, "Patriarchy Stabilized: The Construction of the Male Breadwinner Wage Norm in Nineteenth-Century Britain," *Social History* 11 (1986): 65–67.

6. Medick, "Proto-Industrial Family Economy," pp. 300–313.

7. For a discussion of theories of the origins of gender segregation, see Sonya O. Rose, "Gender Antagonism and Class Conflict: Exclusionary Strategies of Male Trade Unionists in Nineteenth-Century Britain," *Social History* 13 (1988): 191–96.

8. Iorwerth Prothero, *Artisans and Politics in Early Nineteenth Century London* (London: Methuen, 1981), p. 341.

9. George, *London Life*, pp. 158–212.

10. *The Autobiography of Francis Place, 1771–1854*, ed. Mary Thrale (Cambridge: Cambridge University Press, 1972), pp. ix, 22; George, *London Life*, pp. 302–4.

11. The phrase is from Christine Stansell, *City of Women: Sex and Class in New York, 1789–1860* (New York: Knopf, 1986), p. 43.

12. Prothero, *Artisans and Politics*, p. 342; L. D. Schwarz, "Conditions of Life and Work in London, c. 1770–1820, with Special Reference to East London," D.Phil. diss., Oxford University, 1976, p. 66.

13. Quoted in Elizabeth Gilboy, *Wages in Eighteenth-Century England* (Cambridge: Harvard University Press, 1934), p. 7.

14. Michael Anderson, *Family Structure in Nineteenth-Century Lancashire* (Cambridge: Cambridge University Press, 1971), p. 134.

15. John Gillis, *For Better, for Worse: British Marriages, 1600 to the Present* (Oxford: Oxford University Press, 1985), p. 168.

16. Quoted in C. R. Dobson, *Masters and Journeymen: A Prehistory of Industrial Relations, 1717–1800* (London: Croom Helm, 1980), p. 112.

17. Peter Earle, "The Female Labor Market in London in the Late 17th and Early 18th Century," *Economic History Review*, 2d series, 42 (1989): 341–42; K. D. M. Snell, *Annals of the Laboring Poor: Social Change in Agrarian England, 1660–1900* (Cambridge: Cambridge University Press, 1985), ch. 6; Sally Alexander, "Women's Work in Nineteenth-Century London: A Study of the Years 1820–50," in Juliet Mitchell and Ann Oakley, eds., *The Rights and Wrongs of Women* (Harmondsworth: Penguin, 1976), p. 78.

18. Earle, "Female Labor Market," p. 338.

19. George, *London Life*, p. 200.

20. Snell, *Annals*, p. 312.

21. Richard Campbell, *The London Tradesman* (London, 1747); J. Collyer, *The Parents' and Guardians' Directory* (London, 1761); Ivy Pinchbeck, *Women Workers and the Industrial Revolution, 1750–1850* (London: Virago, 1981 [1930]), p. 305.

22. For examples, see George, *London Life*, pp. 425–28.

23. John Overs, *Evenings of a Working Man, Being the Occupation of His Scanty Leisure* (London, 1844), p. viii. Greater London Record Office, London Consistory Court depositions, DL/C 284, 28 Feb. 1789, Smith v. Smith divorce.

24. William Hart, "Autobiography," ed. Lynette Hunter, *London Journal* 8 (1982): 68.

25. Earle, "Female Labor Market," p. 339. Earle may, however, over-emphasize laundry and service as women's trades, since his source, the London Consistory Court files, mainly consist of divorce and defamation records. The women whose occupations he records were the witnesses in these cases, and servants and laundresses were more likely to be able to testify about adultery in divorce cases than craftswomen. But see also Alexander, "Women's Work in Nineteenth-Century London," p. 72.

26. Patricia Malcolmson, *Victorian Laundresses* (Urbana: University of Illinois Press, 1986), pp. 26, 43, 104.

27. "Going out a washing," in British Library Collection 11621.k.4. See also the description in J. T. Smith, *The Cries of London* (London, 1839), p. 81.

28. Hannah More, *The Gamester* (London, 1795), n.p.

29. Schwarz, "Conditions of Life and Work in London," p. 76.

30. John K. Walton, *Lancashire: A Social History* (Manchester: Manchester University Press, 1987), p. 60. For Manchester's growth, see Walton, *Lancashire*, pp. 60–61, 76, 110, 123; Alfred P. Wadsworth and Julia de Lacy Mann, *The Cotton Trade and Industrial Lancashire, 1600–1780* (Manchester: Manchester University Press, 1965 [1931]), p. 510; Craig Calhoun, *The Question of Class Struggle: Social Foundations of Popular Radicalism During the Industrial Revolution* (Chicago: University of Chicago Press, 1982), p. 188.

31. R. A. Cage, *The Scottish Poor Law* (Edinburgh: Scottish Academic Press, 1981), p. 45.

32. T. C. Smout, *A History of the Scottish People 1560–1830* (London: Fontana, 1972), p. 369.

33. Norman Murray, *The Scottish Hand Loom Weavers 1790–1850: A Social History* (Edinburgh: John Donald, 1978), p. 5.

34. Walton, *Lancashire*, pp. 60–61, 76, 110, 123.

35. Brenda Collins, "Sewing and Social Structure: The Flowerers of Scotland and Ireland," in Rosalind Mitchison and Peter Roebuck , eds., *Economy and Society in Scotland and Ireland* (Edinburgh: John Donald, 1988), p. 243; Sir John Sinclair, ed., *The Statistical Account of Scotland*, ed. Donald J. Witrington and Ian R. Grant (Wakefield, England: E. P. Publishing, 1983 [1791–1799]), vol. 7, pp. 250, 296, 677, 730.

36. David Loch, *A Tour Through Most of the Trading Towns and Villages of Scotland* (Edinburgh, 1778), pp. 23, 31, 34.

37. The period of the 1770s through 1815 seems to have been an evanescent time of prosperity for the textile industry. In Lancashire, handloom wages peaked around 1796, then fell, regained strength in 1810–1814, but then declined inexorably. Duncan Bythell, *The Handloom Weavers: A Study in the English Cotton Industry During the Industrial Revolution* (Cambridge: Cambridge University Press, 1969), p. 99. Wages rose for textile workers (and Scottish workers in general) during this period, though some of the rise simply compensated for inflation. During the war years of 1792–1793 to 1815, most workers' wages in Scotland grew more slowly, stagnated, or even declined, but, with some unevenness, textile workers maintained their wage status. J. H. Treble, "The Standard of Living of the Working Class," in T. M. Devine and Rosalind Mitchison, eds., *People and Society in Scotland*. Vol. 1: *1760–1830* (Edinburgh: John Donald, 1988), 197.

38. A. P. Wadsworth, "The Lancashire Wage-Earners Before the Factory System," in Wadsworth and Mann, *The Cotton Trade*, cited in Mary Freifeld, "Technological Change and the 'Self-Acting' Mule: A Study of Skill and the Sexual Division of Labor," *Social History* 11 (1986): 33.

39. *Thoughts on the Use of Machines in the Cotton Manufacture Addressed to the Working People in That Manufacture and to the Poor in General* (Manchester, 1780), p. 14.

40. Berg, *Age of Manufactures*, p. 255.

41. Berg, *Age of Manufactures*, p. 145; also [Ralph Mather], *An Impartial Representation of the Case of the Poor Cotton Spinners* (London, 1780), p. 3.

42. "A Letter from a Journeyman Cotton Spinner," *Black Dwarf* 2 (1818): 622–23.

43. William Lazonick, "Industrial Relations and Technical Change: The Case of the Self-Acting Mule," *Cambridge Journal of Economics* 3 (1979): 232. As Sian Moore demonstrates for the Bradford area, the consequences of mechanization for the gender division of labor were not predictable. In the areas where woolen weaving predominated, which were characterized by a history of artisanal production within the proto-industrial family, men were able to gain control over mechanized spinning. Worsted production had also been carried on in the proto-industrial family, but there patriarchal control was weak, since each member of the family performed a separate task and merchants paid each a separate wage. Hence, when employers introduced mechanized spinning, they could bypass the men and employ young women amd children, who were preferred for their docile dispositions and lower wages. Sian Moore, "Women, Industralization and Protest in Bradford, West Yorkshire, 1780–1845," Ph.D. diss., University of Essex, 1986, pp. 54–67.

44. Anderson, *Family Structure*, p. 134.

45. Smout, *History of the Scottish People*, p. 387.

46. Lazonick, "Industrial Relations and Technical Change," p. 232. The

debate on the sexual division of labor in mule spinning will be discussed more extensively in chs. 7 and 9.

47. M. M. Edwards and R. Lloyd-Jones, "N. J. Smelser and the Cotton Factory Family: A Reassessment," in N. B. Harte and K. G. Ponting, eds., *Textile History and Economic History* (Manchester: Manchester University Press, 1973), p. 302; Michael Anderson, "Sociological History and the Working-Class Family: Smelser Revisited," *Social History* 6 (1976): 325.

48. For a useful comparison and overview, see Per Bolin-Hart, *Work, Family and the State: Child Labor and the Organization of Production in the British Cotton Industry, 1780–1920* (Lund, Sweden: Lund University Press, 1989), p. 54.

49. Tony Clarke and Tony Dickson, "Class and Class Consciousness in Early Industrial Capitalism: Paisley 1770–1850," in Tony Dickson, ed., *Capital and Class in Scotland* (Edinburgh: John Donald, 1982), p. 10.

50. R. A. Houston, "The Demographic Regime," in Devine and Mitchison, eds., *People and Society in Scotland*, vol. 1, pp. 18–19.

51. Frances Collier, *The Family Economy of the Working Class in the Cotton Industry 1784–1833*, ed. R. S. Fitton (Manchester: Manchester University Press, 1964), p. 15.

52. Clarke and Dickson, "Class and Class Consciousness," p. 21.

53. Smout, *History of the Scottish People*, p. 396; David Gilmour, *Reminiscences of the Pen'Folk: Paisley Weavers of Other Days* (2d ed. Paisley, 1879), p. 11.

54. *A Short Account of the Lives and Hardships of a Glasgow Weaver, Written by Himself* (Glasgow, 1834), pp. 3, 4.

55. Autobiography of John Mackinnon, Glasgow, Strathclyde Regional Archives, manuscript TD 743/1, 1859.

56. Gilmour, *Reminiscences of the Pen'Folk*, p. 25.

57. Murray, *Scottish Hand Loom Weavers*, p. 96.

58. Sinclair, ed., *Statistical Account of Scotland*, vol. 7, pp. 250, 730.

59. *A Short Account of the Life and Hardships of a Glasgow Weaver*, p. 3.

60. Murray, *Scottish Hand Loom Weavers*, p. 28; for Manchester, and a discussion of the ramifications of this problem, see E. P. Thompson, *The Making of the English Working Class* (New York: Vintage, 1966), p. 275.

61. Alexander Richmond, *Narrative of the Condition of the Manufacturing Population* (Glasgow, 1825), p. 6.

62. Murray, *Scottish Hand Loom Weavers*, p. 28. According to the Webb Trade Union Collection, section on handloom weavers, 20 percent of the looms in Glasgow were worked by women. London, London School of Economics, Webb Trade Union Collection, E/A/37, p. 288. On the increase in numbers during the Napoleonic wars, see the testimony of Thomas Smith to the Select Committee on Petitions of Several Weavers, PP 1810–1811, vol. II, p. 390.

63. Bythell, *Handloom Weavers*, pp. 60–61.

64. A. Aspinall, *The Early English Trade Unions* (London: Batchworth Press, 1949), p. 20.

65. Murray, *Scottish Hand Loom Weavers*, p. 28.

66. "The Weaver's Lament, by an Operative Weaver," Glasgow, Glasgow University, Collection of Broadsheets. n.d., Mu.23.y.1.

67. John Campbell, *History of the Rise and Progress of Powerloom Weaving and Vindication of the Character of Female Powerloom Weavers* (Rutherglen, 1878), p. 5; Berg, *Age of Manufactures*, p. 249.

68. Thompson, *Making*, p. 308.

69. Maxine Berg, "Women's Work and Mechanization," in Patrick Joyce, ed., *The Historical Meanings of Work* (Cambridge: Cambridge University Press, 1987), p. 82.

CHAPTER THREE: MEN AND WOMEN TOGETHER AND APART

1. E. P. Thompson, *The Making of the English Working Class* (New York: Vintage, 1966), p. 425. Cf. Iorwerth Prothero, *Artisans and Politics in Early Nineteenth Century London* (London: Methuen, 1981), p. 35; E. J. Hobsbawm and Joan Wallach Scott, "Political Shoemakers," *Past and Present* 89 (1980): 86–114; Peter Linebaugh, *The London Hanged: Crime and Civil Society in the Eighteenth Century* (London: Allen Lane Penguin Press, 1991), p. 62.

2. Thompson, *Making*, p. 244.

3. Maxine Berg, "Women's Work, Mechanisation and the Early Phases of Industrialisation in England," in Patrick Joyce, ed., *The Historical Meanings of Work* (Cambridge: Cambridge University Press, 1987), p. 92.

4. E. P. Thompson, *Customs in Common: Studies in Traditional Popular Culture* (New York: New Press, 1991), p. 467.

5. Ruth L. Smith and Deborah M. Valenze, "Mutuality and Marginality: Liberal Moral Theory and Working-Class Women in Nineteenth-Century England," *Signs* 13 (1988): 277–98. Temma Kaplan's work has also been particularly important in pointing out that class consciousness can be rooted in the community as well as the workplace: "Female Consciousness and Collective Action: The Case of Barcelona, 1910–1918," *Signs* 7 (1982): 548.

6. For women as a hindrance, see Craig Calhoun, *The Question of Class Struggle: Social Foundations of Popular Radicalism During the Industrial Revolution* (Chicago: University of Chicago Press, 1982), p. 158.

7. Calhoun, *Question of Class Struggle*, p. 201.

8. For ethnic communities and conflict in London, see L. D. Schwarz, "Conditions of Life and Work in London, c. 1770–1820, with Special Reference to East London," D.Phil. diss., Oxford University, 1976, p. 40; "Church Lane St. Giles," *Journal of the Royal Statistical Society* 2 (1840): 20; Todd Endelmann, *The Jews of Georgian England, 1714–1830* (Phila-

delphia: Jewish Publication Society of America, 1979), p. 268. For Africans escaping slavery, see Peter Fryer, *Staying Power* (London: Pluto Press, 1984). For Glasgow and Irish/Protestant/Catholic conflict, see T. M. Devine, "Urbanisation," in T. M. Devine and Rosalind Mitchison, eds., *People and Society in Scotland*. Vol. 1: *1760–1830* (Edinburgh: John Donald, 1988), pp. 42–43.

9. Schwarz, "Conditions of Life and Work in London," p. 29.

10. J. T. Smith, *The Streets of London* (London, 1849), pp. 76, 173.

11. Rev. Wyatt Edgell, "Moral Statistics of the Parishes of St. James, St. George and St. Ann Soho, Westminster," *Journal of the Royal Statistical Society* 1 (1838): 478.

12. "Church Lane St. Giles," pp. 1–13.

13. W. Felkin, "Moral Statistics of a District near Grays Inn," *Journal of the Royal Statistical Society* 1 (1839): 541–42.

14. Robert Glen, *Urban Workers in the Early Industrial Revolution* (London: Croom Helm, 1984), p. 66.

15. For immigration to Stockport, see Glen, *Urban Workers*, p. 20.

16. Michael Anderson, *Family Structure in Nineteenth Century Lancashire* (Cambridge: Cambridge University Press, 1971), p. 57.

17. John Foster, *Class Struggle and the Industrial Revolution* (London: Weidenfeld and Nicolson, 1974), p. 126.

18. John Gillis, *For Better, for Worse: British Marriages, 1600 to the Present* (Oxford: Oxford University Press, 1985), p. 160.

19. Leonore Davidoff, "The Separation of Home and Work? Landladies and Lodgers in 19th and Early 20th Century England," in Sandra Burman, ed., *Fit Work for Women* (London: Croom Helm, 1979).

20. Anderson, *Family Structure*, p. 45.

21. Eileen Yeo and E. P. Thompson, *The Unknown Mayhew* (New York: Schocken, 1972), p. 337.

22. John Butt, "Housing," in R. A. Cage, *The Working Class in Glasgow 1750–1914* (London: Croom Helm, 1987), p. 41.

23. For a middle-class woman's description, no doubt exaggerated, see Elizabeth Hamilton, *The Cottagers of Glenburnie: A Tale for the Farmer's Inglenook* (Edinburgh, 1822), p. 154.

24. J. E. Handley, *The Irish in Scotland* (Cork: Cork University Press, 1945), p. 242.

25. Hans Medick, "Plebeian Culture in the Transition to Capitalism," in Raphael Samuel and Gareth Stedman Jones, eds., *Culture, Ideology and Politics* (London: Routledge and Kegan Paul, 1983), p. 91.

26. David Gilmour, *Reminiscences of the Pen'Folk: Paisley Weavers of Other Days* (2d ed. Paisley, 1879), p. 109; Joseph Lawson, *Progress in Pudsey* (Firle, Sussex: Caliban Books, 1978 [1887]), p. 28; Mary Taylor, *Miss Miles: Or, A Tale of Yorkshire Life Sixty Years Ago* (Oxford University Press, 1990), p. 127.

27. M. Dorothy George, *London Life in the Eighteenth Century* (Harmondsworth: Penguin, 1966 [1925]), p. 279.

28. Patrick Colquhoun, *Observations and Facts Relative to Public Houses* (London, 1794), p. 49.

29. Report, Select Committee on Drunkenness, PP 1834, vol. 8, p. 3.

30. Glasgow, Strathclyde Regional Archives, Glasgow Police Court books, 1813–1816.

31. Glasgow, Strathclyde Regional Archives, Police notebook, TD 734, July 16, 1835, p. 141.

32. Edinburgh, Scottish Record Office, AD 14/26/248 (Prosecution papers), Precognition of Hugh Dick, 27 June 1826.

33. Engraving by Laurie and Whittle, 1805, British Museum Catalogue of Satirical Prints number 10513. Possession of the author.

34. London, Guildhall Library, Printed Old Bailey Sessions Papers 1819–1820, p. 110, case of Thomas Brophy.

35. *Weekly Dispatch*, 3 March 1833.

36. *A New and Diverting Dialogue Between a Shoemaker and His Wife* (London, 1800), p. 6.

37. Medick, "Plebeian Culture," p. 91.

38. Medick, "Plebeian Culture," p. 91.

39. Mary Anne Clawson, *Constructing Brotherhood: Gender, Class, and Fraternalism* (Princeton: Princeton University Press, 1989), p. 146.

40. John O'Neill, "Fifty Years Experience as an Irish Shoemaker in London," *St. Crispin* 1 (1869): 316.

41. Mary Ann Clawson, "Early Modern Fraternalism and the Patriarchal Family," *Feminist Studies* 6 (1980): 369; Clawson, *Constructing Brotherhood*, p. 47.

42. For the middle class, see Leonore Davidoff and Catherine Hall, *Family Fortunes: Men and Women of the English Middle Class* (London: Hutchinson, 1987).

43. For the debates on libertinism, see James G. Turner, "The Properties of Libertinism," *Eighteenth-Century Life* 9 (1985): pp. 75–87.

44. See, e.g., Pierce Egan, *Life in London: Or, The Day and Night Scenes of Tom and Jerry* (London, 1820).

45. Davidoff and Hall, *Family Fortunes*, pp. 110, 400.

46. J. M. Beattie, *Crime and the Courts in England, 1660–1800* (Oxford: Oxford University Press, 1986), p. 92.

47. London, Guildhall Library, Printed Old Bailey Sessions Papers 1825, vol. 1, p. 181.

48. *Trades' Newspaper*, 17 July 1825.

49. Merry E. Weisner, "Guilds, Male Bonding and Women's Work in Early Modern Germany," *Gender and History* 1 (1989): 131.

50. Clawson, *Constructing Brotherhood*, p. 4.

51. Prothero, *Artisans and Politics*, p. 35.

52. *Universal Register* (*London Times*), 1 Dec. 1786.

53. Alexander Somerville, *The Autobiography of a Working Man* (London, 1848), p. 120.

54. Tony Clarke and Tony Dickson, "Class and Class Consciousness in Early Industrial Capitalism: Paisley 1770–1850," in Tony Dickson, ed., *Capital and Class in Scotland* (Edinburgh: John Donald, 1982), p. 21. At the trial of Charles Campbell, a cotton spinner, for murdering his lover, witnesses commented on the respectability and intelligence of the witnesses who worked in cotton mills. "Trial of Charles Campbell, Before the Circuit Court of the Justiciary," in Charles Campbell, *Memoirs* (Glasgow, 1828), p. 39.

55. John Rule, "The Property of Skill in the Period of Manufacture," in Patrick Joyce, ed., *The Historical Meanings of Work* (Cambridge: Cambridge University Press, 1987), p. 118.

56. Jacques Rancière, "The Myth of the Artisan: Critical Reflections on a Category of Social History," in Steven Laurence Kaplan and Cynthia J. Koepp, *Work in France: Representations, Meaning, Organization and Practice* (Ithaca: Cornell University Press, 1986), p. 318.

57. Thompson, *Making*, p. 193. The depositions of prosecutions of combinations of workmen in Scotland contain descriptions of these customs and membership cards. Edinburgh, Scottish Record Office, AD 14/38/502 (Prosecution papers), bundle 2, item 6 (1838), history of cotton spinners union by George Salmond); AD 14/14/16 (1814), calico printers; AD 14/13/8 (1813), weavers.

58. Clarke and Dickson, "Class and Class Consciousness," p. 18.

59. *The Autobiography of John McAdam 1806–1883*, ed. Janet Fyfe (Edinburgh: Clark Constable Ltd. for Scottish History Society, 1980), p. 3.

60. James Paterson, *Autobiographical Reminiscences: Recollections of the Radical Years 1819–20* (Glasgow, 1871), p. 65.

61. Campbell, *Memoirs*, p. 23.

62. George, *London Life*, pp. 289, 267.

63. Gilmour, *Reminiscences of the Pen'Folk*, p. 25.

64. George, *London Life*, p. 192.

65. Iain MacCalman, *Radical Underworld: Prophets, Revolutionaries and Pornographers in London, 1795–1840* (Cambridge: Cambridge University Press, 1988), pp. 28.

66. For further discussion of stages in life cycles, see John Gillis, *Youth and History: Tradition and Change in European Age Relations, 1770 to the Present* (New York: Academic Press, 1975).

67. Clawson, "Early Modern Fraternalism," p. 369. Cf. her *Constructing Brotherhood*, p. 47; Gillis, *Youth and History*, p. 22.

68. Elspeth King, *Scotland Sober and Free: The Temperance Movement 1829–1879* (Glasgow: Glasgow Museums and Art Galleries, 1979), p. 5.

69. Alexander Thomson, *Random Notes and Rambling Recollections of Drydock* (Glasgow, 1895), pp. 23–26.

70. Sometimes shoemakers' wives could go on tramp with their hus-

bands, according to Prothero, but taking a whole family along must have been difficult, if not impossible. Prothero, *Artisans and Politics*, p. 30.

71. Cynthia Cockburn, *Brothers: Male Dominance and Technological Change* (London: Pluto Press, 1983), p. 134.

72. "What Man Would Be Without a Woman," Oxford, Bodleian Library, John Johnson Collection of Ephemera, Street Ballads Box 7, printed 1832.

73. See Gillis, *For Better, for Worse*, p. 34, for rituals of homosocial leavetaking.

74. [Thomas Wright], *Some Habits and Customs of the Working Classes, by a Journeyman Engineer* (New York: Augustus M. Kelley, 1967 [1867]), p. 100.

75. Charles Manby Smith, *A Working Man's Way in the World* (London: Printing History Society, 1967 [1857]), p. 257.

76. Campbell, *Memoirs*, p. 24; Gilmour, *Reminiscences of the Pen'Folk*, p. 25.

77. Ian Donnachie, "Drinking in Scotland," *Journal of the Scottish Labor History Society* 20 (1985): 13.

78. "The Ladies Club," printed after 1840 by Elizabeth Hodges, British Library Collection 11621.k.4.

79. Ellen Ross, "Survival Networks: Women's Neighborhood Sharing in London Before World War I," *History Workshop Journal* 15 (1983): pp. 6–7. They also differed from the networks Ross describes, however, in that they were more likely to be organized formally.

80. The classic article on women's culture is Carroll Smith-Rosenberg, "The Female World of Love and Ritual," *Signs* 1 (1975): 1–29, reprinted in her *Disorderly Conduct: Visions of Gender in Victorian America* (New York: Alfred A. Knopf, 1985). For an overview of the historiography, see Nancy A. Hewitt, "Beyond the Search for Sisterhood: American Women's History in the 1980s," *Social History* 10 (1985): 309.

81. Numbers from London, Greater London Record Office, "List of Rules of Friendly Societies Deposited with the Clerk of the Peace of Middlesex," 1794–1830, and London, Guildhall Library, "List of Rules of Friendly Societies Deposited with the Clerk of the Peace of London," 1794–1830.

82. Returns of Friendly Societies, PP 1837, vol. 51, p. 195.

83. Returns of Friendly Societies, PP 1842, vol. 26, pp. 22–23.

84. Sheila Lewenhak, *Women and Trade Unions: An Outline History of Women in the British Trade Union Movement* (London: Ernest Benn, 1977), p. 46; Dorothy Thompson, "Women and Radical Politics: The Lost Dimension," in Juliet Mitchell and Ann Oakley, eds., *The Rights and Wrongs of Women* (Harmondsworth: Penguin, 1976), p. 177; P. H. Gosden, *Friendly Societies in England, 1815–1875* (Manchester: Manchester University Press, 1961), p. 62.

85. Glen, *Urban Workers*, p. 110; Chester, Chester Record Office, "A

List of the Friendly Society Rules Filed with the Clerk of the Peace for the County of Chester 1794–1849," QDS2, lists thirteen female societies.

86. Returns of Friendly Societies, PP 1824, vol. 28.

87. Thomas Johnston, *The History of the Working Classes in Scotland* (Totowa, N.J.: Rowman and Littlefield, 1974 [1946]), p. 382.

88. The Kilmarnock Dutiful Female Friendly Society was founded in 1817, registered in 1835; and there were nine other female friendly societies registered in Kilmarnock. Female Friendly Society of Saltcoats, instituted 1831, registered 1846. Three out of six friendly societies in Irvine were women's. Edinburgh, Scottish Record Office, Friendly Society Records, FS1/2/42; *New Statistical Account* (Edinburgh, 1845), vol. 7, p. 312, for Neilston: two societies had been in existence for six years by 1837, one with 328 members, the other with 564; there were also four male societies. The female population was 4,477. *New Statistical Account*, vol. 7, p. 292: two female friendly societies in Paisley were "managed by respectable females of the operative class for relief of sickness." In 1844 sixteen female friendly societies were registered in Scotland, with a total membership of 3,280. Ian Levitt and Christopher Smout, *The State of the Scottish Working Class in 1843: A Statistical and Spatial Enquiry Based on the Data from the Poor Law Commission of 1844* (Edinburgh: Scottish Academic Press, 1979), p. 143.

89. London, Greater London Record Office, "List of Rules of Friendly Societies Deposited with the Clerk of the Peace of Middlesex," 1794–1830, nos. 924 and 1518; servants, no. 899; governesses, in Rules filed 1829–1843, no. 88 (1831) and no. 1077 (1843).

90. *The New Art and Mystery of Gossiping* (London, ca. 1800).

91. Lewenhak, *Women and Trade Unions*, p. 18.

92. For instance, *Rules and Orders to Be Observed by the Sociable Friendly Society of Females at Manchester* (Failsworth, 1799); also *Manchester Friendly Sisters*, Preston, Lancashire Record Office, Friendly Society Rules, QDS/1/5/7, 1813.

93. Rules of the Sisterly Society of Women, London, Public Record Office, Friendly Society papers, FS/1/403/5.

94. *Rules and Orders to Be Observed by a Friendly Society of Women*, held at the Old George, Drury Lane (London, 1787).

95. London, Public Record Office, Friendly Society papers, FS/1/406A/78.

96. *Rules and Orders to Be Observed by a Friendly Society of Women, United for the Mutual Support and Benefit of Each Other When Under Real Afflictions*, held at the Blakeney Head, Norton Folgate (London, 1785). The same rules were established for clubs at the Green Dragon, in Fore Street, Cripplegate (London, 1785); at the Sign of the Three Jolly Butchers, Hoxton Market Place (London, 1795); and at the Old George, Drury Lane (London, 1787) (all in the British Library).

97. London, Public Record Office, Friendly Society papers, FS/1/403/8.

98. *Weekly Free Press*, 6 Dec. 1828, reporting a dispute over the proper payment for conducting such an examination.

99. *Rules to Be Observed by a Society Called the Constant Friend*, London, Public Record Office, Friendly Society papers, FS/1/403/2.

100. *Rules, Orders and Regulations, to Be Observed for the Government and Guidance of a Society of Women* (Sabden Bridge, Burnley, 1813).

101. London, Public Record Office, Friendly Society papers, FS/1/406A/67, Golden Lion, Fore Street; London, Public Record Office, Friendly Society papers, FS/1/406A/75, meeting at Green Dragon, Fore Street, founded 1775.

102. Rules of societies meeting at the Blakeney Head and the Green Dragon.

103. *The New Art and Mystery of Gossiping* (London, ca. 1800), p. 6.

104. *Rules of Society*, meeting in Fore Street (London, 1787).

105. *Rules of a Society of Women, Founded in Battersea* (London, 1788), which was supervised by a patroness who rewarded chastity; and the similar *Female Friendly Society* (London, 1802). For later versions, see Brian Harrison, "The Girls' Friendly Society," *Past and Present* 61 (1973): 107–38.

106. Sir Frederick Eden, *Observations on Friendly Societies* (London, 1801), p. 21.

107. London, Public Record Office, Friendly Society papers, FS/1/403/5.

108. London, Public Record Office, Friendly Society papers, FS/1/406A/109; also Mrs. Campbell's Society (FS/1/403/8); the Society at the Green Dragon, Fore Street, was founded in 1775 (FS/1/406A/75); one at the Golden Lion, Fore Street, was founded in 1775 as well (FS/1/406A/59), and both were registered in 1794.

109. Henry Mayhew, *London Labour and the London Poor* (London, 1860), vol. 1, p. 466.

110. Report of the Select Committee on Drunkenness, p. 274. This was still true in late-nineteenth-century London, although in some areas working-class women did not go to the pub. See Ross, "Survival Networks," p. 11; also Ellen Ross, "'Not the Sort That Would Sit on the Doorstep': Respectability in Pre–World War I London Neighborhoods," *International Labor and Working Class History* 27 (1985): 39–59.

111. "Fuddling Day, or Saint Monday, an Answer to Washing Day," in John Holloway and Joan Black, eds., *Later English Broadside Ballads* (London: Routledge and Kegan Paul, 1979), p. 111. For Saint Monday, see Thompson, *Customs in Common*, pp. 372–73; D. H. Reid, "The Decline of St. Monday, 1776–1876," *Past and Present* 71 (1976): 77, 81–82.

112. Wright, *Some Habits and Customs of the Working Classes*, p. 261.

113. London, Greater London Record Office, London Consistory Court

depositions, Defamation case, Jarman v. Saunders alias Morris, DL/C 283, 2 May 1789.

114. Report on Handloom Weavers, PP 1840, vol. 23, p. 219.

115. Mayhew, *London Labour and the London Poor*, vol. 1, p. 459.

116. Anderson, *Family Structure*, p. 56.

117. Butt, "Housing," p. 41.

118. Glasgow, 1841 Census sample. See Appendix (N=666).

119. R. A. Cage, "Population and Employment Characteristics," in Cage, *Working Class in Glasgow*, p. 17.

120. Greater London Record Office, Rejected Foundling Hospital petition, 1844, no. 10.

121. Mayhew, *London Labour and the London Poor*, vol. 1, p. 463.

122. Mary Ann Ashford, *Life of a Licensed Victualler's Daughter* (London, 1849), p. 20; for an assessment of this autobiography, see Patricia Susan Seleski, "The Women of the Laboring Poor: Love, Work, and Poverty in London, 1750–1820," Ph.D. diss., Stanford University, 1989, p. 102.

123. Seleski, "Women of the Laboring Poor," p. 149.

CHAPTER FOUR: PLEBEIAN SEXUAL MORALITY, 1780 – 1820

1. Case concerning incestuous marriage, London, Greater London Record Office, London Consistory Court depositions, DL/C 285, 26 March 1794, Webb v. Webb.

2. E. A. Wrigley and R. S. Scholefield, *Population History of England* (Cambridge: Harvard University Press, 1981), p. 438; John Gillis, *For Better, for Worse: British Marriages, 1600 to the Present* (New York: Oxford University Press, 1985), p. 110; Steve Humphries, *A Secret World of Sex: Forbidden Fruit, the British Experience 1900–1950* (London: Sidgewick and Jackson, 1991), p. 65.

3. Barbara Taylor, *Eve and the New Jerusalem: Socialism and Feminism in the Nineteenth Century* (New York: Pantheon, 1983), p. 268.

4. For illegitimacy statistics, see Gillis, *For Better, for Worse*, p. 110; Peter Laslett, "Long-term Trends in Bastardy in England," in his *Family Life and Illicit Love* (Cambridge: Cambridge University Press, 1977), p. 119; W. E. Tate, *The Parish Chest* (3d ed. Cambridge: Cambridge University Press, 1961), p. 213. Within this larger social context, however, illegitimacy rates varied considerably from region to region. Albert Leffingwell, *Illegitimacy and the Influence of Seasons upon Conduct* (New York: Arno Press, 1976 [1892]), p. 68; Society for the Diffusion of Useful Knowledge, *British Almanac and Companion* (London, 1834), p. 88.

5. Thomas Laqueur, *Religion and Respectability: Sunday Schools and Working-Class Culture, 1780–1850* (New Haven: Yale University Press, 1976), p. 244.

6. For the debates on libertinism, see James G. Turner, "The Properties of Libertinism," *Eighteenth-Century Life* 9 (1985): 75–87.

7. David Levine, "Production, Reproduction and the Proletarian Family in England, 1500–1851," in David Levine, *Proletarianization and Family History* (Orlando: Academic Press, 1984), p. 99; David Levine, *Family Formation in an Age of Nascent Capitalism* (New York: Academic Press, 1977), pp. 137–45; Patricia Susan Seleski, "The Women of the Laboring Poor: Love, Work, and Poverty in London, 1750–1820," Ph.D. diss., Stanford University, 1989, pp. 21, 76, 126, 226; Gillis, *For Better, for Worse*, ch. 4.

8. P. E. H. Hair, "Bridal Pregnancy in Rural England in Earlier Centuries," *Population Studies* 20 (1966–1967): 233–43; also his "Bridal Pregnancy in Earlier Rural England, Further Examined," *Population Studies* 24 (1970): 59–70.

9. For a debate on this subject, see Edward Shorter, "Illegitimacy, Sexual Revolution, and Social Change in Modern Europe," *Journal of Interdisciplinary History* 2 (1971): 250; Louise A. Tilly, Joan W. Scott, and Miriam Cohen, "Women's Work and European Fertility Patterns," *Journal of Interdisciplinary History* 6 (1976): 465.

10. For a contrast with late-nineteenth-century respectability, see Ellen Ross, " 'Not the Sort That Would Sit on the Doorstep': Respectability in Pre–World War I London Neighborhoods," *International Labor and Working-Class History* 27 (1985): 39–59; Peter Bailey, " 'Will the Real Bill Banks Please Stand Up?' Towards a Role Analysis of Mid-Victorian Working-Class Respectability," *Journal of Social History* 12 (1979): 336–53.

11. Leonore Davidoff and Catherine Hall, *Family Fortunes: Men and Women of the English Middle Class 1780–1850* (London: Hutchinson, 1987), pp. 401–3.

12. M. J. D. Roberts, "Making Victorian Morals? The Society for the Suppression of Vice and Its Critics, 1802–1886," *Historical Studies* 21 (1984): 157–73.

13. Quoted in Ford K. Brown, *Fathers of the Victorians* (Cambridge: Cambridge University Press, 1961), p. 16.

14. For debate on this issue, see William Hale, *Address to the Public upon the Dangerous Tendency of the London Female Penitentiary* (London, 1809), p. 12; *An Account . . . of the Lock Asylum* (London, 1821), pp. 3–4.

15. Patrick Colquhoun, *A Treatise on the Police of the Metropolis* (London, 1797), pp. vii–xi.

16. R. W. Malcolmson, *Popular Recreations in English Society 1700–1850* (Cambridge: Cambridge University Press, 1973), p. 104.

17. Stanley Nash, "Prostitution and Charity: The Magdalen Hospital, a Case Study," *Journal of Social History* 17 (1974): 617–28; Linda Ma-

hood, *The Magdalenes: Prostitution in the Nineteenth Century* (London: Routledge, 1990), pp. 75–83; Donna Andrew, *Philanthropy and Police: London Charity in the Eighteenth Century* (Princeton: Princeton University Press, 1989), pp. 119–27; *Thoughts on the Plan for a Magdalen-House for Repentant Prostitutes . . .* (London, 1757).

18. Ursula Henriques, "Bastardy and the New Poor Law," *Past and Present* 37 (1967): 103–5. J. R. Poynter, *Society and Pauperism* (London: Routledge and Kegan Paul, 1969), p. 311; Rev. C. D. Brereton, *An Inquiry into the Workhouse System and the Law of Maintenance in Agricultural Districts* (Norwich, [1826]), p. 112; Rev. J. T. Becher, *A Letter to the Right Hon. Lord Viscount Melbourne on the Alteration and Amendment of the Laws Relating to Bastardy* (London, 1834), pp. 8–9.

19. R. A. Cage, *The Scottish Poor Law* (Edinburgh: Scottish Academic Press, 1981), p. 30.

20. *Commodity* was in fact a slang term for the female genitals. *The Dictionary of the Vulgar Tongue* (London: Macmillan, 1981 [1811]).

21. "A List of the Several Delinquents, Who Are to Be Tried at Glasgow 19 of September 1786," in C. D. Donald, *Collection of Glasgow Broadsides* (Mitchell Library, Glasgow), vol. 1, fol. 83.

22. Rosalind K. Marshall, *Women in Scotland 1660–1780* (Edinburgh: Trustees of the National Gallery of Scotland, 1979), p. 13.

23. The kirk sessions were the Scottish equivalents of church courts. Elders of the Kirk of Scotland (the established church) would meet to consider moral infractions by members of their congregations. Each "sinner" would be investigated, would be asked to account for his or her behavior, and would then express repentance. Dissenting congregations had their own versions of this institution, to be discussed in the next chapter. Rosalind Mitchison and Leah Leneman, *Sexuality and Social Control: Scotland 1660–1780* (Oxford: Basil Blackwell, 1989), p. 231; also J. S. Marshall, "Irregular Marriages and Kirk Sessions," *Records of the Scottish Church History Society* 18 (1972): 10–25. These authorities seem to think kirk-session discipline dies out by 1800, but kirk sessions minute books for early nineteenth-century Glasgow reveal that irregular marriages continued to be the subject of discipline. Parishes studied which continued to be disciplined are Gorbals, St. John's, Blackfriars, and Rutherglen, and the statistical analysis is based on the first three. Their records are to be found in the Strathclyde Regional Archives, Mitchell Library, Glasgow. See also Callum G. Brown, *The Social History of Religion in Scotland Since 1730* (London: Methuen, 1987), pp. 11, 94.

24. Kirk sessions minute books in Glasgow, Strathclyde Regional Archives, parishes of Blackfriars (CH2/1292/1), 1797–1807; St. John's (CH2/176/1), 1819–1836; Gorbals (contiguous to Glasgow) (CH2/1311/1), 1800–1830; the textile-industry suburb of Rutherglen CH2/315/5, 1792–1819, 1820–1839.

25. Mitchison and Leneman, *Sexuality and Social Control*, p. 158.

26. Kenneth M. Boyd, *Scottish Church Attitudes to Sex, Marriage and the Family 1850–1914* (Edinburgh: John Donald, 1980), p. 55.

27. Mitchison and Leneman, *Sexuality and Social Control*, p. 231; Marshall, "Irregular Marriages and Kirk Sessions," pp. 10–25. Alison testified about common-law unions in the First Report of the Select Committee on Combinations of Workmen, PP VIII (1837–1838), p. 168.

28. John Urie, *Reminescences of Eighty Years* (Paisley, 1908), p. 97.

29. Counter to findings of Laslett and Oosterveen. See studies by Peter Laslett, Karla Oosterveen, and R. W. Smith, eds., *Bastardy in Its Comparative History* (Cambridge: Cambridge University Press, 1980).

30. G. N. Gandy, "Illegitimacy in a Hand-Loom Weaving Community: Fertility Patterns in Culcheth, Lancashire, 1781–1860," D.Phil. diss., Oxford University, 1978, pp. 175–200, quoted in Seleski, "Women of the Laboring Poor," p. 20.

31. William Marcroft, *The Marcroft Family and the Inner Circle of Human Life* (Rochdale, 1888), pp. 20–40.

32. Gillis, *For Better, for Worse*, p. 176; Hans Medick, "The Proto-Industrial Family Economy," in Peter Kriedtke, Hans Medick, and Jürgen Schlumbom, eds., *Industrialization Before Industrialization* (Cambridge: Cambridge University Press, 1981), p. 63.

33. David Loch, *A Tour Through Most of the Trading Towns and Villages of Scotland* (Edinburgh, 1778), p. 35.

34. Note on the Paisley weaver-poet Alexander Tannahill, *Glasgow Evening Post*, 31 Feb. 1834.

35. Gorbals kirk sessions minutes, CH2/1311/1, 7 Sept. 1813.

36. T. C. Smout, "Aspects of Sexual Behavior in Nineteenth-Century Scotland," in A. Allen Maclaren, *Social Class in Scotland* (Edinburgh: John Donald, 1981), p. 70.

37. Female Friendly Society of Saltcoats, Edinburgh, Scottish Record Office, FS1/2/42. The Bluebell Society of Manchester allowed for one lying-in by an unmarried mother: Sheila Lewenhak, *Women and Trade Unions: An Outline History of Women in the British Trade Union Movement* (London: Ernest Benn, 1977), p. 18.

38. Robert Burns, "A Poet's Welcome to His Love-Begotten Daughter," in *Poetical Works of Robert Burns, with Life and Notes by William Wallace* (London: Chambers, n.d.), p. 29; Robert Burns, *The Fornicator's Court* (Mauchline, 1786).

39. *The Swinish Multitudes Push for Reform* (Glasgow, 1816).

40. "Jenny Nettles," in *The Wonderful Age* (Glasgow, n.d.), a chapbook of songs. See also "Oxter My Laddie" (Glasgow, 1801), in British Library Collection 11606.aa.23, no. 29.

41. [Dougal Graham], *The Whole Proceedings of Jockey and Maggy's Courtship . . . , The Comical Tricks of Lothian Tom* and *The History of the*

Haveral Wives in *John Cheap the Chapman's Library: The Scottish Cheap Literature of the Last Century* (Glasgow, 1877).

42. This is lower than in other areas. In Ayrshire, 54 percent of men accused denied paternity. Mitchison and Leneman, *Sexuality and Social Control*, pp. 71–75. As late as 1840, a Rev. Wright of Dumfries complained that "the fathers of illegitimate children contrived by one villainous art or another, to trample on the rights of poor helpless females, and avoid doing anything for the support of their offspring." *Scots Times*, 6 May 1840.

43. St. John's, Glasgow (CH2/176/1), 5 Dec. 1831, case of Elizabeth Patten.

44. St. John's, Glasgow (CH2/176/1), 4 April 1829, case of Agnes Wilson.

45. Gorbals kirk sessions, CH2/1311/1, 7 May 1816, case of Margaret Wilson.

46. William Acton, "Observations on Illegitimacy in the London Parishes of St. Marylebone, St. Pancras . . . During the Year 1857," *Journal of the Statistical Society of London* 22 (1859): 493; John Gillis, "Servants, Sexual Relations, and the Risks of Illegitimacy in London, 1801–1900," in Judith L. Newton et al., eds., *Sex and Class in Women's History* (London: Routledge and Kegan Paul, 1983), p. 129; Seleski, "Women of the Laboring Poor," p. 126.

47. Gillis, *For Better, for Worse*, p. 141.

48. Bastardy examinations from St. Mary LeStrand, 1780–1789, London, Westminster Public Library, Victoria Branch, G1015; St. Sepulchre, 1793–1805, and St. Botolph's Aldgate, 1808–1815, London, Guildhall Library. N=158 for the three together.

49. Nicholas Rogers, "Carnal Knowledge: Illegitimacy in Eighteenth-Century Westminster," *Journal of Social History* 23 (1979): 259–62.

50. *The Autobiography of Francis Place, 1771–1854*, ed. Mary Thrale (Cambridge: Cambridge University Press, 1972), pp. 81–82.

51. *Autobiography of Francis Place*, p. 57.

52. London, Greater London Record Office, London Consistory Court depositions, DL/C 280, 27 Feb. 1777, Hicks v. Hicks. Polly Morris found a similar defamation case from Somerset in 1828 in which neighbors described an unmarried mother as "a person of good life and sober conversation." Polly Morris, "Defamation and Sexual Reputation in Somerset, 1733–1850," Ph.D. diss., University of Warwick, 1985, p. 458.

53. London, Guildhall Library, Printed Old Bailey Sessions Papers, 1821–1822, p. 147.

54. Greater London Record Office, Foundling Hospital Petition, 1815, unnumbered. The babies were accepted by the hospital, but the grandmother kept them anyway.

55. London, Guildhall Library, Printed Old Bailey Sessions Papers, 1809–1810, p. 18.

56. London, Greater London Record Office, London Consistory Court depositions, DL/C 293, 25 Oct. 1810, Evens v. Evens divorce.

57. *Sun*, 19 May 1818.

58. Gillis, *For Better, for Worse*, p. 168.

59. Mary Wollstonecraft, *A Vindication of the Rights of Women*, ed. Miriam Kramnick (Harmondsworth: Penguin, 1978 [1792]), p. 261. For other similar comments, see Mary Ann Radcliffe, *Memoirs and the Female Advocate* (London, 1799), p. 409; *Times*, 10 May 1785, 11 Jan. 1787, 10 Oct. 1803.

60. *Trades Free Press*, 28 March 1829.

61. London, Guildhall Library, Printed Old Bailey Sessions Papers, 1796, vol. 1, p. 40.

62. Morris, "Defamation and Sexual Reputation in Somerset," pp. 134ff.; Susan Dwyer Amussen, "Feminin/Masculin: Le Genre dans l'Angleterre de l'Epoque Moderne," *Annales E.S.C.* 40 (1985): 269–85.

63. Hugh Phillips, *Mid-Georgian London* (London: Collins, 1964), p. 114. For examples of corruption and arrests, see *Public Advertizer*, 21 Aug. 1790; *Universal Register*, 28 April, 17 Nov. 1785; 11 Sept., 14 Oct. 1788; *Times*, 25 Oct. 1803; *Sun*, 14 Dec. 1816; *Weekly Dispatch*, 24 Nov. 1822, 25 April 1824.

64. Max Glucksman, "Gossip and Scandal," *Current Anthropology* 4 (1963): 308. For an overview, see Ralph L. Rosnow and Gary Alan Fine, *Rumor and Gossip* (New York: Elsevier, 1976), pp. 90–95.

65. Susan Harding, "Women and Words in a Spanish Village," in Rayna Rapp Reiter, ed., *Toward an Anthropology of Women* (New York: Monthly Review Press, 1975), p. 303; Julian Pitt-Rivers, "Honor and Social Status in Andalusia," in J. Peristiany, ed., *Honor and Shame: The Values of Mediterrean Society* (Chicago: University of Chicago Press, 1966), p. 61; Yves Castan, *Honnêteté et Relations Sociales en Languedoc c. 1715–1780* (Paris: Plon, 1974), p. 40; Bertram Wyatt-Brown, *Southern Honor: Ethics and Behavior in the Old South* (New York: Oxford University Press, 1982), p. 227.

66. J. A. Sharpe, *Defamation and Sexual Slander in Early Modern England: The Church Courts at York*, Borthwick Papers No. 58 (York: Borthwick Institute, 1980), pp. 19–20; Amussen, "Feminin/Masculin," p. 279.

67. Morris, "Defamation and Sexual Reputation in Somerset," p. 733.

68. For a study of early defamation cases, see Laura Gowing, "Gender and the Language of Insult in Early Modern London," *History Workshop Journal* 35 (1993): 1–21.

69. Morris, "Defamation and Sexual Reputation in Somerset," p. 134.

70. Morris, "Defamation and Sexual Reputation in Somerset," p. 279.

71. "Rules of a Friendly Society of Women Held at Thistle and Crown," London, Public Record Office, Friendly Society papers, FS/1/406A/109, established 1774.

72. *Weekly Dispatch*, 4 Sept. 1825.

73. London, Greater London Record Office, London Consistory Court depositions, DL/C 281, 10 Nov. 1780, Dickers v. Dickers divorce.

74. *Weekly Dispatch*, 17 Aug. 1823.

75. Several paid funeral benefits only for legally married husbands: see Bell Church Friendly Society of Women, reg. 1794, London, Public Record Office, Friendly Society papers, FS/1/406A/78, and Lovers of Amity, FS/1/406A/60; also "Rules of a Friendly Society of Women Held at Thistle and Crown." The City of Refuge for Benefit of Widows cut off benefits for cohabiting women (London, Public Record Office, Friendly Society papers, FS/1/406A/111); the Friendly Society of Women of Fore Street prohibited membership to any woman "that shall be loose upon the town, or live in an unmarried state with any man, so to pass for their husband" (London, Public Record Office, Friendly Society papers, FS/1/406A/59). The Female Forecast Society gave lying-in benefits only to married women (London, Public Record Office, Friendly Society papers, FS/1/406A/62, 1791). Two northern societies had similar rules: Burnley society refused benefits for illegitimate children and for any woman who went along with the hired militia: *Rules, Orders and Regulations to Be Observed for the Government and Guidance of a Society of Women* (Sabden Bridge, Burnley, 1813); and a Manchester society declared that "no common prostitute nor woman of vile character shall be admitted a member of this society": *Rules and Orders to Be Observed by the Sociable Friendly Society of Females, Manchester* (Failsworth, 1799).

76. London, Greater London Record Office, London Consistory Court depositions, DL/C 290, 1804, Rea v. Rea divorce.

77. George Rudé, *Hanoverian London 1714–1808* (London: Secker and Warburg, 1971), pp. 7–10.

78. William Hale, *Letters to Samuel Whitbread on the Condition of the Poor in Spitalfields* (London, 1813), p. 25.

79. Nicole Castan also notes petit-bourgeois women expressing class or status tension by calling each other whores in eighteenth-century Languedoc, in "Contentieux Social et Utilisation Variable du Charivari à la Fin de l'Ancien Régime en Languedoc," in J. Le Goff and J.-C. Schmidt, eds., *Le Charivari* (Paris: Mouton, 1981), p. 202.

80. Disruptive gossips traditionally could be prosecuted as scolds; during this period, occasional cases still appeared in London. *Times*, 6 April 1801; see 3 March 1804, for scolds being ducked in Surrey. London, Greater London Record Office, Middlesex Sessions, Roll 3451, 1785, indictment 101, of Susanna Pardon, and indictment 34, of Marmaduke Riley. It was highly unusual for a man to be indicted as a scold, and although Riley was involved in many assault cases he was not convicted.

81. London, Greater London Record Office, London Consistory Court depositions, DL/C 284, 23 Nov. 1789, Rudolph v. Vanderpump.

82. London, Greater London Record Office, London Consistory Court depositions, DL/C 283, 27 June 1789, Crompton v. Butler. See also DL/C 284, 12 May 1790, Myatt v. Allen.

83. DL/C 284, 26 Jan. 1792, Barmore v. Morris.

84. DL/C 284, 1792, Pritchard v. Dalby; a similar case is Jarman v. Saunders alias Morris, DL/C 283, 2 May 1789.

85. DL/C 284, 24 Nov. 1791, Simpson v. Swan.

86. "The Gossiping Husband," in Oxford, Bodleian Library, John Johnson Collection of Ephemera, Street Ballads Box 2, published by Catnach circa 1828–1832.

87. DL/C 281, 2 Feb. 1782, Greaves v. Kendrick.

88. London, Greater London Record Office, London Consistory Court depositions, DL/C 282, 8 Dec. 1783, Sefton v. Taylor.

89. DL/C 282, 11 Dec. 1783, Spence v. Heberley.

90. Morris, "Defamation and Sexual Reputation in Somerset," p. 291.

91. DL/C 280, 21 Dec. 1776, Clarke v. Price.

92. OBSP 1778–1779, p. 387, July 1779.

93. London, Greater London Record Office, London Consistory Court depositions, DL/C 291, 2 Jan. 1814, Cairns v. Moss; see also Anna Clark, *Women's Silence, Men's Violence: Sexual Assault in England, 1770–1845* (London: Pandora Press, 1987), pp. 35–36, for a discussion of rapists bragging about their exploits.

94. Clark, *Women's Silence*, ch. 6.

95. *Dictionary of the Vulgar Tongue.*

96. John Holloway and Joan Black, eds., *Later English Broadside Ballads* (London: Routledge and Kegan Paul, 1979), pp. 61–62.

97. For further discussion, see Clark, *Women's Silence*, p. 118.

98. *Glasgow Saturday Post*, 24 Sept., 11 Feb. 1842; cf. 8 Oct. 1842.

99. For some egregious examples of misogynist artisan radicals, see Iain MacCalman, *Radical Underworld: Prophets, Revolutionaries and Pornographers in London, 1795–1840* (Cambridge: Cambridge University Press, 1988), pp. 45, 149.

100. *The Autobiography of Francis Place*, p. 77.

101. Christine Stansell, *City of Women: Sex and Class in New York, 1789–1860* (New York: Alfred A. Knopf, 1986), p. 83. See also Seleski, "Women of the Laboring Poor," pp. 242–52.

102. Gillis, *For Better, for Worse*, p. 177.

103. St. John's, Glasgow, kirk sessions, Glasgow, Strathclyde Regional Archives, Kirk sessions minute books, CH2/176/1, Oct. 2, 1826, case of William Taylor and Catherine Hill.

104. Unfortunately, Gray also seduced several other women, and a

"babble about the weans" brought him to the kirk sessions several times. St. John's, Glasgow, kirk sessions, CH2/176/2, 6 June 1831, also 3 Dec. 1832, both involving John Gray.

105. Thomas Whittaker, *Life's Battles in Temperance Armor* (London, 1884), p. 36.

106. Glasgow, Strathclyde Regional Archives, Police notebook, TD 734, p. 74, May 7, 1825.

107. "New Bury Loom," in Martha Vicinus, *Broadsides of the Industrial North* (Newcastle upon Tyne: Frank Graham, 1975), p. 32.

108. Edinburgh, Scottish Record Office, Prosecution papers, AD 14/28/356, case of Richard Bates, 6 Nov. 1828, precognitions to the High Court of the Justiciary.

109. Clark, *Women's Silence*, p. 35.

110. Sian Moore, "Women, Industrialisation and Protest in Bradford, West Yorkshire, 1780–1845," Ph.D diss., University of Essex, 1986, p. 129.

CHAPTER FIVE: THE STRUGGLE FOR THE BREECHES

1. David Love, *Life and Adventures* (Nottingham, 1823), p. 37.

2. John Gillis, *For Better, for Worse: British Marriages, 1600 to the Present* (Oxford: Oxford University Press, 1985), p. 82.

3. Joy Wiltenburg, *Disorderly Women and Female Power in the Street Literature of Early Modern England and Germany* (Charlottesville: University Press of Virginia, 1992), p. 98.

4. William Secker, *A Wedding Ring, Fit for the Finger, Laid Open in a Sermon, Preached at a Wedding in St. Edmond's* (Glasgow, n.d.), in *John Cheap the Chapman's Library* (Glasgow, 1877), pp. 11, 20; see also William Whateley's *Directions for Married Persons* (London, 1763 [1619]), p. 47.

5. John Stephens, *The Advantages Which Man Derives from Woman* (2d ed. London, 1813), p. 12.

6. Sarah Wilks, *Memoirs of the Reverend Mark Wilks* (London, 1821), p. 125.

7. Wiltenburg, *Disorderly Women*, p. 256, makes a similar observation for the seventeenth century.

8. M. Dorothy George, *London Life in the Eighteenth Century* (Harmondsworth: Penguin, 1966 [1925]), p. 177.

9. John Burnett, *Destiny Obscure: Autobiographies of Childhood, Education and Family from the 1820s to the 1920s* (Harmondsworth, Penguin, 1984), p. 258.

10. Quoted in David Vincent, *Bread, Knowledge and Freedom: A Study of Nineteenth Century Working Class Autobiography* (London: Methuen, 1981), p. 42.

11. Love, *Life and Adventures*, p. 28.

12. John O'Neill, "Fifty Years Experience an Irish Shoemaker in London," *St. Crispin* 2 (1869): 212.

13. "The Autobiography of William Hart, Cooper," ed. Pat Hudson and Lynette Hunter, *London Journal* 8 (1982): 68.

14. Robert Tannahill, *Complete Songs and Poems* (Paisley, 1877), p. 12. Tannahill was born in 1774.

15. *The Art of Courtship* (Glasgow, ca. 1807). There were several tales conversely complaining about lazy wives who would not work; [Dougal Graham], "Fun upon Fun, or Leper the Tailor," in *John Cheap*, p. 9; *The New Way of Woo'd an Marry'd* (Glasgow, 1802); "The Spinning Wheel's Garden," "The Married Man's Lament, or Fairly Shot of Her," both in London, British Library, Davison Collection, ca. 1800; *Robin's Cure for a Bad Wife* (Falkirk, ca. 1800–1810, London, British Library, Collection of broadsides, 11606.aa.22 (45).

16. Alexander Somerville, *The Autobiography of a Working Man* (London, 1848), p. 20.

17. Joseph Gutteridge, *Lives and Shadows in the Life of an Artisan*, ed. Valerie Chancellor (London: Evelyn, Adam and Melloy, 1969 [1893]), p. 115.

18. Joseph Livesey, *Autobiography*, ed. Joyce Livesey (Preston, 1887), p. 12.

19. Christopher A. Whatley, "The Experience of Work," in T. M. Devine and Rosalind Mitchison, eds., *People and Society in Scotland*. Vol. 1: *1760–1830* (Edinburgh: John Donald, 1988), p. 242.

20. Report on Handloom Weavers, PP 1840, vol. 23, p. 261.

21. Thomas Whittaker, *Life's Battles in Temperance Armor* (London, 1884), p. 41.

22. Gutteridge, *Lives and Shadows*, pp. 107, 115, 179.

23. London, British Library, Collection of broadsides, 11621.k.5, printed in 1808.

24. James Paterson, *Autobiographical Reminiscences, Including Recollections of the Radical Years 1819–20* (Glasgow, 1871), p. 65.

25. Wilks, *Memoirs*, p. 49.

26. David Gilmour, *Reminiscences of the Pen'Folk: Paisley Weavers of Other Days* (2d ed. Paisley, 1879), p. 59.

27. Gilmour, *Reminiscences of the Pen'Folk*, p. 125.

28. Vincent, *Bread, Knowledge and Freedom*, p. 42.

29. Burnett, *Destiny Obscure*, p. 233.

30. Janet Bathgate, *Aunt Janet's Legacy to Her Nieces: Recollections of Humble Life in Yarrow at the Beginning of the Century* (Selkirk, 1895), pp. 90, 160.

31. Mary Ann Ashford, *Life of a Licensed Victualler's Daughter* (London, 1844), p. 76.

32. Mary Saxby, *Memoirs of a Female Vagrant Written by Herself*, ed. Samuel Greathead (London, 1806), pp. 20–23.

33. Ann Candler, *Poetical Attempts by a Suffolk Cottager, with a Short Narrative of Her Life* (Ipswich, 1803), pp. 8, 10, 14.

34. London, British Library, Collection of broadsides, 1875.d.16. Similar songs include "The Rakish Husband" in Collection 11621.k.4, "Merry and Wise" in Collection 1875.d.16, and "The Crazy London Prentice" in Collection C. 116.bb.11.

35. William Paul, *The Wars of Wedlock, or Davie Glen and Bessy Hill* (Glasgow, 1829); also "A Man Without a Wife," in *The Year That's Awa'* (Glasgow, 1829), in Glasgow, Mitchell Library, Glasgow chapbooks.

36. Laure Beaumont-Maillet, *La Guerre des Sexes XVe–XIVe Siècles* (Paris: Albin Michel, 1984), p. 14. She gives fifteenth- to nineteenth-century versions of caricatures of the struggle for the breeches and other examples of the "sex wars." For German examples, see Keith Moxey, *Peasants, Warriors and Wives: Popular Imagery in the Reformation* (Chicago: University of Chicago, 1989), p. 106; Wiltenburg, *Disorderly Women*, p. 131. To be sure, Wiltenburg points out that German popular literature about marriage stressed male domination much more rigidly, while British literature emphasized that love and companionship were compatible with patriarchy. See also Natalie Zemon Davis, "Women on Top," in her *Society and Culture in Early Modern France* (Palo Alto: Stanford University Press, 1975), p. 134, for the tradition of the Quinze Joyes de Mariage.

37. As far back as the sixteenth century, it was an insult to a woman to say she wore the breeches. Laura Gowing, "Gender and the Language of Insult in Early Modern London," *History Workshop Journal* 35 (1993): 11.

38. "Will the Weaver," in *Four Popular Songs* (Stirling, ca. 1820–1830).

39. "John and His Wife on Using Tea," in Glasgow, Glasgow University Library, Ballads and broadsides, Mu.23.y.1 (ca. 1840–1850). This may have been printed from earlier songs, for tea-drinking was a common theme between 1800 and 1820. A similar scene occurs in Ben Brierley, *Fratchingtons of Fratchingthorpe: A Course in Connubial Crosses, or Fireside Fraps* (London, 1866), p. 48.

40. Wiltenburg, *Disorderly Women*, p. 108. For instance, a play by a soldier affectionately ridiculed a defiant wife. A. M'Laren (a soldier and playwright), *The Humours of Greenock Fair, or the Taylor Made a Man: A Musical Interlude* (Glasgow, 1790).

41. *The Jealous Man . . .* (London, 1800), p. 7.

42. Wiltenburg, *Disorderly Women*, pp. 95, 101.

43. See *A New and Diverting Dialogue Between a Husband and His Wife* (London, 1800), p. 5; also "A Diverting Dialogue, Both Serious and Comical, Which Happened Between a Most Noted Shoemaker and His Wife, Living in This Neighborhood," Glasgow, Mitchell Library, Glasgow ballads, p. 330. This trope of the struggle for the breeches persisted quite late. For instance, the songs "Quarrel Between Man and Wife to See Which Will Be Master," and "The Struggle for the Breeches" (two versions),

printed after 1840, in London, British Library, Collections of broadsides, 11621.k.5.

44. Martha Vicinus, *The Industrial Muse* (London: Croom Helm, 1974), p. 9. See also J. S. Bratton, *The Victorian Popular Ballad* (London: Macmillan, 1975), p. 162, for a discussion of the women's tradition in songs of outwitting male opponents.

45. "A woman Never Knows When Her Days Work Is Done" and "There Is Nothing Can Equal a Wife," both from London, British Library, Collections of broadsides, 11621.k.5; cf. the similar theme in "Drunken Husband," Manchester, Manchester Public Library, Ballad collection, p. 364.

46. "I'll Be No Submissive Wife!" Cambridge, Cambridge University Library, Madden Collection of Ballads.

47. Oxford, Bodleian Library, John Johnson Collection of Ephemera, Street Ballads Box 7 (1832).

48. "The Woman That Wishes She Never Got Married," London, British Library, Collections of broadsides, 11621.k.5, two versions printed after 1840, one published by Anne Ryle and the other by Elizabeth Hodges. "I'm Ninety-Five" in London, British Library, Collections of broadsides, C. 116.i.1.

49. Louis James, *The Print and the People* (Harmondsworth: Penguin, 1978), pp. 321–22.

50. *Trades' Newspaper*, 30 Oct. 1825.

51. "The Bachelor's Litany," Oxford, Bodleian Library, John Johnson Collection of Ephemera, Street Ballads Box 9; "The Birmingham Buttonmaker" (Alnick, 1790), in London, British Library, Davison Collection, 11606.aa.23, no. 10.

52. John Gillis, "Servants, Sexual Relations, and the Risk of Illegitimacy in London, 1801–1900," *Feminist Studies* 5 (1979): 142–73.

53. "The Jovial Batchelor" (Glasgow, 1801), London, British Library, Davison Collection, 11606.aa.23, no. 74.

54. "Advice to Sailors" (n.p., 1802), London, British Library, Davison Collection, 11606.aa.23, no. 19.

55. Alexander Wilson, "Watty and Meg," in Tom Leonard, ed., *Radical Renfrew: Poetry from the French Revolution to the First World War* (Edinburgh: Polygon, 1990), pp. 9, 26. It was thought to have sold over 100,000 copies.

56. "A Fool's Advice to Henpeck'd Husbands" (Manchester, ca. 1800), Manchester, Manchester Public Library, Ballad collection, p. 346. "A stick not much thicker than your thumb" is a clear allusion to Judge Thumb, discussed later in this chapter. A more elegant version of this was Robert Burns's "On the Henpecked Husband":

> Were such the wife had fallen to my part,
> I'd break her spirit or I'd break her heart;

I'd charm her with the magic of a switch,
I'd kiss her maids and kick the perverse bitch.
*Poetical Works of Robert Burns, with Life
and Notes* by William Wallace (London:
Chambers, n.d.), p. 484.

57. John Urie, *Reminiscences of Eighty Years* (Paisley, 1908), p. 51. For Hawkie, see *Hawkie: The Autobiography of a Gangrel,* ed. J. Stratehesk (Glasgow, 1888); for Dougal Graham's possible original, see *John Falkirk's Cariches* (Glasgow, [1779]), p. 1.

58. *Tegg's Caricatures* (London, 1821), vol. 4, pp. 104, 224.

59. *Cambridge Jests* (Newcastle, 1770), p. 9.

60. "The Bold Cobbler," Oxford, Bodleian Library, John Johnson Collection of Ephemera, Street Ballads Box 7.

61. "The Cobler." See also "The Drunken Cobler, or the Prating Magpie," both Newcastle, 1800, in London, British Library, Davison Collection, 11606.23, n. 62, and 11606.24. Also "An Account of a Horrible Dispute Which Took Place Between a Cobler, and His Wife the Day of King Crispian's Procession" (n.p., n.d. [early nineteenth century]), London, British Library, Collections of broadsides, 1875.b.30, no. 39.

62. *Trades' Newspaper,* 3 June 1827.

63. John Wight, *Mornings at Bow Street* (London, 1824), pp. 9–11, 63–65, 205–7.

64. *Weekly Dispatch,* 16 Nov. 1834.

65. *Thistle,* 9 Aug. 1830.

66. Over 90 percent of domestic violence in the Middlesex Sessions of the Peace, 1780–1785, 1790–1795; 89 percent of marital homicides and 78 percent of marital assaults in the Old Bailey Sessions, 1780–1845; 95 percent of domestic violence in Glasgow and Glasgow, Gorbals, and Paisley police and justice of the peace courts, 1813–1824, 1829–1831, 1835–1836, from Glasgow, Strathclyde Regional Archives, Police Court books; John Brownlie, *Police Reports of Causes Tried Before the Justices of the Peace and the Glasgow, Gorbals and Calton Police Courts from 18th July till 3rd October* (Glasgow, 1829), and this journal's successor the *Thistle* (Glasgow, 1830).

67. Richard Burns, *Justice of the Peace* (London, 1776), vol. 4, p. 268, notes that "some say" wife-beating is allowed. William Blackstone, *Commentaries on the Laws of England,* with notes by Edward Christian (12th ed. London, 1793), vol. 1, p. 444, traces the slow contraction of the "right." In Scotland, Patrick Fraser wrote in 1846 that a husband's right of "personal chastisement" of his wife was still allowed in the law, according to an 1813 decision, but Fraser described it as "a rule so utterly inconsistent with modern manners, as not to be one, it is all probable, the court will sanction." *A Treatise on the Law of Scotland as Applicable to the Personal and Domestic Relations,* vol. 1 (Edinburgh, 1846), p. 460. See Anna Clark, "Humanity or Justice? Wifebeating and the Law in the Eighteenth and

Nineteenth Centuries," in Carol Smart, ed., *Regulating Womanhood: Historical Writings on Marriage, Motherhood and Sexuality* (London: Routledge, 1992), and Margaret Hunt, "Wifebeating, Domesticity, and Women's Independence in 18th Century London," *Gender and History* 4 (1992): 18.

68. It is unclear whether Buller ever actually made this statement. Alan Simpson, in his *Biographical Dictionary of the Common Law* (London: Buttersworth, 1984), p. 88, says that Buller did not originate the phrase but that it reflected his attitude; William C. Townsend, in his *Lives of Twelve Eminent Judges* (London, 1846), states that Buller "unpremeditatedly" blurted out the phrase. For popular views, see *Rambler's Magazine* (London, 1783), vol. 1, p. 35.

69. *Glasgow Evening Post*, 1 June 1833.

70. Glasgow, Mitchell Library, Collection of Glasgow broadsides, "Trials and Sentences of the Various Prisoners Who Have Appeared Before the Bar of the Circuit Court of the Justiciary," Glasgow, 7 Sept. 1830; Glasgow University Library, Crime Broadsides, Eph. G/94; "An Account of the Execution of William McFeat for the Horrible Murder of his Wife."

71. *Glasgow Evening Post*, 8 June 1833.

72. *Scots Times*, 5 June 1840.

73. *Thistle*, 18 Jan. 1830.

74. Brownlie, *Police Reports*, pp. 120–21.

75. *Weekly Dispatch*, 25 July 1841.

76. *Weekly Dispatch*, 6 Oct. 1822.

77. Glasgow, Strathclyde Regional Archives, Police Court books, 1813–1824, and Gorbals case books, 1835–1836.

78. R. Emerson Dobash and Russell Dobash, *Violence Against Wives: A Case Against the Patriarchy* (New York: Free Press, 1979); for an overview, see Wini Breines and Linda Gordon, "The New Scholarship on Family Violence," *Signs* 8 (1983): 506–25; Linda Gordon, *Heroes of Their Own Lives: The Politics and History of Family Violence, Boston, 1880–1960* (New York: Viking, 1988); Elizabeth Pleck, *Domestic Tyranny: The Making of Social Policy Against Family Violence from Colonial Times to the Present* (New York: Oxford University Press, 1987).

79. Nancy Tomes, "A 'Torrent of Abuse': Crimes of Violence Between Working-Class Men and Women in London, 1840–1875," *Journal of Social History* 11 (1978): 331–33. See also Ellen Ross, "Fierce Questions and Taunts: Married Life in Working-Class London, 1870–1914," *Feminist Studies* 8 (1982): 575–602, which will be discussed in ch. 14. See also Nicole Castan, "Puissance Conjugale et Violence Maritale," *Penelope* 6 (1982): 85–91, for a portrayal of the more openly domineering, violent husbands of eighteenth-century southern France.

80. Peter Linebaugh presents an interesting, though flawed, explanation for male plebeian violence as being displaced onto women and children

from the "real" causes of violence, that is, wage slavery and proletarianization. He finds such violence exemplified in Punch and Judy. "As Punch puts an end to wife and children . . . he puts an end to the society that give rise to the repression of gender, race, class, and law." *The London Hanged: Crime and Civil Society in the Eighteenth Century* (London: Allen Lane Penguin Press, 1991), p. 441.

81. François Bederida gives 37 percent for semi-skilled workers and 15 percent for unskilled workers, but his semi-skilled category includes workers in textiles, clothing, and printing, whom I categorize as skilled. "Londres au milieu du XIXe siècle," *Annales E.S.C.* 23 (1968): 287–91. For populations of specific artisans, see Iorwerth Prothero, *Artisans and Politics in Early Nineteenth Century London* (London: Methuen, 1981), p. 342.

82. In Lancashire, they accounted for 3.6 percent of the wife-beating cases and 2.7 percent of the occupied male population (N=7 out of 195, not a large enough sample to be conclusive).

83. Sir Frederick Eden, *The State of the Poor* (London, 1797), vol. 1, p. 625.

84. Hannah More, *The Gamester* (London: Cheap Repository Tract, 1795), n.p.

85. "A New Intended Act of Parliament," Oxford, Bodleian Library, John Johnson Collection of Ephemera, Street Ballads Box 1, printed circa 1828–1829.

86. London, Guildhall Library, Printed Old Bailey Sessions Papers 1780–1845 (OBSP) 1829, p. 209.

87. London, Greater London Record Office, Middlesex Sessions, 1781 Roll 3406, unnumbered article of the peace.

88. OBSP 1829, p. 209.

89. OBSP 1818–1819, p. 240.

90. OBSP 1809–1810, pp. 241–42; OBSP 1812–1813, p. 123.

91. Brownlie, *Police Reports*, p. 22.

92. Margaret Hunt similarly found that middle-class women with financial and familial resources were the ones who tried to divorce their husbands in the early eighteenth century. "Wifebeating, Domesticity," p. 20.

93. *Times*, 21 April 1801.

94. London, Greater London Record Office, Middlesex Sessions, 1795 Roll 3582, indictment 32; for similar testimony, see Ann Barras's article of the peace, 1793 Roll 3563, indictment 57; Martha Seldon's article of the peace, 1792 Roll 3553, indictment 47.

95. Middlesex Sessions, 1795 Roll 3582, indictment 32, Feb. 1795. For similar testimony see Ann Barras's article of the peace, Martha Seldon's article of the peace; Fenton bigamy trial, OBSP 1808–1809, p. 9; *Trades' Newspaper*, 29 April 1827.

96. Preston, Lancashire Record Office, Quarter Sessions Rolls, QSB 1/192, 12 July 1818.

97. Oxford, Bodleian Library, John Johnson Collection of Ephemera, Street Ballads Box 6, printed circa 1820–1844.
98. Glasgow, Mitchell Library, C. D. Donald, *Collection of Glasgow Broadsides*, Vol. 1, fol. 12, 1824.
99. *Thistle*, 5 April 1830.
100. *Times*, 10 Sept. 1788.
101. N=256: 210 men and 46 women.
102. Report of the Select Committee on Drunkenness, PP 1834, vol. 8, pp. 308, 310, 315.
103. Christine Stansell, *City of Women: Sex and Class in New York, 1789–1860* (New York: Knopf, 1986), p. 80.
104. Gordon, *Heroes of Their Own Lives*, p. 265.
105. Saxby, *Memoirs*, p. 23.
106. J. P. Malcolm, *Anecdotes of the Manners and Customs of London in the Eighteenth Century* (2d ed. London, 1810), p. 483.
107. *Thistle*, 9 April 1831.
108. *Weekly Dispatch*, 20 May 1838.
109. *Weekly Dispatch*, 6 April 1823.
110. *Weekly Dispatch*, 6 May 1832.
111. John Holloway and Joan Black, eds., *Later English Broadside Ballads* (London: Routledge and Kegan Paul, 1979), vol. 2, p. 110. Later in the century Saint Monday became a holiday families could enjoy together; see Doug Reid, "The Decline of St. Monday," *Past and Present* 71 (1976): 84, and [Thomas Wright], *Some Habits and Customs of the Working Classes, by a Journeyman Engineer* (New York: Augustus M. Kelley, 1967 [1867]), p. 119.
112. *Times*, 1 July 1810.
113. Manchester, Manchester Public Library, Ballads collection, p. 200.
114. Brownlie, *Police Reports*, p. 60.
115. *Thistle*, 27 May 1830.
116. *Times*, 22 Feb. 1800.
117. OBSP 1817–1818, pp. 293–94.
118. Stansell, *City of Women*, p. 78.
119. OBSP 1828, vol. 3, pp. 893–94.
120. Charles Campbell, *Memoirs* (Glasgow, 1828), p. 33; see also Glasgow, Glasgow University Library, Ballads and broadsides, Mu.23.y.1, "Charles Campbell's Lament, Who Is to Be Imprisoned for Life for the Murder of His Wife" (1826).
121. First Report of the Select Committee on Combinations of Workmen, PP vol. 7, 1837–1838, p. 168.
122. Edinburgh, Scottish Record Office, AD 14/23/89, Autumn 1823, precognition against Mary Horn or Muckstraffick.
123. *Times*, 10 Jan. 1785.
124. London, Greater London Record Office, London Consistory Court

depositions, DL/C 281, Dickers v. Dickers, 1780; DL/C 179, Brazier v. Brazier, 1781; DL/C 282, Charlton v. Charlton (divorce cases).

125. *Conjugal Infidelity* (London, 1819), p. 10.

126. *Sun*, 16 Dec. 1804; cf. *Times*, 10 May 1825.

127. *A New and Diverting Dialogue . . . Between a Noted Shoemaker and His Wife* (London, 1800), p. 1; "A Diverting Dialogue, Both Serious and Comical, Which Happened Between a Most Noted Shoemaker and His Wife, Living in This Neighborhood," Glasgow, Mitchell Library, Collection of Glasgow broadsides; *The Jealous Man . . .* , p. 4.

128. Malcolm, *Anecdotes of London*, p. 205; J. Brand, *Popular Antiquities* (London, 1905), vol. 2, p. 53.

129. E. P. Thompson, *Customs in Common: Studies in Traditional Popular Culture* (New York: New Press, 1991), p. 512. For a critique of the literature on rough music, see A. James Hammerton, "The Targets of 'Rough Music': Respectability and Domestic Violence in Victorian England," *Gender and History* 3 (1991): 22–29.

130. *Glasgow Saturday Reformer*, 2 April 1842, example from Maryburgh, Rossshire; for the eighteenth century, see Eunice, *Scottish Women in Bygone Days* (Glasgow, 1930), p. 22.

131. *Trades' Newspaper*, 29 April 1827, reporting on the case of Lindley v. Howards and Kinder, Chester Assizes. This verse was later used against wife-beaters in the north; see William Andrews, *Old Times Punishments* (London, 1881), p. 182. See also *Weekly Dispatch*, 24 Dec. 1843, a Liverpool case; *The Literary and Weekly Record*, 22 Dec. 1821; clipping in Brand's *Popular Antiquities*, "grangerized" (interpellated with clippings) by J. Haslewood, in the British Library, vol. 2 103–7.

132. Tomes, " 'Torrent of Abuse,' " p. 330; Ross, "Fierce Questions and Taunts," p. 591.

133. OBSP 1787, pp. 869–72.

134. OBSP 1786.

135. OBSP 1798, p. 472.

136. OBSP 1793, pp. 364–70.

137. OBSP 1790, pp. 2–4.

138. OBSP 1801, p. 588.

139. Swinton's Scottish Cases, 1835–1837, vol. 1, p. 108.

140. Thompson, *Customs in Common*, pp. 413, 441. For other interpretations of wife-selling as relatively benign, see Gillis, *For Better, for Worse*, pp. 211–19; Randolph Trumbach, "Kinship and Marriage in Early Modern France and England: Four Books," *Annals of Scholarship* 2 (1981): 303. The author of the major work on the subject regards wife-selling in a more negative light while appreciating its ethnographic significance: Samuel Pyeatt Menefee, *Wives for Sale: An Ethnographic Study of Popular Divorce* (Oxford: Basil Blackwell, 1981).

141. *True Briton*, 14 June 1797.

142. *Weekly Dispatch,* 23 May 1841.
143. *Leeds Mercury,* 21 March 1784.
144. Thompson, *Customs in Common,* p. 441.
145. OBSP 1810–1811, p. 159.
146. OBSP 1826, p. 315.
147. *Trades' Newspaper,* 14 Aug. 1825.
148. *Sun,* 9 Feb. 1813.
149. Menefee, *Wives for Sale,* p. 153.
150. For examples, see *Sun,* 5 May and 25 May 1806, 28 Sept. 1819.
151. Menefee, *Wives for Sale,* p. 138.

PART TWO: THE SEARCH FOR SOLUTIONS

1. For the apocalyptic atmosphere inspired by the revolution, see Clarke Garrett, *Respectable Folly: Millenarianism and the French Revolution in France and England* (Baltimore: Johns Hopkins University Press, 1975).

CHAPTER SIX: SIN AND SALVATION

1. Great Hamilton Street Reformed Presbyterian Church, minutes, 14 Sept. 1797. Calton, Glasgow, Strathclyde Regional Archives, CH3/158/1, 1797–1831 (hereafter referred to as Calton Church).

2. Clergymen complained of how few working people attended their city churches and of the inadequate space for them: London, Lambeth Palace, Fulham Papers, London Visitation Returns, 81a and b, 197; Hugh MacLeod, *Religion and the Working Class in Nineteenth Century Britain* (London: Macmillan, 1984), p. 22; Callum G. Brown, *The Social History of Religion in Scotland Since 1730* (London: Methuen, 1987), p. 7.

3. Brown, *Social History of Religion,* p. 157.

4. Alan D. Gilbert, *Religion and Society in Industrial England: Church, Chapel and Social Change 1740–1914* (London: Longman, 1976), 60; Henry Grey Graham, *The Social Life of Scotland in the Eighteenth Century* (London: Adam and Charles Black, 1909), p. 356; Callum G. Brown, "Religion and Social Change," in T. M. Devine and Rosalind Mitchison, eds., *People and Society in Scotland.* Vol. 1: *1760–1830* (Edinburgh: John Donald, 1988), 148–49.

5. E. P. Thompson, *The Making of the English Working Class* (New York: Vintage, 1966), p. 40. For an excellent survey of this debate, see MacLeod, *Religion and the Working Class,* pp. 50–51.

6. E. J. Hobsbawm, *Primitive Rebels* (New York: Norton, 1959), p. 132.

7. Sir John Sinclair, ed., *The Statistical Account of Scotland,* ed. Donald J. Witrington and Ian R. Grant (Wakefield, England: E.P. Publishing, 1983 [1791–1799]), vol. 7, p. 527; William Law Mathieson, *Church and Reform in Scotland: A History from 1797 to 1843* (Glasgow: Maclehose, 1916), pp. 115, 148; Donald J. Withrington, "Schooling, Learning and So-

ciety," in Devine and Mitchison, eds., *People and Society in Scotland,*
p. 179.

8. David Gilmour, *Reminiscences of the Pen'Folk: Paisley Weavers of
Other Days* (2d ed. Paisley, 1879), p. 11; cf. pp. 25, 77, 109, 59.

9. Bernard Semmel, *The Methodist Revolution* (London: Heineman,
1974), p. 20. This also happened in the seventeenth century. See Keith
Thomas, "Women and the Civil War Sects," *Past and Present* 13 (1958):
42–62; Phyllis Mack, "Women as Prophets During the English Civil War,"
Feminist Studies 8 (1982): 23–40.

10. Brown, *Social History of Religion,* p. 251.

11. Henry Abelove, "The Sexual Politics of Early Wesleyan Methodism," and Gail Malmgreen, "Domestic Discords: Women and the Family
in East Cheshire Methodism," in James Obelkovich, Lyndal Roper, and
Raphael Samuel, eds., *Disciplines of Faith: Studies in Religion, Politics and
Patriarchy* (London: Routledge, 1987), pp. 55–70, 86–98; Deborah Valenze, *Prophetic Sons and Daughters: Female Preaching and Popular Religion in Industrial England* (Princeton: Princeton University Press, 1985),
p. 50.

12. Valenze, *Prophetic Sons and Daughters,* p. 6.

13. Quoted in Thompson, *Making,* p. 37.

14. Albert M. Lyles, *Methodism Mocked: The Satiric Reaction to
Methodism in the 18th Century* (London: Epworth Press, 1960), p. 71.

15. Henry Fielding, *The Female Husband and Other Writings,* ed.
Claude E. Jones (Liverpool: Liverpool University Press, 1960), p. 20.

16. R. Polwhele, *Anecdotes of Methodism* (London, 1800), pp. 38–39.
William Benbow made similar allegations from a radical perspective in his
Crimes of the Clergy Laid Open; Or, The Pillars of Priestcraft Shaken
(London, 1823), p. 35.

17. One example is Mary Dickin, described in the *Methodist Magazine*
23 (1800): 63; *Minutes of Several Conversations Between the Rev. John
Wesley A.M. and the Preachers Connected with Him* (London, 1797),
p. 36. See also Malmgreen, "Domestic Discords," p. 61, and Henry Abelove, *Evangelist of Desire: John Wesley and the Methodists* (Palo Alto:
Stanford University Press, 1991), p. 64.

18. John Wesley, *Thoughts on a Single Life* (London, 1765), p. 4; Abelove, *Evangelist,* p. 48.

19. Zechariah Taft, *Biographical Sketches of Female Preachers,* vol. 1
(London, 1825), p. 153; Earl Kent Brown, *Women of Mr. Wesley's Methodism* (New York: Edwin Mellen Press, 1983), p. 135; Abelove, *Evangelist,*
p. 90.

20. William Bramwell, *A Short Account of the Life and Death of Ann
Cutler, with an Appendix by Zechariah Taft, Containing an Account of
Elizabeth Dickinson* (2d ed. York, 1827), p. 11.

21. *Memoirs of the Late Mrs. Mary Cooper of London* (London, 1814),
p. 55.

22. *Memoirs of the Late Mrs. Mary Cooper* (London, 1814), p. 55; Jane Cooper, *Letters* (London, 1764), p. 24; Brown, *Women of Mr. Wesley's Methodism*, pp. 53, 80. See examples of these networks in Taft, *Biographical Sketches*, p. 106.

23. Brown, *Women of Mr. Wesley's Methodism*, p. 166.

24. Valenze, *Prophetic Sons and Daughters*, p. 191.

25. Ann Carr and Martha Williams, *A Selection of Hymns, for the Use of the Female Revivalist Methodists* (Leeds, 1838), p. 2.

26. Malmgreen, "Domestic Discords," p. 58.

27. Taft, *Biographical Sketches*, p. 251; Bramwell, *Short Account of the Life and Death of Ann Cutler*, p. 5; Valenze, *Prophetic Sons and Daughters*, p. 52.

28. B. Moore, *History of Wesleyan Methodism in Burnley and East Lancashire* (Burnley, 1899), p. 63; for further discussion, see Valenze, *Prophetic Sons and Daughters*, p. 62.

29. Bramwell, *Short Account of the Life and Death of Ann Cutler*, p. 8. W. Pilkington, *The Makers of Wesleyan Methodism in Preston, and the Relation of Methodism to the Temperance and Teetotal Movements* (Manchester, 1890), p. 21.

30. Taft, *Biographical Sketches*, p. iii. Taft was married to a prominent female preacher, which may explain his views.

31. Leonore Davidoff and Catherine Hall, *Family Fortunes: Men and Women of the English Middle Class* (London: Hutchinson, 1987), p. 116.

32. Alan Smith, *The Established Church and Popular Religion* (London: Longman, 1971), p. 38.

33. W. F. Richardson, *Preston Methodism's Two Hundred Fascinating Years and Their Background, Local and National* (Preston: Henry L. Kirby, 1975), p. 11.

34. Taft, *Biographical Sketches*, p. 153; Valenze, *Prophetic Sons and Daughters*, p. 69.

35. Valenze, *Prophetic Sons and Daughters*, p. 62.

36. Brown, *Women of Mr. Wesley's Methodism*, p. 49.

37. Valenze, *Prophetic Sons and Daughters*, p. 52; Bramwell, *Short Account of the Life and Death of Ann Cutler*, p. 8.

38. Valenze, *Prophetic Sons and Daughters*, p. 94.

39. *An Extract from the Journal of Elizabeth Harper* (London, 1769), p. 45.

40. H. B. Kendall, *History of Primitive Methodists* (London: Joseph Johnson, 1919), vol. 2, p. 146.

41. Valenze, *Prophetic Sons and Daughters*, p. 56.

42. Bramwell, *Short Account of the Life and Death of Ann Cutler*, p. 34, quoting from letter to Wesley of 1771, p. 34.

43. Robert Currie, *Methodism Divided* (London: Faber and Faber, 1968), p. 17.

44. Semmel, *Methodist Revolution*, p. 20; James Obelkovitch, *Religion and Rural Society* (Oxford: Oxford University Press, 1976), pp. 234–35.

45. *Methodist Magazine* 23 (1800): 299.

46. Valenze, *Prophetic Sons and Daughters*, p. 114.

47. Kendall, *History of Primitive Methodists*, p. 94.

48. Valenze, *Prophetic Sons and Daughters*, p. 193.

49. Brown, *Women of Mr. Wesley's Methodism*, p. 2; *Methodist Magazine* 33 (1810): 482; 43 (1820): 840.

50. John Stephens, *The Advantages Which Man Derives from Woman* (2d ed. London, 1813), p. 12.

51. *Methodist Magazine* 32 (1809): 320.

52. Rev. J. Telford, *Two West End Chapels; Or, A Sketch of London Methodism in Mr. Wesley's Day* (London, 1886), pp. 49, 62, 63. See also Annie E. Keeling, *Eminent Methodist Women* (London, 1889), pp. 25, 164.

53. L. F. Church, *More About the Early Methodist People* (London: Epworth Press, 1949), pp. 6, 28; Gilbert, *Religion and Society*, p. 63.

54. Gilbert, *Religion and Society*, p. 63; for Baptists, see W. T. Whitley, *London Baptists 1612–1912* (London: Kingsgate Press, 1928), p. 24, and the Baptism Register of White's Row Chapel, Spitalfields, London, Greater London Record Office.

55. London, Guildhall Library, Society of Genealogists, Transcripts of Methodist Chapel Registers, 1835–1837 for Clerkenwell, 1827, 1837 for Aldersgate.

56. Gilbert, *Religion and Society*, p. 60; K. S. Inglis, *Churches and the Working Classes in Victorian England* (London: Routledge and Kegan Paul, 1963), p. 13.

57. E. A. Rose, *Methodism in Ashton-Under-Lyne* (Ashton-Under-Lyne: J. Andrew, 1967), p. 31.

58. Brown, "Religion and Social Change," p. 152.

59. Gilbert, *Religion and Society*, p. 74.

60. Theodore Koditschek, *Class Formation and Urban Industrial Society: Bradford, 1750–1850* (Cambridge: Cambridge University Press, 1990), p. 285.

61. Bank Top Sunday School minutes, Manchester, Manchester Public Library, Local History Archives M314, July 1813.

62. Extracts from the diary of Barnabas Battersby, Long Preston, Yorkshire, 1795–1815, manuscript, Preston, Lancashire Record Office.

63. Pilkington, *Makers of Wesleyan Methodism*, p. 21; Richardson, *Preston Methodism's Two Hundred Fascinating Years*, p. 50.

64. Rosalind Mitchison and Leah Leneman, *Sexuality and Social Control: Scotland 1660–1780* (Oxford: Basil Blackwell, 1989), p. 231; also J. S. Marshall, "Irregular Marriages and Kirk Sessions," *Records of the Scottish Church History Society* 18(1972): 10–25. Parishes studied that continued

discipline are Gorbals, St. John's, Blackfriars, and Rutherglen; the statistics derive from first three. Records in Strathclyde Regional Archives, CH12. See also Brown, *Social History of Religion,* pp. 11, 94.

65. Kenneth M. Boyd, *Scottish Church Attitudes to Sex, Marriage and the Family 1850–1914* (Edinburgh: John Donald, 1980), p. 57.

66. For prosecutions for antenuptial fornication, see St. John's, Kirk Sessions minute books, 1819–1836, in Glasgow, Strathclyde Regional Archives, CH2/176/1. The following two books discuss Chalmers's attitudes toward sexuality in general, although they do not mention this particular experiment (other kirks in Glasgow very rarely prosecuted prenuptial conception): Stewart J. Brown, *Thomas Chalmers and the Godly Commonwealth in Scotland* (Oxford: Oxford University Press, 1982), p. 129; Boyd Hilton, *The Age of Atonement: The Influence of Evangelicalism on Social and Economic Thought 1785–1865* (Oxford: Oxford University Press, 1991), p. 82.

67. Macleod, *Religion and the Working Class,* p. 61, quoting A. A. MacLaren, *Religion and Social Class: The Disruption Years in Aberdeen* (1974); P. Hillis, "Presbyterian and Social Class in Mid–Nineteenth Century Glasgow: A Study of Nine Churches," *Journal of Ecclesiastical History* 32 (1981): 57–64.

68. For a brief discussion of a Baptist congregation's discipline in Gloucestershire, see Albion M. Urdank, *Religion and Society in a Cotswold Vale: Nailsworth, Gloucestershire, 1780–1865* (Berkeley: University of California Press, 1990), pp. 300–301; cf. Koditschek, *Class Formation,* p. 286.

69. Robert F. Wearmouth, *Methodism and the Common People of the 18th Century* (London: Epworth Press, 1945), p. 242.

70. W. H. Reid, *The Rise and Dissolution of the Infidel Societies of This Metropolis* (London, 1800), pp. 46–47.

71. Benbow, *Crimes of the Clergy,* p. 157.

72. Hilton, *Age of Atonement,* pp. 66, 11.

73. Old Scots Independent Church minute book, Oswald Street, 1768–1966, Glasgow, Strathclyde Regional Archives, TD 420/1.

74. Great Hamilton Street Reformed Presbyterian Church, minutes, 14 Sept. 1797, Calton Church.

75. Gilmour, *Reminiscences of the Pen'Folk,* p. 11.

76. See Davidoff and Hall, *Family Fortunes,* p. 134, for more detail on gender and church government.

77. Davidoff and Hall, *Family Fortunes,* p. 110.

78. Teachers' minute meeting book, Wesleyan New Connexion, Culcheth, Lancashire, Manchester, Manchester Public Library, Local History Archive M36/11/1/1, 1823.

79. Pat Hudson and Lynette Hunter, eds., "Autobiography of William Hart, Cooper, 1776–1857, Part 2," *London Journal* 8 (1982): 71.

80. New Court Congregational Church minute meeting books, London, Greater London Record Office N/C/69/13/1, 28 Jan. 1742.

81. William Whately, *Directions for Married Persons* (London, 1763 [1619]), p. 10.

82. William Gadsby, *A Sermon, Shewing the Nature and Design of the Marriage Union, Preached at the Baptist Chapel, St. George's Road, Manchester, Dec. 3, 1820, Occasioned by the Late Proceedings in the House of Lords Against the Queen* (Manchester, 1820), pp. 11, 16.

83. Wearmouth, *Methodism and the Common People*, p. 245.

84. Brown, *Social History of Religion*, p. 94; Mitchison and Leneman, *Sexuality and Social Control*, p. 97.

85. Case of Samuel Aitkin and wife, and Alexander Russell and wife, both 1820, Calton Church.

86. New Broad Street Chapel minute meeting books, London, Greater London Record Office N/C/32/1, 30 Aug. 1739, 29 Jan. 1740.

87. Fetter Lane Congregation minute meeting books, London, Greater London Record Office N/C/31/5, 30 Aug. 1809.

88. White's Row Chapel minute meeting books, London, Greater London Record Office, N/C/25/3, 10 Oct. 1809.

89. Obituary of Mary Dickin, *Methodist Magazine* 23 (1800): 63.

90. *The Good Wife*, Cheap Repository Tract (London, n.d.).

91. *Methodist Magazine* 32 (1809): 175; cf. pp. 291, 425.

92. Bridge Street Wesleyan Chapel, minutes, Bolton, 1822–1827, Bolton, Central Library, Local Archives, NMWB/1/7/1.

93. Koditschek, *Class Formation*, p. 286.

94. Great Hamilton Street Reformed Presbyterian Church, 1805, Calton Church.

95. Quoted in Abelove, *Evangelist*, p. 59.

96. William Swan, *The Journal of Two Poor Dissenters* (London: Routledge and Kegan Paul, 1970), pp. 45–52.

97. Great Hamilton Street Reformed Presbyterian Church, 1825, Calton Church.

98. London, Westminster Public Library, Marylebone Branch, Hinde Street Methodist Circuit minutes, 1 Oct. 1816.

99. Hinde Street minutes, 10–17 March 1818.

100. Great Hamilton Street Reformed Presbyterian Church, 1816, 1822, 1826, Calton Church.

101. Fetter Lane Congregation minute meeting books, July 1815.

102. London, Guildhall Library, Printed Old Bailey Sessions Papers, 13 Jan. 1825, pp. 84–85.

103. Hinde Street minutes, 23 Dec. 1817.

104. Benbow, *Crimes of the Clergy*, p. 157.

105. New Broad Street Chapel minute meeting books, 2 Feb. 1769.

106. *Times*, 25 July 1810.

107. London, Guildhall Library, Printed Old Bailey Sessions Papers, Sept. 1798, p. 559.

108. Robert Glen, *Urban Workers in the Early Industrial Revolution* (London: Croom Helm, 1984), p. 231.

109. Case of Mary Miller, 1817, Calton Church.

110. Clarke Garrett, *Millenarianism and the French Revolution in France and England* (Baltimore: Johns Hopkins University Press, 1975), p. 312.

111. Benbow, *Crimes of the Clergy*, p. 124.

112. New Broad Street Chapel minute meeting books, 3 Dec. 1807. The minute books do not specify these "licentious practices."

113. Mack, "Women as Prophets," p. 23.

114. Brown, "Religion and Social Change," p. 160.

115. *Statistical Account of Scotland*, vol. 7, p. 181; *New Statistical Account (Edinburgh*, 1845), vol. 5 p. 634.

116. Garrett, *Millenarianism*, p. 312.

117. Garrett, *Millenarianism*, pp. 190–96, discusses Brothers more fully and mentions Eyre, Flaxmer, and Gott.

118. J. F. C. Harrison, *The Second Coming: Popular Millenarianism 1780–1850* (London: Routledge and Kegan Paul, 1979), pp. 87, 132.

119. E. P. Thompson, *Making*, p.387.

120. Dorothy Gott, *Midnight Cry* (London, 1787), p. 59.

121. Letter to Jane Townley, in Westminster Public Library, Marylebone Branch, 6 Sept. 1804; also collection in London, Greater London Record Office Acc. 1040/223.

122. Sarah Flaxmer, *Satan Revealed* (London, 1795), p. 8.

123. Harrison, *Second Coming*, pp. 31, 66.

124. Dorothy Gott, *The Morning Star* (London, 1798), p. 53.

125. *Oracle*, 22 Jan., 2 April 1795.

126. Gott, *Morning Star*, p. 38.

127. I am indebted to Barbara Taylor's discussion of Joanna Southcott in *Eve and the New Jerusalem: Socialism and Feminism in the Nineteenth Century* (New York: Pantheon, 1983), p. 164; Harrison, *Second Coming*, p. 108.

128. London, Greater London Record Office, Acc. 1040/223.

129. Alice Seymour, *The Express, Containing the Life and Divine Writings of the Late Joanna Southcott* (London, 1909), vol. 1, p. 116.

130. Taylor, *Eve and the New Jerusalem*, p. 164; G. R. Balleine, *Past Finding Out: The Tragic Story of Joanna Southcott and Her Successors* (London: Society for the Promotion of Christian Knowledge, 1956), p. 6; Seymour, *Express*, p. 168.

131. Harrison, *Second Coming*, p. 109.

132. James K. Hopkins, *A Woman to Deliver Her People: Joanna Southcott and English Millenarianism in an Era of Revolution* (Austin: University of Texas Press, 1982), p. 77.

133. Hopkins, *Woman to Deliver Her People*, p. 86.

134. Quoted in Taylor, *Eve and the New Jerusalem*, p. 165.

135. Hopkins, *Woman to Deliver Her People*, p. 113.

136. Balleine, *Past Finding Out*, p. 58.

137. William Bryan, *A Testimony of the Spirit of the Truth Concerning Richard Brothers* (London, 1795); John Wright, *A Revealed Knowledge of Some Things That Will Be Speedily Fulfilled in This World* (London, 1794).

138. Gertrude Huehns, *Antinomians in English History, with Special Reference to the Period 1640–1660* (London: Cresset Press, 1951), pp. 67, 84.

139. Abelove, *Evangelist*, p. 84; Harrison, *Second Coming*, p. 30.

140. Carr and Williams, *Selection of Hymns*, p. 2.

141. Gadsby, *A Sermon*, 43.

142. *Statistical Account*, vol. 7, p. 510.

143. Graham, *Social Life of Scotland*, pp. 399–411.

144. Brown, *Social History of Religion*, p. 137; for the doctrine of atonement, see Hilton, *Age of Atonement*, pp. 3–33.

145. Old Scots Independent Church minute book, Oswald Street.

146. For Relly and Huntington, see *The Dictionary of National Biography*; for Church, *The Infamous Life of John Church, the St. George's Field Preacher* (London, 1817); for Ward, C. B. H., *Memoir of John Ward, Named Zion by the Call of God* (Birmingham, 1882).

147. Reid, *Rise and Dissolution of the Infidel Societies*, p. 41. There was also an antinomian congregation in Bartholomew by the Exchange: London, Lambeth Palace, Fulham Papers, London Visitation Returns, 81a and b, 1790 (Church of England).

148. Fulham Papers 81a and b, St. Andrew, Holborn, 1790.

149. Ebenezer Hooper, *The Celebrated Coalheaver, or Reminiscences of the Rev. William Huntington, S.C.* (London, 1871), p. 19; Oensimus, *Memoirs of the Life and Ministry of the Late William Hintington, S.S.* (London, 1813), p. 32; *Dictionary of National Biography*; Benbow, *Crimes of the Clergy*, p. 200.

150. Thomas Guthrie, ed., *The Street-Preacher, Being the Autobiography of Robert Flockhart* (Edinburgh, 1858), pp. 141, 151.

151. *Religion and Morality Vindicated* (London, 1813).

152. John Church, *The Foundling: Or, The Child of Providence* (London, 1823), p. 159.

153. Randolph Trumbach, "London's Sodomites: Homosexual Behavior and Western Culture in the 18th Century," *Journal of Social History* 11 (1977): 9–11; A. D. Harvey, "Prosecutions for Sodomy in England at the Beginning of the 19th Century," *Historical Journal* 21 (1978): 944; Louis Crompton, *Byron and Greek Love: Homophobia in Nineteenth-Century England* (Berkeley: University of California Press, 1985), pp. 163–69; Anna Clark, "Womanhood and Manhood in the Transition from Plebeian

to Working-Class Culture, London, 1780–1845," Ph.D. diss., Rutgers University, 1987, pp. 186–96.

154. Church, *Foundling*, p. 18.

155. John Church, *The Speedy Appearance of Christ* (London, 1815), p. 10.

156. Hooper, *Celebrated Coalheaver*, p. 34.

157. John Church, *The Nature of a Gospel Church* (London, 1814), p. 23.

158. Benbow, *Crimes of the Clergy*, p. 19.

159. Taylor, *Eve and the New Jerusalem*, p. 173; for radical female biblical rhetoric, see *Poor Man's Guardian*, 3 March 1832; *The Gauntlet*, 25 Aug. 1833.

160. Mack, "Women as Prophets," p. 35. Mack also notes that seventeenth-century Quaker prophetesses drew on feminine symbolism of the irrational and hysterical instead of truly claiming moral authority (p. 35), but neither Joanna Southcott nor the Methodist female preachers fit this pattern.

161. John K. Walton, *Lancashire: A Social History, 1558–1939* (Manchester: Manchester University Press, 1987), p. 184.

162. Thomas Laqueur, *Religion and Respectability: Sunday Schools and Working-Class Culture, 1780–1850* (New Haven: Yale University Press, 1976), p. 244.

163. Hugh MacLeod, *Class and Religion in the Late Victorian City* (London: Croom Helm, 1976), p. 32.

164. Dorothy Thompson, *The Chartists: Popular Politics in the Industrial Revolution* (Aldershot: Wildwood House, 1986), p. 116.

165. Hobsbawn, *Primitive Rebels*, p. 132.

166. Laqueur, *Religion and Respectability*, pp. 94, 239.

167. Brown, "Religion and Social Change," p. 152.

168. Harrison, *Second Coming*, pp. 78–79.

169. Rose, *Methodism in Ashton-Under-Lyne*, p. 31.

CHAPTER SEVEN: THE STRUGGLE OVER
THE GENDER DIVISION OF LABOR, 1780–1826

1. Edinburgh, Scottish Record Office, Prosecution papers (henceforth SRO), AD 14/13/8 Bundle 4, ticket of Annan Associated Weavers.

2. SRO, AD 14/13/8 Bundle 2, correspondence book, 16 Dec. 1809–31 March 1810.

3. K. D. M. Snell, *Annals of the Laboring Poor: Social Change and Agrarian England, 1660–1900* (Cambridge: Cambridge University Press, 1985), pp. 312–13.

4. Iorwerth Prothero, *Artisans and Politics in Early Nineteenth Century London* (London: Methuen, 1981), pp. 22–28, for a survey of these

efforts in London; E. P. Thompson, *The Making of the English Working Class* (New York: Vintage, 1966), p. 253. For "collective property in skill," see John Rule, "The Property of Skill in the Period of Manufacture," in Patrick Joyce, ed., *The Historical Meanings of Work* (Cambridge: Cambridge University Press, 1987), p. 109.

5. In 1802 10 percent of the male labor force was removed for war-time mobilization. Roger Wells, *Wretched Faces: Famine in Wartime England, 1293–1801* (Gloucester: Sutton, 1988), p. 56.

6. Prothero, *Artisans and Politics*, 44.

7. E. P. Thompson, "The Moral Economy of the English Crowd," *Past and Present* 50 (1973): 76–136. Calhoun applies the "moral economy" concept to artisans' struggles: Craig Calhoun, *The Question of Class Struggle: Social Foundations of Popular Radicalism During the Industrial Revolution* (Chicago: University of Chicago Press, 1982), p. 46.

8. A. Aspinall, *The Early English Trade Unions* (London: Batchworth Press, 1949), pp. 107, 322; *Gorgon*, 10 Oct. 1819, p. 158; SRO, AD 14/13/ 8 Bundle 2, correspondence book, 31 March 1810; W. Hamish Fraser, *Conflict and Class: Scottish Workers 1700–1838* (Edinburgh: John Donald, 1980), p. 96.

9. Rule, "Property of Skill," p. 105. See also Thompson, *Making*, p. 542.

10. For the clash between laissez-faire and workers' rhetoric, see John Smail, "New Languages for Capital and Labour: The Transformation of Discourse in the Early Years of the Industrial Revolution," *Social History* 12 (1987): 51. Of course laissez-faire advocacy was not the only tendency in Parliament; for instance, in the Report on Calico Printers Petition (PP 1806–1807, vol. II, p. 6), the Select Committee asked the House to consider "whether it is quite equitable for parties, that on one part there should arise a great accumulation of wealth, while on the other there should prevail a degree of poverty, from which the parties cannot emerge by the utmost exertion of industry, skill, and assiduous application, and may" be forced on the parish, raising rates which the landed interest had to pay. However, as Smail points out (p. 56), laissez-faire or, as he terms them, "industrial discourse" advocates were in the majority on parliamentary committees considering these problems during this era.

11. Adam Smith, *The Wealth of Nations* (New York: Random House, 1937 [1776]), pp. 67–69.

12. Hannah More, "The Riot," in her *Works* (Philadelphia, 1832), vol. 2, p. 49; Hannah More, *Betty Brown, the St. Giles Orange Girl* (London, 1796); Hannah More, *John the Shopkeeper Turned Sailor* (London, 1796); Hannah More, *The Affectionate Daughter* (London, [1795]); for the latter, see also P. E. H. Hair, "The Lancashire Collier Girl, 1795," *Transactions* of the Historical Society of Lancashire and Cheshire, 120 (1969): 63–84, on the real woman on whom Hannah More based her story.

13. *Times*, 10 Oct. 1803.

14. *Report of the Society for Bettering the Condition of the Poor*, vol. 4 (London, 1804), pp. 182–92, Appendix, pp. 61–63, quoted in Ivy Pinchbeck, *Women Workers and the Industrial Revolution, 1750–1850* (London: Virago, 1981 [1930]), p. 305.

15. Judy Lown, *Women and Industrialization: Gender at Work in Nineteenth-Century England* (Minneapolis: University of Minnesota Press, 1990), p. 77.

16. Maxine Berg first suggested that there were differences between artisans and textile workers in mode of organization; this chapter attempts to develop her insight. *The Age of Manufactures: Industry, Innovation and Work in Britain, 1700–1820* (London: Fontana, 1985), p. 159.

17. Rule, "Property of Skill," p. 108.

18. Jacques Rancière has suggested that by the early nineteenth century the mastery of the artisan may have been quite illusory. "The Myth of the Artisan: Critical Reflections on a Category of Social History," in Steven Laurence Kaplan and Cynthia J. Koepp, *Work in France: Representations, Meaning, Organization and Practice* (Ithaca: Cornell University Press, 1986), p. 318.

19. Berg, *Age of Manufactures*, p. 159.

20. As Merry E. Weisner notes, German artisans upheld their masculine honor by keeping separate from females and reacting with hostility to married journeymen or artisans who worked with women. "Guilds, Male Bonding and Women's Work in Early Modern Germany," *Gender and History* 1 (1989): 130.

21. W. Kiddier, *Old Trade Unions from the Unpublished Records of the Brushmakers* (London: George Allen and Unwin, 1931), p. 99.

22. Jean Quataert, "The Shaping of Women's Work in Manufacturing: Guilds, Households, and the State in Central Europe, 1658–1870," *American Historical Review* 90 (1985): 1147; Merry E. Weisner, "Wandervogels and Women: Journeymen's Concepts of Masculinity in Early Modern Germany," *Journal of Social History* 24 (1991): 775.

23. Sheila Lewenhak, *Women and Trade Unions: An Outline History of Women in the British Trade Union Movement* (London: Ernest Benn, 1977), p. 26; Felicity Hunt, "Opportunities Lost and Gained: Mechanization and Women's Work in the London Bookbinding and Printing Trades," in Angela V. John, ed., *Unequal Opportunities: Women's Employment in England, 1800–1918* (Oxford: Basil Blackwell, 1986), p. 74.

24. L. D. Schwarz, "Conditions of Life and Work in London, c. 1770–1820, with Special Reference to East London," D.Phil. diss., Oxford University, 1976, pp. 76, 80.

25. M. Dorothy George, *London Life in the Eighteenth Century* (Harmondsworth: Penguin, 1966 [1925]), p. 261.

26. Barbara Taylor, *Eve and the New Jerusalem: Socialism and Feminism in the Nineteenth Century* (New York: Pantheon, 1983), p. 102; but

Peter Linebaugh cautions against overemphasizing the distinction between Flints and Dungs. *The London Hanged: Crime and Civil Society in the Eighteenth Century* (London: Allen Lane Penguin Press, 1991), p. 248. However this very fluidity impelled tailors to make such efforts to preserve the distinction.

27. Address from the Committee of Master Tailors, 1811, London, British Library, Place manuscripts, Add. Ms. 27,799.

28. *Gorgon*, 10 Oct. 1819, p. 158.

29. As Christine Eisenberg points out, British artisans, unlike their German counterparts, married or cohabited, yet they focused more on horizontal solidarity among men since they had lost the protection of formal guilds. Christiane Eisenberg, "Artisans' Socialization at Work: Workshop Life in Early Nineteenth-Century England and Germany," *Journal of Social History* 24 (1991): 509–16.

30. Iain MacCalman, *Radical Underworld: Prophets, Revolutionaries and Pornographers in London, 1795–1840* (Cambridge: Cambridge University Press, 1988), p. 28.

31. Eisenberg, "Artisans' Socialization," pp. 510–12.

32. *Book of Trades* (London, 1806), pt. 1, p. 27.

33. Aspinall, *Early English Trade Unions*, p. 107. Robert Glen discusses this strike in detail, noting that the Stockport union remained strong until 1816, when it was repressed by government prosecutions. *Urban Workers in the Early Industrial Revolution* (London: Croom Helm, 1984), pp. 101–2.

34. Report of the Committee on Artizans and Machinery, PP 1824, vol. 5, p. 81. In eighteenth-century France, women also engaged in the labor processes of the preparation of the felt, and they themselves were quite militant in organizing unions. In 1749, despite royal Letters Patent prohibiting hatters' combinations, women workers combined on the grounds that they were not considered to be part of the hatters' corporation. Michael Sonenscher, *The Hatters of Eighteenth-Century France* (Berkeley: University of California Press, 1987), p. 91.

35. Report of the Committee on Artizans and Machinery, pp. 81, 73, 97.

36. Report of the Minutes of Evidence Taken Before the Select Committee on the State of Children Employed in the Manufactures of the United Kingdom, PP 1816, vol. 3, p. 341.

37. London, British Library, Place manuscripts, Add. Ms. 27,799, fol. 78.

38. Report of the Committee on Artizans and Machinery, p. 81.

39. Aspinall, *Early English Trade Unions*, p. 84.

40. George, *London Life*, p. 196.

41. James Devlin, *The Shoemakers' Guide to Trade* (London, 1839), pp. 27–28, 98.

42. John O'Neill, "Fifty Years Experience as an Irish Shoemaker in London," *St. Crispin* 2 (1869): 19, 26.

43. There is an allusion to a strike between 1785 and 1795 "for the wages of work done by women shoemakers" which led to the introduction of "inferior species of work," but it is unclear whether the men were striking against or on behalf of the women. *Trades' Newspaper*, 20 Nov. 1825, describing a meeting of the Master Shoemakers.

44. E. J. Hobsbawm and Joan Wallach Scott, "Political Shoemakers," *Past and Present* 89 (1980): 86–114.

45. O'Neill, "Fifty Years Experience," pp. 3, 275.

46. George, *London Life*, p. 199.

47. Prothero, *Artisans and Politics*, p. 30; Nicholas Mansfield, "John Brown: A Shoemaker in Place's London," *History Workshop Journal* 8 (1979): 131.

48. Fraser, *Conflict and Class*, p. 25.

49. Precognitions of the High Court of the Justiciary, SRO, AD 14/16/21, 4 July 1816. There was another strike in 1824 when shoemakers "molested" customers and strikebreakers at Michael McKirdy's shop. Glasgow, Strathclyde Regional Archives, Glasgow Police Court books, 25 Aug. 1824.

50. For a comparative view of such tensions, see Mary H. Blewett, *Men, Women and Work: Class, Gender and Protest in the New England Shoe Industry 1780–1910* (Urbana: University of Illinois Press, 1988); and Mary Blewett, "Work, Gender and the Artisan Tradition in New England Shoemaking, 1780–1860," *Journal of Social History* 17 (1983): 221–48.

51. Report and Minutes of Evidence on Cotton Manufactures, PP 1808, vol. 2, p. 127.

52. Report on Ribbon Weavers' Petitions, PP 1818, vol. 9, p. 88, quoted in Pinchbeck, *Women Workers and the Industrial Revolution*, p. 161.

53. For a survey of the silk weaving industry and industrial action, see Marc W. Steinberg, "Worthy of Hire: Discourse, Ideology and Collective Action Among English Working-Class Trade Groups, 1800–1830," Ph.D. diss., University of Michigan, 1989, pp. 103–202.

54. Richard Campbell, *The London Tradesman* (London, 1747), p. 260; George, *London Life*, p. 185.

55. George, *London Life*, p. 184.

56. House of Commons *Journals*, vol. 30, 1765, pp. 725, 212.

57. Newspaper cutting dated 30 July 1826, in London, British Library, Place Collection of clippings, set 16, vol. 1, p. 61.

58. Samuel Sholl, *A Short Historical Account of the Silk Manufacture in England* (London, 1812), pp. 9, 34; George, *London Life*, pp. 182–84.

59. Report from Assistant Handloom Weavers' Commissioners, PP 1840, vol. 23, Part 2, p. 230.

60. *Morning Chronicle*, 14 Feb. 1826, in Place Collection of clippings, set 16, vol. 2; Report from Assistant Handloom Weavers' Commissioners, 1840, p. 219.

61. Report from Assistant Handloom Weavers' Commissioners, 1840, p. 232.

62. *Trades Free Press,* 13 Jan. 1828, 5 July 1828.

63. *Trades' Newspaper,* 29 Jan. 1826.

64. As Clarke and Dickson point out, "The weavers thus exercised a relatively high degree of control over their own labour, and in addition, a command over their own family labor." Tony Clarke and Tony Dickson, "Class and Class Consciousness in Early Industrial Capitalism: Paisley 1770–1850," in Tony Dickson, ed., *Capital and Class in Scotland* (Edinburgh: John Donald, 1982), p. 17.

65. Norman Murray, *The Scottish Handloom Weavers 1790–1850: A Social History* (Edinburgh: John Donald, 1978), p. 29.

66. Fraser, *Conflict and Class,* p. 60.

67. Kenneth J. Logue, *Popular Disturbances in Scotland, 1780–1815* (Edinburgh: John Donald, 1979), p. 155.

68. Autobiography of John Mackinnon, Glasgow, Strathclyde Regional Archives, manuscript, TD 743/1–3, 1859, p. 27.

69. Murray, *Scottish Handloom Weavers,* p. 29.

70. For the deliberately law-abiding strategy of Scottish weavers in 1808–1813, see H. A. Turner, *Trade Union Growth, Structure and Policy: A Comparative Study of the Cotton Trade Unions* (London: George Allen and Unwin, 1962), p. 90.

71. SRO, AD 14/13/8, 1813, manuscript note in prosecutions for weavers union, and cf. SRO, AD 14/13/8, "The Petition of the Undersigned Operative Weavers," 14 March 1812.

72. "Petition of the Undersigned Operative Weavers." See also Bundle 3, "An Address to the Masters and Journeymen Weavers," 1812.

73. For traditional trades' views on apprenticeship, see Report of the Select Committee on Apprenticeship Laws, PP 1813, vol. 4, p. 941; for Scottish weavers and apprenticeship, see Murray, *Scottish Handloom Weavers,* p. 2.

74. W. Hamish Fraser, "A Note on the Scottish Weavers' Association, 1808–1813," *Journal of the Scottish Labour History Society* 6 (1982): 34.

75. SRO, AD 14/13/8 Bundle 2, correspondence book of Weavers' Association, 16 Dec. 1809; SRO, AD 14/13/8 Bundle 3, articles and regulations of the Clyde, Bell, and Tobago Street Association of the Operative Cotton Weavers of Calton, 26 March 1810.

76. SRO, AD 14/13/8 Bundle 3, letter from William Morrison to Thomas Smith, 11 Mar. 1812.

77. SRO, AD 14/13/8 Bundle 6, precognition of Alexander Sinclair, Glasgow, 17 Dec. 1813.

78. *Weavers Magazine and Literary Companion* (Nov. 1818): 96–97, 101.

79. William Taylor, *A Letter to the Operative Weavers of Scotland* (Glasgow, 1824), p. 5.

80. Murray, *Scottish Handloom Weavers,* p. 192.

81. Fraser, *Conflict and Class,* p. 114.

82. Minutes of Evidence from the Committee on the Petitions of Several Weavers, PP 1810–1811, vol. 2, p. 13.

83. *Glasgow Chronicle*, 3 Aug., 26 Sept. 1816; also broadsheet, "Trials at the Circuit Court of Justiciary, Glasgow 25 Sept. 1816," in Glasgow, Mitchell Library, C. D. Donald, *Collection of Glasgow Broadsides*, vol. 2, fol. 107.

84. A. G. Rose, "Early Cotton Riots in Lancashire, 1769–1779," *Transactions* of the Lancashire and Cheshire Antiquarian Society 73–74 (1963–1964): 87; Lewenhak, *Women and Trade Unions*, p. 28.

85. "Further Accounts of the Dreadful and Alarming Riots Which Have Taken Place Among the Weavers at Manchester," London, British Library 1880.c.20, fol. 186; cf. fol. 97.

86. J. L. Hammond and Barbara Hammond, *The Skilled Labourer* (London, 1919), p. 295.

87. Maxine Berg, "Women's Work, Mechanization, and the Early Stages of Industrialization in England," in Joyce, ed., *Historical Meanings of Work*, p. 82.

88. Thompson, *Making*, 193.

89. Calhoun, *Question of Class Struggle*, p. 201, negatively correlates the number of females in factory towns with the strength of their trade union movements.

90. Robert G. Hall, "Tyranny, Work and Politics: The 1818 Strike Wave in the English Cotton District," *International Review of Social History* 34 (1989): 445.

91. Glen, *Urban Workers*, p. 73.

92. "Chester Assizes," 5 Sept. 1818, newspaper cutting in Manchester, Manchester Public Library, Manchester collection of cuttings.

93. SRO, JC 45/12, Minute Book of Glasgow General Weavers Committee, 1 Sept. 1810; SRO, AD 14/13/8 Bundle 7, deposition of James Duncan, weaver, Pollakshaws (suburb of Glasgow), 15 Dec. 1812; John Campbell, *Recollections of Radical Times* (Glasgow, 1880), p. 17.

94. Campbell, *Recollections of Radical Times*, p. 17; John Campbell, *History of the Rise and Progress of Powerloom Weaving; Vindication of the Character of Female Powerloom Weavers* (Rutherglen, 1878), pp. 8–9.

95. SRO, AD 14/23/239, deposition of John Robertson, son of a weaver, August 1823.

96. Glasgow, Mitchell Library, C. H. Donald, *Collection of Glasgow Broadsides*, vol. 2, p. 178, 9 Sept. 1823, "A Riot Which Took Place Among the Workers of the Cotton Mills in Hutcheson Town." SRO, AD 14/38/502 Item 6, Bundle 2, account by George Salmond, procurator-fiscal for Lanarkshire, of Combined PowerLoom Operatives history, p. 5.

97. Declaration of Jean Kirkwood, 21 Aug. 1823; information and presentment of George Salmond, procurator-fiscal of Lanarkshire; declaration of Isabella McFadyen, 1823, all in SRO, AD 14/23/241.

98. For their reputation for violence, see Mariana Valverde, "Giving the Female a Domestic Turn: The Social, Legal and Moral Regulation of Women's Work in British Cotton Mills, 1820–1850," *Journal of Social History* 21 (1988): 624; Turner, *Trade Union Growth*, p. 92; John T. Ward, "Textile Trade Unionism in Nineteenth-Century Scotland," in John Butt and and Kenneth Ponting, eds., *Scottish Textile History* (Aberdeen: Aberdeen University Press, 1987), p. 133.

99. William Lazonick, "Industrial Relations and Technical Change: The Case of the Self-Acting Mule," *Cambridge Journal of Economics* 3 (1979): 232.

100. John K. Walton, *Lancashire: A Social History* (Manchester: Manchester University Press, 1987), p. 146; SRO, AD 14/38/502, account of cotton spinners' association by George Salmond, 1838. Mary Freifeld, "Technological Change and the 'Self-Acting' Mule: A Study of Skill and the Sexual Division of Labor," *Social History* 11 (1986): 334.

101. Isaac Cohen, "Workers' Control in the Cotton Industry: A Comparative Study of British and American Mulespinning," *Labor History* 26 (1985): 62; Per Bolin-Hart, *Work, Family and the State: Child Labour and the Organization of Production in the British Cotton Industry, 1780–1920* (Lund, Sweden: Lund University Press, 1989), p. 49, echoing John Doherty, Lancashire mule spinner unionist. Cf. R. G. Kirby and A. E. Musson, *The Voice of the People: John Doherty, 1798–1854* (Manchester: Manchester University Press, 1975), p. 109. Doherty said mule spinning was too strenuous for men of forty, but his comment made clear that he really feared the reversal of gender roles.

102. Alan Fowler and Terry Wyke, *Barefoot Aristocrats: A History of the Amalgamated Association of Cotton Spinners* (Littleborough: George Kelsall, 1987), p. 4.

103. John Jones, *The Cotton Mill: A Poem* (Manchester, 1821), p. 13.

104. Eleanor Gordon, *Women and the Labor Movement in Scotland 1850–1914* (Oxford: Oxford University Press, 1991), pp. 48–49. I owe thanks to Dr. Gordon for allowing me to see the proofs of this book before it was published.

105. Lazonick, "Industrial Relations and Technical Change," p. 232.

106. Gordon, *Women and the Labor Movement*, p. 41.

107. Lazonick, "Industrial Relations and Technical Change," p. 236.

108. James Montgomery, *Theory and Practice of Cotton Spinning* (3d ed. Glasgow, 1836), p. 272.

109. Kirby and Musson, *Voice of the People*, p. 13.

110. Aspinall, *Early English Trade Unions*, p. 264.

111. Indeed, they lamented that their wives no longer could take work home from the factories. "A Letter from a Journeyman Cotton Spinner," *Black Dwarf* 2 (1818): 622–23.

112. Hall, "Tyranny, Work and Politics," p. 443.

113. Hall, "Tyranny, Work and Politics," p. 458.

114. Aspinall, *Early English Trade Unions*, p. 310, quoting a letter from James Norris to Viscount Sidmouth.

115. [Elizabeth Salt], *To All Persons Friendly to, and Desirous of Establishing a Union on Legal Principles, for the Purpose of Supporting the Innocent Mothers, Wives and Children of Such Persons as Are . . . Suffering Under a Want of Just Renumeration for Their Labor* (Manchester, [1818]). Signed by four other women as well. For a discussion of this incident, see Hammond and Hammond, *Skilled Labourer*, p. 106.

116. Report on Children in Manufactures, p. 239, testimony of Nathanial Gould.

117. John Butt, "Labor and Industrial Relations in the Scottish Cotton Industry During the Industrial Revolution," in Butt and Ponting, eds., *Scottish Textile History*, p. 145.

118. SRO, AD 14/38/502 Bundle 2, Item 1, deposition of Thomas Stewart, 19 Jan. 1821; Item 6, account by George Salmond of the history of Glasgow mule spinners' union.

119. *Statement of the Proprietors of the Cotton Works of Glasgow* (Glasgow, 1825), p. 7.

120. Neil Smelser interpreted the militant activity of mule spinners as a response to disruption of their trade occasioned by their growing inability to employ their own children, but Calhoun and Anderson have demonstrated that the timing of expansion in the industry cannot explain their militancy and that mule spinners always had to employ other children and young people. Neil Smelser, *Social Change in the Industrial Revolution* (London: Routledge and Kegan Paul, 1959); Calhoun, *Question of Class Struggle*, p. 192; Michael Anderson, "Sociological History and the Working-Class Family: Smelser Revisited," *Social History* 6 (1976): 325–27. However, family structure is relevant to mule spinning. Sonya O. Rose, *Limited Livelihoods: Gender and Class in Nineteenth-Century England* (Berkeley: University of California Press, 1992), pp. 2, 248, on how Smelser's insights should not be dismissed out of hand.

121. SRO, AD 14/20/115, precognition against James MacAlpine, 1820. Also AD 14/20/60, precognition against James McAlpine et al. at Stirling, 1820.

122. SRO, AD 14/22/145, precognition against James McCafferty et al., 1822.

123. SRO, AD 14/25/192, precognition against John Kean, testimony of Mary Cameron, who was his piecer, 20 Dec. 1825; AD 14/26/310, Catherine McMarlane, piecer to Robert Watson, precognition as to assault on Robert Watson, 12 March 1825.

124. In the cardroom, where women were employed "on set wages," "the carding master must act with the utmost vigilance and promptitude, and sometimes with a degree of seeming severity that is not so necessary"

in the spinning room. Montgomery, *Theory and Practice*, p. 272; Report on Children in Manufactures, pp. 341, 190.

125. SRO, AD 14/23/239, declaration of Hugh Donaldson, September 1823.

126. SRO, AD 14/26/310, precognition against James Steel, declaration of Alexander Davidson, 4 April 1823.

127. P.M., *Narrative of the Late Occurrences at the Cotton Mills in Glasgow in Answer to the Statement of the Occurrences by the Proprietors* (Glasgow, 1825), pp. 13, 19; also *Account of the Trial of Ann McGregor* (Glasgow, 1825).

128. SRO, AD 14/25/192; precognition against John Kean, Spring 1825; the song is included in this precognition.

129. SRO, AD 14/25/192.

130. P.M., *Narrative of the Late Occurrences*, p. 8. Also SRO, AD 14/17/8, 1817, for depositions of James McEwan and Peter Gibson on the involvement of cotton spinners in sedition (advocating armed force in order to obtain annual Parliaments and universal suffrage).

131. *Statement of the Proprietors of the Cotton Workers in Glasgow* (Glasgow, 1825), p. 71.

132. SRO, AD 14/25/170, 12 March 1825, declaration of James Robertson.

133. SRO, AD 14/38/502 Bundle 3, Misc. 3, letter to Mr. Clark from Select Committee of Operatives, 17 Feb. 1822.

134. SRO, AD 14/38/502 Bundle 3, letter of 1 Feb. 1827.

135. Berg, *Age of Manufactures*, p. 159.

136. Smail, "New Languages," p. 51.

137. Report on Children in Manufactures, pp. 310, 369, 384.

138. Thompson, *Making*, p. 418.

139. Smail, "New Languages," p. 53.

140. John Gast, "Articles of the Philanthropic Hercules," 2 Dec. 1818, London, British Library, Place manuscripts, Add. Ms. 27,799, fol. 143.

CHAPTER EIGHT: MANHOOD AND CITIZENSHIP

1. Jürgen Habermas, *The Structural Transformation of the Public Sphere*, trans. Thomas Burger (Cambridge: MIT Press, 1989 [1962]), p. 73. Anthony J. La Vopa, "Conceiving a Public: Ideas and Society in Eighteenth-Century Europe," *Journal of Modern History* 64 (1992): esp. 106–15, and for a feminist critique, Joan B. Landes, *Women and the Public Sphere in the Age of the French Revolution* (Ithaca: Cornell University Press, 1988) p. 45.

2. Catherine Hall, "Gender, Class and Politics, 1780–1850," in her *White, Male and Middle Class: Explorations in Feminist History* (Cambridge: Polity, 1992), p. 159; information on exclusion of working men was

kindly shared with me by John Smail: see Smail, *The Origins of Middle-Class Culture* (Cornell: Cornell University Press, 1995), ch. 5.

3. Lord Henry Cockburn, *An Examination of the Trials for Sedition Which Have Hitherto Occurred in Scotland* (New York: Augustus M. Kelley, 1970 [1888]), vol. 1, p. 248.

4. Carl B. Cone, *The English Jacobins: Reformers in the Late Eighteenth Century* (New York: Scribner's, 1968), p. 16.

5. British Museum Add. Ms. 27,814, fol. 238, quoted in Mary Thale, ed., *Selections from the Papers of the London Corresponding Society 1792–1799* (Cambridge: Cambridge University Press, 1982), p. 8. For the classic discussion of the LCS, see E. P. Thompson, *The Making of the English Working Class* (New York: Vintage, 1966), pp. 1–21.

6. Ruth L. Smith and Deborah M. Valenze, "Mutuality and Marginality: Liberal Moral Theory and Working-Class Women in Nineteenth Century England," *Signs* 13 (1988): 289.

7. Geoff Eley, "Rethinking the Political: Social History and Political Culture in Eighteenth and Nineteenth Century Britain," *Archiv für Sozialgeschischte* 32 (1981): 427–57.

8. Leonore Davidoff and Catherine Hall, *Family Fortunes: Men and Women of the English Middle Class* (London: Hutchinson, 1987) p. 155; for a theoretical perspective on the illusory separation, see Mary Poovey, *Uneven Developments: The Ideological Work of Gender in Mid-Victorian England* (Chicago: University of Chicago Press, 1988), p. 12.

9. J. G. A. Pocock, "Cambridge Paradigms and Scotch Philosophers," p. 235; and John Robertson, "The Scottish Enlightenment and the Civil Tradition," p. 138, both in Istvan Hont and Michael Ignatieff, eds., *Wealth and Virtue: The Shaping of Political Economy in the Scottish Enlightenment* (Cambridge: Cambridge University Press, 1983).

10. Susan M. Okin, *Women in Western Political Thought* (Princeton University Press, 1979), p. 91.

11. Carole Pateman, *The Disorder of Women: Democratic Feminism and Political Theory* (Palo Alto: Stanford University Press, 1989), p. 6.

12. Hanna Pitkin, *Fortune Was a Woman: Gender in the Political Thought of Nicolò Machiavelli* (Berkeley: University of California Press, 1984), p. 25.

13. Caroline Robbins, *The Eighteenth Century Commonwealthman* (Harvard University Press, 1959), pp. 43, 49, 182, 201; Robertson, "Scottish Enlightenment," p. 138. This trope was borrowed by American revolutionaries. Linda K. Kerber, "The Paradox of Women's Citizenship in the Early Republic," *American Historical Review* 97 (1992): 354.

14. For citizens as burgesses of city, see the *Oxford English Dictionary*, s.v. "citizen"; Penelope J. Corfield, "Class in Eighteenth Century Britain," in Penelope J. Corfield, ed., *Language, History and Class* (Oxford: Basil Blackwell, 1991), pp. 117, 122.

15. Smail, *Origins of Middle-Class Culture*, ch. 5. Among them, city

radicals overlapped with artisans; provincial merchants and tradesmen struggled for influence with the gentry; independent manufacturers, as in Halifax, made themselves into a ruling elite; professionals were dependent on upper-class patronage. But, as Smail notes, by midcentury these people were acquiring enough solidarity to be identified as the middle class.

16. George Rudé, *Wilkes and Liberty* (London: Lawrence and Wishart, 1983 [1962]), p. 19; J. E. Ross, *Radical Adventurer: The Diaries of Robert Morris 1772–1774* (Bath: Adams and Dart, 1971), pp. 6, 12. Robert Morris, son of a wealthy industrialist, was a key supporter of Wilkes who became a lawyer and helped win Lord Baltimore's acquittal for rape. During Wilkes's heyday as a hero of liberty, he and Morris traded epistolary tips on the seduction of married women, and Morris either seduced or abducted Lord Baltimore's twelve-year-old daughter and married her.

17. G. J. Barker-Benfield, *The Culture of Sensibility: Sex and Society in Eighteenth-Century Britain* (Chicago: University of Chicago Press, 1992), p. 47.

18. Randolph Trumbach, "Sodomy Transformed: Aristocratic Libertinage, Public Reputation and the Gender Revolution of the 18th Century," *Journal of Homosexuality* 19 (1990): 121; J. C. D. Clark, *English Society 1688–1832* (Cambridge: Cambridge University Press, 1985), p. 310. However, it should be noted that there were also anticlerical radical men interested in homoeroticism who were Wilkes's contemporaries; and the son of William Beckford, a politician and Wilkes's ally, had to flee into exile after being tried for sodomy. G. S. Rousseau, "The Sorrows of Priapus: Anticlericalism, Homosocial Desire, and Richard Payne Knight," in G. S. Rousseau and Roy Porter, eds., *Sexual Underworlds of the Enlightenment* (Chapel Hill: University of North Carolina Press, 1988), pp. 122, 141.

19. John Dwyer, *Virtuous Discourse: Sensibility and Community in Late Eighteenth Century Scotland* (Edinburgh: John Donald, 1987), pp. 107, 96, 104; Davidoff and Hall, *Family Fortunes*, p. 110.

20. Cone, *English Jacobins*, pp. 11, 44, 68, 71. For Wilkes on representation, see Wilkes's speech in Parliament in 1776, excerpted in Simon MacCoby, ed., *The English Radical Tradition 1763–1914* (New York: New York University Press, 1957), p. 31.

21. Cone, *English Jacobins*, p. 71; H. T. Dickinson, *Liberty and Property: Political Ideology in Eighteenth-Century Britain* (New York: Holmes and Meier, 1977), p. 229.

22. Albert Goodwin, *The Friends of Liberty: The English Radical Movement in the Age of the French Revolution* (London: Hutchinson, 1979), p. 211. Of course, in the first two years of the French Revolution only the propertied could be "active citizens"; the others were "passive citizens."

23. Cone, *English Jacobins*, p. 88.

24. Goodwin, *Friends of Liberty*, p. 211.

25. T. C. Smout, *A History of the Scottish People 1560–1830* (London: Fontana, 1972), pp. 203, 413; Kenneth J. Logue, *Popular Disturbances in*

Scotland, 1780–1815 (Edinburgh: John Donald, 1979), pp. 169, 199, 203; Henry W. Meikle, *Scotland and the French Revolution* (Glasgow: James Maclehose and Sons, 1912), p. 40.

26. John Brims, "From Reformers to Jacobins: The Scottish Association of the Friends of the People," in T. M. Devine, ed., *Conflict and Stability in Scottish Society 1700–1850* (Edinburgh: John Donald, 1990), p. 35; *The Trial of Thomas Muir . . . for Sedition* (London, 1793), p. 63.

27. Edinburgh, Scottish Record Office (henceforth SRO), RH 2/4, vol. 65, fol. 9, letter of 9 Nov. 1792 from a soldier, possibly D. Scott. He also advocated that in order to prevent sedition from spreading from Scotland to England, the government should spread anti-Scottish propaganda in England against the reformers.

28. Norman MacLeod, *Letters to the People of North Britain* (London, 1793), p. 6.

29. John K. Walton, *Lancashire: A Social History 1558–1939* (Manchester: Manchester University Press, 1987), p. 152. See also Manchester Manchester Public Library, Manchester collection of cuttings, fols. 21, 27, newspaper accounts of large "seditious meetings" in 1792 and 1794; Robert Glen, *Urban Workers in the Early Industrial Revolution* (London: Croom Helm, 1984), p. 123.

30. Thale, ed., *Selections*, p. 303, meeting of London Corresponding Society, 17 Sept. 1795.

31. *The Origin and Plan of the General Association of Householders within the Kingdom of Great Britain . . .* (London, 1796).

32. British Museum Add. Ms. 27,814, fol. 238, quoted in Thale, ed., *Selections*, p. 8.

33. For a discussion of the later ramifications of this trend, see James Epstein, "The Constitutional Idiom: Radical Reasoning, Rhetoric, and Action in Early Nineteenth Century England," *Journal of Social History* 23 (1990): 553–73. In the 1790s, Jacobins accused the Whigs of abandoning the heritage of 1688. *Morning Chronicle*, Oct. 1793, London, British Library, Francis Place Collection of Newspaper Cuttings and Pamphlets, vol. 38 (hereafter referred to as Place Coll. vol. 38), fol. 71; [J. T. Callender], *The Political Progress of Great Britain* (Edinburgh, 1792), p. 32. Jacobins also found classical republicanism inadequate: *Give Us Our Rights! Or, An Address to the People of Britain Clearly Demonstrating That Those Rights Are Universal Suffrage, Annual Parliaments, and the Freedom of Popular Association* (London, 1792[?]). See Cone, *English Jacobins*, p. 37, for free agency. This argument continued for several years: see "The London Corresponding Society's Answer to a Member of Parliament's Letter" (London, 1797), in Place Coll., vol. 38, fol. 145.

34. Gregory Claeys, *Thomas Paine: Social and Political Thought* (Boston: Unwin Hyman, 1989), p. 90; Olivia Smith, *The Politics of Language 1791–1819* (Oxford: Oxford University Press, 1984), discusses the neces-

sity for radicals to create a plebeian political language, since they were excluded from formal philosophical discourse.

35. Dickinson, *Liberty and Property*, p. 253.

36. Okin, *Women in Western Political Thought*, pp. 200–201.

37. Thomas Paine, *Rights of Man* (London: J. M. Dent, Everyman's Library, 1915), p. 42.

38. Jane Abray, "Feminism in the French Revolution," *American Historical Review* 80 (1975): 57; Darline Gay Levy, Harriet Branson Applewhite, and Mary Durham Johnson, *Women in Revolutionary Paris, 1789–1795* (Urbana: University of Illinois Press, 1979).

39. Thomas Cooper, *Reply to Mr. Burke's Invective* (London, 1792), quoted in Claeys, *Thomas Paine*, p. 124.

40. William Hodgson, *The Commonwealth of Reason* (London, 1795), p. 100.

41. "On the Rights of Women," *The Cabinet* 2 (1795): 42–49, quoted in Dickinson, *Liberty and Property*, p. 253.

42. Thomas Spence, *Something to the Purpose: A Receipt to Make a Millenium* (London, n.d.).

43. Mary Wollstonecraft, *A Vindication of the Rights of Woman*, ed. Miriam Kramnick (Harmondsworth: Penguin, 1978 [1792]), pp. 127–54, 259. For rational motherhood, see Pateman, *Disorder of Women*, p. 197.

44. Mary Hays, "To the Editor," *Monthly Magazine*, 2 March 1797, excerpted in Moira Ferguson, ed., *First Feminists: British Women Writers 1578–1799* (Bloomington: Indiana University Press, 1985), p. 418.

45. For an interpretation of this theme, see Barbara Taylor, "Mary Wollstonecraft and the Wild Wish of Early Feminism," *History Workshop Journal* 33 (1992): 216.

46. Wollstonecraft, *Vindication*, pp. 80, 84. See also Catherine Macaulay, who wished to educate "a careless, modest beauty, grave, manly, noble, full of strength and majesty." She believed there was "No characteristic Difference in Sex." "Letters on Education," excerpted in Ferguson, ed., *First Feminists*, pp. 402, 410.

47. Sarah Burks of Spitalfields, for instance, was charged, although not prosecuted, for selling seditious literature. London, Greater London Record Office, Middlesex Sessions, Roll 3579, Recognizance 67, December 1794.

48. Letter from "Tabitha Bramble," 32 Jan. 1792, Home Office Files for Scotland, SRO, RH 2/4, vol. 74, fol. 122.

49. Thale, ed., *Selections*, pp. 43, 155, 83, 79.

50. Thomas Johnston, *The History of the Working Classes in Scotland* (Totowa, N.J.: Rowman and Littlefield, 1974 [1946]), p. 382.

51. [Andrew Larcher], *Fraternal and Philanthropic Policy, or Articles of the British Fraternal and Philanthropic Community, United Against Monopoly and Extortion* (London, 1796), p. 12.

52. For identification of men with reason and women with irrationality, see Landes, *Women and the Public Sphere*, p. 46.

53. James Vernon, *Politics and the People: A Study in English Political Culture c. 1815–1867* (Cambridge: Cambridge University Press, 1993), pp. 315, 319. Thanks are due to James Vernon for allowing me to see this chapter in manuscript. Ian Dyck has also suggested that Paine's ideas were less popular than they might have been because his internationalism did not acknowledge the importance of local, regional, and national identities for working people. "Local Attachments, National Identities and World Citizenship in the Thought of Thomas Paine," *History Workshop Journal* 35 (1993): 125. Mary Wollstonecraft made extensive use of gothic narratives in her novels, depicting women as suffering victims or chaste heroines, not as the sturdy, independent householders she imagined in her political thought.

54. Edmund Burke, "Reflections on the Revolution in France," excerpted in Marilyn Butler, *Burke, Paine, Godwin and the Revolution Controversy* (Cambridge: Cambridge University Press, 1984), pp. 44–45.

55. Paine, *Rights of Man*, p. 242. See p. 169 for a similar statement.

56. *Trial of Thomas Muir*, pp. 5–6, quoting *The Patriot*, a radical tract he was accused of giving to a Kirkintilloch weaver; similar language is found in a broadsheet, "London, Executive Committee, Sitting of Thursday, March 23, 1797," London, British Library, Place Coll., vol. 38, fol. 32.

57. Burke, "Reflections on the Revolution in France," pp. 44–45.

58. Mary Wollstonecraft, "A Vindication of the Rights of Man," (1790), in Butler, *Burke, Paine, Godwin*, p. 74.

59. Talk by Iain MacCalman, Eighteenth-Century History Seminar conducted by John Brewer, London, Victoria and Albert Museum, May 1992.

60. Hodgson, *Commonwealth of Reason*, p. 19.

61. Paine, *Rights of Man*, p. 59.

62. William Godwin, *A Defense of the Rockingham Party*, in Burton R. Pollin, ed., *Four Early Pamphlets* (Gainesville: Scholars' Fascimiles and Reprints, 1966 [1783]), p. 2.

63. *The Rights of Nobles, Consisting of Extracts from Pigott's Political Dictionary* (London, 1794[?]), p. 3.

64. Raymond Williams, *Keywords* (New York: Oxford University Press, 1976), pp. 121–23, traces the evolution of this word.

65. Paine, *Rights of Man*, pp. 42, 253.

66. Goodwin, *Friends of Liberty*, p. 360.

67. Thomas Bentley, *A Short View of Some of the Evils and Grievances Which Oppress the British Empire* (London, 1792), in London, Greater London Record Office, Middlesex Sessions, Roll 3553, Indictment 46, December 1792. This topic persisted in later radicalism. See *A Proposal on Behalf of the Married Poor* (London, 1801). See "Remonstrance of the

Journeymen Carpenters and Joiners," 27 Jan. 1816, Place Manuscripts, British Museum Add. Ms. 27,799, fol. 124; *Black Dwarf*, 1 (1817): 286, argued that soldiers should be allowed to marry.

68. *The Rights of Man, Consisting of Extracts from Pigott's Political Dictionary* (London, 1794[?]), p. 7.

69. "Hampden," "To the Inhabitants of Nottingham," 1793, broadsheet, London, British Library, Collection of political pamphlets from the 1790s, 628.c.26, no. 81.

70. Thomas Spence, *Burke's Address to the Swinish Multitude* (London, 1793).

71. The radical religious linen draper Thomas Bentley called for the "rights of the sober, honest, industrious poor, that they have an equal right with the rich to the . . . privilege of divorcement." Bentley also believed the government should provide wastelands for the poor to cultivate, and education in trades for both boys and girls among the poor. *The Rights of the Poor* (London, 1791), London, British Library, Collection of political pamphlets from the 1790s, 628.c.26, no. 46. The deist William Hodgson argued that illegitimate children should be able to inherit and that divorce should be freely available, for "the hymenal lamp expires when love ceases to furnish oil." Bentley and Hodgson did not derive their arguments only from a philosophical critique; they were also sensitive to the hardships and insecurity of marriage in plebeian life. Hodgson wrote that divorce would "prevent those shameful bickerings that but too frequently send the husband one way and the wife another, to their mutual destruction." Hodgson, *Commonwealth of Reason*, p. 78; for anti-Jacobin propaganda, see Claeys, *Thomas Paine*, p. 151.

72. John Bone, secretary of London Corresponding Society, "Fellow Citizen," 1797, in London, British Library, Place Coll., vol. 38, fol. 31.

73. "London, Executive Committee, Sitting of Thurs. March 23, 1797," in London, British Library, Place Coll., vol. 38, fol. 32.

74. Anon., *The Happy Reign of George the Last: An Address to the Little Tradesmen, and the Labouring Poor of England* (London, 1795), p. 2.

75. *A Warning to Tyrants, Consisting of Extracts from Pigott, Gerald etc.* (London, 1795), pp. 2, 5. Similarly, in 1798, a broadsheet countered the repressive laws of that year by arguing that "your hard and scanty Earnings are to be still further diminished by new Taxes; to provide for a set of Vultures, Cormorants, and Wolves, blood-thirsty Villains and Monsters in human shape, while you, your wives, your tender Infants, and aged Parents, are eating the refuse Scraps." "A Friend to Rational Liberty," "An Exhortation to the Friends of Peaceable Measures and Remonstrance," London, British Library, Place Coll., vol. 38, fol. 95.

76. From the conservative side, "Colonius" claimed that in contemporary Scotland there was no need for the equal distribution of land, because manufactures gave work to women and children, "So if one in each family

beside the Master is employed," the household could earn over thirty-six pounds a year. "Colonius," "To the Manufacturers, Mechanics and Labouring People of Scotland," 1792, in SRO, RH 2/4, vol. 66, fol. 321. The radical Thomas Bentley, even before the second part of *Rights of Man* came out with Paine's welfare proposal, called for the government to provide work for women and girls as well as men and boys, clearly assuming they had to support themselves. Bentley, *The Rights of the Poor*.

77. Hays, in Ferguson, ed., *First Feminists*, p. 418.

78. This may also reflect the influence of Jean-Jacques Rousseau. Brian Rigby, "Radical Spectators of the Revolution: The Case of the *Analytical Review*," in Ceri Crossley and Ian Small, eds., *The French Revolution and British Culture* (Oxford: Oxford University Press, 1989), p. 75.

79. [London Corresponding Society], *Reformers No Rioters* (London, 1794).

80. Thale, ed., *Selections*, p. 87.

81. John Bohstedt, "Gender, Household, and Community Politics: Women in English Riots, 1790–1810," *Past and Present* 120 (1988): 110.

82. SRO, RH 2/4, vol. 70, fol. 175, 9 April 1793, letter from magistrates of Inverness to Sir Hector Munro.

83. *Morning Chronicle*, 5 Sept. 1797, in Place Coll., vol. 38, fol. 147.

84. Home Office 42/50, Legge to John King (?), 1 May 1800, quoted in Clive Emsley, *British Society and the French Wars, 1793–1815* (London: Croom Helm, 1979), p. 52. See also Roger Wells, *Insurrection: The British Experience 1795–1803* (Gloucester: Alan Sutton, 1983), pp. 178–87.

85. Alan Booth, "Food Riots in the North-West of England: 1790–1801," *Past and Present* 77 (1977): 101.

86. These sentiments were not confined to men. As Joan Landes notes, Mary Wollstonecraft's focus on austere virtue led her to stigmatize rioting market women as immoral and unruly and to attack Jacobins for associating with "shameless women of the town." *Women and the Public Sphere*, pp. 149–50.

87. "Minutes of the Proceedings of the General Convention of the Delegates from the Societies of the Friends of the People Throughout Scotland" (1793), SRO, RH 2/4, vol. 69, fol. 222.

88. [London Corresponding Society], *Reformers No Rioters*.

89. [Vicesimus Knox], *The Spirit of Despotism* (5th ed. London, 1820), p. 21.

90. Bohstedt, "Gender, Household, and Community Politics," p. 112. Catherine Hall, "The Tale of Samuel and Jemima: Gender and Working-Class Culture in Early Nineteenth-Century England," in her *White, Male and Middle Class*, says that women's participation lessened as food riots gave way to more formal organization (p. 131).

91. Claeys, *Thomas Paine*, p. 151.

92. "A True and Particular Account of the Trial of Thomas Paine"

(London, [1792 or 1793]), London, British Library, Collection of political pamphlets from the 1790s, 628.c.26, no. 44.

93. [William Jones], *One Pennyworth of Truth, from Thomas Bull, to His Brother John* (Nayland, 1792), London, British Library, Collection of political pamphlets from the 1790s, 628.c.26, no. 7. For a further discussion of the language of this pamphlet, see Smith, *Politics of Language*, pp. 71–72.

94. Hannah More, *Works* (Philadelphia, 1832), vol. 1, p. 49.

95. Brims, "From Reformers to Jacobins," p. 43.

96. Letter from William Carlile of Paisley, 8 Feb. 1794, SRO, RH 2/4, vol. 74, fol. 152.

97. Conservatives were even more adamant about restricting the scope of the constitution: Vernon, *Politics and the People*, p. 301. See also Drohr Wahrman, "Virtual Representation: Parliamentary Reporting and the Languages of Class in the 1790s," *Past and Present* 136 (1992): 91.

98. Quoted in Gregory Claeys, *Thomas Paine*, p. 146.

99. Dwyer, *Virtuous Discourse*, p. 38; Pocock, *Virtue, Commerce and History* (Cambridge: Cambridge University Press, 1985), p. 235.

100. Boyd Hilton, *The Age of Atonement: The Influence of Evangelicalism on Social and Economic Thought 1785–1865* (Oxford: Oxford University Press, 1991), p. 204.

101. Wells, *Insurrection*, p. 22; Meikle, *Scotland*, p. 154.

102. Talk by Iain MacCalman, Eighteenth-Century British History Seminar, May 1992.

103. J. Ann Hone, *For the Cause of Truth: Radicalism in London, 1796–1821* (Oxford: Oxford University Press, 1982), p. 86.

104. Hone, *For the Cause of Truth*, p. 87; Iain MacCalman, *Radical Underworld: Prophets, Revolutionaries and Pornographers in London, 1796–1840* (Cambridge: Cambridge University Press, 1988), p. 45; Iain MacCalman, "Ultra-Radicalism and Convivial Debating Clubs," *English Historical Review* 102 (1987): 311.

105. MacCalman, *Radical Underworld*, pp. 28, 45, 187, 192.

106. "My Dear Countrymen," British Library, Collection 1879.cc.4.

107. Louis Crompton, *Byron and Greek Love: Homophobia in Nineteenth-Century England* (Berkeley: University of California Press, 1985), p. 159.

108. *Times*, 10 July 1810; *The Infamous Life of John Church, the St. George's Field Preacher* (London, 1817), p. 5.

109. Robert Holloway, *The Phoenix of Sodom; Or, The Vere St. Coterie* (London, 1813), pp. 10, 30. For more on the history of this subculture, see Randolph Trumbach, "London's Sodomites: Homosexual Behavior and Western Culture in the 18th Century," *Journal of Social History* 11 (1977): 1–31; Rictor Norton, *Mother Clap's Molly House: The Gay Subculture in England 1700–1830* (London: Gay Men's Press, 1992).

110. MacCalman, *Radical Underworld*, pp. 34–41.

111. Crompton, *Byron and Greek Love*, pp. 269, 308.

112. William Benbow, *Crimes of the Clergy Laid Open; Or, The Pillars of Priestcraft Shaken* (London, 1823).

113. Crompton, *Byron and Greek Love*, pp. 301–5.

114. Hone, *For the Cause of Truth*, p. 232.

115. John Belchem, *Orator Hunt: Henry Hunt and Working-Class Radicalism* (Oxford: Oxford University Press, 1985), p. 196.

116. Polly Morris, "Defamation and Sexual Reputation in Somerset, 1733–1850," Ph.D. diss., University of Warwick, 1985), p. 701.

117. Ellen Moers, *The Dandy: Brummell to Beerbohm* (London: Secker and Warburg, 1960), p. 33; Davidoff and Hall, *Family Fortunes*, pp. 410–15.

118. The best-known dandy, Beau Brummell, opposed the Prince Regent, apparently on grounds of style and taste rather than politics. Samuel Tenenbaum, *The Incredible Beau Brummell* (South Brunswick: A. S. Barnes, 1967), p. 150.

119. *Black Dwarf* 2 (1818): 574.

120. Glasgow, Mitchell Library, C. D. Donald, *Collection of Glasgow Broadsides*, vol. 2, fol. 179, circa 1820.

121. *Spirit of the Union*, 18 Dec. 1819, p. 64. For the Volunteers, John Urie, *Autobiographical Reminiscences and Recollections of the Radical Years 1819–1820* (Glasgow, 1871), p. 82.

122. For this image, see Linda Colley, *Britons: Forging the Nation, 1707–1837* (New Haven: Yale University Press, 1992).

123. *Weavers Magazine and Literary Companion* 1 (1818): 96–97, 101; 2 (1819): 231. The "Hen-Pecked Dandy" was from a caricature of 1818: M. Dorothy George, *Catalogue of Personal and Political Satires* (London: British Museum, 1938), no. 13069.

124. Jonathan Fulcher, "Gender, Politics and Class in the Early Nineteenth-Century English Radical Movement," forthcoming in *Historical Research*. I thank Jonathan Fulcher for sending me this manuscript before its publication.

125. *Gorgon* 1 (1818): 109.

126. Fulcher, "Gender, Politics and Class." For Tocker, see also Ruth Frow and Edmund Frow, eds., *Political Women 1800–1850* (London: Pluto, 1989), pp. 1–12.

127. *Black Dwarf* 2 (1818): 704.

128. *Black Dwarf* 2 (1818): 655.

129. *Weavers Magazine and Literary Companion* 1 (1818): 96–97, 101; 2 (1819): 231.

130. *Black Dwarf* 2 (1818): 655.

131. MacCalman, *Radical Underworld*, p. 131.

132. *Black Dwarf* 1 (1817): 572.

CHAPTER NINE: A WIDER VISION OF COMMUNITY, 1815 – 1820

1. For a discussion of later implications of notions of the "People," see Patrick Joyce, *Visions of the People: Industrial England and the Question of Class, 1840–1914* (Cambridge: Cambridge University Press, 1991); for the "plebeian public," see Geoff Eley, "Rethinking the Political: Social History and Political Culture in Eighteenth and Nineteenth Century Britain," *Archiv für Sozialgeschichte* 32 (1981): 427–57.

2. Olivia Smith, *The Politics of Language 1791–1819* (Oxford: Oxford University Press, 1984).

3. Ruth L. Smith and Deborah M. Valenze, "Mutuality and Marginality: Liberal Moral Theory and Working-Class Women in Nineteenth Century England," *Signs* 13 (1988): 289; Catherine Hall, "The Tale of Samuel and Jemima: Gender and Working-Class Culture in Early Nineteenth-Century England," in her *White, Male and Middle Class: Explorations in Feminism and History* (Cambridge: Polity, 1992), p. 131; John Bohstedt, "Gender, Household, and Community Politics: Women in English Riots, 1790–1810," *Past and Present* 120 (1988): 112. Yet, as Bohstedt also points out, women participated in rioters as members of communities, not just as women, and most rioters were men.

4. For examples of rhetoric linking these concerns, see the 2 Oct. 1816 newspaper clipping from London, British Library, Place collection of clippings (hereafter Place Coll.), vol. 60. See also "Petitioning Weavers Defended in Remarks on the Manchester Police Meeting of Jan. 13, 1817," in London, Public Record Office (henceforth PRO), Home Office files (henceforth HO), 40/9/61.

5. The broadsheet "A Penny a Head! To an Old Townsman" (Manchester, 22 Oct. 1816) claimed that manufacturers, farmers, and tradesmen all suffered from the same causes, but "To the Manchester Tradesmen, and More Particularly the Borough Reeves and Counsellors" criticized tradesmen for refusing to support reform. Manchester, Manchester Public Library, Manchester collection of cuttings, BR F 942.7389.SC 13, fol. 29, 47.

6. *The People* 1 (1817): 1–10, in London, University of London, Goldsmiths Library.

7. Dorothy Thompson, "Women and Radical Politics: A Lost Dimension," in Juliet Mitchell and Ann Oakley, eds., *The Rights and Wrongs of Women* (Harmondsworth: Penguin, 1976), p. 115; Samuel Bamford, *Passages in the Life of a Radical* (Oxford: Oxford University Press, 1984 [1844]) p. 123.

8. Robert Glen, *Urban Workers in the Early Industrial Revolution* (London: Croom Helm, 1984), pp. 231–32; Ruth Frow and Edmund Frow, eds., *Political Women 1800–1850* (London: Pluto, 1989), pp. 16–28.

9. *Glasgow Herald*, 5 Nov. 1819.

10. Bohstedt, "Gender, Household, and Community Politics," p. 99.

11. Glen, *Urban Workers*, p. 110.

12. Rules of Manchester Friendly Sisters, Preston, Lancashire Record Office, Rules of Friendly Societies, QDS 1/5/7, 1813.

13. [Elizabeth Salt], *To All Persons Friendly to, and Desirous of Establishing a Union on Legal Principles, for the Purpose of Supporting the Innocent Mothers, Wives and Children of Such Persons as Are . . . Suffering Under a Want of Just Renumeration for Their Labor* (Manchester, [1818]). Signed by four other women as well.

14. Kenneth J. Logue, *Popular Disturbances in Scotland, 1780–1815* (Edinburgh: John Donald, 1979) p. 199; David Gilmour, *Reminiscences of the Pen'Folk: Paisley Weavers of Other Days* (2d ed. Paisley, 1879), pp. 11, 25, 77, 109, 59.

15. "Manchester Female Reformers' Address," in Frow and Frow, eds., *Political Women*, p. 27.

16. E. P. Thompson, *The Making of the English Working Class* (New York: Vintage, 1966), p. 740.

17. *Spirit of the Union*, 6 Nov. 1819, p. 13.

18. Charles Hutcheson, "Notes on Radicalism in the West of Scotland," diary, National Library of Scotland, MS 2773, fol. 8., 1817–1820.

19. John Urie, *Autobiographical Reminiscences and Recollections of the Radical Years 1819–1820* (Glasgow, 1871), p. 71.

20. John Mackinnon, autobiography (1859), in Glasgow, Strathclyde Regional Archives, TD 743/1, p. 54.

21. Bamford, *Passages*, pp. 146.

22. James Epstein, "Understanding the Cap of Liberty: Symbolic Practice and Social Conflict in Early Nineteenth Century England," *Past and Present* 122 (1989): 103.

23. Glen, *Urban Workers*, p. 232.

24. *Reformer*, 24 Nov. 1819, p. 25; *Glasgow Herald*, 29 Oct. 1819, was also critical.

25. "The Village Disputants," in *Cheap Repository Tracts Suited to the Present Times* (London, 1819), p. 114.

26. *Cobbett's Political Register* 35 (1819): 267.

27. M. Dorothy George, *Catalogue of Personal and Political Satires* (London: British Museum, 1938), no. 12263. See also Jonathan Fulcher, "Gender, Politics and Class in the Early Nineteenth-Century Radical Movement," forthcoming in *Historical Research*.

28. *Black Dwarf* 3 (1818): 510, 452.

29. "Address of the Manchester Female Reformers," "Address of the Blackburn Female Reformers," both 1819, in Frow and Frow, eds., *Political Women*, pp. 26, 23.

30. "Blackburn Female Reformers," *Black Dwarf* 8 (1819): 452.

31. For female sailors, see Anna Clark, "Womanhood and Manhood in the Transition from Plebeian to Working-Class Culture," Ph.D. diss., Rut-

gers University, 1987, ch. 5; Diane Dugaw, "Balladry's Female Warriors: Women, Warfare, and Disguise in the Eighteenth Century," *Eighteenth-Century Life* 9 (1985): 2.

32. E. P. Thompson, *Making*, p. 687; Dorothy Thompson, "Women and Radical Politics," p. 116.

33. Iain MacCalman, *Radical Underworld: Prophets, Revolutionaries and Pornographers in London, 1795–1840* (Cambridge: Cambridge University Press, 1988), p. 135.

34. There was an abortive uprising in Glasgow in 1820, probably incited by spies. However, there had been rumors of insurrection, including pikemaking and drilling, for several years previously. The fullest account is Peter Berresford Ellis and Seumas Mac a'Ghobhaiinn, *The Scottish Insurrection of 1820* (London: Pluto, 1989), which, however, overstates the nationalist element. The insurrection was accompanied by widespread strikes by weavers and cotton spinners: see autobiography of John Mackinnon, Glasgow, Strathclyde Regional Archives, manuscript TD 243/1, 1859, pp. 75–80.

35. John Stevenson, "The Queen Caroline Affair," in John Stevenson, ed., *London in the Age of Reform* (Oxford: Oxford University Press, 1977), p. 141; Iorwerth Prothero, *Artisans and Politics in Early Nineteenth Century London* (London: Methuen, 1981), pp. 141, 156.

36. See *Observations on the Various Accounts of a Late Family Difference in High Life* (London, 1796) for newspaper reports; Thea Holme, *Caroline: A Biography of Caroline of Brunswick* (London: Atheneum, 1979).

37. Extract from *Manchester Courier*, 7 Sept. 1820, and unlabeled cuttings from 17 July 1820, 18 Oct. 1820, and 3 April 1820, Manchester, Manchester Public Library, Manchester collection of cuttings, MPL q. 942.7389.M1, fols. 35, 51, 53, 41.

38. Letter from D. Grant, Bridgend, Perth, 13 July 1821, Edinburgh, Scottish Record Office, Scottish Home Office Papers, RH 2/4, vol. 138, fol. 268; see also PRO, HO, 102/33/393, 17 Nov. 1820, from J. T. Alston to Sidmouth on the riots in Glasgow when the divorce bill was abandoned. The weaver John Mackinnon remembered illuminating his windows for Caroline "with pleasure." "She reigned as Queen in the hearts of the people." Mackinnon autobiography, p. 75.

39. Patricia Hollis, *The Pauper Press: A Study of Working-Class Radicalism of the 1830s* (Oxford: Oxford University Press, 1970), ch. 1. For Manchester, a report of 18 Oct. 1820 recounted that a meeting in Ardwick, near Manchester, to celebrate the queen's "victory" when the bill of divorce was dropped was attended not only by the usual radicals but by a "numerous and respectable" audience of dissenters and those who opposed rates for constables and new parish churches. Manchester, Manchester Public Library, Manchester collection of cuttings, MPL q. 942.7389.M1, fol. 53.

40. Thomas Laqueur, "The Queen Caroline Affair: Politics as Art in the Reign of George IV, "*Journal of Modern History* 54 (1982): 420, opened up the possibilities for interpreting the Queen Caroline affair in the context of popular culture. See also Craig Calhoun, *The Question of Class Struggle: Social Foundations of Popular Radicalism During the Industrial Revolution* (Chicago: University of Chicago Press, 1982), p. 114. For a further development of my argument, see Anna Clark, "Queen Caroline and the Sexual Politics of Popular Culture in London, 1820," *Representations* 31 (1990): 47–68; Iain MacCalman, in his discussion of Caroline in *Radical Underworld*, comes to many of the same conclusions as I do and has augmented my argument.

41. As Linda Colley has demonstrated, in the 1790s royalists had encouraged the populace to think of the domestic bliss of George III and his queen as a pattern for English family life and to regard the pair as the mother and father of the nation. "The Apotheosis of George III: Loyalty, Royalty, and the British Nation, 1760–1820," *Past and Present* 102 (1984): 125.

42. Smith, *Politics of Language*, p. 166; MacCalman, *Radical Underworld*, p. 45.

43. Smith, *Politics of Language*, p. 160. Owenite Allen Davenport proudly remembered that songs of his composed to defend Caroline "were read and sung for months, from Mile End to Brandenburgh House [Caroline's residence]." *Life and Literary Pursuits of Allen Davenport* (Westport, Conn.: Garland, 1986 [1845]), 52. For T. J. Wooler's use of popular forms, see Richard Hendrix, "Popular Humor and the *Black Dwarf*," *Journal of British Studies* 16 (1976): 108–28.

44. Letter from George Wells of Weston, 16 Sept. 1830, PRO, HO, 40/14/273.

45. Prothero, *Artisans and Politics*, p. 136. *Black Dwarf* 5 (1820): 34; *Traveller*, 4 Sept. 1820; *The Queen's Address to the King* (London, 1820), p. 3; "Cotton Weavers," broadsheet PRO, HO, 40/16/388.

46. *Manchester Courier*, 7 Sept. 1820, in Manchester, Manchester Public Library, Manchester collection of cuttings, MPL q. 942.7389.M1, fol. 35. Similarly, the townspeople of Nottingham told her that "the addressers felt for the wrongs of the Queen as they felt for the various oppressions under which they themselves labored." *Black Dwarf* 5 (1820): 173; cuttings from November 1820 in London, British Library, Place Coll., Set 18; Address from 16 Aug. 1820, in *Selections from the Queen's Answers to Various Addresses* (London, 1821). See also "Cotton Weavers" broadsheet; "Answer to the Address from the Weavers of Spitalfields," *Englishman* (September 1820) in Place Coll., Set 18.

47. For multivalent symbolism of female figures, see Marina Warner, *Monuments and Maidens: The Allegory of the Female Form* (London: Picador, 1985, p. 36.

48. On manliness, see *Cobbett's Political Register* 37 (1820): 110; for

the king as a dandy, see William Hone, *The Political House That Jack Built* (London, 1819), p. 9; also "Rational Novel and Grand Amusement," broadsheet, PRO, HO, 40/14/205; for marrow bones and cleavers, as well as devastating insults against George IV's manhood and intelligence, see *A Peep at the P*V****; Or, Boiled Mutton with Caper Sauce at the Temple of Joss* (London, 1820), pp. 8–9. The motif of horns was originally used against Caroline, as in *Horns Forever! A Procession to Blackheath* (London, 1813), but obviously humiliated the king. See also a caricature by John Fairburn, *The King of the Cuckolds Crowned* (1820) in PRO, Treasury Solicitors' papers, 11/115/90. For the popular significance of horns, see J. P. Malcolm, *Anecdotes of the Manners and Customs of London During the Eighteenth Century* (2d ed. London, 1810), p. 205. For more on horns, see Laqueur, "Queen Caroline Affair," pp. 449–50.

49. Clark, "Womanhood and Manhood," p. 275; cf. [Vicesimus Knox], *The Spirit of Despotism* (5th ed. London, 1820), pp. 13, 36, 45; William Godwin, *A Defense of the Rockingham Party*, in Burton R. Pollin, ed., *Four Early Pamphlets* (Gainesville: Scholars' Fascimiles and Reprints, 1966 [1783]), p. 2.

50. In this way the meaning of the Queen Caroline affair was quite different for plebeians than it was for the middle class. Caroline's middle-class supporters viewed her as a symbol of purity, a means of repudiating aristocratic libertinism in favor of middle-class morality. Leonore Davidoff and Catherine Hall, *Family Fortunes: Men and Women of the English Middle Class* (London: Hutchinson, 1987), p. 120.

51. For plebeian sexual values, see John Gillis, *For Better, for Worse: British Marriages, 1600 to the Present* (Oxford: Oxford University Press, 1984), p. 111.

52. Iain MacCalman, "Unrespectable Radicalism: Infidels and Pornography in Early Nineteenth-Century London," *Past and Present* 104 (1984): 66–70. In 1819 the "violently radical and infidel" *Medusa* opposed Alderman Wood's drives against prostitution by arguing that men needed to have access to prostitutes since overtaxation prevented them from marrying. *Medusa*, 27 March 1819, p. 27.

53. London, British Library, Add. Mss. 35, 146, fol. 95, quoted in Prothero, *Artisans and Politics*, p. 137.

54. *Examiner*, 3 Sept. 1820, and *Champion*, 24 Sept. 1820, in Place Coll., Set 18.

55. *Republican* 2 (25 Feb. 1820): 18.

56. W. Bissell Pope, ed., *The Diary of Benjamin Robert Haydon*, 2 vols. (Cambridge: Harvard University Press, 1960), vol. 1, pp. 296–97, quoted in Stevenson, "Queen Caroline Affair," p. 128.

57. PRO, HO, 44/2/61, 156, 17 June 1820.

58. The caricature is in PRO, Treasury Solicitors' papers (henceforth TS) 11/115/326.

59. The caricature is also in PRO, TS 11/115/326. For instances of

women tossing ordinary wife-beaters, see *True Briton*, 15 April 1797, Place Coll., Set 18; *Trades Newspaper*, 4 Sept. 1825.

60. For background, see Hendrix, "Popular Humor," p. 130.

61. *Black Dwarf* 4 (1819): 800; 5 (1820): 149.

62. Oxford, Bodleian Library, John Johnson Collection of Ephemera, Queen Caroline Box. The "Petticoats Is Master" theme surfaced again in a song about the young Queen Victoria's marriage: Louis James, *The Print and the People* (London: Allen Lane, 1979), p. 340. Benbow also published a caricature, "The Filth & Lies of the Green Bag Visiting Their Parents; Or, A Dandy of Sixty Severely Beaten by His Wife," PRO, TS 11/115/21.

63. A spy reported on one 1816 sermon preached by "Johnson" at New Islington, Manchester, where he asked how rulers could riot in luxury while the poor starved, bringing up the parable of the rich man, the camel, and the needle. The king was a sinner and a robber, he claimed. Anonymous letter of 23 Dec. 1816, PRO, HO, 40/9/438–44.

64. *The Voice of Nature*, 1816, PRO, HO, 40/9/506.

65. Lord Henry Cockburn, *An Examination of the Trials for Sedition Which Have Hitherto Occurred in Scotland* (New York: Augustus M. Kelley, 1970 [1888]), vol. 2, pp. 192–203.

66. Report on the Middleton meeting, 16 Dec. 1816, PRO, HO, 40/9/434.

67. Anna Clark, "The Politics of Seduction in English Popular Culture, 1748–1848," in Jean Radford, ed., *The Progress of Romance: The Politics of Popular Fiction* (London: Routledge and Kegan Paul, 1986), pp. 50–51; Martha Vicinus, "Helpless and Unbefriended: Nineteenth Century Domestic Melodrama," *New Literary History* 13 (1981): 143; Peter Brooks, *The Melodramatic Imagination* (New Haven: Yale University Press, 1976), p. 44.

68. Anon., *The Secret Memoirs of a Prince; Or, A Peep Behind the Scenes* (London, 1816).

69. MacCalman, *Radical Underworld*, p. 164.

70. *Gorgon*, 25 July 1818, p. 94.

71. *Black Dwarf* 5 (1820): 177.

72. William Hone, *The King's Treatment of the Queen* (London, 1820), p. 2.

73. Hone, *King's Treatment of the Queen*, p. 3.

74. For the glorified termagant, see Anon., *The Loyal Man in the Moon* (London, 1820) reprinted in Edgell Rickword, ed., *Radical Squibs and Loyal Ripostes: Satirical Pamphlets of the Regency Period, 1819–1821* (Bath: Adams and Dart, 1971), 170.

75. *Cobbett's Political Register* 37 (1820): 289.

76. Laqueur, "Queen Caroline Affair," p. 442.

77. Returns of Friendly Societies, Lancaster and Chepstow, PP 1824, vol. 18.

78. Cutting of 20 Nov. 1820, in Manchester, Manchester Public Library, Manchester collection of cuttings, MPL q. 942.7389.M1, fol. 73.

79. *Traveller*, 12 Sept. 1820, in Place Coll., Set 18.

80. Oxford, Bodleian Library, John Johnson Collection of Ephemera, Queen Caroline Box.

81. 9 Nov. 1820, Place Coll., Set 18.

82. *Traveller*, 13 Sept. 1820, in Place Coll., Set 18.

83. Oxford, Bodleian Library, John Johnson Collection of Ephemera, Queen Caroline Box.

84. *Morning Post*, 4 and 7 Sept. 1820, Place Coll., Set 18; for another middle-class woman attacking Caroline, see *An Address to the Peers of England by an Englishwoman* (London, 1820).

85. John Fairburn also published a caricature entitled "Female Intrepidity" after Caroline refused to accept the king's offer of fifty thousand pounds if she would leave the country. PRO, TS 11/115/84.

86. Oxford, Bodleian Library, John Johnson Collection of Ephemera, Queen Caroline Box. For more examples of Carolinites as intrepid, see Robert Huish, *Memoirs of Her Late Majesty Caroline Queen of Great Britain*, 2 vols. (London, 1821), vol. 1, pp. 8, 11; *Morning Post*, 7 Sept. 1820. For female sailors, see Clark, "Womanhood and Manhood," ch. 5; Dugaw, "Balladry's Female Warriors," p. 2.

87. In Place Coll., Set 17.

88. PRO, TS 11/115/34.

89. Broadsheet in Oxford, Bodleian Library, John Johnson Collection of Ephemera, Queen Caroline Box; also printed in *Black Dwarf* 5 (1820): 63. For more on the theme of Caroline's search for knowledge, see James Mills, *A Letter to Lord Erskine Containing a Full and Complete Expose of the Foul, Detestable Though Impotent Conspiracy Against our Gracious Queen* (London, 1820) p. 39; even her biographer, usually scornful of Caroline, admits her travels were often motivated by her considerable intellectual interests; Holme, *Caroline*, pp. 155, 171.

90. *Black Dwarf* 6 (1821): 135.

91. Quoted in George Spater, *William Cobbett: The Poor Man's Friend* (Cambridge: Cambridge University Press, 1982), p. 401.

92. Quoted in MacCalman, *Radical Underworld*, p. 176.

93. "Oh My Mother!" caricature published by S. Fores, 23 Aug. 1820, Oxford, Bodleian Library, John Johnson Collection of Ephemera, Queen Caroline Box.

94. Resembling the "Republican Motherhood" of the American Revolution as defined by Linda K. Kerber, *Women of the Republic: Intellect and Ideology in Revolutionary America* (Chapel Hill: University of North Carolina Press, 1980).

95. *Black Dwarf* 5 (1821): 135.

PART THREE: DOMESTICITY AND THE MAKING OF
THE WORKING CLASS

1. E. P. Thompson, *The Making of the English Working Class* (New York: Vintage, 1966), p. 807.

2. Gareth Stedman Jones, *Languages of Class: Studies in English Working Class History 1832–1982* (Cambridge: Cambridge University Press, 1983), p. 57; Geoff Eley, "Edward Thompson, Social History, and Political Culture: The Making of a Working-Class Public, 1780–1850," in Harvey J. Kaye and Keith McClelland, eds., *E. P. Thompson: Critical Perspectives* (Philadelphia: Temple University Press, 1990), p. 29.

3. John Foster, *Class Struggles and the Industrial Revolution* (London: Weidenfeld and Nicolson, 1974). For a good survey of debates on class consciousness, see Theodore Koditschek, *Class Formation and Urban Industrial Society: Bradford, 1750–1850* (Cambridge: Cambridge University Press, 1990), pp. 1–5.

4. Barbara Taylor, *Eve and the New Jerusalem: Socialism and Feminism in the Nineteenth Century* (New York: Pantheon, 1983).

CHAPTER TEN: SEXUAL RADICALISM
AND THE PRESSURE OF POLITICS

1. Barbara Taylor, *Eve and the New Jerusalem: Socialism and Feminism in the Nineteenth Century* (New York: Pantheon, 1983), ch. 6.

2. James Kay-Shuttleworth, *The Moral and Physical Condition of the Working Classes Employed in the Cotton Manufacture in Manchester* (London, 1832), pp. 8, 62, analyzed in Frank Mort, *Dangerous Sexualities: Medico-Moral Politics in England Since 1830* (London: Routledge and Kegan Paul, 1987), p. 21.

3. Karl Polanyi, *The Great Transformation* (London: Rinehart, 1944), pp. 114, 123–25.

4. Thomas W. Laqueur, "Sexual Desire and the Market Economy During the Industrial Revolution," in Domna Stanton, ed., *Discourses of Sexuality: From Aristotle to AIDS* (Ann Arbor: University of Michigan Press, 1992), p. 185.

5. Boyd Hilton, *The Age of Atonement: The Influence of Evangelicalism on Social and Economic Thought* (Oxford: Oxford University Press, 1991), p. 78; Thomas Malthus, *An Essay on the Principle of Population* (London, 1803); H. L. Beales, "The Historical Context of the *Essay* on Population," in D. V. Glass, ed., *Introduction to Malthus* (London: Watts, 1953), p. 15.

6. Raymond G. Cowherd, *Political Economists and the English Poor Laws* (Athens: Ohio State University Press, 1977), p. 31.

7. Malthus, *Essay*, pp. 541–43.

8. Cowherd, *Political Economists,* p. 59.

9. Hilton, *Age of Atonement,* p. 82.

10. Iain MacCalman, *Radical Underworld: Prophets, Revolutionaries and Pornographers in London, 1795–1840* (Cambridge: Cambridge University Press, 1988), pp. 193, 208–12.

11. MacCalman, *Radical Underworld,* p. 216.

12. Francis Place, *Illustrations and Proofs of the Principles of Population,* ed. Norman Himes (London: George Allen and Unwin, 1980), p. 137.

13. Place, *Illustrations,* pp. 154, 175.

14. *Black Dwarf* 12 (1824): 17; *Trades' Newspaper,* 5 Nov. 1826; Angus McLaren, "Contraception and the Working Class: The Social Ideology of the English Birth Control Movement in Its Early Years," *Comparative Studies in Society and History* 18 (1976): 239.

15. For instance, the popular sex manual *Aristotle's Masterpiece* accepted sexual pleasure as necessary. There were many publications and versions, such as those of 1749, 1771, and 1812, all published in London. See Janet Blackman, "Popular Theories of Generation: The Evolution of *Aristotle's Works,*" in John Woodward and David Richards, eds., *Health Care and Popular Medicine in 19th Century England* (London: Croom Helm, 1977), p. 69; Thomas Laqueur, *Making Sex: Body and Gender from the Greeks to Freud* (Cambridge: Harvard University Press, 1990).

16. Place, *Illustrations,* p. 325.

17. London, British Library, Place Collection (henceforth Place Coll.), vol. 68, fol. 103, handbill by "Benjamin Aime."

18. Place, *Illustrations,* p. 309, letter to Charles McLaren, 25 Nov. 1830; p. 330, letter to J. Wade, 9 July 1833.

19. Angus McLaren, *Reproductive Rituals* (London: Methuen, 1984), pp. 66, 94.

20. Place Coll., vol. 68, fol. 88, letter to Carlile, 12 Aug. 1822.

21. Place Coll., vol. 68, fol. 103.

22. Place Coll., vol. 68, fol. 91, letter from Benjamin Base, 21 July 1825, and letter to Carlile, unsigned, 4 Nov. 1824.

23. London, University College, Bentham Papers, box 73, folder 11, fols. 9–10, 1770–1774; folder 72, fols. 189–91, 1778–1780; box 68, folder 3, fols. 13, 14, 1824; box 74a, folder 3, long discussion on homosexuality, 1816. See also discussion in Louis Crompton, *Byron and Greek Love: Homophobia in Nineteenth-Century England* (Berkeley: University of California Press, 1985), pp. 256–78.

24. Letter from Carlile to Place, 8 Aug. 1822, and response from Place to Carlile, 17 Aug. 1822, Place Coll., vol. 68, fol. 88.

25. E. P. Thompson, *The Making of the English Working Class* (New York: Vintage, 1966), p. 730; MacCalman, *Radical Underworld,* p. 193; Iain MacCalman, "Females, Feminism, and Free Love in an Early Nineteenth Century Radical Movement," *Labour History* 38 (1980): 1–25.

26. Taylor, *Eve and the New Jerusalem*, pp. 81–82.

27. McLaren, "Contraception and the Working Class," p. 244.

28. Richard Carlile, *Every Woman's Book, or What Is Love* (4th ed. London, 1826), pp. 12, 37.

29. Working people were especially sensitive to any manipulation of their bodies that seemed to reduce them to the level of animals, as in the controversy over the Bentham-inspired Anatomy Acts of 1832, which allowed doctors to dissect unclaimed bodies of paupers who died in workhouses. See Ruth Richardson, *Death, Dissection and the Destitute* (London: Penguin, 1989), p. 267. Thanks to James Epstein for this insight (personal communication).

30. *Trades' Newspaper*, 11 Sept. 1825.

31. Quoted in *Republican*, 21 April 1826.

32. William Cobbett, *Surplus Population and Poor Law Bill: A Comedy* (London, 1833).

33. For pornography and Carlile, see MacCalman, *Radical Underworld*, pp. 216–17; thanks to James Epstein for insight about the cover.

34. Place Coll., vol. 68, fol. 101, 7 Sept. 1823.

35. *Black Dwarf* 8 (1821): 881.

36. *Black Dwarf* 11 (1823): 407.

37. MacCalman, *Radical Underworld*, p. 206.

38. *Trades' Newspaper*, 28 Aug. 1825, p. 105. Although *homosexuality* was not a contemporary term, I am using it to indicate sexual and emotional relationships between men, since the contemporary term, *sodomy*, refers to sex acts only.

39. *Bull Dog* 3 (9 Sept. 1826): 87.

40. *Black Dwarf* 11 (1823): 780.

41. *Trades' Newspaper*, 31 July 1825, p. 33.

42. Taylor, *Eve and the New Jerusalem*, p. 20.

43. *Herald to the Trades' Advocate*, 30 Oct. 1830.

44. *Glasgow Evening Post*, 4 Aug. 1836.

45. Taylor, *Eve and the New Jerusalem*, p. 195.

46. *Glasgow Evening Post*, 4 Aug. 1836.

47. Taylor, *Eve and the New Jerusalem*, pp. 41–45, 199.

48. William Thompson, *Appeal of One Half the Human Race, Women, Against the Pretensions of the Other Half, Men, to Retain Them in Political, and Thence in Civil and Domestic Slavery* (London: Virago, 1983 [1825]); Taylor, *Eve and the New Jerusalem*, pp. 32–44.

49. *Isis*, 7 April 1832.

50. *Trades' Newspaper*, 4 Nov., 30 Dec. 1827.

51. *Pioneer*, 22 March 1834.

52. *Pioneer*, 31 May 1834.

53. *Crisis*, 24 Aug. 1834.

54. *Pioneer*, 12 April 1834.

55. *Pioneer*, 21 June 1834.

56. Taylor, *Eve and the New Jerusalem*, p. 100.

57. Taylor, *Eve and the New Jerusalem*, p. 169.

58. Taylor, *Eve and the New Jerusalem*, ch. 6.

59. Anthony Brundage, *The Making of the New Poor Law* (New Brunswick: Rutgers University Press, 1978), p. 20.

60. For varying influences of Evangelicals and Utilitarians, see Boyd Hilton, *Age of Atonement*, p. 345; Peter Dunkley, *The Crisis of the Old Poor Law in England 1795–1834* (New York: Garland, 1982); Peter Mandler, "The Making of the New Poor Law Redivivus," *Past and Present* 117 (1987): 131–57. The two most influential commissioners, Nassau Senior and Edwin Chadwick, denied the influence of Malthus over their conclusions. They had a more optimistic Benthamite view. See Beales, "Historical Context." An Evangelical bishop sat on the commission: Brundage, *Making of the New Poor Law*, p. 20.

61. Ursula Henriques, "Bastardy and the New Poor Law," *Past and Present* 37 (1967): 111–12.

62. Pat Thane, "Women and the Poor Law in Victorian and Edwardian England," *History Workshop Journal* 6 (1978), 29.

63. Nassau Senior, *Two Lectures on Population* (London, 1928), p. 52; S. Leon Levy, *Nassau W. Senior 1790–1864* (Newton Abbott: David and Charles, 1970), p. 197.

64. See Hilton, *Age of Atonement*, p. 89, generally on doctrine of atonement.

65. Hansard Parliamentary Debates, vol. 25, July 28, 1834, Lords, cols. 601–2, 1080–81.

66. Great Britain Commissioners for Inquiry into the Administration and Practical Operation of the Poor Laws, *Report* (London, 1834), p. 350, 346.

67. Great Britain Commissioners, *Report*, p. 59.

68. Dorothy Thompson notes that the London Working Men's Association, in order to gain support from the Philosophic Radicals, at first declined to oppose the New Poor Law, but soon changed its opinion. *The Chartists: Popular Politics in the Industrial Revolution* (Aldershot: Wildwood House, 1986), p. 32.

69. By not consulting the London radical press and by relying too heavily on Place and Lovett, Nicholas Edsall underestimates the prevalence of anti–Poor Law feeling in London. *The Anti–Poor Law Movement, 1834–1844* (Totowa, N.J.: Rowman and Littlefield, 1971), p. 137. See John Knott, *Popular Opposition to the 1834 New Poor Law* (London: Croom Helm, 1986), pp. 66, 70, 71. For meetings, see *Bronterre's National Reformer*, 28 Jan. 1837.

70. R. L. Hill, *Toryism and the People, 1832–1846* (London: Constable, 1929), p. 194.

71. Cecil Driver, *Tory Radical: The Life of Richard Oastler* (Oxford: Oxford University Press, 1946), p. 339. Cf. Edsall, *Anti-Poor Law Movement*, p. 13; Knott, *Popular Opposition*, p. 80; Stewart Angus Weaver, *John Fielden and the Politics of Popular Radicalism, 1834–1847* (Oxford: Oxford University Press, 1987), p. 163.

72. Address, 13 Oct. 1838, quoted in G. R. Wythen Baxter, *The Book of the Bastiles; Or, The History of the Working of the New Poor Law* (London, 1841), p. 394.

73. *Spitalfields Weavers' Journal* 8 (March 1838): 4.

74. Bentham questioned the condemnation of infanticide, again on the grounds of population control, but also out of sympathy for desperate unmarried mothers. London, University College, Bentham Papers, box 74a, folder 3, fols. 133–34, 1816. See Richardson, *Death, Dissection*, p. 268.

75. *Northern Lights* (Newcastle, 1841), selections from the *Northern Liberator*, Preface, and No. 37, 1 Dec. 1838.

76. *Address of the Nottingham Working Man's Association on the New Poor Laws* (Nottingham, 1838); Robert Blakey, *Cottage Politics; Or, Letters on the New Poor Law Bill* (London, 1837), p. 170.

77. *Weekly Dispatch*, 21 March 1836, quoted in Baxter, *Book of the Bastiles*, p. 131.

78. Rev. John Hart, *The Cause of the Widows and Fatherless Defended by the God of the Bible* (Manchester, [1839]), p. 24.

79. *Bronterre's National Reformer*, 28 Jan. 1837, p. 26.

80. Dorothy Thompson, "Women and Radical Politics: The Lost Dimension," in Juliet Mitchell and Ann Oakley, eds., *The Rights and Wrongs of Women* (Harmondsworth: Penguin, 1976), pp. 122–23.

81. *English Chartist Circular* 1 (1842): 49.

82. Richard Oastler, Letter to the Editor of the *Argus*, 8 Aug. 1834, in Oastler Collection, vol. 1, London, University of London, Goldsmiths Library, 578, no. 1.

83. Anti-Poor Law meeting at Bradford, 9 June 1838, unlabeled newspaper clipping, Place Coll., vol. 56.

84. *Nottingham Journal*, 28 July 1837.

85. Driver, *Tory Radical*, p. 348.

86. *London Dispatch*, 11 March 1838.

87. For Elland, see *London Dispatch*, 25 Feb. 1838. For accounts of other meetings and petitions which unfortunately do not quote from the petitions, see *Northern Star*, 3, 24 Feb. 1838; *Report on Public Petitions* (PP, House of Lords, 1841), nos. 1512, 1752.

88. *Northern Star*, 11 May 1839.

89. *Northern Star*, 10 Dec. 1842.

90. *English Chartist Circular* 1 (1841): 104.

91. Quoted in *London Dispatch*, 1 April 1838; Thompson, *The Chartists*, pp. 134, 183. Although Thompson does not allude directly to their separation, she reports that Hanson's husband, Abram, a radical shoe-

maker, was rather fond of the alehouse and that Elizabeth was described as a "Xantippe" to his Socrates.

92. J. R. Stephens, *The Political Preacher: An Appeal from the Pulpit on Behalf of the Poor* (London, 1839), pp. 18–19.

93. *Pioneer*, 28 June 1834.

94. *Poor Man's Guardian*, 24 May 1834.

95. *London Dispatch*, 18 Feb. 1838; *Cobbett's Political Register*, 23 Aug. 1834.

96. Cutting in Place Coll., Set 56, fol. 310, December 1838.

97. Samuel Roberts, *The Reverend Pye Smith and the New Poor Law* (Sheffield, 1839), pp. 24–29.

98. Baxter, *Book of the Bastiles*, pp. 4, 180.

99. John Gillis, "Servants, Sexual Relations, and the Risk of Illegitimacy in London, 1800–1900," *Feminist Studies* 5 (1979): 142–73; Anna Clark, *Women's Silence, Men's Violence: Sexual Assault in England, 1770–1845* (London: Pandora Press, 1987), chs. 5 and 6.

100. *Pioneer*, 28 June 1834.

101. For a fuller exposition of this argument, see Anna Clark, "The Politics of Seduction in English Popular Culture, 1748–1848," in Jean Radford, ed., *The Progress of Romance* (London: Routledge and Kegan Paul, 1986), p. 61.

102. Place Coll., vol. 56.

103. M. E. Rose, "The Anti-Poor Law Movement in the North of England," *Northern History* 1 (1966): 89–93; *London Dispatch*, 25 Feb. 1838, 20 June 1839; *Weekly Dispatch*, 14 March 1841.

CHAPTER ELEVEN: EQUALITY OR DOMESTICITY

1. Iorwerth Prothero, *Artisans and Politics in Early Nineteenth Century London* (London: Methuen, 1981), pp. 159–62.

2. Sally Alexander, "Women's Work in Nineteenth-Century London," in Juliet Mitchell and Ann Oakley, eds., *The Rights and Wrongs of Women* (Harmondsworth: Penguin, 1976), p. 78.

3. Jane Humphries, "Class Struggle and the Persistence of the Working Class Family," *Cambridge Journal of Economics* 1 (1977): 241–58.

4. Heidi Hartmann, "Capitalism, Patriarchy and Job Segregation by Sex," *Signs* 1 (1976): 137–69.

5. Sonya O. Rose, "Gender Antagonism and Class Conflict: Exclusionary Strategies of Male Trade Unionists in Nineteenth-Century Britain," *Social History* 13 (1988): 202; Sonya O. Rose, *Limited Livelihoods: Gender and Class in Nineteenth Century England* (Berkeley: University of California Press, 1992), pp. 17, 128–32. See also Harold Benenson, "Victorian Sexual Ideology and Marx's Theory of the Working Class," *International Labor and Working-class History* 25 (1984): 1–23.

6. Contra Wally Seccombe, who finds the breadwinner wage to be an

artisan tradition: "Patriarchy Stabilized: The Construction of the Male Breadwinner Wage Norm in Nineteenth-Century Britain," *Social History* 11 (1986): 65.

7. *Trades' Newspaper*, 30 Oct., 28 Aug. 1825.

8. *Trades' Newspaper*, 16 April 1826, quoted in Prothero, *Artisans and Politics*, p. 216.

9. *Trades' Newspaper*, 16 Oct. 1825.

10. *Trades' Newspaper*, 23 Oct. 1825; see also a letter from a journeyman silk weaver to the *Times*, 1 May 1825, in London, British Library, Place Coll., Set 16, vol. 2, fol. 59. Nancy Grey Osterud writes of similar efforts to restore women to subsidiary tasks in "Gender Divisions and the Organization of Work in the Leicestershire Hosiery Industry," in Angela V. John, ed., *Unequal Opportunities: Women's Employment in England, 1800–1918* (Oxford: Basil Blackwell, 1986), p. 53.

11. [Francis Place], *Handloom Weavers and Factory Workers: A Letter to James Turner, Cotton Spinner* (London, 1835).

12. For a discussion of theories of the labor market discussed in the labor press, see Noel W. Thompson, *The People's Science: The Popular Political Economy of Exploitation and Crisis, 1816–1834* (Cambridge: Cambridge University Press, 1984), p. 124.

13. Thompson, *People's Science*, p. 126.

14. Prothero, *Artisans and Politics*, pp. 226, 205; *Trades' Newspaper*, 28 Aug. 1825.

15. Prothero, *Artisans and Politics*, p. 216.

16. Thompson, *People's Science*, pp. 124–28.

17. Barbara Taylor, *Eve and the New Jerusalem: Socialism and Feminism in the Nineteenth Century* (New York: Pantheon, 1983), p. 90; Prothero, *Artisans and Politics*, p. 257.

18. Gregory Claeys, *Machinery, Money and the Millennium: From Moral Economy to Socialism, 1815–1860* (Princeton: Princeton University Press, 1987), p. 40.

19. *Pioneer*, 8 Feb. 1834, excerpted in Ruth Frow and Edmund Frow, eds., *Political Women 1800–1850* (London: Pluto, 1989), p. 142.

20. Taylor, *Eve and the New Jerusalem*, pp. 88–89.

21. Taylor, *Eve and the New Jerusalem*, p. 114.

22. *Manchester Guardian*, 1 Nov. 1834.

23. *Manchester Guardian*, 28 Aug. 1834.

24. *Pioneer*, 29 March 1834, in Frow and Frow, *Political Women*, p. 157.

25. *Pioneer*, 12 April 1834, in Frow and Frow, *Political Women*, p. 161.

26. *Pioneer*, 22 March 1834, in Frow and Frow, *Political Women*, p. 143.

27. *Pioneer*, 29 March 1834, in Frow and Frow, *Political Women*, p. 148.

28. *Pioneer*, 22 March 1834, in Frow and Frow, *Political Women*, p. 143.

29. *Pioneer*, 29 March 1834, in Frow and Frow, *Political Women*, p. 147.

30. *Manchester Guardian*, 3 May, 28 June 1834.

31. "Address of the Journeymen Tailors," in F. W. Galton, *Select Documents Illustrating the History of the Tailoring Trade* (London, 1896), p. 191.

32. John Rule, *The Laboring Classes in Early Industrial England 1750–1850* (London: Longman, 1986), p. 303.

33. R. G. Kirby and A. E. Musson, *The Voice of the People: John Doherty, 1798–1854, Trade Unionist, Radical, and Factory Reformer* (Manchester: Manchester University Press, 1975), pp. 277, 333.

34. *Herald of the Rights of Industry* 1 (1832): 1.

35. *Herald to the Trades' Advocate*, 13 Nov. 1830, p. 116; 20 Nov. 1830, p. 142.

36. *Reid's Glasgow Magazine* (June 1834): 7.

37. *Report of the Calico Printers Committee on Wages* (Manchester 1831), p. 2.

38. *Glasgow Courier*, 29 Jan. 1831.

39. *Herald to the Trades' Advocate*, 19 Feb. 1831. Edinburgh, Scottish Record Office (henceforth SRO), Prosecution papers, AD 14/14/16, declaration of James Millar, 1814, on calico printers combinations; London, London School of Economics, Webb Trade Union Collection, 3/A/XL, p. 246, quoting Cameron on Campsie; Elspeth King, *Scotland Sober and Free: The Temperance Movement 1829–1879* (Glasgow: Glasgow Museums and Art Galleries, 1979), p. 5.

40. *Glasgow Liberator*, 31 May 1834.

41. 1841 Glasgow census, district 206 (Maryhill), Glasgow, Mitchell Library (microfilm; henceforth 1841 census). Out of 138 households, 26 had daughters who were powerloom weavers, 11 had fathers who were agricultural laborers, and only one household included a calico printer.

42. SRO, Prosecution papers, AD 14/34/107, 12 Sept. 1834, precognition with reference to the information concerning the new printers at Dawsholms. For similar incidents of violence by women against strikebreakers, see *Glasgow Herald*, 28 Feb. 1834, reporting a printer's wife given six weeks' imprisonment for intimidating other women in Dumbartonshire; cf. *Glasgow Herald*, 7 Feb. 1834, and see SRO, Prosecution papers, AD 14/38/358, precognition against James Morrison and Robert Bruce, 24 Feb. 1834.

43. Alexander Thomson, *Random Notes and Rambling Recollections of Drydock* (Glasgow, 1895), pp. 23–26.

44. According to the *Oxford English Dictionary*, a loom semple, or simple, was probably a board to which weighted warp threads were strung.

45. SRO, Prosecution papers, AD 14/31/309, precognition from James Hewit, 16 Dec. 1830, and declarations from Cain and Quin. Account in *Thistle*, 18 Dec. 1830, and see *Cases in the Glasgow Circuit* (Glasgow,

1820), 18 Dec. 1830. Around this time, the female powerloom weavers demanded ten shillings and sixpence as the price of teaching a girl the trade, a price, as eleven-year-old Mary McDonald complained to the factory commissioners, her mother could not afford. Report of the Factory Commissioners on the Employment of Women and Children (henceforth 1833 Report), PP 1833, vol. 20, A1, p. 72, A2, pp. 51–54.

46. *Glasgow Evening Post*, 23 Feb. 1833.

47. *Glasgow Evening Post*, 30 March 1833.

48. *Glasgow Evening Post*, 23 March, 4 May 1833.

49. Robert Duncan, *Textiles and Toil: The Factory System and the Industrial Working Class in Early 19th Century Aberdeen* (Aberdeen: City Library, 1981), pp. 1–13.

50. *Tradesman*, 1 March 1834; cf. *Glasgow Herald*, 28 Feb. 1834; Duncan, *Textiles and Toil*, p. 42.

51. Aberdeen Female Operative Union, *Detailed Report of the Proceedings of the Operatives Since the Turn-Out* (Aberdeen, 1834), p. 11.

52. *Third Report of the Female Operative Union: Containing Remarks on the Improper Interference of the Clergy* . . . (Aberdeen, 1834), p. 12.

53. John Campbell, *History of the Rise and Progress of Power Loom Weavers and Vindication of the Character of Female Powerloom Weavers* (Rutherglen, 1878), pp. 15–17, letter from Kate Dalrymple. See also Jan Lambertz, "Sexual Harassment in the Nineteenth Century English Cotton Industry," *History Workshop Journal* 19 (1985): 29–61.

54. Campbell, *History of the Rise*, pp. 21–24.

55. Glasgow, Glasgow University, Ballads and broadsides, Mu.23.y.1, p. 123, dated 1840s or 1850s.

56. *Scots Times*, 14 Feb. 1840.

57. Manchester, Manchester Public Library, Ballad collection, p. 216. Probably printed around 1853–1854, since it alludes to the Lancashire turn-out.

58. *Glasgow Saturday Post*, 24 Sept. 1842; cf. *Glasgow Herald*, 19 Sept. 1842.

59. *Manchester Guardian*, 20 Nov. 27 Nov. 1824, quoted in Neil Smelser, *Social Change in the Industrial Revolution* (London: Routledge and Kegan Paul, 1959), p. 232.

60. Quoted in Kirby and Musson, *Voice of the People*, pp. 73, 109; For the 1829 strike, see Alan Fowler and Terry Wyke, *Barefoot Aristocrats: A History of the Amalgamated Association of Cotton Spinners* (Littleborough: George Kelsall, 1987), p. 27.

61. *A Report . . . on the Delegate Meeting of the Operative Spinners of England, Ireland and Scotland* (Manchester, 1829).

62. London, London School of Economics, Webb Trade Union Collec-

tion, Cotton Spinners, E/A/XXXIV, p. 257; Mary Freifeld, "Technological Change and the 'Self-Acting' Mule: A Study of Skill and the Sexual Division of Labor," *Social History* 11 (1986): 335; Per Bolin-Hart, *Work, Family and the State: Child Labor and the Organization of Production in the British Cotton Industry, 1780–1920* (Lund, Sweden: Lund University Press, 1989), p. 111.

63. *Poor Man's Advocate*, 4 Aug. 1832.

64. *Herald of the Rights of Industry* 1 (1834): 106.

65. Kirby and Musson, *Voice of the People*, p. 5.

66. Marc W. Steinberg, "Worthy of Hire: Discourse, Ideology and Collective Action Among English Working-Class Trade Groups, 1800–1830," Ph.D. diss., University of Michigan, 1989, vol. 2, p. 331.

67. *Manchester Guardian*, 17 May, 3 May, 16 Aug. 1834.

68. William Lazonick, "Industrial Relations and Technical Change: The Case of the Self-Acting Mule," *Cambridge Journal of Economics* 3 (1979): 239–40.

69. Freifeld, "Technological Change," pp. 338–39.

70. For a comparative study of mule spinners, see William Reddy, *The Rise of Market Culture: Textile Trades and French Culture 1750–1900* (Cambridge: Cambridge University Press, 1984), pp. 79–125.

71. H. A. Turner, *Trade Union Growth, Structure and Policy: A Comparative Study of the Cotton Trade Unions* (London: George Allen and Unwin, 1962), p. 97.

72. SRO, Prosecution papers, AD 14/38/502, 2d bundle, item 20, 2 Nov. 1837, James Moat to Mr. Salmon, remembering past events.

73. W. Hamish Fraser, *Conflict and Class: Scottish Workers 1700–1838* (Edinburgh: John Donald, 1980), p. 160; *Herald to the Trades' Advocate*, 30 Oct. 1830, p. 82, letter by Adam Sydsdorff on the dispute over whether members of cotton spinners union could remain members of the Baptist Church, Kilbarchan. They had been expelled from the chapel but wished to be readmitted.

74. *Herald to the Trades' Advocate*, 12 March 1831, p. 397.

75. Report from Select Committee on Bill to Regulate Labor of Children in Mills and Factories (henceforth 1831–1832 Report), PP 1831–1832, vol. 15, p. 239.

76. 1833 Report, A2, p. 68.

77. 1833 Report, p. 77.

78. 1833 Report, p. 77; James M'Nish chairs meeting for the factory acts of cotton spinners and threatens a strike if the acts are not passed: *Glasgow Evening Post*, 20 April 1833.

79. *Glasgow Evening Post*, 29 June 1833; 1833 Report, p. 84, report of David Sloan, manager; Mariana Valverde, "Giving the Female a Domestic

Turn: The Social, Legal and Moral Regulation of Women's Work in British Cotton Mills, 1820–1850," *Journal of Social History* 21 (1988): 623.

80. E. J. Tufnell, *Character, Object, and Effects of Trade Unionism, with Some Remarks on the Law Concerning Them* (London, 1834), p. 22.

81. SRO, Prosecution papers, AD 14/39/460, precognition against Thomas Hunter, 1837, and declaration of James Moat, recalling events of 1833.

82. 1841 census.

83. 1841 Glasgow census, District 156, Charles Street, out of 86 households. R. A. Cage, *The Working Class in Glasgow 1750–1914* (London: Croom Helm, 1987), pp. 17, 41.

84. 1833 Report, p. 86.

85. 1833 Report, A1, pp. 84–85; *Glasgow Evening Post*, 23 March 1833.

86. 1841 Glasgow census, Charles Street, 1841.

87. First Report of the Select Committee on Combinations of Workmen, PP 1837–1838, vol 8, pp. 286–97.

88. *Glasgow Evening Post*, 23 March 1833.

89. Eleanor Gordon, *Women and the Labor Movement in Scotland 1850–1914* (Oxford: Oxford University Press, 1991), p. 46. I am grateful to Eleanor Gordon for allowing me to see her book before publication. Her discussion of the mule spinner controversy is quite insightful.

90. Report of the Select Committee on Combinations, p. 29.

91. 1833 Report, A1, pp. 84–85.

92. 1833 Report, A1, pp. 65–66.

93. Fraser, *Conflict and Class*, p. 91.

94. SRO, Prosecution papers, AD 14/38/502, 1st bundle, precognition of Archibald Alison, 1837.

95. SRO, Prosecution papers, AD 14/39/460, declaration of Donald McMurphy, 8 July 1837; AD 14/39/460, precognition against Thomas Hunter, part 3, declaration of James Smart, November 1837, p. 446; *Trial of the Glasgow Cotton Spinners* (Edinburgh, 1838), p. 70, testimony of police superintendent.

96. *Glasgow Evening Post*, 27 Jan. 1838, meeting of working men of Glasgow to respond to Sheriff's Alison's portrayal of cotton spinners' conspiracy. Turner, *Trade Union Growth*, p. 97.

97. Fraser, *Conflict and Class*, p. 94.

98. *Monthly Liberator*, 13 June 1838.

99. *Glasgow Evening Post*, 28 Oct. 1837, meeting of operatives; "Proclamation to the Cotton Spinners of Britain and Ireland," 7 Sept. 1837, London, British Library, Place Coll., Set 52.

100. SRO, Prosecution papers, AD 14/39/460, precognition against Thomas Hunter, part 3, 14 Nov. 1837, pp. 19–21.

101. This speech was investigated as seditious. SRO, Scottish Home Office Papers, RH 2/4, vol. 168, fol. 125, *New Liberator*, 6 Jan. 1838.

102. Fraser, *Conflict and Class*, p. 97; Gordon, *Women and the Labor Movement*, pp. 46–47.

103. Robert Gray, "The Languages of Factory Reform in Britain, c. 1830–1860," in Patrick Joyce, ed., *The Historical Meanings of Work* (Cambridge: Cambridge University Press, 1987), p. 146.

104. *Report of a Most Important Meeting of the Operatives of Glasgow upon the Ten Hours Bill . . . from the Liberator* (Bradford, 1833).

105. Claeys, *Machinery*, p. 133.

106. Kirkman Finley, Esq., *Letter to the Right Hon. Lord Ashley on the Cotton Factory System and Ten Hours Factory Bill* (Glasgow, 1833), p. 5.

107. R. H. Greg, *The Factory Question* (London, 1837), p. 32.

108. Whigs often tried to impart such ideas to working-class men in Mechanics' Institutes, especially in Scotland, and through such journals as *Chambers' Edinburgh Magazine*. They told workmen to improve their morals and educate themselves rather than relying on strikes and trade unionism. A. Tyrrell, "Political Economy, Whiggism and the Education of Working-Class Adults in Scotland, 1817–1840," *Scottish Historical Review* 48 (1969): 160.

109. Nassau Senior, *Three Lectures on the Rate of Wages* (London, 1830), p. 8.

110. W. R. Greg, *An Enquiry into the State of the Manufacturing Population and the Causes and Cures of the Evils Therein* (London, 1831), pp. 16, 35. A later but similar version focused on health is Ralph Barnes Grindrod, *The Wrongs of Our Youth: An Essay on the Evils of the Late Hour System* (Manchester, 1843), p. 75.

111. 29 Jan. 1832, quoted in Ivy Pinchbeck, *Women Workers and the Industrial Revolution, 1750–1850* (London: Virago, 1981 [1830]), p. 199.

112. James Kay-Shuttleworth, *The Moral and Physical Condition of the Working Classes Employed in the Cotton Manufacture in Manchester* (London, 1832), p. 26.

113. Greg, *Factory Question*, p. 35.

114. *Scots Times*, 28 Feb. 1832.

115. Cecil Driver, *Tory Radical: The Life of Richard Oastler* (Oxford: Oxford University Press, 1946), p. 227; Frank Mort, *Dangerous Sexualities: Medico-Moral Politics in England Since 1830* (London: Routledge and Kegan Paul, 1987), p. 47.

116. Driver, *Tory Radical*, p. 127.

117. Leonore Davidoff, Jean L'Esperance, and Howard Newby, "Landscape with Figures: Home and Community in English Society," in Mitchell and Oakley, eds., *Rights and Wrongs of Women*, p. 152, on Cobbett, who was very similar to Oastler.

118. Richard Oastler, *Eight Letters to the Duke of Wellington* ... (London, 1835), p. 130, in *Richard Oastler, King of Factory Children: Six Pamphlets* (New York: Arno Press, 1972).

119. 1833 Report, pp. 423–25; 1831–1832 Report, p. 413.

120. 1831–1832 Report, p. 48.

121. 1831–1832 Report, p. 99; Abraham Wildman, a Methodist Sunday school teacher from Keighley, made similar comments, p. 154.

122. 1833 Report, C1, p. 87; 1831–1832 Report, p. 545. For school, see pp. 48, 245.

123. 1833 Report, A1, p. 36 (Lawrence Davidson).

124. *Glasgow Evening Post*, 28 Feb. 1833.

125. *Valedictory Address to the Readers of the Herald to the Trades' Advocate* (Glasgow, 1831), p. 15; see also *Herald to the Trades' Advocate*, 23 April 1831; *Voice of the People*, 5 Feb. 1831, letter from William Longson.

126. *Times*, 19 April 1834, quoted in Jill Liddington and Jill Norris, *One Hand Tied Behind Us: The Rise of the Women's Suffrage Movement* (London: Virago, 1978), p. 62.

127. *British Laborers' Protector, and Factory Child's Friend*, 5 Oct. 1832, p. 31.

128. 1833 Report, A1, pp. 62, 81, 95, and A2, pp. 11, 38, 44; Carol Morgan, "Women, Work and Consciousness in the Mid-Nineteenth Century English Cotton Industry," *Social History* 17 (1992): 29.

129. James Vernon, *Politics and the People: A Study in English Political Culture c. 1815–1867* (Cambridge: Cambridge University Press, 1993), p. 300. Thanks are due to James Vernon for allowing me to see this manuscript before publication.

130. Driver, *Tory Radical*, p. 261.

131. Oastler, *Eight Letters*, p. 130.

CHAPTER TWELVE: CHARTISM

1. Dorothy Thompson, *The Chartists: Popular Politics in the Industrial Revolution* (Aldershot: Wildwood House, 1986), is a good overview.

2. "Petition Adopted at the Crown and Anchor Meeting," 1838, in Dorothy Thompson, ed., *The Early Chartists* (Columbia: University of

South Carolina Press, 1971), p. 62; James Epstein, "The Constitutional Idiom: Radical Reasoning, Rhetoric, and Action in Early Nineteenth Century England," *Journal of Social History* 23 (1990): 565.

3. Joan Scott, "On Language, Gender and Working-Class History," in her *Gender and the Politics of History* (New York: Columbia University Press, 1988), p. 53.

4. Sally Alexander, "Women, Class and Sexual Difference in the 1830s and the 1840s: Some Reflections on the Writing of a Feminist History," *History Workshop Journal* 17 (1984): 125–49. My analysis owes a great deal to Sally Alexander for her recognition of sexual antagonism in the working class. See also Ruth L. Smith and Deborah M. Valenze, "Mutuality and Marginality: Liberal Moral Theory and Working-Class Women in Nineteenth Century England," *Signs* 13 (1988): 288.

5. Benedict Anderson, *Imagined Communities* (London: Verso, 1983), applying his discussion of nationalism to class. Gareth Stedman Jones, "Rethinking Chartism," in his *Languages of Class: Studies in English Working Class History 1832–1982* (Cambridge: Cambridge University Press, 1983), pp. 90–95. For a recent critique of his methodology, see David Mayfield and Susan Thorne, "Social History and Its Discontents: Gareth Stedman Jones and the Politics of Language," *Social History* 17 (1992): 165–69. See also Theodore Koditschek, *Class Formation and Urban Industrial Society: Bradford, 1750–1850* (Cambridge: Cambridge University Press, 1990), pp. 484–93. Even if Chartists did not use socialist rhetoric, they defined themselves as a working-class movement. See James Epstein, "Rethinking the Categories of Working-Class History," *Labour/Le Travailleur* 18 (1986): 202; Neville Kirk, "In Defense of Class: A Critique of Gareth Stedman Jones," *International Review of Social History* 32 (1987): 5; John Belchem, "Radical Language and Ideology in Early Nineteenth-Century England: The Challenge of the Platform," *Albion* 20 (1988): 258. Paul Pickering, "Class Without Words: Symbolic Communication in the Chartist Movement," *Past and Present* 112 (1986): 160, points out that Chartist leader Feargus O'Connor, while upper-class in origin, wore a fustian jacket to symbolize his identification with the workers. For a biography of O'Connor, see James Epstein, *The Lion of Freedom: Feargus O'Connor and the Chartist Movement* (London: Croom Helm, 1982), p. 239.

6. For the working-class public sphere, see Geoff Eley, "Rethinking the Political: Social History and Political Culture in Eighteenth and Nineteenth Century Britain," *Archiv für Sozialgeschischte* 32 (1981): 451.

7. James Epstein, "Some Organisational and Cultural Aspects of the Chartist Movement in Nottingham," in James Epstein and Dorothy Thompson, eds., *The Chartist Experience: Studies in Working-Class Radicalism and Culture, 1830–1860* (London: Macmillan, 1982), pp. 221–68; James D. Young, *The Rousing of the Scottish Working Class* (London: Croom Helm, 1979), p. 73.

8. Archibald Alison, "The Chartists and Universal Suffrage," *Blackwood's Edinburgh Magazine* 187 (1839): 296–97.

9. Belchem, "Radical Language and Ideology," p. 257; Robert Gray, "The Deconstructing of the English Working Class," *Social History* 11 (1986): 363–73; James Epstein, "Understanding the Cap of Liberty: Symbolic Practice and Social Conflict in Early Nineteenth Century England," *Past and Present* 122 (1989): 75–118; Koditschek, *Class Formation*, p. 503; Eileen Yeo, "Christianity and Chartist Struggle," *Past and Present* 91 (1981): 109–39; and Eileen Yeo, "Chartist Religious Belief and the Theology of Liberation," in James Obelkevich, Lyndal Roper, and Raphael Samuel, eds., *Disciplines of Faith: Studies in Religion, Politics and Patriarchy* (London: Routledge and Kegan Paul, 1987), pp. 410–20.

10. Nancy Armstrong, *Desire and Domestic Fiction: A Political History of the Novel* (Oxford: Oxford University Press, 1987), p. 252.

11. This plot acquired radical connotations in Jacobin novels of the 1790s: see Marilyn Butler, *Jane Austen and the War of Ideas* (Oxford: Clarendon Press, 1975), pp. 29–50, and Gary Kelly, *The English Jacobin Novel* (Oxford: Clarendon Press, 1976). For melodrama, which originated as a theatrical form during the French Revolution and then became a working-class popular genre in Great Britain, see James C. Smith, *Victorian Melodrama* (London: J. M. Dent, 1976); Louis James, *Fiction for the Working Man* (Harmondsworth: Penguin, 1974), pp. 171–72; Peter Brooks, *The Melodramatic Imagination* (New Haven: Yale University Press, 1976), p. 44; Martha Vicinus, "Helpless and Unbefriended: Nineteenth Century Domestic Melodrama," *New Literary History* 13 (1981): 143; Anna Clark, "The Politics of Seduction in English Popular Culture, 1784–1848," in Jean Radford, ed., *The Progress of Romance* (London: Routledge and Kegan Paul, 1986), pp. 47–72.

12. Gerald Massey, *Poems and Ballads* (New York, 1854), p. 147. Another classic narrative is found in a tale, "English Life," from the *Northern Star* of 5 June 1847, in which a happy family is evicted from a cottage and must move to a factory town. The son is crippled in the army, and the beautiful daughter is seduced by the factory master, deserted, becomes a prostitute, and dies.

13. Massey, *Poems and Ballads*, p. 76. For other examples of golden age rhetoric, see *Northern Star*, 16 May 1840, letter by Feargus O'Connor; 13 June 1840, address from J. Lomax; 9 Jan. 1841, poem by William Hick, "My Five-Acre Cottage That Stands by the Green."

14. For examples of this rhetoric, see *Northern Star*, 7 April 1838; *Scots Times*, 27 Jan. 1841; *Bronterre's National Reformer*, 21 Jan. 1837; *McDouall's Journal*, 3 April 1841, quoted in Kirk, "In Defense of Class," p. 21; and see David Jones, *Chartism and the Chartists* (New York: St. Martin's Press, 1975), p. 113 for this motif in Chartist poetry.

15. On domesticity as independence, see Deborah Valenze, *Prophetic*

Sons and Daughters: Female Preaching and Popular Religion in Industrial England (Princeton: Princeton University Press, 1985), p. 211.

16. *English Chartist Circular* 2 (1842): 5.

17. Victor Turner, "Social Dramas and Stories About Them," *Critical Inquiry* 7 (1980): 144. Turner notes that in social dramas, unlike fiction, the narrative structure is implicit and often alluded to in terms of metaphorical threads which connect the drama with the social situation. For more examples of melodramatic rhetoric, see *Southern Star*, 19 Jan. 1840, and the similar motif in the anonymous poem *The Doom of Toil* (Sunderland, 1841), p. 10. Cf. the contrast of upper-class immorality with the virtue of the poor in *Northern Star*, 27 Jan. 1838, speech by Mr. William Thornton at Halifax anti–Poor Law meeting. Also *Northern Star*, 6 Oct. 1838; a similar speech in *Northern Star*, 29 Sept. 1838, by Mr Beal, at a Sheffield demonstration; and an editorial in the *Northern Star*, 17 Feb. 1838.

18. *Northern Star*, 1 June 1839.

19. *Northern Star*, 13 Oct. 1838.

20. *Scottish Patriot*, 14 Dec. 1839.

21. James Vernon, *Politics and the People: A Study in English Political Culture 1815–1867* (Cambridge: Cambridge University Press, 1993), p. 389. Thanks are due to James Vernon for allowing me to see this before publication.

22. Thomas Ainge Devyr, *The Odd Book of the 19th Century; Or, Chivalry in Modern Days* (New York, 1882), p. 40. Devyr emigrated to America in 1840 to escape prosecution for Chartist activity: Thompson, *Chartists*, p. 271.

23. "Autobiography," in *Robert Lowery, Radical and Chartist*, ed. Brian Harrison and Patricia Hollis (London: Europa Publications, 1979), p. 141.

24. *Scottish Patriot*, 14 Dec. 1839.

25. *Chartist Circular*, 18 Sept. 1841, p. 433.

26. London, British Library, Place Coll., Set 56, July–December 1838.

27. Thompson, *Chartists*, p. 144.

28. O'Connor and Ernest Jones, eds., *The Labourer* (Manchester, 1847), vol. 1, pp. 44–49.

29. John Foster, *Class Struggles and the Industrial Revolution* (New York: St. Martin's Press, 1974), p. 221, tends to portray temperance as part of "liberalization" and the co-optation of the working class. For another view, see Brian Harrison, "Teetotal Chartism," *History* 58 (1973): 193–203. Temperance had been advocated in the 1820s for political reasons by trade unionist John Gast; see Iorwerth Prothero, *Artisans and Politics in Early Nineteenth Century London* (London: Methuen, 1981), p. 216.

30. *Trades' Newspaper*, 30 Oct., 28 Aug. 1825, on domestic mistreatment.

31. Harrison, "Teetotal Chartism," p. 194.

32. *Carlisle Journal*, 6 Oct. 1838, quoted in *Robert Lowery*, p. 33.

33. *Lifeboat*, 9 Dec. 1843 (Westport, Ct.: Garland, 1972).

34. Renee Sofer, "Attitudes and Allegiances in the Unskilled North," *International Review of Social History* 10 (1965): 429–54.

35. This originated with R. G. Gammage, *History of the Chartist Movement 1837–1854* (New York; Augustus M. Kelley, 1969 [1894]); J. T. Ward, *Chartism* (New York: Harper and Row, 1973), pp. 111–42.

36. Clive Behagg, *Politics and Production in the Early Nineteenth Century* (London: Routledge, 1990), p. 212; Thompson, *Chartists*, p. 58; Epstein, *Lion of Freedom*, p. 239. Robert Sykes points out that there was an overlap in tactics between the two wings. "Physical Force Chartism: The Cotton District and the Chartist Crisis of 1839," *International Review of Social History* 30 (1985): 211.

37. For evidence of this debate, see *Northern Star*, 27 Jan., 24 March, 23 June, 7 July, 28 Sept., 13 Oct., 3 Nov., 17 Nov., 22 Dec., 29 Dec. 1838. While the Scottish Chartist movement has often been described as inclining more toward moral force, other historians have pointed out that proponents of physical force were strong, especially in Glasgow. Leslie C. Wright, *Scottish Chartism* (Edinburgh: Oliver and Boyd, 1953), p. 45; Alexander Wilson, *The Chartist Movement in Scotland* (New York: Augustus M. Kelley, 1970), p. 101; Young, *Rousing*, p. 82.

38. Tony Clarke, "Early Chartism in Scotland: A Moral Force Movement?" in T. M. Devine, ed., *Conflict and Stability in Scottish Society 1700–1850* (Edinburgh: John Donald, 1990), pp. 111, 114. In another book, Clarke points out that this debate was also complicated by ethnic divisions, for Daniel O'Connell, who opposed physical-force Chartism, won the allegiance of the Glasgow Irish, who often violently disrupted O'Connorite meetings that refused to denounce physical force: *Scottish Capitalism: Class, State and Nation from Before the Union to the Present* (London: Lawrence and Wishart, 1980), p. 205.

39. *Address and Rules of the Working Men's Association, for Benefitting Politically, Socially, and Morally the Useful Classes* (London, 1836), p. 2.

40. William Lovett, *Social and Political Morality* (London, 1853), p. 83.

41. Edward Swaine, *The Political Franchise a Public Trust, Demanding an Intelligent and Virtuous Care for the Public Good* (London, n.d.), p. 28.

42. This form of rough yet radical manhood is discussed by Iain MacCalman in *Radical Underworld: Prophets, Revolutionaries and Pornographers in London, 1795–1840* (Cambridge: Cambridge University Press, 1988), p. 149.

43. David Goodway, *London Chartism* (Cambridge: Cambridge University Press, 1982), p. 45; Christopher Godfrey, *Chartist Lives: The Anatomy of a Working-Class Movement* (Westport, Ct.: Garland, 1987),

p. 119, for disruption of an anti–Poor Law meeting; and *Glasgow Constitutional*, 7 Nov. 1840, for disruption of a meeting about a house of refuge; 5 Dec. 1840, for a meeting to celebrate the queen's birthday; 25 Dec. 1839, interrupting an anti–Corn Law meeting.

44. *London Democrat*, 11 May 1839.

45. *Northern Star*, 16 Oct., 22 Dec. 1838.

46. Goodway, *London Chartism*, p. 25; Jennifer Bennett, "The London Democratic Association 1837–41: A Study in London Radicalism," in Epstein and Thompson, eds., *Chartist Experience*, pp. 87–119.

47. *Northern Star*, 1 May 1841, in the context of Lovett and Collins's "New Move," which broke away from Feargus O'Connor and the National Charter Association.

48. Speech at Wigan Chartist meeting reported in *Northern Star*, 17 Nov. 1838; see also Jones, *Chartism*, p. 115.

49. *Northern Star*, 1 June 1839.

50. *Northern Star*, 18 May 1839. While Stephens's support of universal suffrage was ephemeral, fading by 1840, he had very strong support among the Chartists in the first years of Chartism. Thompson, *Chartists*, p. 265.

51. *Northern Star*, 18 May 1839.

52. *English Chartist Circular* 1 (1841): 166.

53. Goodway, *London Chartism*, p. 16.

54. *Northern Star*, 11 May 1839.

55. Sykes, "Physical Force Chartism," p. 213; Goodway, *London Chartism*, p. 34.

56. Thompson, *Chartists*, p. 141; also Wright, *Scottish Chartism*, pp. 105, 148.

57. *Scots Times*, 11 Nov. 1840.

58. *True Scotsman*, 28 Nov. 1840.

59. Alexander Somerville, *Dissuasive Warnings to the People on Street Warfare* (London, 1839), letter 5, p. 5.

60. Thomas Milton Kremitz, "Approaches to the Chartist Movement: Feargus O'Connor and Chartist Strategy," *Albion* 5 (1973): 57–73; William Henry Maehl, Jr., "The Dynamics of Violence in Chartism: A Case Study in North-East England," *Albion* 7 (1975): 102.

61. Thompson, *Chartists*, p. 259.

62. *Scottish Patriot*, 14 Sept. 1839.

63. *Northern Star*, 9 June 1838.

64. *Northern Star*, 10 Dec. 1842.

65. Wright, *Scottish Chartism*, p. 43.

66. Jutta Schwarzkopf, *Women in the Chartist Movement* (London: Macmillan, 1991), p. 199; for Scotland, Wilson, *Chartist Movement*, p. 273, lists twenty; cf., for Barrhead and Paisley, *Scottish Patriot*, 27 July 1839; for Campsie, *Scots Times*, 27 Jan. 1841; for Dundee, *True Scotsman*, 8 Feb. 1840. Also see David Jones, "Women and Chartism," *History* 68

(1983): 1–21; Jutta Schwarzkopf, "The Sexual Division in the Chartist Family," *British Society for the Study of Labor History Bulletin* 54 (1989): 12–14.

67. Schwarzkopf, *Women in the Chartist Movement*, pp. 80–81; Thompson, *Chartists*, p. 62.

68. Koditschek, *Class Formation*, p. 504.

69. Wilson, *Chartist Movement*, p. 273.

70. Robert Duncan, "Artisans and Proletarians: Chartism and Working-Class Allegiance in Aberdeen, 1838–42," *Northern Scotland* 4 (1981): 56.

71. *Scottish Patriot*, 19 Oct. 1839.

72. Thompson, *Chartists*, p. 144.

73. Catherine Hall, "The Tale of Samuel and Jemima: Gender and Working-Class Culture in Early Nineteenth-Century England," in her *White, Male and Middle Class: Explorations in Feminism and History* (Cambridge: Polity, 1992), pp. 124–50.

74. This vision is similar to that of the "republican motherhood" of the American Revolution. See Linda K. Kerber, *Women of the Republic: Intellect and Ideology in Revolutionary America* (Chapel Hill: University of North Carolina Press, 1980).

75. *Birmingham Journal*, 18 July 1838, in London, British Library, Place Coll., Set 56, July–December 1838; for very similar sentiments see also the London Female Democratic Association, reported in the *Northern Star*, 11 May 1839.

76. *Northern Star*, 24 July 1841, quoted in Ruth Frow and Edmund Frow, eds., *Political Women 1800–1850* (London: Pluto, 1989), pp. 199–200.

77. *Northern Star*, 16 Feb. 1839.

78. *Northern Star*, 2 Feb. 1839.

79. The pages of the *National Association Gazette* contained both such bitter feminism and celebrations of domesticity, sometimes in the same article. Cf. 30 April and 5 Feb. 1842.

80. *True Scotsman*, 20 Oct. 1839.

81. *Scottish Patriot*, 21 Dec. 1839; cf. the similar sentiment in *Scots Times*, 13 March 1840.

82. Epstein, "Understanding the Cap of Liberty," p. 103.

83. *Scots Times*, 1 May 1840.

84. *Scots Times*, 18 Nov. 1840.

85. *Scots Times*, 30 Dec. 1840.

86. *True Scotsman*, 22 Dec. 1838.

87. Jones, "Women and Chartism," pp. 2–3; Thompson, *Chartists*, p. 126; Schwarzkopf, *Women in the Chartist Movement*, p. 59.

88. *Northern Star*, 23 June 1838.

89. Quoted in Schwarzkopf, *Women in the Chartist Movement*, p. 62; Thompson, *Chartists*, p. 124.

90. *Northern Star*, 2 Feb. 1839.

91. R. J. Richardson, *The Rights of Woman* (1840), in Thompson, ed., *Early Chartists*, pp. 115–27; cf. Barbara Taylor, *Eve and the New Jerusalem: Socialism and Feminism in the Nineteenth Century* (New York: Pantheon, 1983), p. 269.

92. *London Dispatch,* 11 Feb. 1838.

93. Schwarzkopf, *Women in the Chartist Movement,* p. 63.

94. Taylor, *Eve and the New Jerusalem,* p. 270.

95. *Northern Star,* 26 Oct. 1846, 30 Oct. 1847.

96. Quoted in *National Association Gazette,* 30 April 1842, p. 141.

97. *Scottish Patriot,* 3 Aug. 1839. The *Southern Star,* 19 Jan. 1840, quoted Cobbett as saying that women's feminine duties disqualified them.

98. See ch. 8, above.

99. *Northern Star,* 19 Sept. 1840, 2 Jan. 1841.

100. Quoted (in all capital letters) in Taylor, *Eve and the New Jerusalem,* p. 271; cf. pp. 270–72; also Thompson, *Chartists,* p. 126.

CHAPTER THIRTEEN: CHARTISM AND
THE PROBLEM OF WOMEN WORKERS

1. Carol Morgan, "Women, Work and Consciousness in the Mid-Nineteenth Century English Cotton Industry," *Social History* 17 (1992): 30.

2. For the Chartist notion of property in skill as masculine, see Joan Scott, *Gender and the Politics of History* (New York: Columbia University Press, 1988), p. 54.

3. R. J. Richardson, *The Rights of Women* (1840), in Dorothy Thompson, ed., *The Early Chartists* (Columbia: University of South Carolina Press, 1971), p. 117.

4. Clive Behagg, *Politics and Production in the Early Nineteenth Century* (London: Routledge, 1990), p. 233.

5. Richardson, *Rights of Women,* p. 122.

6. *Northern Star,* 9 Feb. 1839.

7. *Northern Star,* 24 July 1841, quoted in Ruth Frow and Edmund Frow, eds., *Political Women 1800–1850* (London: Pluto, 1989), pp. 199–200.

8. *Birmingham Journal,* 1, 29 Sept. 1838, from London, British Library, Place Coll., Set 56.

9. Bronterre O'Brien, editorial in the *Northern Star,* 8 Sept. 1838, was an exception who addressed women as workers. See also Sally Alexander, "Women, Class, and Sexual Difference in the 1830s and the 1840s: Some Reflections on the Writing of a Feminist History," *History Workshop Journal* 17 (1984): 148; Sonya O. Rose, *Limited Livelihoods: Gender and Class in Nineteenth-Century England* (Berkeley: University of California Press, 1992), p. 148.

10. *Weekly Dispatch,* 12 May 1839.

11. *English Chartist Circular*, 2 (1842): 165, 361, 136. Contemporary American radical working men used very similar rhetoric; see Christine Stansell, *City of Women: Sex and Class in New York, 1789–1860* (New York: Knopf, 1986), p. 140.

12. *Northern Star*, 10 Dec. 1842.

13. Dorothy Thompson, *The Chartists: Popular Politics in the Industrial Revolution* (Aldershot: Wildwood House, 1986), p. 139.

14. Speech by Mr. Lowry, *Northern Star*. 8 Dec. 1838.

15. Morgan, "Women, Work and Consciousness," p. 30.

16. Malcolm Thomis and Jennifer Grimmet, *Women in Protest: 1800–1850* (London: Macmillan, 1982), p. 78.

17. *Northern Star*, 17 Oct. 1840.

18. *Northern Star*, 17 Oct. 1840.

19. Carol Edyth Morgan, "Working-Class Women and Labor and Socialist Movements of Mid-Nineteenth Century Britain," Ph.D. diss., University of Iowa, 1979, p. 293.

20. *The Trial of Feargus O'Connor, and Fifty-eight Others, on a Charge of Sedition, Conspiracy, Tumult and Riot* (New York: Augustus M. Kelley, 1970 [1843]), p. 249.

21. *Northern Star*, 2 July 1840.

22. *Northern Star*, 17 Oct. 1840.

23. *Northern Star*, 2 May 1840.

24. Report on Bolton from Thomas Thomasson, cotton spinner, from the *Charter*, quoted in *Scottish Patriot*, 21 March 1840.

25. *Northern Star*, 18 Sept. 1841.

26. Morgan, "Working-Class Women," pp. 249–60; Marianna Valverde, "'Giving the Female a Domestic Turn': The Social, Legal and Moral Regulation of Women's Work in British Cotton Mills, 1820–1850," *Journal of Social History* 21 (1988): 628.

27. Robert Blakey, *The Political Pilgrim's Progress, from the Northern Liberator* (Newcastle, 1839) p. 5.

28. *Poor Man's Guardian and Repealers Friend* (1843): 15; *MacDouall's Chartist Journal and Trades Advocate*, 18 Sept. 1841, p. 196.

29. *Chartist Circular* 3 (1841): 519; *English Chartist Circular* 2 (1842): 225.

30. First Report of the Select Committee on Combinations of Workmen, PP 1837–1838, vol. 8.

31. *Scots Times*, 14 Feb. 1840.

32. *Glasgow Saturday Post [Saturday Reformer]*, 24 Sept. 1842.

33. Friedrich Engels, *The Condition of the Working Class in England*, trans. and ed. W. O. Henderson and W. H. Chaloner (Stanford: Stanford University Press, 1968 [1845]), p. 162; cf. discussion on pp. 162–64. See also Rose, *Limited Livelihoods*, p. 128.

34. *Northern Star*, 30 June 1849.

35. William Dodd, *The Factory System Illustrated* (London, 1842), pp. 63–64, quoted in Caroline Davidson, *A Woman's Work Is Never Done: A History of Housework in the British Isles* (London: Chatto and Windus, 1986), p. 187.

36. Sian Moore, "Women, Industrialisation and Protest in Bradford, West Yorkshire, 1780–1845," Ph.D. diss., University of Essex, 1986, p. 112.

37. Moore, "Women, Industrialisation and Protest," p. 113. A similar theme appears in a Chartist placard in 1842, which claims that cotton mills "reduced thousands of tender mothers to a worse state than brute beasts." Quoted in Thompson, *Chartists*, p. 298.

38. Robert Duncan, "Artisans and Proletarians: Chartism and Working-Class Allegiance in Aberdeen, 1838–42," *Northern Scotland* 4 (1981): 56.

39. *English Chartist Circular* 2 (1842): 225; the same passage was later cited in Samuel Smiles, "The Condition of Factory Women—What Is Doing for Them," *The People's Journal* 2 (1846): 259; and in the *Ten Hours' Advocate* 1 (1846–1847): 123.

40. [Samuel Kydd], *The History of the Factory Movement* (New York: Augustus M. Kelley, 1966 [1857]), vol. 2, p. 214; later echoed by Smiles: "Condition of Factory Women," p. 259.

41. *Northern Star*, 8 Jan. 1842.

42. *Address of the Lancashire Short-Time Central Committee to the Right Hon. Lord Ashley, with His Lordship's Reply* (Manchester, 1843), in *The Battle for the Ten Hours Day Continues: Four Pamphlets, 1837–1843* (New York: Arno Press, 1972); unlike the West Riding Committee, the Lancashire Committee stressed the advisability of shortening the hours children worked rather than emphasizing the deleterious effects of women's labor.

43. Robert Gray, "Factory Legislation and the Gendering of Jobs in the North of England, 1830–1860," *Gender and History* 5 (1993): 64.

44. *Northern Star*, 3 Dec. 1842.

45. Nancy Grey Osterud, "Gender Divisions and the Organization of Work in the Leicestershire Hosiery Industry," in Angela V. John, ed., *Unequal Opportunities: Women's Employment in England, 1800–1918* (Oxford: Basil Blackwell, 1986), p. 55.

46. Ralph Grindrod, *The Wrongs of Our Youth* (London, 1843), pp. 25–26.

47. *Northern Star*, 8 Jan. 1842.

48. There were sporadic strikes and riots in Scotland, but nothing comparable to the Lancashire outbreak. See *Manchester Guardian*, 17 Aug. 1842, *Northern Star*, 27 Aug. 1842.

49. Editorial, *Northern Star*, 13 Aug. 1842.

50. Thompson, *Chartists*, pp. 290–98. See also Mick Jenkins, *The General Strike of 1842* (London: Lawrence and Wishart, 1980), who argues, in

a more traditionally Marxist way, that this was a general strike for political ends.

51. T. D. W. Reid and Naomi Reid, "The 1842 'Plug Plot' in Stockport," *International Review of Social History* 24 (1979): 72.

52. *Trial of Feargus O'Connor*, p. 96.

53. A. G. Rose, "The Plug Riots of 1842," *Transactions of the Antiquarian Society of Lancashire and Cheshire* 67 (1957): 89.

54. *Manchester Guardian*, 10 Aug. 1842.

55. *Manchester Guardian*, 17 Aug. 1842.

56. *Northern Star*, 20 Aug. 1842.

57. Rose, "Plug Riots," p. 92.

58. *Northern Star*, 13 Aug. 1842.

59. Trial, p. 78, PRO, HO 45/249A, fols. 23, 63.

60. *Trial of Feargus O'Connor*, p. 62.

61. *Manchester Guardian*, 17 Aug. 1842.

62. *Northern Star*, 20 Aug. 1842.

63. *Manchester Guardian*, 17 Aug. 1842.

64. Thomis and Grimmet, *Women in Protest*, p. 84.

65. Jenkins, *General Strike*, p. 217, quoting *Manchester Guardian*, 3 Sept. 1842.

66. S. S., "The Women of the Working Classes," *The Union* 1 (1843): 424.

67. *Northern Star*, 10, 17 Sept. 1842.

68. *Northern Star*, 20 Aug. 1842.

69. Trial, p. 380; *Preston Chronicle*, 13 Aug. 1842, in PRO, HO 45/249A, fol. 23.

70. S. S., "The Women of the Working Classes," p. 426.

71. Quoted in Anna Jameson, *Memoirs and Essays Illustrative of Art, Literature and Social Morals* (London, n.d.), pp. 201–2.

72. *Address of the Lancashire Short-Time Central Committee*, p. 8.

73. Trial, p. 253. For a comment on Pilling's rhetoric, see Thompson, *Chartists*, p. 286.

74. Trial, pp. 196, 212.

75. Jenkins, *General Strike*, p. 255.

76. *Northern Star*, 5 Dec., 14 Nov., 19 Aug. 1846, for meeting in Lancashire and Glasgow.

77. *Ten Hours' Advocate* 1 (1846–1847): 106.

78. Morgan, "Women, Work and Consciousness," pp. 34–35.

79. *Ten Hours' Advocate* 1 (1846–1847): 160, 12.

80. Gray, "Factory Legislation," p. 74.

81. Morgan, "Working-Class Women," p. 293; *Northern Star*, 24 April, 31 July, 25 Sept. 1847.

82. Quoted in Thompson, *Chartists*, p. 136.

83. Moore, "Women, Industrialisation and Protest," p. 177.

84. *Glasgow Courier*, 26 April 1849.

85. Rose, *Limited Livelihoods*, p. 177. See H. I. Dutton, *Ten Percent and No Surrender: The Preston Strike of 1853–54* (Cambridge: Cambridge University Press, 1981), for more on this strike.

86. Alexander, "Women, Class and Sexual Difference," p. 138.

87. Gareth Stedman Jones, *Languages of Class: Studies in English Working Class History 1832–1982* (Cambridge: Cambridge University Press, 1983), p. 173.

88. John Saville, *1848: The British State and the Chartist Movement* (Cambridge: Cambridge University Press, 1987), p. 218.

89. David Jones, *Chartism and the Chartists* (London: Allen Lane, 1975), p. 138. Feargus O'Connor proposed in his Land Plan that every working-class family should obtain a small plot of land to attain self-sufficiency.

90. Theodore Koditschek, *Class Formation and Urban Industrial Society: Bradford, 1750–1850* (Cambridge: Cambridge University Press, 1990), p. 503.

91. Alexander Wilson, *The Chartist Movement in Scotland* (New York: Augustus M. Kelley, 1970), p. 172; *Northern Star*, 1 Oct. 1842; Tony Clarke, *Scottish Capitalism: Class, State and Nation from Before the Union to the Present* (London: Lawrence and Wishart, 1980), p. 211; Fiona Ann Montgomery, "Glasgow Radicalism 1830–1848," Ph.D. diss., University of Glasgow, 1974, p. 226; *Northern Star*, 1 Oct. 1842, where David Thompson admitted that most of the working-class Chartists in Scotland were committed to strikes and other industrial action, although he believed they should have espoused more moderate reforms. Donald Read, "Chartism in Manchester," in Asa Briggs, ed., *Chartist Studies* (London: Macmillan, 1967), pp. 58–61; Jones, *Chartism and the Chartists*, p. 118.

92. Thompson, *Chartists*, p. 122.

93. *Glasgow Saturday Post and Evening Post*, 22 Oct. 1842.

94. Quoted in Jutta Schwarzkopf, *Women in the Chartist Movement* (London: Macmillan, 1991), p. 249.

95. Goodway, *London Chartism* (Cambridge: Cambridge University Press, 1982), p. 59.

96. *English Chartist Circular* 1 (1841): 92.

97. Eileen Yeo, "Mayhew as a Social Investigator," in Eileen Yeo and E. P. Thompson, eds., *The Unknown Mayhew* (New York: Schocken, 1972), p. 85.

98. John Belchem, "1848: Feargus O'Connor and the Collapse of the Mass Platform," in James Epstein and Dorothy Thompson, eds., *The Chartist Experience: Studies in Working-Class Radicalism and Culture* (London: Macmillan, 1982), pp. 269–310; Saville, *1848*, p. 218.

99. Quoted in Leslie C. Wright, *Scottish Chartism* (Edinburgh: Oliver and Boyd, 1953), p. 227.

CHAPTER FOURTEEN: A DIFFICULT IDEAL

1. Tom Leonard, ed., *Radical Renfrew: Poetry from the French Revolution to the First World War* (Edinburgh: Polygon, 1990), pp. 124–43.

2. "Respectability" remained quite difficult to achieve and fluid in definition throughout the nineteenth century, and the distinction between image and reality was always sharp. See Ellen Ross, "'Not the Sort That Would Sit on the Doorstep': Respectability in Pre–World War I London Neighborhoods," *International Labor and Working-Class History* 27 (1985): 39–58; Peter Bailey, "'Will the Real Bill Banks Please Stand Up?' Towards a Role Analysis of Mid-Victorian Working-Class Respectability," *Journal of Social History* 12 (1979): 336–53.

3. Adam Clarke, *Christian Theology, with a Life of the Author* by Samuel Dunn (2d ed. London, 1835), p. 299.

4. Jutta Schwarzkopf, *Women in the Chartist Movement* (London: Macmillan, 1991), p. 46.

5. *True Scotsman*, 25 April 1840; Henry Vincent and others, *An Address to the Working Men of England, Scotland and Wales*, Five a Penny Tracts for the People (London, [1840]).

6. *English Chartist Circular* 1 (1841): 160; a similar argument may be found in *True Scotsman*, 25 April 1840.

7. John O'Neill, "Fifty Years Experience as an Irish Shoemaker in London," *St. Crispin* 2 (1869): 295, 316.

8. Charles Manby Smith, *A Working Man's Way in the World* (London: Printing History Society, 1967 [1857]), p. 247.

9. Schwarzkopf, *Women in the Chartist Movement*, pp. 151, 162.

10. Smith, *Working Man's Way*, 247.

11. *English Chartist Circular* 1 (1841): 49.

12. Ernest Jones, "Woman's Wrongs," in his *Notes for the People*, vol. 2 (London, 1852), pp. 3–6.

13. John Jacob Bezer, "Autobiography of One of the Chartist Rebels of 1848," in David Vincent, ed., *Testaments of Radicalism* (London: Europa, 1977), p. 170.

14. Mary Leman Gillies in *The People's Journal* 2 (1846): 133–34.

15. Catherine Barmby, "Woman and Domestics," *The People's Journal* 3 (1847): 37.

16. *Ten Hours' Advocate* 2 (1846–1847): 303.

17. "Address from the London Working Men's Association to the Citizens of the American Republic" (1837), in William Lovett, *Life and Struggles* (London: Bell, 1920), pp. 137.

18. *Northern Star*, 13 Oct. 1849; apparently this novel was based on Wheeler's own life. See William Stevens, *A Memoir of Thomas Martin Wheeler* (London, 1862).

19. *Northern Star*, 20 Oct. 1849; for a further discussion of this novel, see Schwarzkopf, *Women in the Chartist Movement*, pp. 265–68.

20. William Lovett, *Woman's Mission* (London, 1856); according to Schwarzkopf, *Women in the Chartist Movement*, p. 158, this poem was written in 1842.

21. *English Chartist Circular* 1 (1841): 108, 87, 63.

22. *Northern Star*, 15 Dec. 1849.

23. *Ten Hours' Advocate* 2 (1846–1847): 277.

24. *Ten Hours' Advocate* 2 (1846–1847): 293.

25. London, British Library, Collection of broadsides, 11621.k.5, printed between 1833 and 1841; similar songs are "Good Advice to Bachelors and Maids on Choosing Husbands and Wives," "My Old Girl at Home," and "A Woman's the Pride of a Man," in 11621.k.4.

26. Manchester, Manchester Public Library, Ballad collection, fol. 550.

27. "John and Mary's Discussion on Matrimony"; see also "The Struggle for the Breeches," in Manchester, Manchester Public Library, Ballad collection, fols. 550, 275.

28. Smith, *Working Man's Way*, p. 20.

29. Eileen Yeo and E. P. Thompson, eds., *The Unknown Mayhew* (New York: Schocken, 1972), p. 338.

30. John Overs, *Evenings of a Working Man, Being the Occupation of His Scanty Leisure* (London, 1844), p. viii.

31. M. Dorothy George, *London Life in the Eighteenth Century* (Harmondsworth: Penguin, 1966 [1925]), p. 208.

32. Yeo and Thompson, eds., *Unknown Mayhew*, p. 188.

33. Yeo and Thompson, eds., *Unknown Mayhew*, p. 209.

34. Yeo and Thompson, eds., *Unknown Mayhew*, p. 264.

35. Patricia Malcolmson, "Victorian Kensington," *London Journal* 1 (1975): 43–45.

36. Dr. G. J. M. Ritchie, "The Medical Topography of Neilston," *Glasgow Medical Journal* (1828): 26, quoted in Eleanor Gordon, *Women and the Labor Movement in Scotland 1850–1914* (Oxford: Oxford University Press, 1991), p. 76.

37. John C. Holley comes to this conclusion based on census material: "The Two Family Economies of Industrialism: Factory Workers in Victorian Scotland," *Journal of Family History* 6 (1981): 57–69. Contemporary observer Angus Reach came to the same conclusion: *Labour and the Poor in England and Wales 1849–1851*, vol. 1 (London: Frank Cass, 1983), pp. 13–15.

38. Reach, *Labour and the Poor*, pp. 84–86.

39. "Life of a Cotton Spinner," *Commonwealth*, 27 Dec. 1856.

40. Patrick Joyce, *Work, Society, and Politics: The Culture of the Factory in Later Victorian England* (New Brunswick: Rutgers University Press, 1984), p. 112.

41. Carol Edyth Morgan, "Working-Class Women and Labor and Socialist Movements of Mid-Nineteenth Century Britain," Ph.D. diss.,

University of Iowa, 1979, p. 140; Michael Anderson, *Family Structure in Nineteenth-Century Lancashire* (Cambridge: Cambridge University Press, 1971), p. 72.

42. Ben Brierly, *Home Memories and Recollections of a Life* (Manchester, 1886), p. 48.

43. Ellen Johnston, "The Factory Girl," in her *Autobiography, Poems and Songs* (Glasgow, 1867), p. 123.

44. M. Brigg, "Life in East Lancashire, 1856–60: Newly Discovered Diary of John O'Neil (John Ward), Weaver, of Clitheroe," *Transactions of the Historical Society of Lancashire and Cheshire* 120 (1968): 95.

45. John Burnett, *Destiny Obscure: Autobiographies of Childhood, Education and Family from the 1820s to the 1920s* (Harmondsworth: Penguin, 1984), p. 219.

46. J. Ginswick, ed., *Labour and the Poor in England and Wales 1849–1851: Letters to the Morning Chronicle.* Vol. 1: *Lancashire, Cheshire, Yorkshire* (London: Frank Cass, 1983), p. 23.

47. Sonya O. Rose, *Limited Livelihoods: Gender and Class in Nineteenth-Century England* (Berkeley: University of California Press, 1992), pp. 164–65.

48. Caroline Davidson, *A Woman's Work Is Never Done: A History of Housework in the British Isles* (London: Chatto and Windus, 1986), p. 187.

49. [Thomas Wright], *Some Habits and Customs of the Working Classes, by a Journeyman Engineer* (New York: Augustus M. Kelley, 1967 [1867]), p. 194.

50. For the older tradition, see "The Churlish Husband," and for the newer, "The Molly Coddle," in John Holloway and Joan Black, eds., *Later English Broadside Ballads* (London: Routledge and Kegan Paul, 1979), and "The Dandy Man" in London, British Library, Collections of broadsides, 11621.k.5 and C.116.i.1.

51. "There's No Mistake in That," in London, British Library, Collections of broadsides, 11621.k.5, printed 1839.

52. "Scotch Bloomers," also "A Woman Is the Torment of Man," in Glasgow, Glasgow University, Ballads and broadsides, Mu.23.y.1, fols, 54, 144.

53. Davidson, *Woman's Work Is Never Done*, pp. 183, 184, 207.

54. Ginswick, *Labour and the Poor*, vol. 1, p. 21.

55. Overs, *Evenings of a Working Man*, p. 197.

56. Ellen Ross, "'Fierce Questions and Taunts': Married Life in Working-Class London, 1870–1914," *Feminist Studies* 8 (1982): 580.

57. William Marcroft, *The Marcroft Family and the Inner Circle of Human Life* (Rochdale, 1888), p. 51.

58. Smith, *Working Man's Way*, p. 247.

59. Thomas Carter, *Memoirs of a Working Man* (London, 1845), p. 168.

60. Ross, "'Fierce Questions and Taunts,'" p. 580; Laura Oren, "The

Welfare of Women in Laboring Families, 1860–1950," *Feminist Studies* 1 (1973): 111–12.

61. Louis James, *Print and the People 1819–1851* (Harmondsworth: Penguin, 1978), p. 127; Manchester, Manchester Public Library, Ballad collection, fol. 90; John Johnson Collection, Street Ballads Box 4 ("Eighteen Shillings") and Box 9 ("Hint to Husbands").

62. Carter, *Memoirs*, p. 206.

63. Marcroft, *Marcroft Family*, p. 51.

64. Smith, *Working Man's Way*, p. 260.

65. Jones, "Woman's Wrongs," p. 4. Emphasis in original.

66. Smith, *Working Man's Way*, p. 260.

67. Smith, *Working Man's Way*, p. 247.

68. Thomas Brierly, "God Bless These Poor Wimmen That's Childer," in John Harland, ed., *Lancashire Lyrics* (London, 1866). See also James Hammerton, "The Targets of 'Rough Music': Respectability and Domestic Violence in Victorian England," *Gender and History* 3 (1991): 38, for a similar poem.

69. Gorbals case books, 1835. All in Glasgow, Strathcylde Regional Archives.

70. Nancy Tomes, "A 'Torrent of Abuse': Crimes of Violence Between Working-Class Men and Women in London, 1840–1875," *Journal of Social History* 11 (1978): 330.

71. John Brownlie, *Police Reports of Causes Tried Before the Justices of the Peace and the Glasgow, Gorbals and Calton Police Courts from 18th July to 3rd October* (Glasgow, 1829), p. 90.

72. Brownlie, *Police Reports*, p. 111.

73. *Thistle, or Literary, Theatrical and Police Reporter*, 9 Aug. 1830.

74. *Thistle, or Literary, Theatrical and Police Reporter*, 26 Feb. 1831, Paisley.

75. Hammerton, "The Targets of 'Rough Music,'" p. 36, tables 5 and 6.

76. *Thistle, or Literary, Theatrical and Police Reporter*, 14 May 1831.

77. London, Guildhall Library, Printed Old Bailey Sessions Papers (henceforth OBSP), 11 July 1839, vol. 3, p. 539.

78. OBSP, 1836, vol. 1, pp. 391–401.

79. OBSP, 1840, vol. 4, p. 922.

80. Henry Mayhew, *The Morning Chronicle Survey of Labor and the Poor: The Metropolitan Districts* (Horsham: Caliban Books, 1981), vol. 2, p. 259.

81. *Glasgow City Mission Annual Report* (1854), quoted in Elspeth King, *Scotland Sober and Free: The Temperance Movement 1829–1879* (Glasgow: Museums and Art Galleries, 1979), p. 17.

82. *True Scotsman*, 4 July 1840.

83. OBSP, 1844, vol. 3, pp. 814–16.

84. Mayhew, *The Morning Chronicle Survey*, vol. 2, p. 156; Report of the Select Committee on Drunkenness, PP 1834, vol. 8, p. 4–5.

85. OBSP, Sept 1830, vol. 3, p. 767; 1837–1838, vol. 1, p. 280.
86. *Scots Times,* 20 Oct. 1832.
87. Michael R. Booth, "Early Victorian Farce: Dionysus Domesticated," in Kenneth Richards and Peter Thomson, eds., *Nineteenth Century British Theatre* (London: Methuen, 1971), p. 106.
88. "I Should Dearly Like to Marry," in London, British Library, Collections of broadsides, 11621.k.4, fol. 326.
89. Jan Lambertz and Pat Ayers, "Marriage Relations, Money and Domestic Violence in Working-Class Liverpool," in Jane Lewis, ed., *Labour and Love* (Oxford: Basil Blackwell, 1986), p. 197.
90. Nancy Tomes also found many disputes over domestic tasks: "'Torrent of Abuse,'" p. 331.
91. *Weekly Dispatch,* 22 Jan. 1843.
92. *Trades' Newspaper,* 30 July 1820.
93. *Glasgow Evening Post and Saturday Reformer,* 24 Dec. 1842.
94. R. Emerson Dobash and Russell Dobash, *Violence Against Wives: A Case Against the Patriarchy* (New York: Free Press, 1979), p. 127.
95. *London Dispatch,* 20 May 1838. For further discussion of the legal issues surrounding domestic violence, see Anna Clark, "Humanity or Justice? Wifebeating and the Law in the Eighteenth and Nineteenth Centuries," in Carol Smart, ed., *Regulating Womanhood: Historical Writings on Marriage, Motherhood and Sexuality* (London: Routledge, 1992), pp. 187–206.
96. OBSP, 1843, vol. 2, p. 181.
97. OBSP, 1845, vol. 1, p. 263.
98. *Scots Times,* 17 June 1840.
99. *Glasgow Evening Post,* 27 April 1833.
100. OBSP, 1842–1843, vol. 1, p. 16.
101. OBSP, 1843, vol. 2, p. 994.
102. For the problem of feminist politicization or lack thereof concerning wife-beating, see Jan Lambertz, "Feminists and the Politics of Wife-beating," in Harold L. Smith, ed., *British Feminism in the Twentieth Century* (Amherst: University of Massachusetts Press, 1990), pp. 25–27. For a comparative perspective, see Elizabeth Pleck, *Domestic Tyranny: The Making of Social Policy Against Family Violence from Colonial Times to the Present* (New York: Oxford University Press, 1987), and Linda Gordon, *Heroes of Their Own Lives: The Politics and History of Family Violence, Boston, 1880–1960* (New York: Viking, 1988).

CHAPTER FIFTEEN: CONCLUSION

1. Patrick Joyce, *Visions of the People: Industrial England and the Question of Class, 1840–1914* (Cambridge: Cambridge University Press, 1991), p. 27.
2. For an interesting discussion of the Reform Act, see James Vernon,

"Re-Reading the Constitution: New Narratives in 19th Century English Political History," unpublished ms. Thanks are due to James Vernon for allowing me to see this manuscript.

3. Quoted in Leonore Davidoff and Catherine Hall, *Family Fortunes: Men and Women of the English Middle Class 1780–1850* (London: Hutchinson, 1987), p. 184.

4. Drohr Wahrman, "'Middle-Class' Domesticity Goes Public: Gender, Class and Politics from Queen Caroline to Queen Victoria," *Journal of British Studies* 32 (1993) p. 422. Wahrman is absolutely correct to point out the absence of discussion of domesticity from the debates over reform in 1831-2 and its increasing importance later in the 1830s, but does not provide a compelling reason for the shift. Chartism may be the answer.

5. Alastair Reid, "Intelligent Artisans and Aristocrats of Labor: The Essays of Thomas Wright," in Jay Winter, ed., *The Working Class in Modern British History* (Cambridge: Cambridge University Press, 1983), p. 173. For instance, the journal *The British Workman* (1855) tried to persuade men to reform their domestic habits before claiming the vote. See also James Hammerton, "The Targets of 'Rough Music': Respectability and Domestic Violence in Victorian England," *Gender and History* 3 (1991): 34.

6. Frances Elma Gillespie, *Labor and Politics in England 1850–1867* (Durham: Duke University Press, 1927), pp. 30, 90, 264.

7. From a debate in Parliament, 6 July 1848, quoted in Patricia Hollis, *Class and Conflict in Nineteenth Century England 1815–1850* (London: Routledge and Kegan Paul, 1973), p. 354.

8. Gladstone was very attached to the notion of household suffrage, but he eventually added a limited lodger franchise which included men of a more middle-class social level, due to pressure both from working men and from educated professional middle-class men, who were often bachelor lodgers. Disraeli, of course, probably passed the bill for reasons of political opportunism, as well as hoping to gain working-class votes. For the complexities of the Reform Act, which cannot be reduced to class, see Royden Harrison, *Before the Socialists: Studies in Labour and Politics 1861–1881* (London: Routledge and Kegan Paul, 1965), p. 99. For further development of these ideas, see Anna Clark, "Gender, Class and Suffrage," in James Vernon, ed., *Rereading the Constitution* (Cambridge University Press, forthcoming).

9. See Joyce, *Visions of the People*, pp. 54, 62, 64, for Liberal and Tory attempts to enfold working men into this notion of "the people" and thereby to defuse class conflict; for several explorations of changing notions of masculinity, see essays in Michael Roper and John Tosh, *Manful Assertions: Masculinity in Britain Since 1800* (London: Routledge, 1991), especially Keith McClelland, "Masculinity and the Representative Artisan in Britain, 1850–1900," p. 84, who notes that the figure of the respectable artisan was essential for mid-nineteenth-century class stability.

10. Dickson and Clarke point out that "focussing on the excess supply

of labor rather than the relationship to capitalism . . . tended to mitigate class tension." Tony Dickson and Tony Clarke, "Class and Class Consciousness in Early Industrial Capitalism: Paisley 1770–1850," in Tony Dickson, ed., *Capital and Class in Scotland* (Edinburgh: John Donald, 1982), p. 47.

11. Sonya O. Rose, *Limited Livelihoods: Gender and Class in Nineteenth-Century England* (Berkeley: University of California Press, 1992), ch. 2; Patrick Joyce, *Work, Society and Politics: The Culture of the Factory in Later Victorian England* (New Brunswick: Rutgers University Press, 1984), p. 181.

12. Maxine Berg, *The Machinery Question and the Making of Political Economy* (Cambridge: Cambridge University Press, 1980), p. 296.

13. Barbara Taylor, *Eve and the New Jerusalem: Socialism and Feminism in the Nineteenth Century* (New York: Pantheon, 1983), p. 275; Joyce, *Work, Society and Politics*, p. 113. For a critique of Joyce on deference, see Neville Kirk, *The Growth of Working Class Reformism in Mid-Victorian England* (Urbana: University of Illinois Press, 1985), pp. 1–32.

14. Eric Hobsbawm, *Workers: Worlds of Labor* (New York: Pantheon, 1984), p. 182.

15. Peter Bailey, *Leisure and Class in Victorian England* (London: Methuen, 1987), pp. 169–82.

16. Eleanor Gordon, *Women and the Labor Movement in Scotland 1850–1914* (Oxford: Oxford University Press, 1991), p. 26.

17. Ellen Ross, *Love and Toil: Motherhood in Outcast London, 1870–1918* (New York: Oxford University Press, 1993), p. 576.

18. Keith McClelland, "Time to Work, Time to Live: Some Aspects of Work and the Re-formation of Class in Britain, 1850–1880," in Patrick Joyce, ed., *The Historical Meanings of Work* (Cambridge: Cambridge University Press, 1987), p. 207.

19. Ellen Ross, "'Fierce Questions and Taunts': Married Life in Working-Class London, 1870–1914," *Feminist Studies* 8 (1982): 576.

20. Gareth Stedman Jones, "Working-Class Culture and Working-Class Politics in London, 1870–1900: Notes on the Remaking of a Working Class," in his *Languages of Class: Studies in English Working Class History 1832–1982* (Cambridge: Cambridge University Press, 1983), p. 220.

21. Judith Walkowitz, *City of Dreadful Delight: Narratives of Sexual Danger in Late Victorian London* (Chicago: University of Chicago Press, 1992), pp. 85–87, 93; Judith R. Walkowitz, *Prostitution and Victorian Society: Women, Class, and the State* (Cambridge: Cambridge University Press, 1980).

22. Ross McKibbin, *The Ideologies of Class: Social Relations in Britain, 1880–1950* (Oxford: Oxford University Press, 1990), p. 38.

23. Jane Lawson, Mike Savage, and A. Warde, "Gender and Local Politics: Struggles over Welfare Policies," in L. Murgatroyd et al., eds., *Locali-*

ties, Class and Gender (London: Plon, 1985), pp. 195–217. For an overview, see Neville Kirk, " 'Traditional' Working-Class Culture and the 'Rise of Labor': Some Preliminary Questions and Observations," *Social History* 16 (1991): 203–16.

24. Pat Thane, "Labour and Local Politics: Radicalism, Democracy and Social Reform, 1880–1914," in Eugenio F. Biagini and Alastair J. Reid, eds., *Currents of Radicalism: Popular Radicalism, Organized Labour, and Party Politics in Britain 1850–1914* (Cambridge: Cambridge University Press, 1991), p. 253.

25. Cynthia Cockburn, *Brothers: Male Dominance and Technological Change* (London: Pluto Press, 1983); Sylvia Walby, *Patriarchy at Work: Patriarchal and Capitalist Relations in Employment* (Minneapolis: University of Minnesota Press, 1986); Judy Lown, *Women and Industrialization: Gender at Work in Nineteenth-Century England* (Minneapolis: University of Minnesota Press, 1990).

26. Renato Rosaldo, "Celebrating Thompson's Heroes: Social Analysis in History and Anthropology," in Harvey J. Kaye and Keith McClelland, eds., *E. P. Thompson: Critical Perspectives* (Philadelphia: Temple University Press, 1990), pp. 115–17.

Select Bibliography

COLLECTIONS OF PRINTED AND
MANUSCRIPT PRIMARY SOURCES

For more detailed bibliographical information, especially on the many
pamphlets and broadsheets cited, consult the endnotes.

Bolton, Central Library, Local Archives
    Bridge Street Methodist Chapel meeting minutes
Cambridge, Cambridge University Library
    Madden Collection of Ballads
Chester, Chester Record Office
    "A List of the Friendly Society Rules Filed with the Clerk of the Peace
      for the County of Chester 1796–1849." QDS2
Edinburgh, Scottish Record Office
    Friendly society rules. FS
    Prosecution papers. AD 14
    Scottish Home Office Papers. RH
Glasgow, Glasgow University Library
    Ballads and broadsides. Mu.23.y.1
Glasgow, Mitchell Library, Local History Room
    Collection of Glasgow broadsheets
    Donald, C. H. *Collection of Glasgow Broadsides*
    Glasgow chapbooks
    Glasgow ballads
    Microfilm of 1841 Glasgow census
Glasgow, Mitchell Library, Strathclyde Regional Archives
    Anderston Police Court books, 1824, 1831–1832
    Kirk sessions minute books. CH2
    Glasgow Police Court books, 1813–1824

Gorbals case books, 1835–1836
Great Hamilton Street Reformed Presbyterian Calton Church, 1797–1831. CH3/158/1
Old Scots Independent Church minute book, 1768–1966. TD 420/1
Police notebook, 1825–1835. TD 734
London, British Library
Collections of broadsides. 11621.k.4, 11621.k.5, 1875.d.16, 1875.b.30, C. 116.bb.11, C.116.i.l, 11606.aa.22, 11606.aa.23
Collection of political pamphlets from the 1790s. 628.c.26
Davison Collection
Place, Francis, Collection of newspaper cuttings and pamphlets
Place, Francis, manuscripts
London, British Museum, Department of Prints and Drawings
Caricatures
London, Greater London Record Office
Joanna Southcott Collection. Acc. 1040
Chapel minute meeting books. N/C
"List of Rules of Friendly Societies Deposited with the Clerk of the Peace of Middlesex," 1794–1830
London Consistory Court depositions. DL/C
Middlesex Sessions, indictments and recognizances, articles of the peace, 1780–1800
London, Guildhall Library
Bastardy examinations from St. Sepulchre, 1793–1805
Bastardy examinations from St. Botolph's Aldgate, 1808–1815
"List of Rules of Friendly Societies Deposited with the Clerk of the Peace of London," 1794–1830
Printed Old Bailey Sessions Papers 1780–1845
Society of Genealogists, Transcripts of Methodist Chapel Registers
London, Lambeth Palace
Fulham Papers, London Visitation Returns, 1790 and 1810
London, London School of Economics
Webb Trade Union Collection
London, Public Record Office (PRO)
Friendly Society papers. FS/1.
Home Office files 40, 42, 44, 45, 102
Treasury Solicitors' papers, file 11
London, University College
Bentham Papers
London, University of London, Goldsmiths Library
Collection of pamphlets on social and economic literature
London, Westminster Public Library, Marylebone Branch
Hinde Street Methodist Circuit minutes 1814–1845
Joanna Southcott manuscripts

London, Westminster Public Library, Victoria Branch
    Bastardy examinations from St. Mary LeStrand. G1015
Manchester, Manchester Public Library
    Ballad collection
Manchester, Manchester Public Library, Local History Archive
    Bank Top Sunday School minutes. M.314.1813
    Manchester collection of cuttings. BR F 942.7389.SC 13; MPL
       q. 942.7389.M1
    Local History Archives
    Teachers' minute meeting book, Wesleyan New Connexion, Culcheth,
       Lancashire. M36/11/1/1, 1823
Oxford, Bodleian Library
    John Johnson Collection of Ephemera
Preston, Lancashire Record Office
    Quarter Sessions Rolls. QSB 1, 1799–1834
    Rules of Friendly Societies. QDS 1

CONTEMPORARY NEWSPAPERS AND PERIODICALS

Place of publication is London unless otherwise indicated.

Black Dwarf
Blackwood's Edinburgh Magazine
The British Workman
Bronterre's National Reformer
Chambers' Edinburgh Journal
Cobbett's Political Register
Crisis
English Chartist Circular
The Gauntlet
Glasgow Chronicle
Glasgow Constitutional
Glasgow Courier
Glasgow Evening Post
Glasgow Herald
Glasgow Liberator
Glasgow Saturday Post
Glasgow Saturday Reformer
Gorgon
Herald of the Rights of Industry (Manchester)
Herald to the Trades' Advocate (Glasgow)
Isis
Leeds Mercury
London Democrat

London Dispatch
MacDouall's Chartist Journal and Trades Advocate
Manchester Guardian
Medusa
Methodist Magazine
Monthly Liberator (Glasgow)
National Association Gazette
Northern Star (Leeds)
Nottingham Journal
The People
The People's Journal
Pioneer
Poor Man's Advocate (Manchester)
Poor Man's Guardian
Poor Man's Guardian and Repealer's Friend
Rambler's Magazine
Reid's Glasgow Magazine
Republican
Scots Times (Glasgow)
Scottish Patriot (Glasgow)
Southern Star
Spirit of the Union (Glasgow)
Spitalfields Weavers' Journal
Sun
Ten Hours' Advocate (Manchester)
Thistle, or Literary, Theatrical and Police Reporter (Glasgow)
Times
Trades Free Press
Trades' Newspaper
True Briton
True Scotsman (Glasgow)
The Union (Manchester)
Voice of the People (Manchester)
Weavers Magazine and Literary Companion (Paisley)
Weekly Dispatch

PARLIAMENTARY PAPERS

Minutes of Evidence from the Committee on the Petitions of Several Weavers, PP 1810–1811, vol. 2

First Report of the Select Committee on Combinations of Workmen. 1837–1838, vol. 8.

Report from Assistant Handloom Weavers' Commissioners. 1840, vol. 23.

Report on Calico Printers Petition. 1806–1807, vol. II.

Report of Commissioners, Factories Inquiry Commission. 1833, vol. 20.

Report on the Committee on Artizans and Machinery. 1824, vol. 5.

Report of the Factory Commissioners on the Employment of Women and Children. 1833, vol. 20.

Report and Minutes of Evidence on Cotton Manufactures. 1808, vol. 2.

Report of the Minutes of Evidence Taken Before the Select Committee on the State of Children Employed in the Manufactures of the United Kingdom. 1816, vol. 3.

Report on Public Petitions. 1841.

Report of the Select Committee on Apprenticeship Laws. 1813, vol. 4.

Report from Select Committee on Bill to Regulate Labor of Children in Mills and Factories. 1831–1832, vol. 15.

Report of the Select Committee on Drunkenness. 1834, vol. 8.

Returns of Friendly Societies. 1824, vol. 18; 1837, vol. 51; 1842, vol. 26.

SELECTED SECONDARY SOURCES

Abelove, Henry. *Evangelist of Desire: John Wesley and the Methodists.* Palo Alto: Stanford University Press, 1991.

Abray, Jane. "Feminism in the French Revolution." *American Historical Review* 80 (1975).

Alexander, Sally. "Women, Class and Sexual Difference in the 1830s and the 1840s: Some Reflections on the Writing of a Feminist History." *History Workshop Journal* 17 (1984): 125–149.

——— "Women's Work in Nineteenth-Century London: A Study of the Years 1820–50." In Juliet Mitchell and Ann Oakley, eds., *The Rights and Wrongs of Women.* Harmondsworth: Penguin, 1976.

Anderson, Benedict. *Imagined Communities.* London: Verso, 1983.

Anderson, Michael. *Family Structure in Nineteenth Century Lancashire.* Cambridge: Cambridge University Press, 1971.

——— "Sociological History and the Working-Class Family: Smelser Revisited." *Social History* 6 (1976).

Andrew, Donna. *Philanthropy and Police: London Charity in the Eighteenth Century.* Princeton: Princeton University Press, 1989.

Armstrong, Nancy. *Desire and Domestic Fiction: A Political History of the Novel.* Oxford: Oxford University Press, 1987.

Aspinall, A. *The Early English Trade Unions.* London: Batchworth Press, 1949.

Bailey, Peter. "'Will the Real Bill Banks Please Stand Up?' Towards a Role Analysis of Mid-Victorian Working-Class Respectability." *Journal of Social History* 12 (1979).

Bakhtin, Mikhail. *The Dialogic Imagination,* trans. Michael Holquist. Austin: University of Texas Press, 1981.

Balleine, G. R. *Past Finding Out: The Tragic Story of Joanna Southcott and Her Successors.* London: Society for the Promotion of Christian Knowledge, 1956.

Barker-Benfield, G. J. *The Culture of Sensibility: Sex and Society in Eighteenth-Century Britain.* Chicago: University of Chicago Press, 1992.

Beales, H. L. "The Historical Context of the *Essay* on Population." In D. V. Glass, ed., *Introduction to Malthus.* London: Watts, 1953.

Beattie, J. M. *Crime and the Courts in England, 1660–1800.* Oxford: Oxford University Press, 1986.

Behagg, Clive. *Politics and Production in the Early Nineteenth Century.* London: Routledge, 1990.

Belchem, John. *Orator Hunt: Henry Hunt and Working-Class Radicalism.* Oxford: Oxford University Press, 1985.

—— "Radical Language and Ideology in Early Nineteenth-Century England: The Challenge of the Platform." *Albion* 20 (1988): 247–259.

Benenson, Harold. "Victorian Sexual Ideology and Marx's Theory of the Working Class." *International Labor and Working-Class History* 25 (1984): 1–23.

Berg, Maxine. *The Age of Manufactures: Industry, Innovation and Work in Britain, 1700–1820.* London: Fontana, 1985.

—— *The Machinery Question and the Making of Political Economy.* Cambridge: Cambridge University Press, 1980.

—— "What Difference Did Women's Work Make to the Industrial Revolution?" *History Workshop Journal* 35 (1993): 22–44.

Berg, Maxine, and Pat Hudson. "Rehabilitating the Industrial Revolution." *Economic History Review* 45 (1992): 24–50.

Bezer, John Jacob. "Autobiography of One of the Chartist Rebels of 1848." In David Vincent, ed., *Testaments of Radicalism.* London: Europa, 1977.

Blackman, Janet. "Popular Theories of Generation: The Evolution of *Aristotle's Works.*" In John Woodward and David Richards, eds., *Health Care and Popular Medicine in 19th Century England.* London: Croom Helm, 1977.

Blewett, Mary H. *Men, Women and Work: Class, Gender and Protest in the New England Shoe Industry 1780–1910.* Urbana: University of Illinois Press, 1988.

—— "Work, Gender and the Artisan Tradition in New England Shoemaking, 1780–1860." *Journal of Social History* 17 (1983): 221–248.

Bohstedt, John. "Gender, Household, and Community Politics: Women in English Riots, 1790–1810." *Past and Present* 120 (1988).

—— *Riots and Community Politics in England and Wales.* Cambridge: Harvard University Press, 1983.

Bolin-Hart, Per. *Work, Family and the State: Child Labor and the Organization of Production in the British Cotton Industry, 1780–1920.* Lund, Sweden: Lund University Press, 1989.

Booth, Alan. "Food Riots in the North-West of England: 1790–1801." *Past and Present* 77 (1977).

Booth, Michael R. "Early Victorian Farce: Dionysus Domesticated." In

Kenneth Richards and Peter Thomson, eds., *Nineteenth Century British Theatre*. London: Methuen, 1971.

Bourdieu, Pierre. "What Makes a Social Class?" *Berkeley Journal of Sociology* 32 (1987).

Boyd, Kenneth M. *Scottish Church Attitudes to Sex, Marriage and the Family 1850–1914*. Edinburgh: John Donald, 1980.

Bratton, J. S. *The Victorian Popular Ballad*. London: Macmillan, 1975.

Breines, Wini, and Linda Gordon. "The New Scholarship on Family Violence." *Signs* 8 (1983): 506–525.

Brooks, Peter. *The Melodramatic Imagination*. New Haven: Yale University Press, 1976.

Brown, Callum G. *The Social History of Religion in Scotland Since 1730*. London: Methuen, 1987.

Brown, Earl Kent. *Women of Mr. Wesley's Methodism*. New York: Edwin Mellen Press, 1983.

Brown, Ford K. *Fathers of the Victorians*. Cambridge: Cambridge University Press, 1961.

Brown, Stewart J. *Thomas Chalmers and the Godly Commonwealth in Scotland*. Oxford: Oxford University Press, 1982.

Brundage, Anthony. *The Making of the New Poor Law*. New Brunswick: Rutgers University Press, 1978.

Burman, Sandra, ed. *Fit Work for Women*. London: Croom Helm, 1979.

Burnett, John. *Destiny Obscure: Autobiographies of Childhood, Education and Family from the 1820s to the 1920s*. Harmondsworth, Penguin, 1984.

Butler, Marilyn. *Burke, Paine, Godwin and the Revolution Controversy*. Cambridge: Cambridge University Press, 1984.

——— *Jane Austen and the War of Ideas*. Oxford: Clarendon Press, 1975.

Bythell, Duncan. *The Handloom Weavers: A Study in the English Cotton Industry During the Industrial Revolution*. Cambridge: Cambridge University Press, 1969.

Cage, R. A. *The Scottish Poor Law*. Edinburgh: Scottish Academic Press, 1981.

——— *The Working Class in Glasgow 1750–1914*. London: Croom Helm, 1987.

Calhoun, Craig. *The Question of Class Struggle: Social Foundations of Popular Radicalism During the Industrial Revolution*. Chicago: University of Chicago Press, 1982.

Church, L. F. *More About the Early Methodist People*. London: Epworth Press, 1949.

Claeys, Gregory. *Machinery, Money and the Millennium: From Moral Economy to Socialism, 1815–1860*. Princeton: Princeton University Press, 1987.

——— *Thomas Paine: Social and Political Thought*. Boston: Unwin Hyman, 1989.

Clark, Alice. *The Working Life of Women in the Seventeenth Century.* London: Virago, 1982 (1919).

Clark, Anna. "Humanity or Justice? Wifebeating and the Law in the Eighteenth and Nineteenth Centuries." In Carol Smart, ed., *Regulating Womanhood: Historical Writings on Marriage, Motherhood and Sexuality.* London: Routledge, 1992.

———— "The Politics of Seduction in English Popular Culture, 1748–1848." In Jean Radford, ed., *The Progress of Romance: The Politics of Popular Fiction.* London: Routledge and Kegan Paul, 1986.

———— "Queen Caroline and the Sexual Politics of Popular Culture in London, 1820." *Representations* 31 (1990): 47–68.

———— "Womanhood and Manhood in the Transition from Plebeian to Working-Class Culture, London, 1780–1845." Ph.D. diss., Rutgers University, 1987.

———— *Women's Silence, Men's Violence: Sexual Assault in England, 1770–1845.* London: Pandora Press, 1987.

Clark, J. C. D. *English Society 1688–1832.* Cambridge: Cambridge University Press, 1985.

Clarke, Tony. *Scottish Capitalism: Class, State and Nation from Before the Union to the Present.* London: Lawrence and Wishart, 1980.

Clarke, Tony, and Tony Dickson. "Class and Class Consciousness in Early Industrial Capitalism: Paisley 1770–1850." In Tony Dickson, ed., *Capital and Class in Scotland.* Edinburgh: John Donald, 1982.

Clawson, Mary Anne. *Constructing Brotherhood: Gender, Class, and Fraternalism.* Princeton: Princeton University Press, 1989.

———— "Early Modern Fraternalism and the Patriarchal Family," *Feminist Studies* 6 (1980).

Cockburn, Cynthia. *Brothers: Male Dominance and Technological Change.* London: Pluto Press, 1983.

Cohen, Isaac. "Workers' Control in the Cotton Industry: A Comparative Study of British and American Mulespinning." *Labor History* 26 (1985).

Colley, Linda. "The Apotheosis of George III: Loyalty, Royalty, and the British Nation, 1760–1820." *Past and Present* 102 (1984).

———— *Britons: Forging the Nation, 1707–1837.* New Haven: Yale University Press, 1992.

Collier, Frances. *The Family Economy of the Working Class in the Cotton Industry 1784–1833,* ed. R. S. Fitton. Manchester: Manchester University Press, 1964.

Cone, Carl B. *The English Jacobins: Reformers in the Late Eighteenth Century.* New York: Scribner's, 1968.

Corfield, Penelope J. "Class in Eighteenth Century Britain." In Penelope J. Corfield, ed., *Language, History and Class.* Oxford: Basil Blackwell, 1991.

Cowherd, Raymond G. *Political Economists and the English Poor Laws.* Athens: Ohio State University Press, 1977.

Crompton, Louis. *Byron and Greek Love: Homophobia in Nineteenth-Century England.* London: University of California Press, 1985.

Currie, Robert. *Methodism Divided.* London: Faber and Faber, 1968.

Davidoff, Leonore, and Catherine Hall. *Family Fortunes: Men and Women of the English Middle Class 1780–1850.* London: Hutchinson, 1987.

Davidson, Caroline. *A Woman's Work Is Never Done: A History of Housework in the British Isles.* London: Chatto and Windus, 1986.

Davis, Natalie Zemon. *Society and Culture in Early Modern France.* Palo Alto: Stanford University Press, 1975.

Devine, T. M., ed. *Conflict and Stability in Scottish Society 1700–1850.* Edinburgh: John Donald, 1990.

Devine, T. M., and Rosalind Mitchison, eds. *People and Society in Scotland 1700–1850.* Vol. 1: *1760–1830.* Edinburgh: John Donald, 1988.

Dickinson, H. T. *Liberty and Property: Political Ideology in Eighteenth-Century Britain.* New York: Holmes and Meier, 1977.

The Dictionary of the Vulgar Tongue. London: Macmillan, 1981 (1811).

Dobash, R. Emerson, and Russell Dobash. *Violence Against Wives: a Case Against the Patriarchy.* New York: Free Press, 1979.

Dobson, C. R. *Masters and Journeymen: A Prehistory of Industrial Relations, 1717–1800.* London: Croom Helm, 1980.

Downs, Laura Lee. "If Woman Is Just an Empty Category, Then Why Am I Afraid to Walk Alone at Night? Identity Politics Meets the Post-Modern Subject," and Reply by Joan Scott. *Comparative Studies in Society and History* 35 (1993): 415–451.

Driver, Cecil. *Tory Radical: The Life of Richard Oastler.* Oxford: Oxford University Press, 1946.

Dugaw, Diane. "Balladry's Female Warriors: Women, Warfare, and Disguise in the Eighteenth Century." *Eighteenth-Century Life* 9 (1985).

Duncan, Robert. "Artisans and Proletarians: Chartism and Working-Class Allegiance in Aberdeen, 1838–42." *Northern Scotland* 4 (1981).

——— *Textiles and Toil: The Factory System and the Industrial Working Class in Early 19th Century Aberdeen.* Aberdeen: City Library, 1981.

Dunkley, Peter. *The Crisis of the Old Poor Law in England 1795–1834.* New York: Garland, 1982.

Dutton, H. I. *Ten Percent and No Surrender: The Preston Strike of 1853–54.* Cambridge: Cambridge University Press, 1981.

Dwyer, John. *Virtuous Discourse: Sensibility and Community in Late Eighteenth Century Scotland.* Edinburgh: John Donald, 1987.

Dyck, Ian. "Local Attachments, National Identities and World Citizenship in the Thought of Thomas Paine." *History Workshop Journal* 35 (1993).

Eagleton, Terry. *Literary Theory: An Introduction.* Minneapolis: University of Minnesota Press, 1983.

Earle, Peter. "The Female Labor Market in London in the Late 17th and Early 18th Century." *Economic History Review,* 2d series, 42 (1989).

Edsall, Nicholas. *The Anti–Poor Law Movement, 1834–1844.* Totowa, N.J.: Rowman and Littlefield, 1971.

Eisenberg, Christiane. "Artisans' Socialization at Work: Workshop Life in Early Nineteenth-Century England and Germany." *Journal of Social History* 24 (1991).

Eley, Geoff. "Rethinking the Political: Social History and Political Culture in Eighteenth and Nineteenth Century Britain." *Archiv für Sozialgeschischte* 32 (1981): 427–457.

Ellis, Peter Berresford, and Seumas Mac a'Ghobhaiinn. *The Scottish Insurrection of 1820.* London: Pluto, 1989.

Epstein, James. "The Constitutional Idiom: Radical Reasoning, Rhetoric, and Action in Early Nineteenth Century England." *Journal of Social History* 23 (1990): 553–573.

——— *The Lion of Freedom: Feargus O'Connor and the Chartist Movement.* London: Croom Helm, 1982.

——— "Rethinking the Categories of Working-Class History." *Labour/ Le Travailleur* 18 (1986): 195–208.

——— "Understanding the Cap of Liberty: Symbolic Practice and Social Conflict in Early Nineteenth Century England." *Past and Present* 122 (1989): 74–118.

Epstein, James, and Dorothy Thompson, eds. *The Chartist Experience: Studies in Working-Class Radicalism and Culture, 1830–1860.* London: Macmillan, 1982.

Ferguson, Moira, ed. *First Feminists: British Women Writers 1578–1799.* Bloomington: Indiana University Press, 1985.

Foster, John. *Class Struggles and the Industrial Revolution.* New York: St. Martin's Press, 1974.

Fowler, Alan, and Terry Wyke. *Barefoot Aristocrats: A History of the Amalgamated Association of Cotton Spinners.* Littleborough: George Kelsall, 1987.

Fraser, W. Hamish. *Conflict and Class: Scottish Workers 1700–1838.* Edinburgh: John Donald, 1980.

Fraser, W. Hamish, and R. J. Morris, eds. *People and Society in Scotland.* Vol. 2: *1830–1914.* Edinburgh: John Donald, 1990.

Freifeld, Mary. "Technological Change and the 'Self-Acting' Mule: A Study of Skill and the Sexual Division of Labor." *Social History* 11 (1986): 319–343.

Frow, Ruth, and Edmund Frow, eds. *Political Women 1800–1850.* London: Pluto, 1989.

Fulcher, Jonathan. "Gender, Politics and Class in the Early Nineteenth-

Century English Radical Movement." Forthcoming in *Historical Research*.

Gammage, R. G. *History of the Chartist Movement 1837–1854*. New York; Augustus M. Kelley, 1969 (1894).

Garrett, Clarke. *Millenarianism and the French Revolution in France and England*. Baltimore: Johns Hopkins University Press, 1975.

Geertz, Clifford. *The Interpretation of Cultures*. New York: Basic Books, 1973.

George, M. Dorothy. *London Life in the Eighteenth Century*. Harmondsworth: Penguin, 1966 [1925].

Gilbert, Alan D. *Religion and Society in Industrial England: Church, Chapel and Social Change 1740–1914*. London: Longman, 1976.

Gilboy, Elizabeth. *Wages in Eighteenth-Century England*. Cambridge: Harvard University Press, 1934.

Gillis, John. *For Better, for Worse: British Marriages, 1600 to the Present*. Oxford: Oxford University Press, 1985.

————— "Servants, Sexual Relations, and the Risk of Illegitimacy in London, 1801–1900." In Judith L. Newton et al., eds., *Sex and Class in Women's History*. London: Routledge and Kegan Paul, 1983.

————— *Youth in History: Tradition and Change in European Age Relations, 1770 to the Present*. New York: Academic Press, 1975.

Gillespie, Frances Elma. *Labor and Politics in England 1850–1867*. Durham: Duke University Press, 1927.

Glen, Robert. *Urban Workers in the Early Industrial Revolution*. London: Croom Helm, 1984.

Godfrey, Christopher. *Chartist Lives: The Anatomy of a Working-Class Movement*. Westport, Ct.: Garland, 1987.

Godwin, William. *A Defense of the Rockingham Party*. In Burton R. Pollin, ed., *Four Early Pamphlets*. Gainesville: Scholars' Fascimiles and Reprints, 1966 (1783).

Goodway, David. *London Chartism*. Cambridge: Cambridge University Press, 1982.

Goodwin, Albert. *The Friends of Liberty: The English Radical Movement in the Age of the French Revolution*. London: Hutchinson, 1979.

Gordon, Eleanor. *Women and the Labor Movement in Scotland 1850–1914*. Oxford: Oxford University Press, 1991.

Gordon, Linda. *Heroes of Their Own Lives: The Politics and History of Family Violence, Boston, 1880–1960*. New York: Viking, 1988.

Gosden, P. H. *Friendly Societies in England, 1815–1875*. Manchester: Manchester University Press, 1961.

Gowing, Laura. "Gender and the Language of Insult in Early Modern London." *History Workshop Journal* 35 (1993).

Graham, Henry Grey. *The Social Life of Scotland in the Eighteenth Century*. London: Adam and Charles Black, 1909.

Gray, Robert. "The Deconstructing of the English Working Class." *Social History* 11 (1986).

——— "Factory Legislation and the Gendering of Jobs in the North of England, 1830–1860." *Gender and History* 5 (1993): 56–80.

Habermas, Jurgen. *The Structural Transformation of the Public Sphere*, trans. Thomas Burger. Cambridge: MIT Press, 1989 (1962).

Hair, P. E. H. "Bridal Pregnancy in Earlier Rural England, Further Examined," *Population Studies* 24 (1970).

——— "Bridal Pregnancy in Rural England in Earlier Centuries," *Population Studies* 20 (1966–1967).

——— "The Lancashire Collier Girl, 1795." *Transactions* of the Historical Society of Lancashire and Cheshire, 120 (1969): 63–84.

Hall, Catherine. "The Tale of Samuel and Jemima: Gender and Working-Class Culture in Early Nineteenth-Century England." In Catherine Hall, *White, Male and Middle Class: Explorations in Feminism and History*. Cambridge: Polity, 1992.

——— *White, Male and Middle Class: Explorations in Feminist History*. Cambridge: Polity, 1992.

Hall, Robert G. "Tyranny, Work and Politics: The 1818 Strike Wave in the English Cotton District." *International Review of Social History* 34 (1989).

Hammerton, A. James. "The Targets of 'Rough Music': Respectability and Domestic Violence in Victorian England." *Gender and History* 3 (1991): 21–42.

Hammond, J. L., and Barbara Hammond. *The Skilled Labourer 1760–1832*. New York: Augustus M. Kelley, 1967.

——— *The Town Laborer*. London: Longman, 1978 [1917].

Handley, J. E. *The Irish in Scotland*. Cork: Cork University Press, 1945.

Harrison, Brian. "Teetotal Chartism." *History* 58 (1973): 193–203.

Harrison, J. F. C. *The Second Coming: Popular Millenarianism 1780–1850*. London: Routledge and Kegan Paul, 1979.

Harrison, Royden. *Before the Socialists: Studies in Labour and Politics 1861–1881*. London: Routledge and Kegan Paul, 1965.

Harte, N. B., and K. G. Ponting, eds. *Textile History and Economic History*. Manchester: Manchester University Press, 1973.

Hartmann, Heidi. "Capitalism, Patriarchy, and Job Segregation by Sex." *Signs* 1 (1976): 137–169.

Harvey, A. D. "Prosecutions for Sodomy in England at the Beginning of the 19th Century." *Historical Journal* 21 (1978).

Hendrix, Richard. "Popular Humor and the *Black Dwarf*." *Journal of British Studies* 16 (1976).

Henriques, Ursula. "Bastardy and the New Poor Law." *Past and Present* 37 (1967).

Hewitt, Nancy A. "Beyond the Search for Sisterhood: American Women's History in the 1980s." *Social History* 10 (1985).

Hill, R. L. *Toryism and the People, 1832–1846.* London: Constable, 1929.

Hillis, P. "Presbyterian and Social Class in Mid–Nineteenth Century Glasgow: A Study of Nine Churches." *Journal of Ecclesiastical History* 32 (1981): 57–64.

Hilton, Boyd. *The Age of Atonement: The Influence of Evangelicalism on Social and Economic Thought 1785–1865.* Oxford: Oxford University Press, 1991.

Hobsbawm, E. J. *Primitive Rebels.* New York: Norton, 1959.

———— *Workers: Worlds of Labor.* New York: Pantheon Books, 1984.

Holley, John C. "The Two Family Economies of Industrialism: Factory Workers in Victorian Scotland." *Journal of Family History* 6 (1981).

Hollis, Patricia. *Class and Conflict in Nineteenth Century England 1815–1850.* London: Routledge and Kegan Paul, 1973.

———— *The Pauper Press: A Study of Working-Class Radicalism of the 1830s.* Oxford: Oxford University Press, 1970.

Holloway, John, and Joan Black, eds. *Later English Broadside Ballads.* London: Routledge and Kegan Paul, 1979.

Holme, Thea. *Caroline: A Biography of Caroline of Brunswick.* London: Atheneum, 1980.

Hone, J. Ann. *For the Cause of Truth: Radicalism in London, 1796–1821.* Oxford: Oxford University Press, 1982.

Hont, Istvan, and Michael Ignatieff, eds. *Wealth and Virtue: The Shaping of Political Economy in the Scottish Enlightenment.* Cambridge: Cambridge University Press, 1983.

Hopkins, James K. *A Woman to Deliver Her People: Joanna Southcott and English Millenarianism in an Era of Revolution.* Austin: University of Texas Press, 1982.

Huehns, Gertrude. *Antinomians in English History, with Special Reference to the Period 1640–1660.* London: Cresset Press, 1951.

Humphries, Jane. "Class Struggle and the Persistence of the Working Class Family." *Cambridge Journal of Economics* 1 (1977): 241–258.

Hunt, Lynn, ed. *Eroticism and the Body Politic.* Baltimore: Johns Hopkins University Press, 1991.

Hunt, Margaret. "Wifebeating, Domesticity, and Women's Independence in 18th Century London." *Gender and History* 4 (1992).

Inglis, K. S. *Churches and the Working Classes in Victorian England.* London: Routledge and Kegan Paul, 1963.

James, Louis. *Fiction for the Working Man.* Harmondsworth: Penguin, 1974.

———— *The Print and the People.* London: Allen Lane, 1976.

Jenkins, Mick. *The General Strike of 1842.* London: Lawrence and Wishart, 1980.

John, Angela V., ed. *Unequal Opportunities: Women's Employment in England, 1800–1918.* Oxford: Basil Blackwell, 1986.

Johnston, Thomas. *The History of the Working Classes in Scotland*. To-towa, N.J.: Rowman and Littlefield, 1974 (1946).

Jones, David. *Chartism and the Chartists*. London: Allen Lane, 1975.

———— "Women and Chartism." *History* 68 (1983): 1–21.

Jones, Gareth Stedman. *Languages of Class: Studies in English Working Class History 1832–1982*. Cambridge: Cambridge University Press, 1983.

Joyce, Patrick. *Visions of the People: Industrial England and the Question of Class 1840–1914*. Cambridge: Cambridge University Press, 1991.

———— *Work, Society, and Politics: The Culture of the Factory in Later Victorian England*. New Brunswick: Rutgers University Press, 1984.

Joyce, Patrick, ed. *The Historical Meanings of Work*. Cambridge: Cambridge University Press, 1987.

Katznelson, Ira. "Working-Class Formation: Constructing Classes and Comparisons." In Ira Katznelson and Aristide Zohlberg, *Working-Class Formation: Nineteenth-Century Patterns in Western Europe and the United States*. Princeton: Princeton University Press, 1986.

Kaye, Harvey J., and Keith McClelland, eds. *E. P. Thompson: Critical Perspectives*. Philadelphia: Temple University Press, 1990.

Kelly, Gary. *The English Jacobin Novel*. Oxford: Clarendon Press, 1976.

Kendall, H. B. *History of Primitive Methodists*. London: Joseph Johnson, 1919.

Kerber, Linda K. "The Paradox of Women's Citizenship in the Early Republic." *American Historical Review* 97 (1992).

———— *Women of the Republic: Intellect and Ideology in Revolutionary America*. Chapel Hill: University of North Carolina Press, 1980.

Kiddier, W. *Old Trade Unions from the Unpublished Records of the Brushmakers*. London: George Allen and Unwin, 1931.

King, Elspeth. *Scotland Sober and Free: The Temperance Movement 1829–1879*. Glasgow: Glasgow Museums and Art Galleries, 1979.

Kirby, R. G., and A. E. Musson. *The Voice of the People: John Doherty, 1798–1854, Trade Unionist, Radical, and Factory Reformer*. Manchester: Manchester University Press, 1975.

Kirk, Neville. "In Defense of Class: A Critique of Gareth Stedman Jones." *International Review of Social History* 32 (1987): 2–47.

———— *The Growth of Working Class Reformism in Mid-Victorian England*. Urbana: University of Illinois Press, 1985.

———— "'Traditional' Working-Class Culture and the 'Rise of Labor': Some Preliminary Questions and Observations." *Social History* 16 (1991).

Knott, John. *Popular Opposition to the 1834 New Poor Law*. London: Croom Helm, 1986.

Koditschek, Theodore. *Class Formation and Urban Industrial Society: Bradford, 1750–1850*. Cambridge: Cambridge University Press, 1990.

Kremitz, Thomas Milton. "Approaches to the Chartist Movement: Feargus O'Connor and Chartist Strategy." *Albion* 5 (1973).

Kriedtke, Peter, Hans Medick, and Jurgen Schlumbom, eds. *Industrialization Before Industrialization*. Cambridge: Cambridge University Press, 1981.

Laclau, Ernesto, and Chantal Mouffe. *Hegemony and Socialist Strategy: Toward a Radical Democratic Politics*. London: Verso, 1985.

Lambertz, Jan. "Feminists and the Politics of Wifebeating." In Harold L. Smith, ed., *British Feminism in the Twentieth Century*. Amherst: University of Massachusetts Press, 1990.

———— "Sexual Harassment in the Nineteenth Century English Cotton Industry." *History Workshop Journal* 19 (1985): 29–61.

Lambertz, Jan, and Pat Ayers. "Marriage Relations, Money and Domestic Violence in Working-Class Liverpool." In Jane Lewis, ed., *Labour and Love*. Oxford: Basil Blackwell, 1986.

Landes, Joan B. *Women and the Public Sphere in the Age of the French Revolution*. Ithaca: Cornell University Press, 1988.

Laqueur, Thomas. *Making Sex: Body and Gender from the Greeks to Freud*. Cambridge: Harvard University Press, 1990.

———— "Orgasms, Generation and the Politics of Reproductive Biology." *Representations* 14 (1986): 1–41.

———— "The Queen Caroline Affair: Politics as Art in the Reign of George IV." *Journal of Modern History* 54 (1982): 417–466.

———— *Religion and Respectability: Sunday Schools and Working-Class Culture, 1780–1850*. New Haven: Yale University Press, 1976.

———— "Sexual Desire and the Market Economy During the Industrial Revolution." In Domna Stanton, ed., *Discourses of Sexuality: From Aristotle to AIDS*. Ann Arbor: University of Michigan Press, 1992.

Laslett, Peter. *Family Life and Illicit Love*. Cambridge: Cambridge University Press, 1977.

Laslett, Peter, Karla Oosterveen, and R. W. Smith, eds. *Bastardy in Its Comparative History*. Cambridge: Cambridge University Press, 1980.

La Vopa, Anthony J. "Conceiving a Public: Ideas and Society in Eighteenth-Century Europe." *Journal of Modern History* 64 (1992).

Lazonick, William. "Industrial Relations and Technical Change: The Case of the Self-Acting Mule." *Cambridge Journal of Economics* 3 (1979): 231–262.

Leffingwell, Albert. *Illegitimacy and the Influence of Seasons upon Conduct*. New York: Arno Press, 1976 (1892).

Leonard, Tom, ed. *Radical Renfrew: Poetry from the French Revolution to the First World War*. Edinburgh: Polygon, 1990.

Levine, David. *Family Formation in an Age of Nascent Capitalism*. New York: Academic Press, 1977.

—— *Proletarianization and Family History.* Orlando: Academic Press, 1984.

Levitt, Ian, and Christopher Smout. *The State of the Scottish Working Class in 1843: A Statistical and Spatial Enquiry Based on the Data from the Poor Law Commission of 1844.* Edinburgh: Scottish Academic Press, 1979.

Levy, Darline Gay, Harriet Branson Applewhite, and Mary Durham Johnson. *Women in Revolutionary Paris, 1789–1795.* Urbana: University of Illinois Press, 1979.

Lewenhak, Sheila. *Women and Trade Unions: An Outline History of Women in the British Trade Union Movement.* London: Ernest Benn, 1977.

Liddington, Jill, and Jill Norris. *One Hand Tied Behind Us: The Rise of the Women's Suffrage Movement.* London: Virago, 1978.

Linebaugh, Peter. *The London Hanged: Crime and Civil Society in the Eighteenth Century.* London: Allen Lane Penguin Press, 1991.

Logue, Kenneth J. *Popular Disturbances in Scotland, 1780–1815.* Edinburgh: John Donald, 1979.

Lovett, William. *Life and Struggles.* London: Bell, 1920.

Lown, Judy. *Women and Industrialization: Gender at Work in Nineteenth-Century England.* Minneapolis: University of Minnesota Press, 1990.

Lyles, Albert M. *Methodism Mocked: The Satiric Reaction to Methodism in the 18th Century.* London: Epworth Press, 1960.

MacCalman, Iain. "Females, Feminism, and Free Love in an Early Nineteenth Century Radical Movement." *Labour History* 38 (1980): 1–25.

—— *Radical Underworld: Prophets, Revolutionaries and Pornographers in London, 1795–1840.* Cambridge: Cambridge University Press, 1988.

—— "Ultra-Radicalism and Convivial Debating Clubs." *English Historical Review* 102 (1987).

—— "Unrespectable Radicalism: Infidels and Pornography in Early Nineteenth-Century London." *Past and Present* 104 (1984).

MacCoby, Simon, ed. *The English Radical Tradition 1763–1914.* New York: New York University Press, 1957.

Mack, Phyllis. "Women as Prophets During the English Civil War." *Feminist Studies* 8 (1982): 23–40.

McKibbin, Ross. *The Ideologies of Class: Social Relations in Britain, 1880–1950.* Oxford: Oxford University Press, 1990.

Maclaren, A. Allen. *Social Class in Scotland.* Edinburgh: John Donald, 1981.

McLaren, Angus. "Contraception and the Working Class: The Social Ideology of the English Birth Control Movement in Its Early Years." *Comparative Studies in Society and History* 18 (1976): 236–251.

———— *Reproductive Rituals*. London: Methuen, 1984.

MacLeod, Hugh. *Class and Religion in the Late Victorian City*. London: Croom Helm, 1976.

———— *Religion and the Working Class in Nineteenth Century Britain*. London: Macmillan, 1984.

Maehl, William Henry Jr. "The Dynamics of Violence in Chartism: A Case Study in North-East England." *Albion* 7 (1975).

Mahood, Linda. *The Magdalenes: Prostitution in the Nineteenth Century*. London: Routledge, 1990.

Malcolmson, Patricia. "Victorian Kensington." *London Journal* 1 (1975).

———— *Victorian Laundresses*. Urbana: University of Illinois Press, 1986.

Malcolmson, R. W. *Popular Recreations in English Society 1700–1850*. Cambridge: Cambridge University Press, 1973.

Mandler, Peter. "The Making of the New Poor Law Redivivus." *Past and Present* 117 (1987): 131–157.

Mansfield, Nicholas. "John Brown: A Shoemaker in Place's London." *History Workshop Journal* 8 (1979).

Mark-Lawson, Jane, and Anne Witz. "From 'Family Labor' to 'Family Wage': The Case of Women's Labor in Nineteenth-Century Coalmining." *Social History* 13 (1988).

Marshall, J. S. "Irregular Marriages and Kirk Sessions." *Records of the Scottish Church History Society* 18 (1972).

Marshall, Rosalind K. *Women in Scotland 1660–1780*. Edinburgh: Trustees of the National Gallery of Scotland, 1979.

Mathieson, William Law. *Church and Reform in Scotland: A History from 1797 to 1843*. Glasgow: Maclehose, 1916.

Mayfield, David, and Susan Thorne. "Social History and Its Discontents: Gareth Stedman Jones and the Politics of Language." *Social History* 17 (1992): 165–188.

Mayhew, Henry. *London Labour and the London Poor*. London, 1860.

Medick, Hans. "Plebeian Culture in the Transition to Capitalism." In Raphael Samuel and Gareth Stedman Jones, eds., *Culture, Ideology and Politics*. London: Routledge and Kegan Paul, 1983.

Meikle, Henry W. *Scotland and the French Revolution*. Glasgow: James Maclehose and Sons, 1912.

Menefee, Samuel Pyeatt. *Wives for Sale: An Ethnographic Study of Popular Divorce*. Oxford: Basil Blackwell, 1981.

Mitchison, Rosalind, and Leah Leneman. *Sexuality and Social Control: Scotland 1660–1780*. Oxford: Basil Blackwell, 1989.

Mitchison, Rosalind, and Peter Roebuck, eds. *Economy and Society in Scotland and Ireland*. Edinburgh: John Donald, 1988.

Moers, Ellen. *The Dandy: Brummell to Beerbohm*. London: Secker and Warburg, 1960.

Montgomery, Fiona Ann. "Glasgow Radicalism 1830–1848." Ph.D. diss., University of Glasgow, 1974.

Moore, Sian. "Women, Industrialisation and Protest in Bradford, West Yorkshire, 1780–1845." Ph.D. diss., University of Essex, 1986.

Morgan, Carol. "Women, Work and Consciousness in the Mid-Nineteenth Century English Cotton Industry." *Social History* 17 (1992).

——— "Working-Class Women and Labor and Socialist Movements of Mid-Nineteenth Century Britain." Ph.D. diss., University of Iowa, 1979.

Morris, Polly. "Defamation and Sexual Reputation in Somerset, 1733–1850." Ph.D. diss., University of Warwick, 1985.

Mort, Frank. *Dangerous Sexualities: Medico-Moral Politics in England Since 1830.* London: Routledge and Kegan Paul, 1987.

Moxey, Keith. *Peasants, Warriors and Wives: Popular Imagery in the Reformation.* Chicago: University of Chicago, 1989.

Murray, Norman. *The Scottish Hand Loom Weavers 1790–1850: A Social History.* Edinburgh: John Donald, 1978.

Nash, Stanley. "Prostitution and Charity: The Magdalen Hospital, a Case Study." *Journal of Social History* 17 (1974).

Obelkovitch, James. *Religion and Rural Society.* Oxford: Oxford University Press, 1976.

Obelkovich, James, Lyndal Roper, and Raphael Samuel, eds. *Disciplines of Faith: Studies in Religion, Politics and Patriarchy.* London: Routledge, 1987.

Okin, Susan M. *Women in Western Political Thought.* Princeton University Press, 1979.

Paine, Thomas. *Rights of Man.* London: J. M. Dent, Everyman's Library, 1915.

Pateman, Carole. *The Disorder of Women: Democratic Feminism and Political Theory.* Palo Alto: Stanford University Press, 1989.

Phillips, Hugh. *Mid-Georgian London.* London: Collins, 1964.

Pickering, Paul. "Class Without Words: Symbolic Communication in the Chartist Movement." *Past and Present* 112 (1986): 144–162.

Pilkington, W. *The Makers of Wesleyan Methodism in Preston, and the Relation of Methodism to the Temperance and Teetotal Movements.* Manchester, 1890.

Pinchbeck, Ivy. *Women Workers and the Industrial Revolution, 1750–1850.* London: Virago, 1981 [1930].

Pitkin, Hanna. *Fortune Was a Woman: Gender in the Political Thought of Nicolò Machiavelli.* Berkeley: University of California Press, 1984.

Place, Francis. *The Autobiography of Francis Place, 1771–1854,* ed. Mary Thrale. Cambridge: Cambridge University Press, 1972.

——— *Illustrations and Proofs of the Principles of Population,* ed. Norman Himes. London: George Allen and Unwin, 1980.

Pleck, Elizabeth. *Domestic Tyranny: The Making of Social Policy Against*

Family Violence from Colonial Times to the Present. New York: Oxford University Press, 1987.

Polanyi, Karl. *The Great Transformation.* London: Rinehart, 1944.

Poovey, Mary. *Uneven Developments: The Ideological Work of Gender in Mid-Victorian England.* Chicago: University of Chicago Press, 1988.

Poynter, J. R. *Society and Pauperism.* London: Routledge and Kegan Paul, 1969.

Prothero, Iorwerth. *Artisans and Politics in Early Nineteenth Century London.* London: Methuen, 1981.

Quataert, Jean. "The Shaping of Women's Work in Manufacturing: Guilds, Households, and the State in Central Europe, 1658–1870." *American Historical Review* 90 (1985).

Rancière, Jacques. *The Nights of Labor: The Workers' Dream in Nineteenth-Century France,* trans. John Drury. Philadelphia: Temple University Press, 1989.

Read, Donald. "Chartism in Manchester." In Asa Briggs, ed., *Chartist Studies.* London: Macmillan, 1967.

Reddy, William. *The Rise of Market Culture: Textile Trades and French Culture 1750–1900.* Cambridge: Cambridge University Press, 1984.

Reid, Alastair. "Intelligent Artisans and Aristocrats of Labor: The Essays of Thomas Wright." In Jay Winter, ed., *The Working Class in Modern British History.* Cambridge: Cambridge University Press, 1983.

Reid, Doug. "The Decline of St. Monday." *Past and Present* 71 (1976).

Reid, T. D. W., and Naomi Reid. "The 1842 'Plug Plot' in Stockport." *International Review of Social History* 24 (1979).

Richardson, Ruth. *Death, Dissection and the Destitute.* London: Penguin, 1989.

Rigby, Brian. "Radical Spectators of the Revolution: The Case of the *Analytical Review.*" In Ceri Crossley and Ian Small, eds., *The French Revolution and British Culture.* Oxford: Oxford University Press, 1989.

Robbins, Caroline. *The Eighteenth Century Commonwealthman.* Harvard University Press, 1959.

Roberts, M. J. D. "Making Victorian Morals? The Society for the Suppression of Vice and Its Critics, 1802–1886." *Historical Studies* 21 (1984).

Rogers, Nicholas. "Carnal Knowledge: Illegitimacy in Eighteenth-Century Westminster." *Journal of Social History* 23 (1979).

Roper, Michael, and John Tosh. *Manful Assertions: Masculinity in Britain Since 1800.* London: Routledge, 1991.

Rose, A. G. "Early Cotton Riots in Lancashire, 1769–1779." *Transactions of the Lancashire and Cheshire Antiquarian Society* 73–74 (1963–1964).

——— "The Plug Riots of 1842." *Transactions of the Antiquarian Society of Lancashire and Cheshire* 67 (1957).

Rose, E. A. *Methodism in Ashton-Under-Lyne.* Ashton-Under-Lyne: J. Andrew, 1967.

Rose, M. E. "The Anti-Poor Law Movement in the North of England." *Northern History* 1 (1966): 89–93.

Rose, Sonya O. "Gender Antagonism and Class Conflict: Exclusionary Strategies of Male Trade Unionists in Nineteenth-Century Britain." *Social History* 13 (1988): 131–208.

——— "Gender Segregation in the Transition to the Factory." *Feminist Studies* 13 (1987): 163–184.

——— "Gender at Work: Sex, Class, and Industrial Capitalism." *History Workshop Journal* 21 (1986): 113–131.

——— *Limited Livelihoods: Gender and Class in Nineteenth-Century England.* Berkeley: University of California Press, 1992.

Ross, Ellen. "'Fierce Questions and Taunts': Married Life in Working-Class London, 1870–1914." *Feminist Studies* 8 (1982): 575–602.

——— *Love and Toil: Motherhood in Outcast London, 1870–1918.* New York: Oxford University Press, 1993.

——— "'Not the Sort That Would Sit on the Doorstep': Respectability in Pre–World War I London Neighborhoods." *International Labor and Working-Class History* 27 (1985).

——— "Survival Networks: Women's Neighborhood Sharing in London Before World War I." *History Workshop Journal* 15 (1983): 4–27.

Rousseau, G. S. "The Sorrows of Priapus: Anticlericalism, Homosocial Desire, and Richard Payne Knight." In G. S. Rousseau and Roy Porter, eds., *Sexual Underworlds of the Enlightenment.* Chapel Hill: University of North Carolina Press, 1988.

Rudé, George. *Hanoverian London 1714–1808.* London: Secker and Warburg, 1971.

——— *Wilkes and Liberty.* London: Lawrence and Wishart, 1983 (1962).

Rule, John. *The Experience of Labor in Eighteenth Century Industry.* London: Croom Helm, 1981.

——— *The Laboring Classes in Early Industrial England 1750–1850.* London: Longman. 1986.

——— "The Property of Skill in the Period of Manufacture." In Patrick Joyce, ed., *The Historical Meaning of Work.* Cambridge: Cambridge University Press, 1987.

Samuel, Raphael. "The Workshop of the World: Steam Power and Hand Technology in Mid-Victorian Britain." *History Workshop* 3 (1977): 6–72.

Samuel, Raphael, and Gareth Stedman Jones, eds. *Culture, Ideology and Politics.* London: Routledge and Kegan Paul, 1979.

Saville, John. *1848: The British State and the Chartist Movement.* Cambridge: Cambridge University Press, 1987.

Schwarz, L. D. "Conditions of Life and Work in London, c. 1770–1820, with Special Reference to East London." D.Phil. diss., Oxford University, 1976.

Schwarzkopf, Jutta. "The Sexual Division in the Chartist Family." *British Society for the Study of Labor History Bulletin* 54 (1989).

——— *Women in the Chartist Movement*. London: Macmillan, 1991.

Scott, Joan. "Experience." In Judith Butler and Joan W. Scott, eds., *Feminists Theorize the Political*. New York: Routledge, 1992.

——— *Gender and the Politics of History*. New York: Columbia University Press, 1988.

Scott, Joan Wallach, and E. J. Hobsbawm. "Political Shoemakers." *Past and Present* 89 (1980).

Seccombe, Wally. "Patriarchy Stabilized: The Construction of the Male Breadwinner Wage Norm in Nineteenth-Century Britain." *Social History* 11 (1986).

Seleski, Patricia Susan. "The Women of the Laboring Poor: Love, Work, and Poverty in London, 1750–1820." Ph.D. diss., Stanford University, 1989.

Semmel, Bernard. *The Methodist Revolution*. London: Heineman, 1974.

Shorter, Edward. "Illegitimacy, Sexual Revolution, and Social Change in Modern Europe." *Journal of Interdisciplinary History* 2 (1971).

Smail, John. "New Languages for Capital and Labour: The Transformation of Discourse in the Early Years of the Industrial Revolution." *Social History* 12 (1987): 49–71.

——— *The Origins of Middle-Class Culture*. Cornell: Cornell University Press, 1994.

Smelser, Neil. *Social Change in the Industrial Revolution*. London: Routledge and Kegan Paul, 1959.

Smith, Alan. *The Established Church and Popular Religion*. London: Longman, 1971.

Smith, James C. *Victorian Melodrama*. London: J. M. Dent, 1976.

Smith, Olivia. *The Politics of Language 1791–1819*. Oxford: Oxford University Press, 1984.

Smith, Ruth L., and Deborah M. Valenze. "Mutuality and Marginality: Liberal Moral Theory and Working-Class Women in Nineteenth-Century England." *Signs* 13 (1988): 277–298.

Smout, T. C. *A History of the Scottish People 1560–1830*. London: Fontana, 1972.

Snell, K. D. *Annals of the Laboring Poor: Social Change in Agrarian England, 1660–1900*. Cambridge: Cambridge University Press, 1985.

Sofer, Renee. "Attitudes and Allegiances in the Unskilled North." *International Review of Social History* 10 (1965).

Sonenscher, Michael. *The Hatters of Eighteenth-Century France*. Berkeley: University of California Press, 1987.

Spater, George. *William Cobbett: The Poor Man's Friend*. Cambridge: Cambridge University Press, 1982.

Speigel, Gabrielle M. "History, Historicism and the Social Logic of the Text." *Speculum* 65 (1990): 59–86.

Stansell, Christine. *City of Women: Sex and Class in New York, 1789–1860.* New York: Knopf, 1986.

Steinberg, Marc W. "The Re-making of the English Working Class?" *Theory and Society* 20 (1991): 173–197.

——— "Worthy of Hire: Discourse, Ideology and Collective Action Among English Working-Class Trade Groups, 1800–1830." Ph.D. diss., University of Michigan, 1989.

Sykes, Robert. "Physical Force Chartism: The Cotton District and the Chartist Crisis of 1839." *International Review of Social History* 30 (1985).

Tate, W. E. *The Parish Chest.* 3d ed. London: Cambridge University Press, 1961.

Taylor, Barbara. *Eve and the New Jerusalem: Socialism and Feminism in the Nineteenth Century.* New York: Pantheon, 1983.

——— "Mary Wollstonecraft and the Wild Wish of Early Feminism." *History Workshop Journal* 33 (1992).

Taylor, Barbara, and Anne Phillips. "Sex and Skill: Notes Toward a Feminist Economics." *Feminist Review* 6 (1980): 1–15.

Tenenbaum, Samuel. *The Incredible Beau Brummell.* South Brunswick: A. S. Barnes, 1967.

Thale, Mary, ed. *Selections from the Papers of the London Corresponding Society 1792–1799.* Cambridge: Cambridge University Press, 1982.

Thane, Pat. "Labour and Local Politics: Radicalism, Democracy and Social Reform, 1880–1914." In Eugenio F. Biagini and Alastair J. Reid, eds., *Currents of Radicalism: Popular Radicalism, Organized Labour, and Party Politics in Britain 1850–1914.* Cambridge: Cambridge University Press, 1991.

——— "Women and the Poor Law in Victorian and Edwardian England." *History Workshop Journal* 6 (1978): 29–51.

Tholfsen, Tryve. *Working-Class Radicalism in Mid-Victorian Britain.* London: Croom Helm, 1976.

Thomas, Keith. "Women and the Civil War Sects." *Past and Present* 13 (1958): 42–62.

Thomis, Malcolm, and Jennifer Grimmet. *Women in Protest: 1800–1850.* London: Macmillan, 1982.

Thompson, Dorothy. *The Chartists: Popular Politics in the Industrial Revolution.* Aldershot: Wildwood House, 1986.

——— "Women and Radical Politics: A Lost Dimension." In Juliet Mitchell and Ann Oakley, eds., *The Rights and Wrongs of Women.* Harmondsworth: Penguin, 1976.

Thompson, Dorothy, ed. *The Early Chartists.* Columbus: University of South Carolina Press, 1971.

Thompson, E. P. *Customs in Common: Studies in Traditional Popular Culture.* New York: New Press, 1991.

—— *The Making of the English Working Class.* New York: Vintage, 1966.

—— "The Moral Economy of the English Crowd." *Past and Present* 50 (1973): 76–136.

Thompson, Noel W. *The People's Science: The Popular Political Economy of Exploitation and Crisis, 1816–1834.* Cambridge: Cambridge University Press, 1984.

Tilly, Louise A., Joan W. Scott, and Miriam Cohen. "Women's Work and European Fertility Patterns." *Journal of Interdisciplinary History* 6 (1976).

Toews, John E. "Intellectual History After the Linguistic Turn: The Autonomy of Meaning and the Irreducibility of Experience." *American Historical Review* 92 (1987): 879–907.

Tomes, Nancy. "A 'Torrent of Abuse': Crimes of Violence Between Working-Class Men and Women in London, 1840–1875." *Journal of Social History* 11 (1978): 328–345.

Trumbach, Randolph. "London's Sodomites: Homosexual Behavior and Western Culture in the 18th Century." *Journal of Social History* 11 (1977).

—— "Sodomy Transformed: Aristocratic Libertinage, Public Reputation and the Gender Revolution of the 18th Century." *Journal of Homosexuality* 19 (1990).

Turner, H. A. *Trade Union Growth, Structure and Policy: A Comparative Study of the Cotton Trade Unions.* London: George Allen and Unwin, 1962.

Turner, James G. "The Properties of Libertinism." *Eighteenth-Century Life* 9 (1985).

Turner, Victor. "Social Dramas and Stories About Them." *Critical Inquiry* 7 (1980).

Urdank, Albion M. *Religion and Society in a Cotswold Vale: Nailsworth, Gloucestershire, 1780–1865.* Berkeley: University of California Press, 1990.

Valenze, Deborah. *Prophetic Sons and Daughters: Female Preaching and Popular Religion in Industrial England.* Princeton: Princeton University Press, 1985.

Valverde, Mariana. "'Giving the Female a Domestic Turn': The Social, Legal and Moral Regulation of Women's Work in British Cotton Mills, 1820–1850." *Journal of Social History* 21 (1988): 619–634.

Veeser, H. Aram, ed. *The New Historicism.* London: Routledge, 1989.

Vernon, James. *Politics and the People: A Study in English Political Culture c. 1815–1867.* Cambridge: Cambridge University Press, 1993.

Vicinus, Martha. *Broadsides of the Industrial North.* Newcastle upon Tyne: Frank Graham, 1975.

—— "Helpless and Unbefriended: Nineteenth Century Domestic Melodrama." *New Literary History* 13 (1981).

—— *The Industrial Muse.* London: Croom Helm, 1974.

Vincent, David. *Bread, Knowledge and Freedom: A Study of Nineteenth Century Working Class Autobiography.* London: Methuen, 1981.

Volosinov, V. N. *Marxism and the Philosophy of Language.* Trans. Ladislav Matejka and I. R. Titunik. Cambridge: Harvard University Press, 1986.

Wadsworth, Alfred P., and Julia de Lacy Mann. *The Cotton Trade and Industrial Lancashire, 1600–1780.* Manchester: Manchester University Press, 1965 (1931).

Wahrman, Drohr. "Virtual Representation: Parliamentary Reporting and the Languages of Class in the 1790s." *Past and Present* 136 (1992).

Walby, Sylvia. *Patriarchy at Work: Patriarchal and Capitalist Relations in Employment.* Minneapolis: University of Minnesota Press, 1986.

Walkowitz, Judith. *City of Dreadful Delight: Narratives of Sexual Danger in Late Victorian London.* Chicago: University of Chicago Press, 1992.

—— *Prostitution and Victorian Society: Women, Class, and the State.* Cambridge: Cambridge University Press, 1980.

Walton, John K. *Lancashire: A Social History, 1558–1939.* Manchester: Manchester University Press, 1987.

Ward, J. T. *Chartism.* New York: Harper and Row, 1973.

—— "Textile Trade Unionism in Nineteenth-Century Scotland." In John Butt and and Kenneth Ponting, eds., *Scottish Textile History.* Aberdeen: Aberdeen University Press, 1987.

Warner, Marina. *Monuments and Maidens: The Allegory of the Female Form.* London: Picador, 1985.

Wearmouth, Robert F. *Methodism and the Common People of the 18th Century.* London: Epworth Press, 1945.

Weaver, Stewart Angus. *John Fielden and the Politics of Popular Radicalism, 1834–1847.* Oxford: Oxford University Press, 1987.

Webb, R. K. *The British Working-Class Reader.* London: George Allen and Unwin, 1955.

Weisner, Merry E. "Guilds, Male Bonding and Women's Work in Early Modern Germany." *Gender and History* 1 (1989).

—— "Wandervogels and Women: Journeymen's Concepts of Masculinity in Early Modern Germany." *Journal of Social History* 24 (1991).

Wells, Roger. *Insurrection: The British Experience 1795–1803.* Gloucester: Alan Sutton, 1983.

Whitley, W. T. *London Baptists 1612–1912.* London: Kingsgate Press, 1928.

Wiener, Joel. *Radicalism and Freethought: The Life of Richard Carlile.* Westport, Conn.: Greenwood Press, 1983.

Williams, Raymond. *Keywords*. New York: Oxford University Press, 1976.

Wilson, Alexander. *The Chartist Movement in Scotland*. New York: Augustus M. Kelley, 1970.

Wiltenburg, Joy. *Disorderly Women and Female Power in the Street Literature of Early Modern England and Germany*. Charlottesville: University Press of Virginia, 1992.

Wollstonecraft, Mary. *A Vindication of the Rights of Women*. Harmondsworth: Penguin, 1978 (1792).

Wright, Leslie C. *Scottish Chartism*. Edinburgh: Oliver and Boyd, 1953.

Yeo, Eileen. "Chartist Religious Belief and the Theology of Liberation." In James Obelkevich, Lyndal Roper, and Raphael Samuel, eds., *Disciplines of Faith: Studies in Religion, Politics and Patriarchy*. London: Routledge and Kegan Paul, 1987.

——— "Christianity and Chartist Struggle." *Past and Present* 91 (1981).

Yeo, Eileen, and E. P. Thompson, eds. *The Unknown Mayhew*. New York: Schocken, 1972.

Young, James D. *The Rousing of the Scottish Working Class*. London: Croom Helm, 1979.

Index

Compositor: G & S Typesetters, Inc.
Text: 10/13 Aldus
Display: Aldus
Printer and Binder: BookCrafters, Inc.